Jewish Theology

By Kaufmann Kohler

Published by Pantianos Classics

ISBN-13: 978-1537549248

First published in 1918

Table of Contents

Dedication 5
Preface 6
Introductory 8
    Chapter I. The Meaning of Theology 8
    Chapter II. What is Judaism? 10
    Chapter III. The Essence of the Religion of Judaism 12
    Chapter IV. The Jewish Articles of Faith 14
Part I. God 18
    A. God As He Makes Himself Known To Man 18
    Chapter V. Man's Consciousness of God and Belief in God 18
    Chapter VI. Revelation, Prophecy, and Inspiration 19
    Chapter VII. The Torah—the Divine Instruction 21
    Chapter VIII. God's Covenant 23
    B. The Idea Of God In Judaism 24
    Chapter IX. God and the Gods 24
    Chapter X. The Name of God 26
    Chapter XI. The Existence of God 28
    Chapter XII. The Essence of God 30
    Chapter XIII. The One and Only God 33
    Chapter XIV. God's Omnipotence and Omniscience 36
    Chapter XV. God's Omnipresence and Eternity 38
    Chapter XVI. God's Holiness 39
    Chapter XVII. God's Wrath and Punishment 41
    Chapter XVIII. God's Long-suffering and Mercy 43
    Chapter XIX. God's Justice 44
    Chapter XX. God's Love and Compassion 47
    Chapter XXI. God's Truth and Faithfulness 49
    Chapter XXII. God's Knowledge and Wisdom 50
    Chapter XXIII. God's Condescension 52
    C. God In Relation To The World 53
    Chapter XXIV. The World and its Master 53
    Chapter XXV. Creation As the Act of God 55
    Chapter XXVI. The Maintenance and Government of the World 56
    Chapter XXVII. Miracles and the Cosmic Order 57

Chapter XXVIII. Providence and the Moral Government of the World 59

Chapter XXIX. God and the Existence of Evil 62

Chapter XXX. God and the Angels 63

Chapter XXXI. Satan and the Spirits of Evil 66

Chapter XXXII. God and the Intermediary Powers 68

Part II. Man 72

Chapter XXXIII. Man's Place in Creation 72

Chapter XXXIV. The Dual Nature of Man 73

Chapter XXXV. The Origin and Destiny of Man 75

Chapter XXXVI. God's Spirit in Man 78

Chapter XXXVII. Free Will and Moral Responsibility 79

Chapter XXXVIII. The Meaning of Sin 81

Chapter XXXIX. Repentance Or the Return To God 84

Chapter XL. Man, the Child of God 87

Chapter XLI. Prayer and Sacrifice 89

Chapter XLII. The Nature and Purpose of Prayer 92

Chapter XLIII. Death and the Future Life 94

Chapter XLIV. The Immortal Soul of Man 97

Chapter XLV. Divine Retribution: Reward and Punishment 100

Chapter XLVI. The Individual and the Race 104

Chapter XLVII. The Moral Elements of Civilization 106

Part III. Israel And The Kingdom Of God 109

Chapter XLVIII. The Election of Israel 109

Chapter XLIX. The Kingdom of God and the Mission of Israel 111

Chapter L. The Priest-people and its Law of Holiness 114

Chapter LI. Israel, the People of the Law, and its World Mission 118

Chapter LII. Israel, the Servant of the Lord, Martyr and Messiah Of the Nations 122

Chapter LIII. The Messianic Hope 125

Chapter LIV. Resurrection, a National Hope 130

Chapter LV. Israel and the Heathen Nations 131

Chapter LVI. The Stranger and the Proselyte 134

Chapter LVII. Christianity and Mohammedanism, the Daughter-Religions Of Judaism 140

Chapter LVIII. The Synagogue and its Institutions 146

Chapter LIX. The Ethics of Judaism and the Kingdom of God 155

List Of Abbreviations 161

Footnotes 163

Dedication

To The Memory

Of

Edward L. Heinsheimer

The Lamented President of the Board of Governors of

The Hebrew Union College

In Whom Zeal for the High Ideals of Judaism and Patriotic Devotion to Our Blessed Country Were Nobly Embodied In Friendship And Affection

Preface

In offering herewith to the English-reading public the present work on Jewish Theology, the result of many years of research and of years of activity as President and teacher at the Hebrew Union College of Cincinnati, I bespeak for it that fairness of judgment to which every pioneer work is entitled. It may seem rather strange that no such work has hitherto been written by any of the leading Jewish scholars of either the conservative or the progressive school. This can only be accounted for by the fact that up to modern times the Rabbinical and philosophical literature of the Middle Ages sufficed for the needs of the student, and a systematic exposition of the Jewish faith seemed to be unnecessary. Besides, a real demand for the specific study of Jewish theology was scarcely felt, inasmuch as Judaism never assigned to a creed the prominent position which it holds in the Christian Church. This very fact induced Moses Mendelssohn at the beginning of the new era to declare that Judaism "contained only truths dictated by reason and no dogmatic beliefs at all." Moreover, as he was rather a deist than a theist, he stated boldly that Judaism "is not a revealed religion but a revealed law intended solely for the Jewish people as the vanguard of universal monotheism." By taking this legalistic view of Judaism in common with the former opponents of the Maimonidean articles of faith—which, by the way, he had himself translated for the religious instruction of the Jewish youth—he exerted a deteriorating influence upon the normal development of the Jewish faith under the new social conditions. The fact is that Mendelssohn emancipated the modern Jew from the thraldom of the Ghetto, but not Judaism. In the Mendelssohnian circle the impression prevailed, as we are told, that Judaism consists of a system of forms, but is substantially no religion at all. The entire Jewish renaissance period which followed, characteristically enough, made the cultivation of the so-called science of Judaism its object, but it neglected altogether the whole field of Jewish theology. Hence we look in vain among the writings of Rappaport, Zunz, Jost and their followers, the entire Breslau school, for any attempt at presenting the contents of Judaism as a system of faith. Only the pioneers of Reform Judaism, Geiger, Holdheim, Samuel Hirsch, Formstecher, Ludwig Philippson, Leopold Stein, Leopold Loew, and the Reform theologian par excellence David Einhorn, and likewise, Isaac M. Wise in America, made great efforts in that direction. Still a system of Jewish theology was wanting. Accordingly when, at the suggestion of my dear departed friend, Dr. Gustav Karpeles, President of the Society for the Promotion of the Science of Judaism in Berlin, I undertook to write a compendium (Grundriss) of Systematic Jewish Theology, which appeared in 1910 as Vol. IV in a series of works on Systematic Jewish Lore (Grundriss der Gesammtwissenschaft des Judenthums), I had no work before me that might have served me as pattern or guide. Solomon Schechter's valuable studies were in the main confined to Rabbinical Theology. As a matter of fact I accepted the task only with the understanding that it should be written from the view-point of historical research, instead of a mere dogmatic or doctrinal system. For in my opinion the Jewish religion has never been static, fixed for all time by an ecclesiastical authority, but has ever been and still is the result of a dynamic process of growth and development. At the same time I felt that I could not omit the mystical element which pervades the Jewish religion in common with all others. As our prophets were seers and not philosophers or moralists, so divine inspiration in varying degrees constituted a factor of Synagogal as well as Scriptural Judaism. Revelation, therefore, is to be considered as a continuous force in shaping and reshaping the Jewish faith. The religious genius of the Jew falls within the domain of ethnic psychology concerning which science still gropes in the dark, but which progressive Judaism is bound to recognize in its effects throughout the ages.

It is from this standpoint, taken also by the sainted founder of the Hebrew Union College, Isaac M. Wise, that I have written this book. At the same time I endeavored to be, as it behooves the historian, just and fair to Conservative Judaism, which will ever claim the reverence we owe to our cherished past, the mother that raised and nurtured us.

While a work of this nature cannot lay claim to completeness, I have attempted to cover the whole field of Jewish belief, including also such subjects as no longer form parts of the religious consciousness of the modern Jew. I felt especially called upon to elucidate the historical relations of Judaism to the Christian and Mohammedan religions and dwell on the essential points of divergence from them. If my language at times has been rather vigorous in defense of the Jewish faith, it was because I was forced to correct and refute the prevailing view of the Christian world, of both theologians and others, that Judaism is an inferior religion, clannish and exclusive, that it is, in fact, a cult of the Old Testament Law.

It was a matter of great personal satisfaction to me that the German work on its appearance met with warm appreciation in the various theological journals of America, England, and France, as well as of Germany, including both Jewish and Christian. I was encouraged and urged by many "soon to make the book accessible to wider circles in an English translation." My friend, Dr. Israel Abrahams of Cambridge, England, took such interest in the book that he induced a young friend of his to prepare an English version. While this did not answer the purpose, it was helpful to me in making me feel that, instead of a literal translation, a thorough revision and remolding of the book was necessary in order to present it in an acceptable English garb. In pursuing this course, I also enlarged the book in many ways, especially adding a new chapter on Jewish Ethics, which, in connection with the idea of the Kingdom of God, appeared to me to form a fitting culmination of Jewish theology. I have thus rendered it practically a new work. And here I wish to acknowledge my great indebtedness to my young friend and able pupil, Rabbi Lee J. Levinger, for the valuable aid he has rendered me and the painstaking labor he has kindly and unselfishly performed in going over my manuscript from beginning to end, with a view to revising the diction and also suggesting references to more recent publications in the notes so as to bring it up to date.

I trust that the work will prove a source of information and inspiration for both student and layman, Jew and non-Jew, and induce such as have become indifferent to, or prejudiced against, the teachings of the Synagogue, or of Reform Judaism in particular, to take a deeper insight into, and look up with a higher regard to the sublime and eternal verities of Judaism.

"Give to a wise man, and he will be yet wiser; teach a righteous man, and he will increase in learning."

Cincinnati, November, 1917

Introductory

Chapter I. The Meaning of Theology

1. The name Theology, "the teaching concerning God," is taken from Greek philosophy. It was used by Plato and Aristotle to denote the knowledge concerning God and things godly, by which they meant the branch of Philosophy later called Metaphysics, after Aristotle. In the Christian Church the term gradually assumed the meaning of systematic exposition of the creed, a distinction being made between Rational, or Natural Theology, on the one hand, and Dogmatic Theology, on the other.1 In common usage Theology is understood to be the presentation of one specific system of faith after some logical method, and a distinction is made between Historical and Systematic Theology. The former traces the various doctrines of the faith in question through the different epochs and stages of culture, showing their historical process of growth and development; the latter presents these same doctrines in comprehensive form as a fixed system, as they have finally been elaborated and accepted upon the basis of the sacred scriptures and their authoritative interpretation.

2. Theology and Philosophy of Religion differ widely in their character. Theology deals exclusively with a specific religion; in expounding one doctrinal system, it starts from a positive belief in a divine revelation and in the continued working of the divine spirit, affecting also the interpretation and further development of the sacred books. Philosophy of Religion, on the other hand, while dealing with the same subject matter as Theology, treats religion from a general point of view as a matter of experience, and, as every philosophy must, without any foregone conclusion. Consequently it submits the beliefs and doctrines of religion in general to an impartial investigation, recognizing neither a divine revelation nor the superior claims of any one religion above any other, its main object being to ascertain how far the universal laws of human reason agree or disagree with the assertions of faith.2

3. It is therefore incorrect to speak of a Jewish religious philosophy. This has no better right to exist than has Jewish metaphysics or Jewish mathematics.3 The Jewish thinkers of the Spanish-Arabic period who endeavored to harmonize revelation and reason, utilizing the Neo-Platonic philosophy or the Aristotelian with a Neo-Platonic coloring, betray by their very conceptions of revelation and prophecy the influence of Mohammedan theology; this was really a graft of metaphysics on theology and called itself the "divine science," a term corresponding exactly with the Greek "theology." The so-called Jewish religious philosophers adopted both the methods and terminology of the Mohammedan theologians, attempting to present the doctrines of the Jewish faith in the light of philosophy, as truth based on reason. Thus they claimed to construct a Jewish theology upon the foundation of a philosophy of religion.

But neither they nor their Mohammedan predecessors succeeded in working out a complete system of theology. They left untouched essential elements of religion which do not come within the sphere of rational verities, and did not give proper appreciation to the rich treasures of faith deposited in the Biblical and Rabbinical literature. Nor does the comprehensive theological system of Maimonides, which for centuries largely shaped the intellectual life of the Jew, form an exception. Only the mystics, Bahya at their head, paid attention to the spiritual side of Judaism, dwelling at length on such themes as prayer and repentance, divine forgiveness and holiness.

4. Closer acquaintance with the religious and philosophical systems of modern times has created a new demand for a Jewish theology by which the Jew can comprehend his own religious truths in the light of modern thought, and at the same time defend them against the aggressive attitude of the ruling religious sects. Thus far, however, the attempts made in this direction are but feeble and sporadic; if the structure is not to stand altogether in the air, the necessary material must be brought together from its many sources with painstaking labor.4 The special difficulty in the task lies in the radical difference which exists between our view of the past and that of the Biblical and medieval writers. All those things which have heretofore been taken as facts because related in the sacred books or other traditional sources, are viewed to-day with critical eyes, and are now regarded as more or less colored by human impression or conditioned by human judgment. In other words, we have learned to distinguish between subjective and objective truths,5 whereas theology by its very nature deals with truth as absolute. This makes it imperative for us to investigate historically the leading idea or fundamental principle underlying a doctrine, to note

the different conceptions formed at various stages, and trace its process of growth. At times, indeed, we may find that the views of one age have rather taken a backward step and fallen below the original standard. The progress need not be uniform, but we must still trace its course.

5. We must recognize at the outset that Jewish theology cannot assume the character of apologetics, if it is to accomplish its great task of formulating religious truth as it exists in our consciousness to-day. It can no more afford to ignore the established results of modern linguistic, ethnological, and historical research, of Biblical criticism and comparative religion, than it can the undisputed facts of natural science, however much any of these may conflict with the Biblical view of the cosmos. Apologetics has its legitimate place to prove and defend the truths of Jewish theology against other systems of belief and thought, but cannot properly defend either Biblical or Talmudic statements by methods incompatible with scientific investigation. Judaism is a religion of historical growth, which, far from claiming to be the final truth, is ever regenerated anew at each turning point of history. The fall of the leaves at autumn requires no apology, for each successive spring testifies anew to nature's power of resurrection.

The object of a systematic theology of Judaism, accordingly, is to single out the essential forces of the faith. It then will become evident how these fundamental doctrines possess a vitality, a strength of conviction, as well as an adaptability to varying conditions, which make them potent factors amidst all changes of time and circumstance. According to Rabbinical tradition, the broken tablets of the covenant were deposited in the ark beside the new. In like manner the truths held sacred by the past, but found inadequate in their expression for a new generation, must be placed side by side with the deeper and more clarified truths of an advanced age, that they may appear together as the one divine truth reflected in different rays of light.

6. Jewish theology differs radically from Christian theology in the following three points:

A. The theology of Christianity deals with articles of faith formulated by the founders and heads of the Church as conditions of salvation, so that any alteration in favor of free thought threatens to undermine the very plan of salvation upon which the Church was founded. Judaism recognizes only such articles of faith as were adopted by the people voluntarily as expressions of their religious consciousness, both without external compulsion and without doing violence to the dictates of reason. Judaism does not know salvation by faith in the sense of Paul, the real founder of the Church, who declared the blind acceptance of belief to be in itself meritorious. It denies the existence of any irreconcilable opposition between faith and reason.

B. Christian theology rests upon a formula of confession, the so-called Symbolum of the Apostolic Church,6 which alone makes one a Christian. Judaism has no such formula of confession which renders a Jew a Jew. No ecclesiastical authority ever dictated or regulated the belief of the Jew; his faith has been voiced in the solemn liturgical form of prayer, and has ever retained its freshness and vigor of thought in the consciousness of the people. This partly accounts for the antipathy toward any kind of dogma or creed among Jews.

C. The creed is a conditio sine qua non of the Christian Church. To disbelieve its dogmas is to cut oneself loose from membership. Judaism is quite different. The Jew is born into it and cannot extricate himself from it even by the renunciation of his faith, which would but render him an apostate Jew. This condition exists, because the racial community formed, and still forms, the basis of the religious community. It is birth, not confession, that imposes on the Jew the obligation to work and strive for the eternal verities of Israel, for the preservation and propagation of which he has been chosen by the God of history.

7. The truth of the matter is that the aim and end of Judaism is not so much the salvation of the soul in the hereafter as the salvation of humanity in history. Its theology, therefore, must recognize the history of human progress, with which it is so closely interwoven. It does not, therefore, claim to offer the final or absolute truth, as does Christian theology, whether orthodox or liberal. It simply points out the way leading to the highest obtainable truth. Final and perfect truth is held forth as the ideal of all human searching and striving, together with perfect justice, righteousness, and peace, to be attained as the very end of history.

A systematic theology of Judaism must, accordingly, content itself with presenting Jewish doctrine and belief in relation to the most advanced scientific and philosophical ideas of the age, so as to offer a comprehensive view of life and the world ("Lebens- und Weltanschauung"); but it by no means claims for them the character of finality. The unfolding of Judaism's truths will be completed only when all mankind has attained the heights of Zion's mount of vision, as beheld by the prophets of Israel.7

Chapter II. What is Judaism?

1. It is very difficult to give an exact definition of Judaism because of its peculiarly complex character.8 It combines two widely differing elements, and when they are brought out separately, the aspect of the whole is not taken sufficiently into account. Religion and race form an inseparable whole in Judaism. The Jewish people stand in the same relation to Judaism as the body to the soul. The national or racial body of Judaism consists of the remnant of the tribe of Judah which succeeded in establishing a new commonwealth in Judæa in place of the ancient Israelitish kingdom, and which survived the downfall of state and temple to continue its existence as a separate people during a dispersion over the globe for thousands of years, forming ever a cosmopolitan element among all the nations in whose lands it dwelt. Judaism, on the other hand, is the religious system itself, the vital element which united the Jewish people, preserving it and regenerating it ever anew. It is the spirit which endowed the handful of Jews with a power of resistance and a fervor of faith unparalleled in history, enabling them to persevere in the mighty contest with heathenism and Christianity. It made of them a nation of martyrs and thinkers, suffering and struggling for the cause of truth and justice, yet forming, consciously or unconsciously, a potent factor in all the great intellectual movements which are ultimately to win the entire gentile world for the purest and loftiest truths concerning God and man.

2. Judaism, accordingly, does not denote the Jewish nationality, with its political and cultural achievements and aspirations, as those who have lost faith in the religious mission of Israel would have it. On the other hand, it is not a nomistic or legalistic religion confined to the Jewish people, as is maintained by Christian writers, who, lacking a full appreciation of its lofty world-wide purpose and its cosmopolitan and humanitarian character, claim that it has surrendered its universal prophetic truths to Christianity. Nor should it be presented as a religion of pure Theism, aiming to unite all believers in one God into a Church Universal, of which certain visionaries dream. Judaism is nothing less than a message concerning the One and holy God and one, undivided humanity with a world-uniting Messianic goal, a message intrusted by divine revelation to the Jewish people. Thus Israel is its prophetic harbinger and priestly guardian, its witness and defender throughout the ages, who is never to falter in the task of upholding and unfolding its truths until they have become the possession of the whole human race.

3. Owing to this twofold nature of a universal religious truth and at the same time a mission intrusted to a specially selected nation or race, Judaism offers in a sense the sharpest contrasts imaginable, which render it an enigma to the student of religion and history, and make him often incapable of impartial judgment. On the one hand, it shows the most tenacious adherence to forms originally intended to preserve the Jewish people in its priestly sanctity and separateness, and thereby also to keep its religious truths pure and free from encroachments. On the other hand, it manifests a mighty impulse to come into close touch with the various civilized nations, partly in order to disseminate among them its sublime truths, appealing alike to mind and heart, partly to clarify and deepen those truths by assimilating the wisdom and culture of these very nations. Thus the spirit of separatism and of universalism work in opposite directions. Still, however hostile the two elements may appear, they emanate from the same source. For the Jewish people, unlike any other civilization of antiquity, entered history with the proud claim that it possessed a truth destined to become some day the property of mankind, and its three thousand years of history have verified this claim.

Israel's relation to the world thus became a double one. Its priestly world-mission gave rise to all those laws and customs which were to separate it from its idolatrous surroundings, and this occasioned the charge of hostility to the nations. The accusation of Jewish misanthropy occurred as early as the Balaam and Haman stories. As the separation continued through the centuries, a deep-seated Jew-hatred sprang up, first in Alexandria and Rome, then becoming a consuming fire throughout Christendom, unquenched through the ages and bursting forth anew, even from the midst of would-be liberals. In contrast to this, Israel's prophetic ideal of a humanity united in justice and peace gave to history a new meaning and a larger outlook, kindling in the souls of all truly great leaders and teachers, seers and sages of mankind a love and longing for the broadening of humanity which opened new avenues of progress and liberty. Moreover, by its conception of man as the image of God and its teaching of righteousness as the true path of life, Israel's Law established a new standard of human worth and put the imprint of Jewish idealism upon the entire Aryan civilization.

Owing to these two opposing forces, the one centripetal, the other centrifugal, Judaism tended now inward, away from world-culture, now outward toward the learning and the thought of all nations; and this makes it doubly difficult to obtain a true estimate of its character. But, after all, these very currents and counter-currents at the different eras of history kept Judaism in continuous tension and fluctuation, preventing its stagnation by dogmatic formulas and its division by ecclesiastical dissensions. "Both words are the words of the living God" became the maxim of the contending schools.9

4. If we now ask what period we may fix as the beginning of Judaism, we must by no means single out the decisive moment when Ezra the Scribe established the new commonwealth of Judæa, based upon the Mosaic book of Law, and excluding the Samaritans who claimed to be the heirs of ancient Israel. This important step was but the climax, the fruitage of that religious spirit engendered by the Judaism of the Babylonian exile. The Captivity had become a refining furnace for the people, making them cling with a zeal unknown before to the teachings of the prophets, now offered by their disciples, and to the laws, as preserved by the priestly guilds; so the religious treasures of the few became the common property of the many, and were soon regarded as "the inheritance of the whole congregation of Jacob." As a matter of fact, Ezra represents the culmination rather than the starting point of the great spiritual reawakening, when he came from Babylon with a complete Code of Law, and promulgated it in the Holy City to a worshipful congregation.10 It was Judaism, winged with a new spirit, which carried the great unknown seer of the Exile to the very pinnacle of prophetic vision, and made the Psalmists ring forth from the harp of David the deepest soul-stirring notes of religious devotion and aspiration that ever moved the hearts of men. Moreover, all the great truths of prophetic revelation, of legislative and popular wisdom, were then collected and focused, creating a sacred literature which was to serve the whole community as the source of instruction, consolation, and edification. The powerful and unique institutions of the Synagogue, intended for common instruction and devotion, are altogether creations of the Exile, and replaced the former priestly Torah by the Torah for the people. More wonderful still, the priestly lore of ancient Babylon was transformed by sublime monotheistic truths and utilized in the formation of a sacred literature; it was placed before the history of the Hebrew patriarchs, to form, as it were, an introduction to the Bible of humanity.

Judaism, then, far from being the late product of the Torah and tradition, as it is often considered, was actually the creator of the Law. Transformed and unfolded in Babylonia, it created its own sacred literature and shaped it ever anew, filling it always with its own spirit and with new thoughts. It is by no means the petrifaction of the Mosaic law and the prophetic teachings, as we are so often told, but a continuous process of unfolding and regeneration of its great religious truth.

5. True enough, traditional or orthodox Judaism does not share this view. The idea of gradual development is precluded by its conception of divine revelation, by its doctrine that both the oral and the written Torah were given at Sinai complete and unchangeable for all time. It makes allowance only for special institutions begun either by the prophets, by Ezra and the Men of the Great Synagogue, his associates, or by the masters of the Law in succeeding centuries. Nevertheless, tradition says that the Men of the Great Synagogue themselves collected and partly completed the sacred books, except the five books of Moses, and that the canon was made under the influence of the holy spirit. This holy spirit remained in force also during the creative period of Talmudism, sanctioning innovations or alterations of many kinds.11 Modern critical and historical research has taught us to distinguish the products of different periods and stages of development in both the Biblical and Rabbinical sources, and therefore compels us to reject the idea of a uniform origin of the Law, and also of an uninterrupted chain of tradition reaching back to Moses on Sinai. Therefore we must attach still more importance to the process of transformation which Judaism had to undergo through the centuries.12

Judaism manifested its wondrous power of assimilation by renewing itself to meet the demands of the time, first under the influence of the ancient civilizations, Babylonia and Persia, then of Greece and Rome, finally of the Occidental powers, molding its religious truths and customs in ever new forms, but all in consonance with its own genius. It adopted the Babylonian and Persian views of the hereafter, of the upper and the nether world with their angels and demons; so later on it incorporated into its religious and legal system elements of Greek and Egyptian gnosticism, Greek philosophy, and methods of jurisprudence from Egypt, Babylon, and Rome. In fact, the various parties which arose during the second Temple beside each other or successively—Sadducees and Pharisees, Essenes and Zealots—represent, on closer observation, the different stages in the process of assimilation which Judaism had to undergo. In like manner, the Hellenistic, Apocryphal and Apocalyptic literature, which was rejected and lost to sight by traditional Judaism, and which partly fills the gap between the Bible and the Talmudic writings, casts a flood of light upon the development of the Halakah and the Haggadah. Just as the book of Ezekiel, which was almost excluded from the Canon on account of its divergence from the Mosaic Law, has been helpful in tracing the development of the Priestly Code,13 so the Sadduceean book of Ben Sira14 and the Zealotic book of Jubilees15—not to mention the various Apocalyptic works—throw their searchlight upon pre-Talmudic Judaism.

6. Instead of representing Judaism—as the Christian theologians do under the guise of scientific methods—as a nomistic religion, caring only for the external observance of the Law, it is necessary to distinguish two opposite fundamental tendencies; the one expressing the spirit of legalistic nationalism, the other that of ethical or prophetic universalism. These two work by turn, directing the general trend in the one or the other direction according to circumstances. At one time the center and focus of Israel's religion is the Mosaic Law, with its sacrificial cult in charge of the priesthood of Jerusalem's Temple; at another time it is the Synagogue, with its congregational devotion and public instruction, its inspiring song of the Psalmist and its prophetic consolation and hope confined to no narrow territory, but opened wide for a listening world. Here it is the reign of the Halakah holding fast to the form of tradition, and there the free and fanciful Haggadah, with its appeal to the sentiments and views of the people. Here it is the spirit of ritualism, bent on separating the Jews from the influence of foreign elements, and there again the spirit of rationalism, eager to take part in general culture and in the progress of the outside world.

The liberal views of Maimonides and Gersonides concerning miracle and revelation, God and immortality were scarcely shared by the majority of Jews, who, no doubt, sided rather with the mystics, and found their mouthpiece in Abraham ben David of Posquieres, the fierce opponent of Maimonides. An impartial Jewish theology must therefore take cognizance of both sides; it must include the mysticism of Isaac Luria and Sabbathai Horwitz as well as the rationalism of Albo and Leo da Modena. Wherever is voiced a new doctrine or a new view of life and life's duty, which yet bears the imprint of the Jewish consciousness, there the well-spring of divine inspiration is seen pouring forth its living waters.

7. Even the latest interpretation of the Law, offered by a disciple who is recognized for true conscientiousness in religion, was revealed to Moses on Sinai, according to a Rabbinical dictum.16 Thus is exquisitely expressed the idea of a continuous development of Israel's religious truth. As a safeguard against arbitrary individualism, there was the principle of loyalty and proper regard for tradition, which is aptly termed by Professor Lazarus a "historical continuity."17 The Midrashic statement is quite significant that other creeds founded on our Bible can only adhere to the letter, but the Jewish religion possesses the key to the deeper meaning hidden and presented in the traditional interpretation of the Scriptures.18 That is, for Judaism Holy Scripture in its literal sense is not the final word of God; the Bible is rather a living spring of divine revelation, to be kept ever fresh and flowing by the active force of the spirit. To sum up: Judaism, far from offering a system of beliefs and ceremonies fixed for all time, is as multifarious and manifold in its aspects as is life itself. It comprises all phases and characteristics of both a national and a world religion.

Chapter III. The Essence of the Religion of Judaism

1. We have seen how difficult it is to define Judaism clearly and adequately, including its manifold tendencies and institutions. Still it is necessary that we reach a full understanding of the essence of Judaism as it manifested itself in all periods of its history,19 and that we single out the fundamental idea which underlies its various forms of existence and its different movements, both intellectual and spiritual. There can be no disputing the fact that the central idea of Judaism and its life purpose is the doctrine of the One Only and Holy God, whose kingdom of truth, justice and peace is to be universally established at the end of time. This is the main teaching of Scripture and the hope voiced in the liturgy; while Israel's mission to defend, to unfold and to propagate this truth is a corollary of the doctrine itself and cannot be separated from it. Whether we regard it as Law or a system of doctrine, as religious truth or world-mission, this belief pledged the little tribe of Judah to a warfare of many thousands of years against the hordes of heathendom with all their idolatry and brutality, their deification of man and their degradation of deity to human rank. It betokened a battle for the pure idea of God and man, which is not to end until the principle of divine holiness has done away with every form of life that tends to degrade and to disunite mankind, and until Israel's Only One has become the unifying power and the highest ideal of all humanity.

2. Of this great world-duty of Israel only the few will ever become fully conscious. As in the days of the prophets, so in later periods, only a "small remnant" was fully imbued with the lofty ideal. In times of oppression the great multitude of the people persisted in a conscientious observance of the Law and underwent suffering without a

murmur. Yet in times of liberty and enlightenment this same majority often neglects to assimilate the new culture to its own superior spirit, but instead eagerly assimilates itself to the surrounding world, and thereby loses much of its intrinsic strength and self-respect. The pendulum of thought and sentiment swings to and fro between the national and the universal ideals, while only a few maturer minds have a clear vision of the goal as it is to be reached along both lines of development. Nevertheless, Judaism is in a true sense a religion of the people. It is free from all priestly tutelage and hierarchical interference. It has no ecclesiastical system of belief, guarded and supervised by men invested with superior powers. Its teachers and leaders have always been men from among the people, like the prophets of yore, with no sacerdotal privilege or title; in fact, in his own household each father is the God-appointed teacher of his children.20

3. Neither is Judaism the creation of a single person, either prophet or a man with divine claims. It points back to the patriarchs as its first source of revelation. It speaks not of the God of Moses, of Amos and Isaiah, but of the God of Abraham, Isaac, and Jacob, thereby declaring the Jewish genius to be the creator of its own religious ideas. It is therefore incorrect to speak of a "Mosaic," "Hebrew," or "Israelitish," religion. The name Judaism alone expresses the preservation of the religious heritage of Israel by the tribe of Judah, with a loyalty which was first displayed by Judah himself in the patriarchal household, and which became its characteristic virtue in the history of the various tribes. Likewise the rigid measures of Ezra in expelling all foreign elements from the new commonwealth proved instrumental in impressing loyalty and piety upon Jewish family life.

4. As it was bound up with the life of the Jewish people, Judaism remained forever in close touch with the world. Therefore it appreciated adequately the boons of life, and escaped being reduced to the shadowy form of "otherworldliness."21 It is a religion of life, which it wishes to sanctify by duty rather than by laying stress on the hereafter. It looks to the deed and the purity of the motive, not to the empty creed and the blind belief. Nor is it a religion of redemption, contemning this earthly life; for Judaism repudiates the assumption of a radical power of evil in man or in the world. Faith in the ultimate triumph of the good is essential to it. In fact, this perfect confidence in the final victory of truth and justice over all the powers of falsehood and wrong lent it both its wondrous intellectual force and its high idealism, and adorned its adherents with the martyr's crown of thorns, such as no other human brow has ever borne.

5. Christianity and Islam, notwithstanding their alienation from Judaism and frequent hostility, are still daughter-religions. In so far as they have sown the seeds of Jewish truth over all the globe and have done their share in upbuilding the Kingdom of God on earth, they must be recognized as divinely appointed emissaries and agencies. Still Judaism sets forth its doctrine of God's unity and of life's holiness in a far superior form than does Christianity. It neither permits the deity to be degraded into the sphere of the sensual and human, nor does it base its morality upon a love bereft of the vital principle of justice. Against the rigid monotheism of Islam, which demands blind submission to the stern decrees of inexorable fate, Judaism on the other hand urges its belief in God's paternal love and mercy, which educates all the children of men, through trial and suffering, for their high destiny.

6. Judaism denies most emphatically the right of Christianity or any other religion to arrogate to itself the title of "the absolute religion" or to claim to be "the finest blossom and the ripest fruit of religious development." As if any mortal man at any time or under any condition could say without presumption: "I am the Truth" or "No one cometh unto the Father but by me."22 "When man was to proceed from the hands of his Maker," says the Midrash, "the Holy One, Blessed be His name, cast truth down to the earth, saying, 'Let truth spring forth from the earth, and righteousness look down from heaven.' "23 The full unfolding of the religious and moral life of mankind is the work of countless generations yet to come, and many divine heralds of truth and righteousness have yet to contribute their share. In this work of untold ages, Judaism claims that it has achieved and is still achieving its full part as the prophetic world-religion. Its law of righteousness, which takes for its scope the whole of human life, in its political and social relations as well as its personal aspects, forms the foundation of its ethics for all time; while its hope for a future realization of the Kingdom of God has actually become the aim of human history. As a matter of fact, when the true object of religion is the hallowing of life rather than the salvation of the soul, there is little room left for sectarian exclusiveness, or for a heaven for believers and a hell for unbelievers. With this broad outlook upon life, Judaism lays claim, not to perfection, but to perfectibility; it has supreme capacity for growing toward the highest ideals of mankind, as beheld by the prophets in their Messianic visions.

Chapter IV. The Jewish Articles of Faith

1. In order to reach a clear opinion, whether or not Judaism has articles of faith in the sense of Church dogmas, a question so much discussed since the days of Moses Mendelssohn, it seems necessary first to ascertain what faith in general means to the Jew.24 Now the word used in Jewish literature for faith is Emunah, from the root Aman, to be firm; this denotes firm reliance upon God, and likewise firm adherence to him, hence both faith and faithfulness. Both Scripture and the Rabbis demanded confiding trust in God, His messengers, and His words, not the formal acceptance of a prescribed belief.25 Only when contact with the non-Jewish world emphasized the need for a clear expression of the belief in the unity of God, such as was found in the Shema,26 and when the proselyte was expected to declare in some definite form the fundamentals of the faith he espoused, was the importance of a concrete confession felt.27 Accordingly we find the beginnings of a formulated belief in the synagogal liturgy, in the Emeth we Yatzib28 and the Alenu,29 while in the Haggadah Abraham is represented both as the exemplar of a hero of faith and as the type of a missionary, wandering about to lead the heathen world towards the pure monotheistic faith.30 While the Jewish concept of faith underwent a certain transformation, influenced by other systems of belief, and the formulation of Jewish doctrines appeared necessary, particularly in opposition to the Christian and Mohammedan creeds, still belief never became the essential part of religion, conditioning salvation, as in the Church founded by Paul. For, as pointed out above, Judaism lays all stress upon conduct, not confession; upon a hallowed life, not a hollow creed.

2. There is no Biblical nor Rabbinical precept, "Thou shalt believe!" Jewish thinkers felt all the more the need to point out as fundamentals or roots of Judaism those doctrines upon which it rests, and from which it derives its vital force. To the rabbis, the "root" of faith is the recognition of a divine Judge to whom we owe account for all our doings.31 The recital of the Shema, which is called in the Mishnah "accepting the yoke of God's sovereignty," and which is followed by the solemn affirmation, "True and firm belief is this for us"32 (Emeth we Yatzib or Emeth we Emunah), is, in fact, the earliest form of the confession of faith.33 In the course of time this confession of belief in the unity of God was no longer deemed sufficient to serve as basis for the whole structure of Judaism; so the various schools and authorities endeavored to work out in detail a series of fundamental doctrines.

3. The Mishnah, in Sanhedrin, X, 1, which seems to date back to the beginnings of Pharisaism, declares the following three to have no share in the world to come: he who denies the resurrection of the dead; he who says that the Torah—both the written and the oral Law—is not divinely revealed; and the Epicurean, who does not believe in the moral government of the world.34 We find here (in reverse order, owing to historical conditions), the beliefs in Revelation, Retribution, and the Hereafter singled out as the three fundamentals of Rabbinical Judaism. Rabbi Hananel, the great North African Talmudist, about the middle of the tenth century, seems to have been under the influence of Mohammedan and Karaite doctrines, when he speaks of four fundamentals of the faith: God, the prophets, the future reward and punishment, and the Messiah.35

4. The doctrine of the One and Only God stands, as a matter of course, in the foreground. Philo of Alexandria, at the end of his treatise on Creation, singles out five principles which are bound up with it, viz.: 1, God's existence and His government of the world; 2, His unity; 3, the world as His creation; 4, the harmonious plan by which it was established; and 5, His Providence. Josephus, too, in his apology for Judaism written against Apion,36 emphasizes the belief in God's all-encompassing Providence, His incorporeality, and His self-sufficiency as the Creator of the universe.

The example of Islam, which had very early formulated a confession of faith of speculative character for daily recitation,37 influenced first Karaite and then Rabbanite teachers to elaborate the Jewish doctrine of One Only God into a philosophic creed. The Karaites modeled their creed after the Mohammedan pattern, which gave them ten articles of faith; of these the first three dwelt on: 1, creation out of nothing; 2, the existence of God, the Creator; 3, the unity and incorporeality of God.38

Abraham ben David (Ibn Daud) of Toledo sets forth in his "Sublime Faith" six essentials of the Jewish faith: 1, the existence; 2, the unity; 3, the incorporeality; 4, the omnipotence of God (to this he subjoins the existence of angelic beings); 5, revelation and the immutability of the Law; and 6, divine Providence.39 Maimonides, the greatest of all medieval thinkers, propounded thirteen articles of faith, which took the place of a creed in the Synagogue for the following centuries, as they were incorporated in the liturgy both in the form of a credo (Ani Maamin) and in a poetic version. His first five articles were: 1, the existence; 2, the unity; 3, the incorporeality; 4, the eternity of God;

and 5, that He alone should be the object of worship; to which we must add his 10th, divine Providence.40 Others, not satisfied with the purely metaphysical form of the Maimonidean creed, accentuated the doctrines of creation out of nothing and special Providence.41

This speculative form of faith, however, has been most severely denounced by Samuel David Luzzatto (1800-1865) as "Atticism";42 that is, the Hellenistic or philosophic tendency to consider religion as a purely intellectual system, instead of the great dynamic force for man's moral and spiritual elevation. He holds that Judaism, as the faith transmitted to us from Abraham, our ancestor, must be considered, not as a mere speculative mode of reasoning, but as a moral life force, manifested in the practice of righteousness and brotherly love. Indeed, this view is supported by modern Biblical research, which brings out as the salient point in Biblical teaching the ethical character of the God taught by the prophets, and shows that the essential truth of revelation is not to be found in a metaphysical but in an ethical monotheism. At the same time, the fact must not be overlooked that the Jewish doctrine of God's unity was strengthened in the contest with the dualistic and trinitarian beliefs of other religions, and that this unity gave Jewish thought both lucidity and sublimity, so that it has surpassed other faiths in intellectual power and in passion for truth. The Jewish conception of God thus makes truth, as well as righteousness and love, both a moral duty for man and a historical task comprising all humanity.

5. The second fundamental article of the Jewish faith is divine revelation, or, as the Mishnah expresses it, the belief that the Torah emanates from God (min ha shamayim). In the Maimonidean thirteen articles, this is divided into four: his 6th, belief in the prophets; 7, in the prophecy of Moses as the greatest of all; 8, in the divine origin of the Torah, both the written and the oral Law; and 9, its immutability. The fundamental character of these, however, was contested by Hisdai Crescas and his disciples, Simon Duran and Joseph Albo.43 As a matter of fact, they are based not so much upon Rabbinical teaching as upon the prevailing views of Mohammedan theology,44 and were undoubtedly dictated by the desire to dispute the claims of Christianity and Islam that they represented a higher revelation. Our modern historical view, however, includes all human thought and belief; it therefore rejects altogether the assumption of a supernatural origin of either the written or the oral Torah, and insists that the subject of prophecy, revelation, and inspiration in general be studied in the light of psychology and ethnology, of general history and comparative religion.

6. The third fundamental article of the Jewish faith is the belief in a moral government of the world, which manifests itself in the reward of good and the punishment of evil, either here or hereafter. Maimonides divides this into two articles, which really belong together, his 10th, God's knowledge of all human acts and motives, and 11, reward and punishment. The latter includes the hereafter and the last Day of Judgment, which, of course, applies to all human beings.

7. Closely connected with retribution is the belief in the resurrection of the dead, which is last among the thirteen articles. This belief, which originally among the Pharisees had a national and political character, and was therefore connected especially with the Holy Land (as will be seen in Chapter LIV below), received in the Rabbinical schools more and more a universal form. Maimonides went so far as to follow the Platonic view rather than that of the Bible or the Talmud, and thus transformed it into a belief in the continuity of the soul after death. In this form, however, it is actually a postulate, or corollary, of the belief in retribution.

8. The old hope for the national resurrection of Israel took in the Maimonidean system the form of a belief in the coming of the Messiah (article 12), to which, in the commentary on the Mishnah, he gives the character of a belief in the restoration of the Davidic dynasty. Joseph Albo, with others, disputes strongly the fundamental character of this belief; he shows the untenability of Maimonides' position by referring to many Talmudic passages, and at the same time he casts polemical side glances upon the Christian Church, which is really founded on Messianism in the special form of its Christology.45 Jehuda ha Levi, in his Cuzari, substitutes for this as a fundamental doctrine the belief in the election of Israel for its world-mission.46 It certainly redounds to the credit of the leaders of the modern Reform movement that they took the election of Israel rather than the Messiah as their cardinal doctrine, again bringing it home to the religious consciousness of the Jew, and placing it at the very center of their system. In this way they reclaimed for the Messianic hope the universal character which was originally given it by the great seer of the Exile.47

9. The thirteen articles of Maimonides, in setting forth a Jewish Credo, formed a vigorous opposition to the Christian and Mohammedan creeds; they therefore met almost universal acceptance among the Jewish people, and were given a place in the common prayerbook, in spite of their deficiencies, as shown by Crescas and his school.

Nevertheless, we must admit that Crescas shows the deeper insight into the nature of religion when he observes that the main fallacy of the Maimonidean system lies in founding the Jewish faith on speculative knowledge, which is a matter of the intellect, rather than love which flows from the heart, and which alone leads to piety and goodness. True love, he says, requires the belief neither in retribution nor in immortality. Moreover, in striking contrast to the insistence of Maimonides or the immutability of the Mosaic Law, Crescas maintains the possibility of its continuous progress in accordance with the intellectual and spiritual needs of the time, or, what amounts to the same thing, the continuous perfectibility of the revealed Law itself.48 Thus the criticism of Crescas leads at once to a radically different theology than that of Maimonides, and one which appeals far more to our own religious thought.

10. Another doctrine of Judaism, which was greatly underrated by medieval scholars, and which has been emphasized in modern times only in contrast to the Christian theory of original sin, is that man was created in the image of God. Judaism holds that the soul of man came forth pure from the hand of its Maker, endowed with freedom, unsullied by any inherent evil or inherited sin. Thus man is, through the exercise of his own free will, capable of attaining to an ever higher degree his mental, moral, and spiritual powers in the course of history. This is the Biblical idea of God's spirit as immanent in man; all prophetic truth is based upon it; and though it was often obscured, this theory was voiced by many of the masters of Rabbinical lore, such as R. Akiba and others.49

11. Every attempt to formulate the doctrines or articles of faith of Judaism was made, in order to guard the Jewish faith from the intrusion of foreign beliefs, never to impose disputed beliefs upon the Jewish community itself. Many, indeed, challenged the fundamental character of the thirteen articles of Maimonides. Albo reduced them to three, viz.: the belief in God, in revelation, and retribution; others, with more arbitrariness than judgement, singled out three, five, six, or even more as principal doctrines;50 while rigid conservatives, such as Isaac Abravanel and David ben Zimra, altogether disapproved the attempt to formulate articles of faith. The former maintained that every word in the Torah is, in fact, a principle of faith, and the latter51 pointed in the same way to the 613 commandments of the Torah, spoken of by R. Simlai the Haggadist in the third century.52

The present age of historical research imposes the same necessity of restatement or reformulation upon us. We must do as Maimonides did,—as Jews have always done,—point out anew the really fundamental doctrines, and discard those which have lost their holdup on the modern Jew, or which conflict directly with his religious consciousness. If Judaism is to retain its prominent position among the powers of thought, and to be clearly understood by the modern world, it must again reshape its religious truths in harmony with the dominant ideas of the age.

Many attempts of this character have been made by modern rabbis and teachers, most of them founded upon Albo's three articles. Those who penetrated somewhat more deeply into the essence of Judaism added a fourth article, the belief in Israel's priestly mission, and at the same time, instead of the belief in retribution, included the doctrine of man's kinship with God, or, if one may coin the word, his God-childship.53 Few, however, have succeeded in working out the entire content of the Jewish faith from a modern viewpoint, which must include historical, critical, and psychological research, as well as the study of comparative religion.

12. The following tripartite plan is that of the present attempt to present the doctrines of Judaism systematically along the lines of historical development:

I. God

a. Man's consciousness of God, and divine revelation.

b. God's spirituality, His unity, His holiness, His perfection.

c. His relation to the world: Creation and Providence.

d. His relation to man: His justice, His love and mercy.

II. Man

a. Man's God-childship; his moral freedom and yearning for God.

b. Sin and repentance; prayer and worship; immortality, reward and punishment.

c. Man and humanity: the moral factors in history.

III. Israel and the Kingdom of God

a. The priest-mission of Israel, its destiny as teacher and martyr among the nations, and its Messianic hope.

b. The Kingdom of God: the nations and religions of the world in a divine plan of universal salvation.

c. The Synagogue and its institutions.

d. The ethics of Judaism and the Kingdom of God.

Part I. God

A. God As He Makes Himself Known To Man

Chapter V. Man's Consciousness of God and Belief in God

1. Holy Writ employs two terms for religion, both of which lay stress upon its moral and spiritual nature: Yirath Elohim—"fear of God"—and Daath Elohim—"knowledge or consciousness of God." Whatever the fear of God may have meant in the lower stages of primitive religion, in the Biblical and Rabbinical conceptions it exercises a wholesome moral effect; it stirs up the conscience and keeps man from wrongdoing. Where fear of God is lacking, violence and vice are rife;54 it keeps society in order and prompts the individual to walk in the path of duty. Hence it is called "the beginning of wisdom."55 The divine revelation of Sinai accentuates as its main purpose "to put the fear of God into the hearts of the people, lest they sin."56

2. God-consciousness, or "knowledge of God," signifies an inner experience which impels man to practice the right and to shun evil, the recognition of God as the moral power of life. "Because there is no knowledge of God," therefore do the people heap iniquity upon iniquity, says Hosea, and he hopes to see the broken covenant with the Lord renewed through faithfulness grounded on the consciousness of God.57 Jeremiah also insists upon "the knowledge of God" as a moral force, and, like Hosea, he anticipates the renewal of the broken covenant when "the Lord shall write His law upon the heart" of the people, and "they shall all know Him from the least of them unto the greatest of them."58 Wherever Scripture speaks of "knowledge of God,"59 it always means the moral and spiritual recognition of the Deity as life's inmost power, determining human conduct, and by no means refers to mere intellectual perception of the truth of Jewish monotheism, which is to refute the diverse forms of polytheism. This misconception of the term "knowledge of God," as used in the Bible, led the leading medieval thinkers of Judaism, especially the school of Maimonides, and even down to Mendelssohn, into the error of confusing religion and philosophy, as if both resulted from pure reason. It is man's moral nature rather than his intellectual capacity, that leads him "to know God and walk in His ways."60

3. It is mainly through the conscience that man becomes conscious of God. He sees himself, a moral being, guided by motives which lend a purpose to his acts and his omissions, and thus feels that this purpose of his must somehow be in accord with a higher purpose, that of a Power who directs and controls the whole of life. The more he sees purpose ruling individuals and nations, the more will his God-consciousness grow into the conviction that there is but One and Only God, who in awful grandeur holds dominion over the world. This is the developmental process of religious truth, as it is unfolded by the prophets and as it underlies the historic framework of the Bible. In this light Jewish monotheism appears as the ripe fruitage of religion in its universal as well as its primitive form of God-consciousness, as the highest attainment of man in his eternal seeking after God. Polytheism, on the other hand, with its idolatrous and immoral practices, appeared to the prophets and lawgivers of Israel to be, not a competing religion, but simply a falling away from God. They felt it to be a loss or eclipse of the genuine God-consciousness. The object of revelation, therefore, is to lead back all mankind to the God whom it had deserted, and to restore to all men their primal consciousness of God, with its power of moral regeneration.

4. In the same degree as this God-consciousness grows stronger, it crystallizes into belief in God, and culminates in love of God. As stated above,61 in Judaism belief—Emunah—never denotes the acceptance of a creed. It is rather the confiding trust by which the frail mortal finds a firm hold on God amidst the uncertainties and anxieties of life, the search for His shelter in distress, the reliance on His ever-ready help when one's own powers fail. The believer is like a little child who follows confidingly the guidance of his father, and feels safe when near his arm. In fact, the double meaning of Emunah, faith and faithfulness, suggests man's child-like faith in the paternal faithfulness of God. The patriarch Abraham is presented in both Biblical and Rabbinical writings as the pattern of such a faith,62 and the Jewish people likewise are characterized in the Talmud as "believers, sons of believers."63 The Midrash extols such life-cheering faith as the power which inspires true heroism and deeds of valor.64

5. The highest triumph of God-consciousness, however, is attained in love of God such as can renounce cheerfully all the boons of life and undergo the bitterest woe without a murmur. The book of Deuteronomy inculcates love of God as the beginning and the end of the Law,65 and the rabbis declare it to be the highest type of human perfection. In commenting upon the verse, "Thou shalt love the Lord thy God with all thy heart, with all thy soul, and with all thy might," they say: "Love the Law, even when thy life is demanded as its price, nay, even with the last breath of thy body, with a heart that has no room for dissent, amid every visitation of destiny!"66 They point to the tragic martyrdom of R. Akiba as an example of such a love sealed by death. In like manner they refer the expression, "they that love Thee,"67 to those who bear insults without resentment; who hear themselves abused without retort; who do good unselfishly, without caring for recognition; and who cheerfully suffer as a test of their fortitude and their love of God.68 Thus throughout all Rabbinical literature love of God is regarded as the highest principle of religion and as the ideal of human perfection, which was exemplified by Job, according to the oldest Haggadah, and, according to the Mishnah, by Abraham.69 Another interpretation of the verse cited from Deuteronomy reads, "Love God in such a manner that thy fellow-creatures may love Him owing to thy deeds."70

All these passages and many others71 show what a prominent place the principle of love occupied in Judaism. This is, indeed, best voiced in the Song of Songs:72 "For love is strong as death; the flashes thereof are flashes of fire, a very flame of the Lord. Many waters cannot quench that love, neither can the floods drown it." It set the heart of the Jew aglow during all the centuries, prompting him to sacrifice his life and all that was dear to him for the glorification of his God, to undergo for his faith a martyrdom without parallel in history.

Chapter VI. Revelation, Prophecy, and Inspiration

1. Divine revelation signifies two different things: first, God's self-revelation, which the Rabbis called Gilluy Shekinah, "the manifestation of the divine Presence," and, second, the revelation of His will, for which they used the term Torah min ha Shamayim, "the Law as emanating from God."73 The former appealed to the child-like belief of the Biblical age, which took no offense at anthropomorphic ideas, such as the descent of God from heaven to earth, His appearing to men in some visible form, or any other miracle; the latter appears to be more acceptable to those of more advanced religious views. Both conceptions, however, imply that the religious truth of revelation was communicated to man by a special act of God.

2. Each creative act is a mystery beyond the reach of human observation. In all fields of endeavor the flashing forth of genius impresses us as the work of a mysterious force, which acts upon an elect individual or nation and brings it into close touch with the divine. In the religious genius especially is this true; for in him all the spiritual forces of the age seem to be energized and set into motion, then to burst forth into a new religious consciousness, which is to revolutionize religious thought and feeling. In a child-like age when the emotional life and the imagination predominate, and man's mind, still receptive, is overwhelmed by mighty visions, the Deity stirs the soul in some form perceptible to the senses. Thus the "seer" assumes a trance-like state where the Ego, the self-conscious personality, is pushed into the background; he becomes a passive instrument, the mouthpiece of the Deity; from Him he receives a message to the people, and in his vision he beholds God who sends him. This appearance of God upon the background of the soul, which reflects Him like a mirror, is Revelation.74

3. The states of the soul when men see such visions of the Deity predominate in the beginnings of all religions. Accordingly, Scripture ascribes such revelations to non-Israelites as well as to the patriarchs and prophets of Israel,—to Abimelek and Laban, Balaam, Job, and Eliphaz.75 Therefore the Jewish prophet is not distinguished from the rest by the capability to receive divine revelation, but rather by the intrinsic nature of the revelation which he receives. His vision comes from a moral God. The Jewish genius perceived God as the moral power of life, whether in the form expressed by Abraham, Moses, Elijah, or by the literary prophets, and all of these, coming into touch with Him, were lifted into a higher sphere, where they received a new truth, hitherto hidden from man. In speaking through them, God appeared actually to have stepped into the sphere of human life as its moral Ruler. This self-revelation of God as the Ruler of man in righteousness, which must be viewed in the life of any prophet as a providential act, forms the great historical sequence in the history of Israel, upon which rests the Jewish religion.76

4. The divine revelation in Israel was by no means a single act, but a process of development, and its various stages correspond to the degrees of culture of the people. For this reason the great prophets also depended largely upon

dreams and visions, at least in their consecration to the prophetic mission, when one solemn act was necessary. After that the message itself and its new moral content set the soul of the prophet astir. Not the vision or its imagery, but the new truth itself seizes him with irresistible force, so that he is carried away by the divine power and speaks as the mouthpiece of God, using lofty poetic diction while in a state of ecstasy. Hence he speaks of God in the first person. The highest stage of all is that where the prophet receives the divine truth in the form of pure thought and with complete self-consciousness. Therefore the Scripture says of Moses and of no other, "The Lord spoke to Moses face to face, as a man speaks to another."77

5. The story of the giving of the Law on Mount Sinai is in reality the revelation of God to the people of Israel as part of the great world-drama of history. Accordingly, the chief emphasis is laid upon the miraculous element, the descent of the Lord to the mountain in fire and storm, amid thunder and lightning, while the Ten Words themselves were proclaimed by Moses as God's herald.78 As a matter of fact, the first words of the narrative state its purpose, the consecration of the Jewish people at the outset of their history to be a nation of prophets and priests.79 Therefore the rabbis lay stress upon the acceptance of the Law by the people in saying: "All that the Lord sayeth we shall do and hearken."80 From a larger point of view, we see here the dramatized form of the truth of Israel's election by divine Providence for its historic religious mission.

6. The rabbis ascribed the gifts of prophecy to pagans as well as Israelites at least as late as the erection of the Tabernacle, after which the Divine Presence dwelt there in the midst of Israel.81 They say that each of the Jewish prophets was endowed with a peculiar spiritual power that corresponded with his character and his special training, the highest, of course, being Moses, whom they called "the father of the prophets."82

The medieval Jewish thinkers, following the lead of Mohammedan philosophers or theologians, regard revelation quite differently, as an inner process in the mind of the prophet. According to their mystical or rationalistic viewpoint, they describe it as the result of the divine spirit, working upon the soul either from within or from without. These two standpoints betray either the Platonic or the Aristotelian influence.83 Indeed, the rabbis themselves showed traces of neo-Platonism when they described the ecstatic state of the prophets, or when they spoke of the divine spirit speaking through the prophet as through a vocal instrument, or when they made distinctions between seeing the Deity "in a bright mirror" or "through a dark glass."84

The view most remote from the simple one of the Bible is the rationalistic standpoint of Maimonides, who, following altogether in the footsteps of the Arabic neo-Aristotelians, assumed that there were different degrees of prophecy, depending upon the influence exerted upon the human intellect by the sphere of the Highest Intelligence. He enumerates eleven such grades, of which Moses had the highest rank, as he entered into direct communication with the supreme intellectual sphere. Still bolder is his explanation of the revelation on Sinai. He holds that the first two words were understood by the people directly as logical evidences of truth, for they enunciated the philosophical doctrines of the existence and unity of God, whereas the other words they understood only as sounds without meaning, so that Moses had to interpret them.85 In contrast to this amazing rationalism of Maimonides is the view of Jehuda ha Levi, who asserts that the gift of prophecy became the specific privilege of the descendants of Abraham after their consecration as God's chosen people at Sinai, and that the holy soil of Palestine was assigned to them as the habitation best adapted to its exercise.86 The other attempt of some rationalistic thinkers of the Middle Ages to have a "sound created for the purpose"87 of uttering the words "I am the Lord thy God," rather than accepting the anthropomorphic Deity, merits no consideration whatever.

7. It is an indisputable fact of history that the Jewish people, on account of its peculiar religious bent, was predestined to be the people of revelation. Its leading spirits, its prophets and psalmists, its law-givers and inspired writers differ from the seers, singers, and sages of other nations by their unique and profound insight into the moral nature of the Deity. In striking contrast is the progress of thought in Greece, where the awakening of the ethical consciousness caused a rupture between the culture of the philosophers and the popular religion, and led to a final decay of the political and social life. The prophets of Israel, however, the typical men of genius of their people, gradually brought about an advance of popular religion, so that they could finally present as their highest ideal the God of the fathers, and make the knowledge of His will the foundation of the law of holiness, by which they desired to regulate the entire conduct of man. Thus, religion was no longer confined by the limits of nationality, but was transformed into a spiritual force for all mankind, to lead through a revelation of the One and Holy God toward the highest morality.

8. The development of thought brought the God-seeking spirits to the desire to know His will, or, in Scriptural language, His ways, in order to attain holiness in their pursuit. The natural consequence was the gradual receding of the power of imagination which had made the enraptured seer behold God Himself in visions. As the Deity rose more and more above the realm of the visible, the newly conceived truth was realized as coming to the sacred writer through the spirit of God or an angel. Inspiration took the place of revelation. This, however, still implies a passive attitude of the soul carried away by the truth it receives from on high. This supernatural element disappears gradually and passes over into sober, self-conscious thought, in which the writer no longer thinks of God as the Ego speaking through him, but as an outside Power spoken of in the third person.

A still lower degree of inspiration is represented by those writings which lack altogether the divine afflatus, and to which is ascribed a share of the holy spirit only through general consensus of opinion. Often this imprint of the divine is not found in them by the calm judgment of a later generation, and the exact basis for the classification of such writings among the holy books is sometimes difficult to state. We can only conclude that in the course of time they were regarded as holy by that very spirit which was embodied in the Synagogue and its founders, "the Men of the Great Synagogue," who in their work of canonizing the Sacred Scriptures were believed to have been under the influence of the holy spirit.88

9. Except for the five books of Moses, the idea of a mechanical inspiration of the Bible is quite foreign to Judaism. Not until the second Christian century did the rabbis finally decide on such questions as the inspiration of certain books among the Hagiographa or even among the Prophets, or whether certain books now excluded from the canon were not of equal rank with the canonical ones.89 In fact, the influence of the holy spirit was for some time ascribed, not only to Biblical writers, but also to living masters of the law.90 The fact is that divine influence cannot be measured by the yardstick or the calendar. Where it is felt, it bursts forth as from a higher world, creating for itself its proper organs and forms. The rabbis portray God as saying to Israel, "Not I in My higher realm, but you with your human needs fix the form, the measure, the time, and the mode of expression for that which is divine."91

10. While Christianity and Islam, its daughter-religions, must admit the existence of a prior revelation, Judaism knows of none. It claims its own prophetic truth as the revelation, admits the title Books of Revelation (Bible) only for its own sacred writings, and calls the Jewish nation alone the People of Revelation. The Church and the Mosque achieved great things in propagating the truths of the Sinaitic revelation among the nations, but added to it no new truths of an essential nature. Indeed, they rather obscured the doctrines of God's unity and holiness. On the other hand, the people of the Sinaitic revelation looked to it with a view of ever revitalizing the dead letter, thus evolving ever new rules of life and new ideas, without ever placing new and old in opposition, as was done by the founder of the Church. Each generation was to take to heart the words of Scripture as if they had come "this very day" out of the mouth of the Lord.92

Chapter VII. The Torah—the Divine Instruction

1. During the Babylonian Exile the prophetic word became the source of comfort and rejuvenation for the Jewish people. Now in its place Ezra the Scribe made the Book of the Law of Moses the pivot about which the entire life of the people was to revolve. By regular readings from it to the assembled worshipers, he made it the source of common instruction. Instead of the priestly Law, which was concerned only with the regulation of the ritual life, the Law became the people's book of instruction, a Torah for all alike,93 while the prophetic books were made secondary and were employed by the preacher at the conclusion of the service as "words of consolation."94 Upon the Pentateuch was built up the divine service of the Synagogue as well as the whole system of communal life, with both its law and ethics. The prophets and other sacred books were looked upon only as means of "opening up" or illustrating the contents of the Torah. These other parts of the Mikra ("the collection of books for public reading") were declared to be inferior in holiness, so that, according to the Rabbinical rule, they were not even allowed to be put into the same scroll as the Pentateuch.95 Moreover, neither the number, order, nor the division of the Biblical books was fixed. The Talmud gives 24, Josephus only 22.96 Tradition claims a completely divine origin only for the Pentateuch or Torah, while the rabbis often point out the human element in the other two classes of the Biblical collection.97

2. The traditional belief in the divine origin of the Torah includes not only every word, but also the accepted interpretation of each letter, for both written and oral law are ascribed to the revelation to Moses on Mt. Sinai, to be transmitted thence from generation to generation. Whoever denies the divine origin of either the written or the oral law is declared to be an unbeliever who has no share in the world to come, according to the Tannaitic code, and consequently according to Maimonides[98] also. But here arises a question of vital importance: What becomes of the Torah as the divine foundation of Judaism under the study of modern times? Even conservative investigators, such as Frankel, Graetz, and Isaac Hirsch Weiss, not to mention such radicals as Zunz and Geiger, admit the gradual progress and growth of this very system of law, both oral and written. And if different historical conditions have produced the development of the law itself, we must assume a number of human authors in place of a single act of divine revelation.[99]

3. But another question of equal importance confronts us here, the meaning of Torah. Originally, no doubt, Torah signified the instruction given by the priests on ritual or juridical matters. Out of these decisions arose the written laws (Toroth), which the priesthood in the course of time collected into codes. After a further process of development they appeared as the various books of Moses, which were finally united into the Code or Torah. This Torah was the foundation of the new Judean commonwealth, the "heritage of the congregation of Jacob."[100] The priestly Torah, lightly regarded during the prophetic period, was exalted by post-exilic Judaism, so that the Sadducean priesthood and their successors, the rabbis, considered strict observance of the legal form to be the very essence of religion. Is this, then, the true nature of Judaism? Is it really—as Christian theologians have held ever since the days of Paul, the great antagonist of Judaism—mere nomism, a religion of law, which demanded formal compliance with its statutes without regard to their inner value? Or shall we rather follow Rabbi Simlai, the Haggadist, who first enumerated the 613 commandments of the Torah (mandatory and prohibitive), considering that their one aim is the higher moral law, in that they are all summed up by a few ethical principles, which he finds in the 15th Psalm, Isaiah XXXIII, 15; Micah VI, 8; Isaiah LVI, 1; and Amos V, 4?[101]

4. All these questions have but one answer, a reconciling one, Judaism has the two factors, the priest with his regard for the law and the prophet with his ethical teaching; and the Jewish Torah embodies both aspects, law and doctrine. These two elements became more and more correlated, as the different parts of the Pentateuch which embodied them were molded together into the one scroll of the Law. In fact, the prophet Jeremiah, in denouncing the priesthood for its neglect of the principles of justice, and rebuking scathingly the people for their wrongdoing, pointed to the divine law of righteousness as the one which should be written upon the hearts of men.[102] Likewise, in the book of Deuteronomy, which was the product of joint activity by prophet and priest, the Law was built upon the highest moral principle, the love of God and man. In a still larger sense the Pentateuch as a whole contains priestly law and universal religion intertwined. In it the eternal verities of the Jewish faith, God's omnipotence, omniscience, and moral government of the world, are conveyed in the historical narratives as an introduction to the law.

5. Thus the Torah as the expression of Judaism was never limited to a mere system of law. At the outset it served as a book of instruction concerning God and the world and became ever richer as a source of knowledge and speculation, because all knowledge from other sources was brought into relation with it through new modes of interpretation. Various systems of philosophy and theology were built upon it. Nay more, the Torah became divine Wisdom itself,[103] the architect of the Creator, the beginning and end of creation.[104]

While the term Torah thus received an increasingly comprehensive meaning, the rabbis, as exponents of orthodox Judaism, came to consider the Pentateuch as the only book of revelation, every letter of which emanated directly from God. The other books of the Bible they regarded as due only to the indwelling of the holy spirit, or to the presence of God, the Shekinah. Moreover, they held that changes by the prophets and other sacred writers were anticipated, in essentials, in the Torah itself, and were therefore only its expansions and interpretations. Accordingly, they are frequently quoted as parts of the Torah or as "words of tradition."[105]

6. Orthodox Judaism, then, accepted as a fundamental doctrine the view that both the Mosaic Law and its Rabbinical interpretation were given by God to Moses on Mt. Sinai. This viewpoint is contradicted by all our knowledge and our whole mode of thinking, and thus both our historical and religious consciousness constrain us to take the position of the prophets. To them and to us the real Torah is the unwritten moral law which underlies the precepts of both the written law and its oral interpretation. From this point of view, Moses, as the first of the prophets, becomes the first mediator of the divine legislation, and the original Decalogue is seen to be the starting

point of a long process of development, from which grew the laws of righteousness and holiness that were to rule the life of Israel and of mankind.106

7. The time of composition of the various parts of the Pentateuch, including the Decalogue, must be decided by independent critical and historical research. It is sufficient for us to know that since the time of Ezra the foundation of Judaism has been the completed Torah, with its twofold aspect as law and as doctrine. As law it contributed to the marvelous endurance and resistance of the Jewish people, inasmuch as it imbued them with the proud consciousness of possessing a law superior to that of other nations, one which would endure as long as heaven and earth.107 Furthermore, it permeated Judaism with a keen sense of duty and imprinted the ideal of holiness upon the whole of life. At the same time it gave rise also to ritualistic piety, which, while tenaciously clinging to the traditional practice of the law, fostered hair-splitting casuistry and caused the petrifaction of religion in the codified Halakah. As doctrine it impressed its ethical and humane idealism upon the people, lifting them far above the narrow confines of nationality, and making them a nation of thinkers. Hence their eagerness for their mission to impart the wisdom stored in their writings to all humanity as its highest boon and the very essence of divine wisdom.

Chapter VIII. God's Covenant

1. Judaism has one specific term for religion, representing the moral relation between God and man, namely, Berith, covenant. The covenant was concluded by God with the patriarchs and with Israel by means of sacrificial blood, according to the primitive custom by which tribes or individuals became "blood brothers," when they were both sprinkled with the sacrificial blood or both drank of it.108 The first covenant of God was made after the flood, with Noah as the representative of mankind; it was intended to assure him and all coming generations of the perpetual maintenance of the natural order without interruption by flood, and at the same time to demand of all mankind the observance of certain laws, such as not to shed, or eat, blood. Here at the very beginning of history religion is taken as the universal basis of human morality, so developing at the outset the fundamental principle of Judaism that it rests upon a religion of humanity, which it desires to establish in all purity. As the universal idea of man forms thus its beginning, so Judaism will attain its final goal only in a divine covenant comprising all humanity. Both the rabbis and the Hellenistic writers consider the covenant of Noah with its so-called Noahitic commandments as unwritten laws of humanity. In fact, they are referred to Adam also, so that religion appears in its essence as nothing else than a covenant of God with all mankind.109

2. Accordingly, Judaism is a special basis of relationship between God and Israel. Far from superseding the universal covenant with Noah, or confining it to the Jewish people, this covenant aims to reclaim all members of the human family for the wider covenant from which they have relapsed. God chose for this purpose Abraham as the one who was faithful to His moral law, and made a special covenant with him for all his descendants, that they might foster justice and righteousness, at first within the narrow sphere of the nation, and then in ever-widening circles of humanity.110 Yet the covenant with Abraham was only the precursor of the covenant concluded with Israel through Moses on Mt. Sinai, by which the Jewish people were consecrated to be the eternal guardians of the divine covenant with mankind, until the time when it shall encompass all the nations.111

3. In this covenant of Sinai, referred to by the prophet Elijah, and afterward by many others, the free moral relationship of man to God is brought out; this forms the characteristic feature of a revealed religion in contradistinction to natural religion. In paganism the Deity formed an inseparable part of the nation itself; but through the covenant God became a free moral power, appealing for allegiance to the spiritual nature of man. This idea of the covenant suggested to the prophet Hosea the analogy with the conjugal relation,112 a conception of love and loyalty which became typical of the tender relation of God to Israel through the centuries. In days of direst woe Jeremiah and the book of Deuteronomy invested this covenant with the character of indestructibility and inviolability.113 God's covenant with Israel is everlasting like that with the heaven and the earth; it is ever to be renewed in the hearts of the people, but never to be replaced by a new covenant. Upon this eternal renewal of the covenant with God rests the unique history of Judaism, its wondrous preservation and regeneration throughout the ages. Paul's doctrine of a new covenant to replace the old114 conflicts with the very idea of the covenant, and even with the words of Jeremiah.

4. The Israelitish nation inherited from Abraham, according to the priestly Code, the rite of circumcision as a "sign of the covenant,"115 but under the prophetic influence, with its loathing of all sacrificial blood, the Sabbath was placed in the foreground as "the sign between God and Israel."116 In ancient Israel and in the Judean commonwealth the Abrahamitic rite formed the initiation into the nationality for aliens and slaves, by which they were made full-fledged Jews. With the dispersion of the Jewish people over the globe, and the influence of Hellenism, Judaism created a propaganda in favor of a world-wide religion of "God-fearing" men pledged to the observance of the Noahitic or humanitarian laws. Rabbinism in Palestine called such a one Ger Toshab—sojourner, or semi-proselyte; while the full proselyte who accepted the Abrahamitic rite was called Ger Zedek, or proselyte of righteousness.117 Not only the Hellenistic writings, but also the Psalms, the liturgy, and the older Rabbinical literature give evidence of such a propaganda,118 but it may be traced back as far as Deutero-Isaiah, during the reign of Cyrus. His outlook toward a Jewish religion which should be at the same time a religion of all the world, is evident when he calls Israel "a mediator of the covenant between God and the nations," a "light to the peoples,"—a regenerator of humanity.119

5. This hope of a universal religion, which rings through the Psalms, the Wisdom books and the Hellenistic literature, was soon destined to grow faint. The perils of Judaism in its great struggles with the Syrian and Roman empires made for intense nationalism, and the Jewish covenant shared this tendency. The early Christian Church, the successor of the missionary activity of Hellenistic Judaism, labored also at first for the Noahitic covenant.120 Pauline Christianity, however, with a view to tearing down the barrier between Jew and Gentile, proclaimed a new covenant, whose central idea is belief in the atoning power of the crucified son of God.121 Indeed, one medieval Rabbinical authority holds that we are to regard Christians as semi-proselytes, as they practically observe the Noahitic laws of humanity.122

6. Progressive Judaism of our own time has the great task of re-emphasizing Israel's world-mission and of reclaiming for Judaism its place as the priesthood of humanity. It is to proclaim anew the prophetic idea of God's covenant with humanity, whose force had been lost, owing to inner and outer obstacles. Israel, as the people of the covenant, aims to unite all nations and classes of men in the divine covenant. It must outlast all other religions in its certainty that ultimately there can be but the one religion, uniting God and man by a single bond.123

B. The Idea Of God In Judaism

Chapter IX. God and the Gods

1. Judaism centers upon its sublime and simple conception of God. This lifts it above all other religions and satisfies in unique measure the longing for truth and inner peace amidst the futility and incessant changes of earthly existence. This very conception of God is in striking contrast to that of most other religions. The God of Judaism is not one god among many, nor one of many powers of life, but is the One and holy God beyond all comparison. In Him is concentrated all power and the essence of all things; He is the Author of all existence, the Ruler of life, who lays down the laws by which man shall live. As the prophet says to the heathen world: "The gods that have not made the heavens and the earth, these shall perish from the earth and from under the heavens.... Not like these is the portion of Jacob; for He is the Former of all things.... The Lord is the true God; He is the living God and the everlasting King; at His wrath the earth trembleth, and the nations are not able to abide His indignation."124

2. This lofty conception of the Deity forms the essence of Judaism and was its shield and buckler in its lifelong contest with the varying forms of heathenism. From the very first the God of Judaism declared war against them all, whether at any special time the prevailing form was the worship of many gods, or the worship of God in the shape of man, the perversion of the purity of God by sensual concepts, or the division of His unity into different parts or personalities. The Talmudic saying is most striking: "From Sinai, the Mount of revelation of the only God, there came forth Sinah, the hostility of the nations toward the Jew as the banner-bearer of the pure idea of God."125 Just as day and night form a natural contrast, divinely ordained, so do the monotheism of Israel and the polytheism of the nations constitute a spiritual contrast which can never be reconciled.

3. The pagan gods, and to some extent the triune God of the Christian Church, semi-pagan in origin also, are the outcome of the human spirit's going astray in its search for God. Instead of leading man upwards to an ideal which

will encompass all material and moral life and lift it to the highest stage of holiness, paganism led to depravity and discord. The unrelenting zeal displayed by prophet and law-giver against idolatry had its chief cause in the immoral and inhuman practices of the pagan nations—Canaan, Egypt, Assyria, and Babylon—in the worship of their deities.126 The deification of the forces of nature brutalized the moral sense of the pagan world; no vice seemed too horrible, no sacrifice too atrocious for their cults. Baal, or Moloch, the god of heaven, demanded in times of distress the sacrifice of a son by the father. Astarte, the goddess of fecundity, required the "hallowing" of life's origin, and this was done by the most terrible of sexual orgies. Such abominations exerted their seductive influence upon the shepherd tribes of Israel in their new home in Canaan, and thus aroused the fiercest indignation of prophet and law-giver, who hurled their vials of wrath against those shocking rites, those lewd idols, and those who "whored after them."127 If Israel was to be trained to be the priest people of the Only One in such an environment, tolerance of such practices was out of the question. Thus in the Sinaitic law God is spoken of as "the jealous God"128 who punishes unrelentingly every violation of His laws of purity and holiness.

4. The same sharp contrast of Jewish ethical and spiritual monotheism remained also when it came in contact with the Græco-Syrian and Roman culture. Here, too, the myths and customs of the cult and the popular religion offended by their gross sensuality the chaste spirit of the Jewish people. Indeed, these were all the more dangerous to the purity of social life, as they were garbed with the alluring beauty of art and philosophy.129 The Jew then felt all the more the imperative duty to draw a sharp line of demarcation between Judaism with its chaste and imageless worship and the lascivious, immoral life of paganism.

5. This wide gulf which yawned between Israel's One and holy God and the divinities of the nations was not bridged over by the Christian Church when it appeared on the stage of history and obtained world-dominion. For Christianity in its turn succeeded by again dragging the Deity into the world of the senses, adopting the pagan myths of the birth and death of the gods, and sanctioning image worship. In this way it actually created a Christian plurality of gods in place of the Græco-Roman pantheon; indeed, it presented a divine family after the model of the Egyptian and Babylonian religions,130 and thus pushed the ever-living God and Father of mankind into the background. This tendency has never been explained away, even by the attempts of certain high-minded thinkers among the Church fathers. Judaism, however, insists, as ever, upon the words of the Decalogue which condemn all attempts to depict the Deity in human or sensual form, and through all its teachings there is echoed forth the voice of Him who spoke through the seer of the Exile: "I am the Lord, that is My name, and My glory will I not give to another, neither My praise to graven images."131

6. When Moses came to Pharaoh saying, "Thus speaketh JHVH the God of Israel, send off My people that they may serve Me," Pharaoh—so the Midrash tells—took his list of deities to hand, looked it over, and said, "Behold, here are enumerated the gods of the nations, but I cannot find thy God among them." To this Moses replied, "All the gods known and familiar to thee are mortal, as thou art; they die, and their tomb is shown. The God of Israel has nothing in common with them. He is the living, true, and eternal God who created heaven and earth; no people can withstand His wrath."132 This passage states strikingly the difference between the God of Judaism and the gods of heathendom. The latter are but deified powers of nature, and being parts of the world, themselves at one with nature, they are subject to the power of time and fate. Israel's God is enthroned above the world as its moral and spiritual Ruler, the only Being whom we can conceive as self-existent, as indivisible as truth itself.

7. As long as the pagan conception prevailed, by which the world was divided into many divine powers, there could be no conception of the idea of a moral government of the universe, of an all-encompassing purpose of life. Consequently the great thinkers and moralists of heathendom were forced to deny the deities, before they could assert either the unity of the cosmos or a design in life. On the other hand, it was precisely this recognition of the moral nature of God, as manifested both in human life and in the cosmic sphere, which brought the Jewish prophets and sages to their pure monotheism, in which they will ultimately be met by the great thinkers of all lands and ages. The unity of God brings harmony into the intellectual and moral world; the division of the godhead into different powers or personalities leads to discord and spiritual bondage. Such is the lesson of history, that in polytheism, dualism, or trinitarianism one of the powers must necessarily limit or obscure another. In this manner the Christian Trinity led mankind in many ways to the lowering of the supreme standard of truth, to an infringement on justice, and to inhumanity to other creeds, and therefore Judaism could regard it only as a compromise with heathenism.

8. Judaism assumed, then, toward paganism an attitude of rigid exclusion and opposition which could easily be taken for hostility. This prevailed especially in the legal systems of the Bible and the rabbis, and was intended primarily to guard the monotheistic belief from pagan pollution and to keep it intact. Neither in the Deuteronomic law nor in the late codes of Maimonides and Joseph Caro is there any toleration for idolatrous practices, for instruments of idol-worship, or for idolaters.133 This attitude gave the enemies of the Jew sufficient occasion for speaking of the Jewish God as hating the world, as if only national conceit underlay the earnest rigor of Jewish monotheism.

9. As a matter of fact, since the time of the prophets Judaism has had no national God in any exclusive sense. While the Law insists upon the exclusive worship of the one God of Israel, the narratives of the beginnings in the Bible have a different tenor. They take the lofty standpoint that the heathen world, while worshiping its many divinities, had merely lost sight of the true God after whom the heart ever longs and searches. This implies that a kernel of true piety underlies all the error and delusion of paganism, which, rightly guided, will lead back to the God from whom mankind had strayed. The Godhead, divided into gods—as is hinted even in the Biblical name, Elohim—must again become the one God of humanity. Thus the Jew holds that all worship foreshadows the search for the true God, and that all humanity shall at one time acknowledge Him for whom they have so long been searching. Surely the Psalms express, not national narrowness, but ardent love for humanity when they hail the God of Israel, the Maker of heaven and earth, as the world's great King, and tell how He will judge the nations in justice, while the gods of the nations will be rejected as "vanities."134 Nor does the divine service of the Jew bear the stamp of clannishness. For more than two thousand years the central point in the Synagogue liturgy every morning and evening has been the battle-cry, "Hear, O Israel, the Lord our God, the Lord is One." And so does the conclusion of every service, the Alenu, the solemn prayer of adoration, voice the grand hope of the Jew for the future, that the time may speedily come when "before the kingdom of Almighty all idolatry shall vanish, and all the inhabitants of the earth perceive that unto Him alone every knee must bend, and all flesh recognize Him alone as God and King."135

Chapter X. The Name of God

1. Primitive men attached much importance to names, for to them the name of a thing indicated its nature, and through the name one could obtain mastery over the thing or person named. Accordingly, the name of God was considered to be the manifestation of His being; by invoking it man could obtain some of His power; and the place where that name was called became the seat of His presence. Therefore the name must be treated with the same reverential awe as the Deity Himself. None dare approach the Deity, nor misuse the Name. The pious soul realized the nearness of the Deity in hearing His name pronounced. Finally, the different names of God reflect the different conceptions of Him which were held in various periods.136

2. The Semites were not like the Aryan nations, who beheld the essence of their gods in the phenomena of nature such as light, rain, thunder, and lightning,—and gave them corresponding names and titles. The more intense religious emotionalism of the Semites137 perceived the Godhead rather as a power working from within, and accordingly gave it such names as El ("the Mighty One"), Eloha or Pahad ("the Awful One"), or Baal ("the Master"). Elohim, the plural form of Eloha, denoted originally the godhead as divided into a number of gods or godly beings, that is, polytheism. When it was applied to God, however, it was generally understood as a unity, referring to one undivided Godhead, for Scripture regarded monotheism as original with mankind. While this view is contradicted by the science of comparative religion, still the ideal conception of religion, based on the universal consciousness of God, postulates one God who is the aim of all human searching, a fact which the term Henotheism fails to recognize.138

3. For the patriarchal age, the preliminary stage in the development of the Jewish God-idea, Scripture gives a special name for God, El Shaddai—"the Almighty God." This probably has a relation to Shod, "storm" or "havoc" and "destruction," but was interpreted as supreme Ruler over the celestial powers.139 The name by which God revealed Himself to Moses and the prophets as the God of the covenant with Israel is JHVH (Jahveh). This name is inseparably connected with the religious development of Judaism in all its loftiness and depth. During the period of the Second Temple this name was declared too sacred for utterance, except by the priests in certain parts of the service, and for mysterious use by specially initiated saints. Instead, Adonai—"the Lord"—was substituted for it in the Biblical reading, a usage which has continued for over two thousand years. The meaning of the name in pre-

Mosaic times may be inferred from the fiery storms which accompanied each theophany in the various Scriptural passages, as well as from the root havah, which means "throw down" and "overthrow."140

To the prophets, however, the God of Sinai, enthroned amid clouds of storm and fire, moving before His people in war and peace, appeared rather as the God of the Covenant, without image or form, unapproachable in His holiness. As the original meaning of JHVH had become unintelligible, they interpreted the name as "the ever present One," in the sense of Ehyeh asher Ehyeh, "I shall be whatever (or wherever) I am to be"; that is, "I am ever ready to help." Thus spoke God to Moses in revealing His name to him at the burning bush.141

4. The prophetic genius penetrated more and more into the nature of God, recognising Him as the Power who rules in justice, mercy, and holiness. This process brought them to identify JHVH, the God of the covenant, with the One and only God who overlooks all the world from his heavenly habitation, and gives it plan and purpose. At the same time, all the prophets revert to the covenant on Sinai in order to proclaim Israel as the herald and witness of God among the nations. In fact, the God of the covenant proclaimed His universality at the very beginning, in the introduction to the Decalogue: "Ye shall be Mine own peculiar possession from among all peoples, for all the earth is Mine. And ye shall be unto Me a kingdom of priests and a holy nation."142 In other words,—you have the special task of mediator among the nations, all of which are under My dominion.

5. In the Wisdom literature and the Psalms the God of the covenant is subordinated to the universality of JHVH as Creator and Ruler of the world. In a number of the Psalms and in some later writings the very name JHVH was avoided probably on account of its particularistic tinge. It was surrounded more and more with a certain mystery. Instead, God as the "Lord" is impressed on the consciousness and adoration of men, in all His sublimity and in absolute unity. The "Name" continues its separate existence only in the mystic lore. The name Jehovah, however, has no place whatsoever in Judaism. It is due simply to a misreading of the vowel signs that refer to the word Adonai, and has been erroneously adopted in the Christian literature since the beginning of the sixteenth century.143

6. Perhaps the most important process of spiritualization which the idea of God underwent in the minds of the Jewish people was made when the name JHVH as the proper name of the God of the covenant was given up and replaced by Adonai—"the Lord." As long as the God of Israel, like other deities, had His proper name, he was practically one of them, however superior in moral worth. As soon as He became the Lord, that is, the only real God over all the world, a distinctive proper noun was out of place. Henceforth the name was invested with a mysterious and magic character. It became ineffable, at least to the people at large, and its pronunciation sinful, except by the priests in the liturgy. In fact, the law was interpreted so as directly to forbid this utterance.144 Thus JHVH is no longer the national God of Israel. The Talmud guards against the very suspicion of a "Judaized God" by insisting that every benediction to Him as "God the Lord" must add "King of the Universe" rather than the formula of the Psalms, "God of Israel."145

7. The Midrash makes a significant comment on the words of the Shema: "Why do the words, 'the Lord is our God' precede the words, 'the Lord is One'? Does not the particularism of the former conflict with the universalism of the latter sentence? No. The former expresses the idea that the Lord is 'our God' just so far as His name is more intertwined with our history than with that of any other nation, and that we have the greater obligation as His chosen people. Wherever Scripture speaks of the God of Israel, it does not intend to limit Him as the universal God, but to emphasize Israel's special duty as His priest-people."146

8. Likewise is the liturgical name "God of our fathers" far from being a nationalistic limitation. On the contrary, the rabbis single out Abraham as the missionary, the herald of monotheism in its march to world-conquest. For his use of the term, "the God of heaven and the God of the earth"147 they offer a characteristic explanation: "Before Abraham came, the people worshiped only the God of heaven, but Abraham by winning them for his God brought Him down and made Him also the God of the earth."148

9. Reverence for the Deity caused the Jew to avoid not only the utterance of the holy Name itself, but even the common use of its substitute Adonai. Therefore still other synonyms were introduced, such as "Master of the universe," "the Holy One, blessed be He," "the Merciful One," "the Omnipotence" (ha Geburah),149 "King of the kings of kings" (under Persian influence—as the Persian ruler called himself the King of Kings);150 and in Hasidean circles it became customary to invoke God as "our Father" and "our Father in heaven."151 The rather strange appellations for God, "Heaven"152 and (dwelling) "Place" (ha Makom) seem to originate in certain

formulas of the oath. In the latter name the rabbis even found hints of God's omnipresence: "As space—Makom—encompasses all things, so does God encompass the world instead of being encompassed by it."153

10. The rabbis early read a theological meaning into the two names JHVH and Elohim, taking the former as the divine attribute of mercy and the latter as that of justice.154 In general, however, the former name was explained etymologically as signifying eternity, "He who is, who was, and who shall be." Philo shows familiarity with the two attributes of justice and mercy, but he and other Alexandrian writers explained JHVH and Ehyeh metaphysically, and accordingly called God, "the One who is," that is, the Source of all existence. Both conceptions still influence Jewish exegesis and account for the term "the Eternal" sometimes used for "the Lord."

Chapter XI. The Existence of God

1. For the religious consciousness, God is not to be demonstrated by argument, but is a fact of inner and outer experience. Whatever the origin and nature of the cosmos may be according to natural science, the soul of man follows its natural bent, as in the days of Abraham, to look through nature to the Maker, Ordainer, and Ruler of all things, who uses the manifold world of nature only as His workshop, and who rules it in freedom as its sovereign Master. The entire cosmic life points to a Supreme Being from whom all existence must have arisen, and without whom life and process would be impossible. Still even this mode of thought is influenced and determined by the prevalent monotheistic conceptions.

Far more original and potent in man is the feeling of limitation and dependency. This brings him to bow down before a higher Power, at first in fear and trembling, but later in holy awe and reverence. As soon as man attains self-consciousness and his will acquires purpose, he encounters a will stronger than his own, with which he often comes into conflict, and before which he must frequently yield. Thus he becomes conscious of duty—of what he ought and ought not to do. This is not, like earlier limitations, purely physical and working from without; it is moral and operates from within. It is the sense of duty, or, as we call it, conscience, the sense of right and wrong. This awakened very early in the race, and through it God's voice has been perceived ever since the days of Adam and of Cain.155

2. According to Scripture, man in his natural state possesses the certainty of God's existence through such inner experience. Therefore the Bible contains no command to believe in God, nor any logical demonstration of His existence. Both the Creation stories and those of the beginnings of mankind assume as undisputed the existence of God as the Creator and Judge of the world. Arguments appealing to reason were resorted to only in competition with idolatry, as in Deuteronomy, Jeremiah, and Deutero-Isaiah, and subsequently by the Haggadists in legends such as those about Abraham. Nor does the Bible consider any who deny the existence of God;156 only much later, in the Talmud, do we hear of those who "deny the fundamental principle" of the faith. The doubt expressed in Job, Koheleth, and certain of the Psalms, concerns rather the justice of God than His existence. True, Jeremiah and the Psalms157 mention some who say "There is no God," but these are not atheists in our sense of the word; they are the impious who deny the moral order of life by word or deed. It is the villain (Nabal), not the "fool" who "says in heart, there is no God." Even the Talmud does not mean the real atheist when speaking of "the denier of the fundamental principle," but the man who says, "There is neither a judgment nor a Judge above and beyond."158 In other words, the "denier" is the same as the Epicurean (Apicoros), who refuses to recognize the moral government of the world.159

3. After the downfall of the nation and Temple, the situation changed through the contemptuous question of the nations, "Where is your God?" Then the necessity became evident of proving that the Ruler of nations still held dominion over the world, and that His wondrous powers were shown more than ever before through the fact of Israel's preservation in captivity. This is the substance of the addresses of the great seer of the Exile in chapters XL to LIX of Isaiah, in which he exposes the gods of heathendom to everlasting scorn, more than any other prophet before or afterward. He declares these deities to be vanity and naught, but proclaims the Holy One of Israel as the Lord of the universe. He hath "meted out the heavens with the span," and "weighed the mountains in scales, and the hills in a balance." Before Him "the nations are as a drop of the bucket," and "the inhabitants of the earth as grasshoppers." "He bringeth out the hosts of the stars by number, and calleth them all by name," "He hath assigned to the generations of men their lot from the beginning, and knoweth at the beginning what will be their end."160 Measured by such passages as these and such as Psalms VIII, XXIV, XXXIII, CIV, and CXXXIX, where God is felt as a

living power, all philosophical arguments about His existence seem to be strange fires on the altar of religion. The believer can do without them, and the unbeliever will hardly be convinced by them.

4. Upon the contact of the Jew with Greek philosophy doubt arose in many minds, and belief entered into conflict with reason. But even then, the defense of the faith was still carried on by reasoning along the lines of common sense.161 Thus the regularity of the sun, moon, and stars,—all worshiped by the pagans as deities—was considered a proof of God's omnipotence and rule of the universe, a proof which the legend ascribes to Abraham in his controversy with Nimrod.162 In like manner, the apocryphal Book of Wisdom163 says that true wisdom, as opposed to the folly of heathenism, is "to reason from the visible to the Invisible One, and from the cosmos, the great work of art, to the Supreme Artificer."

5. Philo was the first who tried to refute the "atheistic" views of materialists and pantheists by adducing proofs of God's existence from nature and the human intellect. In the former he pointed out order as evidence of the wisdom underlying the cosmos, and in the latter the power of self-determination as shadowing forth a universal mind which determines the entire universe.164 Still, with his mystical attitude, Philo realized that the chief knowledge of God is through intuition, by the inner experience of the soul.

6. Two proofs taken from nature owe their origin to Greek philosophy. Anaxagoras and Socrates, from their theory of design in nature, deduced that there is a universal intelligence working for higher aims and purposes. This so-called teleological proof, as worked out in detail by Plato, was the unfailing reliance of subsequent philosophers and theologians.165 Plato and Aristotle, moreover, from the continuous motion of all matter, inferred a prime cause, an unmoved mover. This is the so-called cosmological proof, used by different schools in varying forms.166 It occupies the foremost place in the systems of the Arabic Aristotelians, and consequently is dominant among the Jewish philosophers, the Christian scholastics, and in the modern philosophic schools down to Kant. It is based upon the old principle of causality, and therefore takes the mutability and relativity of all beings in the cosmos as evidence of a Being that is immutable, unconditioned, and absolutely necessary, causa sui, the prime cause of all existence.

7. The Mohammedan theologians added a new element to the discussion. In their endeavor to prove that the world is the work of a Creator, they pointed as evidence to the multiformity and composite structure, the contingency and dependency of the cosmos; thus they concluded that it must have been created, and that its Creator must necessarily be the one, absolute, and all-determining cause. This proof is used also by Saadia and Bahya ben Joseph.167 Its weakness, however, was exposed by Ibn Sina and Alfarabi among the Mohammedans, and later by Abraham ibn Daud and Maimonides, their Jewish successors as Aristotelians. These proposed a substitute argument. From the fact that the existence of all cosmic beings is merely possible,—that is, they may exist and they may not exist,—these thinkers concluded that an absolutely necessary being must exist as the cause and condition of all things, and this absolutely unconditioned yet all-conditioning being is God, the One who is.168 Of course, the God so deduced and inferred is a mere abstraction, incapable of satisfying the emotional craving of the heart.

8. While the cosmological proof proceeds from the transitory and imperfect nature of the world, the ontological proof, first proposed by Anselm of Canterbury, the Christian scholastic of the XI century, and further elaborated by Descartes and Mendelssohn, proceeds from the human intellect. The mind conceives the idea of God as an absolutely perfect being, and, as there can be no perfection without existence, the conclusion is that this idea must necessarily be objectively true. Then, as the idea of God is innate in man, God must necessarily exist,—and for proof of this they point to the Scriptural verse, "The fool hath said in his heart, there is no God," and other similar passages. In its improved form, this argument uses the human concept of an infinitely perfect God as evidence, or, at least, as postulate that such a Being exists beyond the finite world of man.169

Another argument, rather naïve in character, which was favored by the Stoics and adopted by the Church fathers, is called de consensu gentium, and endeavored to prove the reality of God's existence from the universality of His worship. It speaks well for the sound reasoning of the Jewish thinkers that they refused to follow the lead of the Mohammedans in this respect, and did not avail themselves of an argument which can be used just as easily in support of a plurality of gods.170

9. All these so-called proofs were invalidated by Immanuel Kant, the great philosopher of Königsberg, whose critical inquiry into the human intellect showed that the entire sum of our knowledge of objects and also of the formulation of our ideas is based upon our limited mode of apperception, while the reality or essence, "the thing in

itself," will ever remain beyond our ken. If this is true of physical objects, it is all the more true of God, whom we know through our minds alone and not at all through our five senses. Accordingly, he shows that all the metaphysical arguments have no basis, and that we can know God's existence only through ethics, as a postulate of our moral nature. The inner consciousness of our moral obligation, or duty, implies a moral order of life, or moral law; and this, in turn, postulates the existence of God, the Ruler of life, who assigns to each of us his task and his destiny.171

10. It is true that God is felt and worshiped first as the supreme power in the world, before man perceives Him as the highest ideal of morality. Therefore man will never cease looking about him for vestiges of divinity and for proofs of his intuitive knowledge of God. The wondrous order, harmony, and signs of design in nature, as well as the impulse of the reason to search for the unity of all things, corroborate this innate belief in God. Still more do the consciousness of duty in the individual—conscience—and the progress of history with its repeated vindication of right and defeat of wrong proclaim to the believer unmistakably that the God of justice reigns. But no proof, however convincing, will ever bring back to the skeptic or unbeliever the God he has lost, unless his pangs of anguish or the void within fill his desolate world anew with the vivifying thought of a living God.

11. Among all the Jewish religious philosophers the highest rank must be accorded to Jehudah ha Levi, the author of the Cuzari,172 who makes the historical fact of the divine revelation the foundation of the Jewish religion and the chief testimony of the existence of God. As a matter of fact, reason alone will not lead to God, except where religious intuition forms, so to speak, the ladder of heaven, leading to the realm of the unknowable. Philosophy, at best, can only demonstrate the existence of a final Cause, or of a supreme Intelligence working toward sublime purposes; possibly also a moral government of the world, in both the physical and the spiritual life. Religion alone, founded upon divine revelation, can teach man to find a God, to whom he can appeal in trust in his moments of trouble or of woe, and whose will he can see in the dictates of conscience and the destiny of nations. Reason must serve as a corrective for the contents of revelation, scrutinizing and purifying, deepening and spiritualizing ever anew the truths received through intuition, but it can never be the final source of truth.

12. The same method must apply also to modern thought and research, which substituted historical methods for metaphysics in both the physical and intellectual world, and which endeavors to trace the origin and growth of both objects and ideas in accordance with fixed laws. The process of evolution, our modern key with which to unlock the secrets of nature, points most significantly to a Supreme Power and Energy. But this energy, entering into the cosmic process at its outset, causing its motion and its growth, implies also an end, and thus again we have the Supreme Intelligence reached through a new type of teleology.173 But all these conceptions, however they may be in harmony with the Jewish belief in creation and revelation, can at best supplement it, but can certainly neither supplant nor be identified with it.

Chapter XII. The Essence of God

1. An exquisite Oriental fable tells of a sage who had been meditating vainly for days and weeks on the question, What is God? One day, walking along the seashore, he saw some children busying themselves by digging holes in the sand and pouring into them water from the sea. "What are you doing there?" he asked them, to which they replied, "We want to empty the sea of its water." "Oh, you little fools," he exclaimed with a smile, but suddenly his smile vanished in serious thought. "Am I not as foolish as these children?" he said to himself. "How can I with my small brain hope to grasp the infinite nature of God?"

All efforts of philosophy to define the essence of God are futile. "Canst thou by searching find out God?" Zophar asks of his friend Job.174 Both Philo and Maimonides maintain that we can know of God only that He is; we can never fathom His innermost being or know what He is. Both find this unknowability of God expressed in the words spoken to Moses: "If I withdraw My hand, thou shall see My back—that is, the effects of God's power and wisdom—but My face—the real essence of God—thou shalt not see."175

2. Still, a divinity void of all essential qualities fails to satisfy the religious soul. Man demands to know what God is—at least, what God is to him. In the first word of the Decalogue God speaks through His people Israel to the religious consciousness of all men at all times, beginning, "I am the Lord, thy God." This word I lifts God at once above all beings and powers of the cosmos, in fact, above all other existence, for it expresses His unique self-consciousness. This attribute above all is possessed by no being in the world of nature, and only by man, who is the

image of his Maker. According to the Midrash, all creation was hushed when the Lord spoke on Sinai, "I am the Lord."176 God is not merely the supreme Being, but also the supreme Self-consciousness. As man, in spite of all his limitations and helplessness, still towers high above all his fellow creatures by virtue of his free will and self-conscious action, so God, who knows no bounds to His wisdom and power, surpasses all beings and forces of the universe, for He rules over all as the one completely self-conscious Mind and Will. In both the visible and invisible realms He manifests Himself as the absolutely free Personality, moral and spiritual, who allots to every thing its existence, form, and purpose. For this reason Scripture calls Him "the living God and everlasting King."177

3. Judaism, accordingly, teaches us to recognize God, above all, as revealing Himself in self-conscious activity, as determining all that happens by His absolutely free will, and thus as showing man how to walk as a free moral agent. In relation to the world, His work or workshop, He is the self-conscious Master, saying "I am that which I am"; in relation to man, who is akin to Him as a self-conscious rational and moral being, He is the living Fountain of all that knowledge and spirituality for which men long, and in which alone they may find contentment and bliss.

Thus the God of Judaism, the world's great I Am, forms a complete contrast, not only to the lifeless powers of nature and destiny, which were worshiped by the ancient pagans, but also to the God of modern paganism, a God divested of all personality and self-consciousness, such as He is conceived of by the new school of Christian theology, with its pantheistic tendency. I refer to the school of Ritschl, which strives to render the myth of the man-god philosophically intelligible by teaching that God reaches self-consciousness only in the perfect type of man, that is, Christ, while otherwise He is entirely immanent, one with the world. All the more forcibly does Jewish monotheism insist upon its doctrine that God, in His continual self-revelation, is the supermundane and self-conscious Ruler of both nature and history. "I am the Lord, that is My name, and My glory will I not give to another,"—so says the God of Judaism.178

4. The Jewish God-idea, of course, had to go through many stages of development before it reached the concept of a transcendental and spiritual god. It was necessary first that the Decalogue and the Book of the Covenant prohibit most stringently polytheism and every form of idolatry, and second that a strictly imageless worship impress the people with the idea that Israel's God was both invisible and incorporeal.179 Yet a wide step still intervened from that stage to the complete recognition of God as a purely spiritual Being, lacking all qualities perceptible to the senses, and not resembling man in either his inner or his outer nature. Centuries of gradual ripening of thought were still necessary for the growth of this conception. This was rendered still more difficult by the Scriptural references to God in His actions and His revelations, and even in His motives, after a human pattern. Israel's sages required centuries of effort to remove all anthropomorphic and anthropopathic notions of God, and thus to elevate Him to the highest realm of spirituality.180

5. In this process of development two points of view demand consideration. We must not overlook the fact that the perfectly clear distinction which we make between the sensory and the spiritual does not appeal to the child-like mind, which sees it rather as external. What we call transcendent, owing to our comprehension of the immeasurable universe, was formerly conceived only as far remote in space or time. Thus God is spoken of in Scripture as dwelling in heaven and looking down upon the inhabitants of the earth to judge them and to guide them.181 According to Deuteronomy, God spoke from heaven to the people about Mt. Sinai, while Exodus represents Him as coming down to the mountain from His heavenly heights to proclaim the law amid thunder and lightning.182 The Babylonian conception of heaven prevailed throughout the Middle Ages and influenced both the mystic lore about the heavenly throne and the philosophic cosmology of the Aristotelians, such as Maimonides. Yet Scripture offers also another view, the concept of God as the One enthroned on high, whom "the heavens and the heaven's heavens cannot encompass."183

The fact is that language still lacked an expression for pure spirit, and the intellect freed itself only gradually from the restrictions of primitive language to attain a purer conception of the divine. Thus we attain deeper insight into the spiritual nature of God when we read the inimitable words of the Psalmist describing His omnipresence,184 or that other passage: "He that planted the ear, shall He not hear? He that formed the eye, shall He not see? He that chastiseth the nations, shall He not correct, even He that teaches man knowledge?"185

The translators and interpreters of the Bible felt the need of eliminating everything of a sensory nature from God and of avoiding anthropomorphism, through the influence of Greek philosophy. This spiritualization of the God idea was taken up again by the philosophers of the Spanish-Arabic period, who combated the prevailing mysticism.

Through them Jewish monotheism emphasized its opposition to every human representation of God, especially the God-Man of the Christian Church.

6. On the other hand, we must bear in mind that we naturally ascribe to God a human personality, whether we speak of Him as the Master-worker of the universe, as the all-seeing and all-hearing Judge, or the compassionate and merciful Father. We cannot help attributing human qualities and emotions to Him the moment we invest Him with a moral and spiritual nature. When we speak of His punitive justice, His unfailing mercy, or His all-wise providence, we transfer to Him, imperceptibly, our own righteous indignation at the sight of a wicked deed, or our own compassion with the sufferer, or even our own mode of deliberation and decision. Moreover, the prophets and the Torah, in order to make God plain to the people, described Him in vivid images of human life, with anger and jealousy as well as compassion and repentance, and also with the organs and functions of the senses,—seeing, hearing, smelling, speaking, and walking.

7. The rabbis are all the more emphatic in their assertions that the Torah merely intends to assist the simple-minded, and that unseemly expressions concerning Deity are due to the inadequacy of language, and must not be taken literally.186 "It is an act of boldness allowed only to the prophets to measure the Creator by the standard of the creature," says the Haggadist, and again, "God appeared to Israel, now as a heroic warrior, now as a venerable sage imparting knowledge, and again as a kind dispenser of bounties, but always in a manner befitting the time and circumstance, so as to satisfy the need of the human heart."187 This is strikingly illustrated in the following dialogue: "A heretic came to Rabbi Meir asking, 'How can you reconcile the passage which reads, "Do I not fill heaven and earth, says the Lord," with the one which relates that the Lord appeared to Moses between the cherubim of the ark of the covenant?' Whereupon Rabbi Meir took two mirrors, one large and the other small, and placed them before the interrogator. 'Look into this glass,' he said, 'and into that. Does not your figure seem different in one than in the other? How much more will the majesty of God, who has neither figure nor form, be reflected differently in the minds of men! To one it will appear according to his narrow view of life, and to the other in accordance with his larger mental horizon.'"188

In like manner Rabbi Joshua ben Hanania, when asked sarcastically by the Emperor Hadrian to show him his God, replied: "Come and look at the sun which now shines in the full splendor of noonday! Behold, thou art dazzled. How, then, canst thou see without bewilderment the majesty of Him from whom emanates both sun and stars?"189 This rejoinder, which was familiar to the Greeks also, is excelled by the one of Rabban Gamaliel II to a heathen who asked him "Where does the God dwell to whom you daily pray?" "Tell me first," he answered, "where does your soul dwell, which is so close to thee? Thou canst not tell. How, then, can I inform thee concerning Him who dwells in heaven, and whose throne is separated from the earth by a journey of 3500 years?" "Then do we not do better to pray to gods who are near at hand, and whom we can see with our eyes?" continued the heathen, whereupon the sage struck home, "Well, you may see your gods, but they neither see nor help you, while our God, Himself unseen, yet sees and protects us constantly."190 The comparison of the invisible soul to God, the invisible spirit of the universe, is worked out further in the Midrash to Psalm CIII.

8. From the foregoing it is clear that, while Judaism insists on the Deity's transcending all finite and sensory limitations, it never lost the sense of the close relationship between man and his Maker. Notwithstanding Christian theologians to the contrary, the Jewish God was never a mere abstraction.191 The words, "I am the Lord thy God," betoken the intimate relation between the redeemed and the heavenly Redeemer, and the song of triumph at the Red Sea, "This is my God, I will extol Him," testifies—according to the Midrash—that even the humblest of God's chosen people were filled with the feeling of His nearness.192 In the same way the warm breath of union with God breathes through all the writings, the prayers, and the whole history of Judaism. "For what great nation is there that hath God so nigh unto them as the Lord our God is, whenever we call upon Him?" exclaims Moses in Deuteronomy, and the rabbis, commenting upon the plural form used here, Kerobim, = "nigh," remark: "God is nigh to everyone in accordance with his special needs."193

9. Probably the rabbis were at their most profound mood in their saying, "God's greatness lies in His condescension, as may be learned from the Torah, the Prophets, and the Writings. To quote only Isaiah also: 'Thus saith the High and Lofty One, I dwell in high and holy places, with him that is of a contrite and humble spirit.'194 For this reason God selected as the place of His revelation the humble Sinai and the lowly thornbush."195 In fact, the absence of any mediator in Judaism necessitates the doctrine that God—with all His transcendent majesty—is

at the same time "an ever present helper in trouble,"196 and that His omnipotence includes care for the greatest and the smallest beings of creation.197

10. The doctrine that God is above and beyond the universe, transcending all created things, as well as time and space, might lead logically to the view of the deist that He stands outside of the world, and does not work from within. But this inference has never been made even by the boldest of Jewish thinkers. The Psalmist said, "Who is like the Lord our God, that hath His seat on high, that humbleth Himself to behold what is in heaven and on earth?"198—words which express the deepest and the loftiest thought of Judaism. Beside the all-encompassing Deity no other divine power or personality can find a place. God is in all; He is over all; He is both immanent and transcendent. His creation was not merely setting into motion the wheels of the cosmic fabric, after which He withdrew from the world. The Jew praises Him for every scent and sight of nature or of human life, for the beauty of the sea and the rainbow, for every flash of lightning that illumines the darkened clouds and every peal of thunder that shakes the earth. On every such occasion the Jew utters praise to "Him who daily renews the work of creation," or "Him who in everlasting faithfulness keepeth His covenant with mankind." Such is the teaching of the men of the Great Synagogue,199 and the charge of the Jewish God idea being a barren and abstract transcendentalism can be urged only by the blindness of bigotry.200

11. The interweaving of the ideas of God's immanence and transcendency is shown especially in two poems embodied in the songs of the Synagogue, Ibn Gabirol's "Crown of Royalty" and the "Songs of Unity" for each day of the week, composed by Samuel ben Kalonymos, the father of Judah the Pious of Regensburg. Here occur such sentences as these: "All is in God and God is in all"; "Sufficient unto Himself and self-determining, He is the ever-living and self-conscious Mind, the all-permeating, all-impelling, and all-accomplishing Will"; "The universe is the emanation of the plenitude of God, each part the light of His infinite light, flame of His eternal empyrean"; "The universe is the garment, the covering of God, and He the all-penetrating Soul."201 All these ideas were borrowed from neo-Platonism, and found a conspicuous place in Ibn Gabirol's philosophy, later influencing the Cabbalah.

Similarly the appellation, Makom, "Space," is explained by both Philo and the rabbis as denoting "Him who encompasses the world, but whom the world cannot encompass."202 An utterance such as this, well-nigh pantheistic in tone, leads directly to theories like those of Spinoza or of David Nieto, the well-known London Rabbi, who was largely under Spinozistic influence203 and who still was in accord with Jewish thought. Certainly, as long as Jewish monotheism conceives of God as self-conscious Intellect and freely acting Will, it can easily accept the principle of divine immanence.

12. We accept, then, the fact that man, child-like, invests God with human qualities,—a view advanced by Abraham ben David of Posquieres in opposition to Maimonides.204 Still, the thinkers of Judaism have ever labored to divest the Deity of every vestige of sensuousness, of likeness to man, in fact, of every limitation to action or to free will. Every conception which merges God into the world or identifies Him with it and thus makes Him subject to necessity, is incompatible with the Jewish idea of God, which enthrones Him above the universe as its free and sovereign Master. "Am I a God near at hand, saith the Lord, and not a God afar off? Can any hide himself in secret places that I shall not see him? saith the Lord. Do I not fill heaven and earth?"205 "To whom will you liken Me, that I should be equal?"206

Chapter XIII. The One and Only God

1. From the very beginning no Jewish doctrine was so firmly proclaimed and so heroically defended as the belief in the One and Only God. This constitutes the essence and foundation of Judaism. However slowly the people learned that there could be no gods beside the One God, and that consequently all the pagan deities were but "naught and vanity," the Judaism of the Torah starts with the proclamation of the Only One, and later Judaism marches through the nations and ages of history with a never-silent protest against polytheism of every kind, against every division of the Godhead into parts, powers, or persons.

2. It is perfectly clear that divine pedagogy could not well have demanded of a people immature and untrained in religion, like Israel in the wilderness period, the immediate belief in the only one God and in none else. Such a belief is the result of a long mental process; it is attained only after centuries of severe struggle and crisis. Instead of this, the Decalogue of Sinai demanded of the people that they worship only the God of the Covenant who had delivered them from Egypt to render them His people.207 But, as they yielded more and more to the seductive worship of

the gods of the Canaanites and their other neighbors, the law became more rigid in prohibiting such idolatrous practices, and the prophets poured forth their unscathing wrath against the "stiff-necked people" and endeavored by unceasing warnings and threats to win them for the pure truth of monotheism.208

3. The God of Sinai proclaims Himself in the Decalogue as a "jealous God," and not in vain. He cannot tolerate other gods beside Himself. Truth can make no concession to untruth, nor enter into any compromise with it without self-surrender. A pagan religion could well afford to admit foreign gods into its pantheon without offending the ruling deities of the land. On the contrary, their realm seemed rather to be enlarged by the addition. It was also easy to blend the cults of deities originally distinct and unite many divinities under a composite name, and by this process create a system of worship which would either comprise the gods of many lands or even merge them into one large family. This was actually the state of the various pagan religions at the time of the decline of antiquity. But such a procedure could never lead towards true monotheism. It lacks the conception of an inner unity, without which its followers could not grasp the true idea of God as the source and essence of all life, both physical and spiritual. Only the One God of revelation made the world really one. In Him alone heaven and earth, day and night, growth and decay, the weal and woe of individuals and nations, appear as the work of an all-ruling Power and Wisdom, so that all events in nature and history are seen as parts of one all-comprising plan.209

4. It is perfectly true that a wide difference of view exists between the prohibition of polytheism and idolatry in the Decalogue and the proclamation in Deuteronomy of the unity of God, and, still more, between the law of the Pentateuch and the prophetic announcement of the day when Israel's God "shall be King of the whole earth, and His name shall be One."210 Yet Judaism is based precisely upon this higher view. The very first pages of Genesis, the opening of the Torah, as well as the exilic portions of Isaiah which form the culmination of the prophets, and the Psalms also, prove sufficiently that at their time monotheism was an axiom of Judaism. In fact, heathenism had become synonymous with both image-worship and belief in many gods beside the Only One of Israel, and accordingly had lost all hold upon the Jewish people. The heathen gods were given a place in the celestial economy, but only as subordinate rulers or as the guardian angels of the nations, and always under the dominion of God on high.211

5. Later, in the contest against Græco-Egyptian paganism, the doctrine of God's unity was emphasized in the Alexandrian propaganda literature, of which only a portion has been preserved for us. Here antagonism in the most forcible form is expressed against the delusive cults of paganism, and exclusive worship claimed for "the unseen, yet all-seeing God, the uncreated Creator of the world."212 The Rabbinical Haggadah contains but dim reminiscences of the extensive propaganda carried on previous to Hillel, the Talmudic type of the propagandist. Moreover, this period fostered free inquiry and philosophical discussion, and therefore the doctrine of unity emerged more and more from simple belief to become a matter of reason. The God of truth put to flight the gods of falsehood. Hence many gentiles espoused the cause of Judaism, becoming "God-fearing men."213

6. In this connection it seems necessary to point out the difference between the God of the Greek philosophers—Xenophanes and Anaxagoras, Plato and Aristotle—and the God of the Bible. In abandoning their own gods, the Greek philosophers reached a deistic view of the cosmos. As their study of science showed them plan and order everywhere, they concluded that the universe is governed by an all-encompassing Intelligence, a divine power entirely distinct from the capricious deities of the popular religion. Reflection led them to a complete rupture with their religious belief. The Biblical belief in God underwent a different process. After God had once been conceived of, He was held up as the ideal of morality, including both righteousness and holiness. Then this doctrine was continuously elucidated and deepened, until a stage was reached where a harmony could be established between the teachings of Moses and the wisdom of Plato and Aristotle. To the noble thinkers of Hellas truth was an object of supreme delight, the highest privilege of the sage. To the adherents of Judaism truth became the holiest aim of life for the entire people, for which all were taught to battle and to die, as did the Maccabean heroes and Daniel and his associates, their prototypes.

7. A deeper meaning was attached to the doctrine of God's unity under Persian rule, in contact with the religious system of Zoroaster. To the Persians life was a continual conflict between the principles of good and of evil, until the ultimate victory of good shall come. This dualistic view of the world greatly excels all other heathen religious systems, insofar as it assigns ethical purpose to the whole of life. Yet the great seer of the Exile opposes this system in the name of the God of Judaism, speaking to Cyrus, the king of Persia; "I am the Lord and there is none else; beside Me there is no God. I will gird thee, though thou dost not know Me, in order that the people shall know from

the rising of the sun and from the west that there is none beside Me. I form the light and create darkness; I make peace and also create evil, I am the Lord that doeth these things."214 This declaration of pure monotheism is incompatible with dualism in both the physical and the moral world; it regards evil as being mere semblance without reality, an opposing force which can be overcome and rendered a source of new strength for the victory of the good. "Out of the mouth of the Most High cometh there not the evil and the good?"215

8. The division of the world into rival realms of good and evil powers, of angelic and demoniacal forces, which originated in ancient Chaldea and underlies the Zoroastrian dualism, finally took hold of Judaism also. Still this was not carried to such an extent that Satan, the supreme ruler of the demon world, was given a dominion equal to that of God, or interfering with it, so as to impair thereby the principle of monotheism, as was done by the Church later on. As a matter of fact, at the time of nascent Christianity the leaders of the Synagogue took rigid measures against those heretics (Minim) who believed in two divine powers,216 because they recognized the grave danger of moral degeneracy in this Gnostic dualism. In the Church it led first to the deification of Christ (i.e. the Messiah) as the vanquisher of Satan; afterwards, owing to a compromise with heathenism, the Trinity was adopted to correspond with the three-fold godhead,—father, mother, and son,—the place of the mother deity being taken by the Holy Ghost, which was originally conceived as a female power (the Syrian Ruha being of the feminine gender).217

9. The churchmen have attempted often enough to harmonize the dualism or trinitarianism of Christianity with the monotheism of the Bible. Still Judaism persists in considering such an infringement upon the belief in Israel's one and only God as really a compromise with heathenism. "A Jew is he who opposes every sort of polytheism," says the Talmud.218

10. The medieval Jewish thinkers therefore made redoubled efforts to express with utmost clearness the doctrine of God's unity. In this effort they received special encouragement from the example of the leaders of Islam, whose victorious march over the globe was a triumph for the one God of Abraham over the triune God of Christianity. A great tide of intellectual progress arose, lending to the faith of the Mohammedans and subsequently also to that of the Jews an impetus which lasted for centuries. The new thought and keen research of that period had a lasting influence upon the whole development of western culture. An alliance was effected between religion and philosophy, particularly by the leading Jewish minds, which proved a liberating and stimulating force in all fields of scientific investigation. Thus the pure idea of monotheism became the basis for modern science and the entire modern world-view.219

11. The Mohammedan thinkers devoted their attention chiefly to elucidating and spiritualizing the God idea, beginning as early as the third century of Islamism, so to interpret the Koran as to divest God of all anthropomorphic attributes and to stress His absolute unity, uniqueness, and the incomparability of His oneness. Soon they became familiar with neo-Platonic and afterward with Aristotelian modes of speculation through the work of Syrian and Jewish translators. With the help of these they built up a system of theology which influenced Jewish thought also, first in Karaite and then in Rabbanite circles.220 Thus sprang up successively the philosophical systems of Saadia, Jehuda ha Levi, Ibn Gabirol, Bahya, Ibn Daud, and Maimonides. The philosophical hymns and the articles of faith, both of which found a place in the liturgy of the Synagogue, were the work of their followers. The highest mode of adoring God seemed to be the elaboration of the idea of His unity to its logical conclusion, which satisfied the philosophical mind, though often remote from the understanding of the multitude. For centuries the supreme effort of Jewish thought was to remove Him from the possibility of comparison with any other being, and to abolish every conception which might impair His absolute and simple unity. This mental activity filled the dwellings of Israel with light, even when the darkness of ignorance covered the lands of Christendom, dispelled only here and there by rays of knowledge emanating from Jewish quarters.221

12. The proofs of the unity of God adduced by Mohammedan and Jewish thinkers were derived from the rational order, design, and unity of the cosmos, and from the laws of the mind itself. These aided in endowing Judaism with a power of conviction which rendered futile the conversionist efforts of the Church, with its arguments and its threats. Israel's only One proved to be the God of truth, high and holy to both the mind and the heart. The Jewish masters of thought rendered Him the highest object of their speculation, only to bow in awe before Him who is beyond all human ken; the Jewish martyrs likewise cheerfully offered up their lives in His honor; and thus all hearts echoed the battle-cry of the centuries, "Hear O Israel, the Lord our God, the Lord is One," and all minds were illumined by the radiant hope, "The Lord will be King of the earth; on that day the Lord shall be One, and His name shall be One."

13. Under all conditions, however, the doctrine of unity remained free from outward compulsion and full of intrinsic vigor and freshness. There was still room for differences of opinion, such as whether God's life, power, wisdom, and unity are attributes—distinct from His being, and qualifying it,—or whether they are inherent in His nature, comprising His very essence. This controversy aimed to determine the conception of God, either by Aristotelian rationalism, as represented by Maimonides, or by the positive religious assumptions of Crescas and others.

This is Maimonides' statement of the unity: "God is one; that is, He is unlike any other unit, whether made one in point of numbers or species, or by virtue of composition, separation, and simplification. He is one in Himself, there being no multiplicity in Him. His unity is beyond all definition."222

Ibn Gabirol in his "Crown of Royalty" puts the same thought into poetic form: "One art Thou; the wise wonder at the mystery of Thy unity, not knowing what it is. One art Thou; not like the one of dimension or number, as neither addition nor change, neither attribute nor quality affects Thy being. Thou art God, who sustainest all beings by Thy divinity, who holdest all creatures in Thy unity. Thou art God, and there is no distinction between Thy unity, Thy eternity, and Thy being. All is mystery, and however the names may differ, they all tell that Thou art but one."223

14. Side by side with this rationalistic trend, Judaism always contained a current of mysticism. The mystics accepted literally the anthropomorphic pictures of the Deity in the Bible, and did not care how much they might affect the spirituality and unity of God. The philosophic schools had contended against the anthropomorphic views of the older mystics, and thus had brought higher views of the Godhead to dominance; but when the rationalistic movement had spent its force, the reaction came in the form of the Cabbalah, the secret lore which claimed to have been "transmitted" (according to the meaning of the word) from a hoary past. The older system of thought had stripped the Deity of all reality and had robbed religion of all positiveness; now, in contrast, the soul demanded a God of revelation through faith in whom might come exaltation and solace.224

Nevertheless the Maimonidean articles of faith were adopted into the liturgy because of their emphasis on the absolute unity and indivisibility of God, by which they constituted a vigorous protest against the Christian dogma. Judaism ever found its strength in God the only One, and will find Him ever anew a source of inspiration and rejuvenation.

Chapter XIV. God's Omnipotence and Omniscience

1. Among all the emotions which underlie our God-consciousness the foremost is the realization of our own weakness and helplessness. This makes us long for One mightier than ourselves, for the Almighty whose acts are beyond comparison. The first attribute, therefore, with which we feeble mortals invest our Deity is omnipotence. Thus the pagan ascribes supreme power over their different realms to his various deities. Hence the name for God among all the Semites is El—"the Powerful One."225 Judaism claims for God absolute and unlimited power over all that is. It declares Him to be the source and essence of all strength, the almighty Creator and Ruler of the universe. All that exists is His creation; all that occurs is His achievement. He is frequently called by the rabbis ha Geburah, the Omnipotence.226

2. The historical method of study seems to indicate that various cosmic potencies were worshiped in primitive life either singly or collectively under the name of Elohim, "divine powers," or Zibeoth Elohim, "hosts of divine powers." With the acceptance of the idea of divine omnipotence, these were united into a confederacy of divine forces under the dominion of the one God, the "Lord of Hosts." Still these powers of heaven, earth and the deep by no means at once surrendered their identity. Most of them became angels, "messengers" of the omnipotent God, or "spirits" roaming in the realms where once they ruled, while a few were relegated as monsters to the region of superstition. The heathen deities, which persisted for a while in popular belief, were also placed with the angels as "heavenly rulers" of their respective lands or nations about the throne of the Most High. At all events, Israel's God was enthroned above them all as Lord of the universe. In fact, the Alexandrian translators and some of the rabbis actually explained in this sense the Biblical names El Shaddai and J.H.V.H. Zebaoth.227 The medieval philosophers, however, took a backward step away from the Biblical view when, under the influence of Neoplatonism, they represented the angels and the spirits of the stars as intermediary forces.228

3. According to the Bible, both the Creation and the order of the universe testify to divine omnipotence. God called all things into existence by His almighty word, unassisted by His heavenly messengers. He alone stretched out the heavens, set bounds to the sea, and founded the earth on pillars that it be not moved; none was with Him to partake in the work. This is the process of creation according to the first chapter of Genesis and the fortieth chapter of Isaiah. So He appears throughout the Scriptures as "the Doer of wonders," "whose arm never waxes short" to carry out His will. "He fainteth not, neither is He weary." His dominion extends over the sea and the storm, over life and death, over high and low. Intermediary forces participating in His work are never mentioned. They are referred to only in the poetic description of creation in the book of Job: "Where wast thou when I laid the foundations of the earth?... When the morning stars sang together, and all the sons of God shouted for joy."229

Proof of God's supreme power was found particularly in history, either in His miraculous changing of the natural order, or in His defeat of the mighty hostile armies which bade Him defiance.230 Often the heathen deities or the celestial powers are introduced as dramatic figures to testify to the triumph of the divine omnipotence, as when the Lord is said to "execute judgment against the gods of Egypt" or when "the stars in their courses fought against Sisera."231

4. God's power is limited only by His own volition. "He doeth what He willeth."232 In man the will and the power for a certain act are far apart, and often directly conflicting. Not so with God, for the very idea of God is perfection, and His will implies necessarily the power to accomplish the desired end. His will is determined only by such factors as His knowledge and His moral self-restraint.

5. Therefore the idea of God's omnipotence must be coupled with that of His omniscience. Both His power and His knowledge are unlike man's in being without limitation. When we repeat the Biblical terms of an all-seeing, all-hearing, and all-knowing God, we mean in the first instance that the limitation of space does not exist for Him. He beholds the extreme parts of the earth and observes all that happens under the heavens; nothing is hidden from His sight. He not only sees the deeds of men, He also searches their thoughts. Looking into their hearts, He knows the word, ere it is upon the tongue. Looking into the future, he knows every creature, ere it enters existence. "The darkness and the light are alike to Him." With one glance He surveys all that is and all that happens.233 He is, as the rabbis express it, "the all-seeing Eye and the all-hearing Ear."234

In like manner the distinctions of time disappear before Him. The entire past is unrolled before His sight; His book records all that men do or suffer, even their tears;235 and there is no forgetfulness with Him. The remotest future also is open before Him, for it is planned by Him, and in it He has allotted to each being its days and its steps.236 Yea, as He beholds events ere they transpire, so He reveals the secrets of the future to His chosen ones, in order to warn men of the judgments that threaten them.237

6. The idea of divine omniscience could ripen only gradually in the minds of the people. The older and more child-like conception still remains in the stories of the Deluge and the Tower of Babel, where God descended from heaven to watch the doings of men, and repented of what He had done.238 Obviously the idea of divine omniscience took hold of the people as a result of the admonitions of the prophets.

7. Philosophical inquiry into the ideas of the divine omnipotence and omniscience, however, discloses many difficulties. The Biblical assertion that nothing is impossible to God will not stand the test as soon as we ask seriously whether God can make the untrue true,—as making two times two to equal five—or whether He can declare the wrong to be right. Obviously He cannot overturn the laws of mathematical truth or of moral truth, without at the same time losing His nature as the Source and Essence of all truth. Nor can He abrogate the laws of nature, which are really His own rules for His creation, without detracting from both His omniscience and the immutability of His will. This question will be discussed more fully in connection with miracles, in chapter XXVII.

Together with the problem of the divine omniscience arises the difficulty of reconciling this with our freedom of will and our moral responsibility. Would not His foreknowledge of our actions in effect determine them? This difficulty can only be solved by a proper conception of the freedom of the will, and will be discussed in that connection in chapter XXXVII.

Altogether, we must guard against applying our human type of knowledge to God. Man, limited by space and time, obtains his knowledge of things and events by his senses, becoming aware of them separately as they exist either beside each other or in succession. With God all knowledge is complete; there is no growth of knowledge from yesterday to to-day, no knowledge of only a part instead of the whole of the world. His omniscience and omnipotence are bound up with His omnipresence and eternity. "For My thoughts are not your thoughts, neither are your ways My ways, saith the Lord. For as the heavens are higher than the earth, so are My ways higher than your ways, and My thoughts than your thoughts."239

Chapter XV. God's Omnipresence and Eternity

1. As soon as man awakens to a higher consciousness of God, he realizes the vast distance between his own finite being limited by space and time, and the Infinite Being which rules everywhere and unceasingly in lofty grandeur and unlimited power. His very sense of being hedged in by the bounds and imperfections of a finite existence makes him long for the infinite God, unlimited in might, and brings to him the feeling of awe before His greatness. But this conception of God as the omnipresent and everlasting Spirit, as distinct from any created being, is likewise the result of many stages of growing thought.

2. The primitive mind imagines God as dwelling in a lofty place, whence He rules the earth beneath, descending at times to take part in the affairs of men, to tarry among them, or to walk with them.240 The people adhered largely to this conception during the Biblical period, as they considered as the original seat of the Deity, first Paradise, later on Sinai or Zion, and finally the far-off heavens. It required prophetic vision to discern that "the heavens and the heavens' heavens do not encompass God's majesty," expressed also in poetic imagery that "the heaven is My throne and the earth My footstool."241 The classic form of this idea of the divine omnipresence is found in the oft-quoted passage from Psalm CXXXIX.242

3. The dwelling places of God are to give way the moment His omnipresence is understood as penetrating the universe to such an extent that nothing escapes His glance nor lies without His dominion.243 They are then transformed into places where He had manifested His Name, His Glory, or His Presence ("Countenance," in the Hebrew). In this way certain emanations or powers of God were formed which could be located in a certain space without impairing the divine omnipresence. These intermediary powers will be the theme of chapter XXXII.

The following dialogue illustrates this stage of thought: A heretic once said sarcastically to Gamaliel II, "Ye say that where ten persons assemble for worship, there the divine majesty (Shekinah) descends upon them; how many such majesties are there?" To which Gamaliel replied: "Does not the one orb of day send forth a million rays upon the earth? And should not the majesty of God, which is a million times brighter than the sun, be reflected in every spot on earth?"244

4. Nevertheless a conception of pure spirit is very difficult to attain, even in regard to God. The thought of His omnipresence is usually interpreted by imagining some ethereal substance which expands infinitely, as Ibn Ezra and Saadia before him were inclined to do,245 or by picturing Him as a sort of all-encompassing Space, in accordance with the rabbis.246 The New Testament writers and the Church fathers likewise spoke of God as Spirit, but really had in mind, for the most part, an ethereal substance resembling light pervading cosmic space. The often-expressed belief that man may see God after death rests upon this conception of God as a substance perceptible to the mind.247

A higher standpoint is taken by a thinker such as Ibn Gabirol, who finds God's omnipresence in His all-pervading will and intellect.248 But this type of divine omnipresence is rather divine immanence. The religious consciousness has a quite different picture of God, a self-conscious Personality, ever near to man, ever scanning his acts, his thoughts, and his motives. Here philosophy and religion part company. The former must abstain from the assumption of a divine personality; the latter cannot do without it. The God of religion must partake of the knowledge and the feelings of His worshiper, must know his every impulse and idea, and must feel with him in his suffering and need. God's omnipresence is in this sense a postulate of religion.

5. The second earthly and human limitation is that of time. Confined by space and time, man casts his eyes upward toward a Being who shall be infinite and eternal. Whatever time begets, time swallows up again. Transitoriness is the fate of all things. Everything which enters existence must end at last. "Also heaven and earth perish and wax old like a garment. Only God remains forever the same, and His years have no end. He is from everlasting to everlasting, the first and the last." So speak prophet and psalmist, voicing a universal thought249; and our liturgical poet sings:

"The Lord of all did reign supreme

Ere yet this world was made and formed;

When all was finished by His will,

Then was His name as King proclaimed.

"And should these forms no more exist,

He still will rule in majesty;

He was, He is, He shall remain,

His glory never shall decrease."250

6. But the idea of God's eternity also presents certain difficulties to the thinking mind. As Creator and Author of the universe, God is the First Cause, without beginning or end, the Source of all existence; as Ruler and Master of the world, He maintains all things through all eternity; though heaven and earth "wax old like a garment," He outlasts them all. Now, if He is to manifest these powers from everlasting to everlasting, He must ever remain the same. Consequently, we must add immutability as a corollary of eternity, if the latter is to mean anything. It is not enough to state that God is without beginning and without end; the essential part of the doctrine is His transcendence above the changes and conditions of time. We mortals cannot really entertain a conception of eternity; our nearest approach to it is an endless succession of periods of time, a ceaseless procession of ages and eons following each other. Endless time is not at all the same as timelessness. Therefore eternity signifies transcendence above all existence in time; its real meaning is supermundaneity.251

7. This seems the best way to avoid the difficulty which seemed almost insuperable to the medieval thinkers, how to reconcile a Creation at a certain time and a Creator for whom time does not exist. In the effort to solve the difficulty, they resorted to the Platonic and Aristotelian definition of time as the result of the motions of the heavenly bodies; thus they declared that time was created simultaneously with the world. This is impossible for the modern thinker, who has learned from Kant to regard time and space, not as external realities, but as human modes of apperception of objects. So the contrast between the transient character of the world and the eternity of God becomes all the greater with the increasing realization of the vast gap between the material world and the divine spirit.

At this point arises a still greater difficulty. The very idea of creation at a certain time becomes untenable in view of our knowledge of the natural process; the universe itself, it seems to us, extends over an infinity of space and time. Indeed, the modern view of evolution in place of creation has the grave danger of leading to pantheism, to a conception of the cosmos which sees in God only an eternal energy (or substance) devoid of free volition and self-conscious action.252 We can evade the difficulty only by assuming God's transcendence, and this can be done in such a way as not to exclude His immanence, or—what is the same thing—His omnipresence.

8. Both God's omnipresence and His eternity are intended only to raise Him far above the world, out of the confines of space and time, to represent His sublime loftiness as the "Rock of Ages," as holding worlds without number in "His eternal arms." "Nothing can be hidden from Him who has reared the entire universe and is familiar with every part of it, however remote."253

Chapter XVI. God's Holiness

1. Judaism recognizes two distinct types of divine attributes. Those which we have so far considered belong to the metaphysical group, which chiefly engage the attention of the philosopher. They represent God as a transcendental Being who is ever beyond our comprehension, because our finite intellect can never grasp the infinite Spirit. They are not descriptions, but rather inferences from the works of the Master of the world to the Master himself. But there are other divine attributes which we derive from our own moral nature, and which invest our whole life with a higher moral character. Instead of arising from the external necessity which governs nature in its causes and effects, these rest upon our assumption of inner freedom, setting the aims for all that we achieve. This moral nature is realized to some extent even by the savage, when he trembles before his deity in pangs of conscience, or endeavors to propitiate him by sacrifices. Still, Judaism alone fully realized the moral nature of the Deity; this was done by investing the term "holiness" with the idea of moral perfection, so that God became the ideal and pattern of

the loftiest morality. "Be ye holy, for I the Lord your God am holy."254—This is the central and culminating idea of the Jewish law.255

2. Holiness is the essence of all moral perfection; it is purity unsullied by any breath of evil. True holiness can be ascribed only to Divinity, above the realm of the flesh and the senses. "There is none holy but the Lord, for there is none beside Thee," says Scripture.256 Whether man stands on a lower or higher level of culture, he has in all his plans and aspirations some ideal of perfection to which he may never attain, but which serves as the standard for his actions. The best of his doings falls short of what he ought to do; in his highest efforts he realizes the potentiality of better things. This ideal of moral perfection works as the motive power of the will in setting for it a standard; it establishes human freedom in place of nature's compulsion, but such an ideal can emanate only from the moral power ruling life, which we designate as the divine Holiness.

3. Scripture says of God that He "walketh in holiness,"257 and accordingly morality in man is spoken of as "walking in the ways of God."258 "Walk before Me and be perfect!" says God to Abraham.259 Moses approached God with two petitions,—the one, "Show me Thy ways that I may know Thee!" the other, "Show me, I pray Thee, Thy glory!" In response to the latter God said, "No man can see Me and live", but the former petition was granted in that the Lord revealed Himself in His moral attributes.260 These alone can be understood and emulated by man; in regard to the so-called metaphysical attributes God will ever remain beyond human comprehension and emulation.

4. In order to serve as vehicle for the expression of the highest moral perfection, the Biblical term for holiness, Kadosh, had to undergo a long process of development, obscuring its original meaning. The history of this term gives us the deepest insight into the working of the Jewish genius towards the full revelation of the God of holiness. At first the word Kadosh261 seems to have denoted unapproachableness in the sense in which fire is unapproachable, that is, threatening and consuming. This fiery nature was ascribed by primitive man to all divine beings. Hence the angels are termed "the holy ones" in Scripture.262 According to both priestly practice and popular belief, the man who approached one of these holy ones with hand or foot, or even with his gaze, was doomed to die.263 Out of such crude conceptions evolved the idea of God's majesty as unapproachable in the sense of the sublime, banishing everything profane from its presence, and visiting with punishment every violation of its sanctity. The old conception of the fiery appearance of the Deity served especially as a figurative expression of the moral power of God, which manifests itself as a "consuming fire,"264 exterminating evil, and making man long for the good and the true, for righteousness and love.

5. The divine attribute of holiness has accordingly a double meaning. On the one hand, it indicates spiritual loftiness transcending everything sensual, which works as a purging power of indignation at evil, rebuking injustice, impurity and falsehood, and punishing transgression until it is removed from the sight of God. On the other hand, it denotes the condescending mercy of God, which, having purged the soul of wrong, wins it for the right, and which endows man with the power of perfecting himself, and thus leads him to the gradual building up of the kingdom of goodness and purity on earth. This ethical conception of holiness, which emanates from the moral nature of God, revealed to the prophetic genius of Israel, must not be confused with the old Semitic conception of priestly or ritual holiness. Ritual holiness is purely external, and is transferable to persons and things, to times and places, according to their relation to the Deity. Hence the various cults applied the term "holy" to the most abominable forms of idolatry and impure worship.265 The Mosaic law condemned all these as violations of the holiness of Israel's God, but could not help sanctioning many ordinances and rites of priestly holiness which originated in ancient Semitic usages. Hence the two conceptions of holiness, the priestly or external and the prophetic or ethical, became interwoven in the Mosaic code to such an extent as to impair the standard of ethical holiness stressed by the prophets, the unique and lofty possession of Judaism. Hence the letter of the Law caused a deplorable confusion of ideas, which was utilized by the detractors of Judaism. The liberal movement of modern Judaism, in pointing to the prophetic ideals as the true basis of the Jewish faith, is at the same time dispelling this ancient confusion of the two conceptions of holiness.

6. The Levitical holiness adheres outwardly to persons and things and consists in their separation or their reservation from common use. In striking contrast to this, the holiness which Judaism attributes to God denotes the highest ethical purity, unattainable to flesh and blood, but designed for our emulation.

The contemplation of the divine holiness is to inspire man with fear of sin and to exert a healthful influence upon his conduct. Thus God became the hallowing power in Judaism and its institutions, truly the "Holy One of Israel" according to the term of Isaiah and his great exilic successor, the so-called Deutero-Isaiah.266 Thus His holiness invested His people with special sanctity and imposed upon it special obligations. In the words of Ezekiel, God became the "Sanctifier of Israel."267

The rabbis penetrated deeply into the spirit of Scripture, at the same time that they adhered strictly to its letter. While they clung tenaciously to the ritual holiness of the priestly codes, they recognized the ideal of holiness which is so sharply opposed in every act and thought to the demoralizing cults of heathenism.268

7. Accordingly, holiness is not the metaphysical concept which Jehuda ha Levi considers it,269 but the principle and source of all ethics, the spirit of absolute morality, lending purpose and value to the whole of life. As long as men do good or shun evil through fear of punishment or hope for reward, whether in this life or the hereafter, so long will ideal morality remain unattained, and man cannot claim to stand upon the ground of divine holiness. The holy God must penetrate and control all of life—such is the essence of Judaism. The true aim of human existence is not salvation of the soul,—a desire which is never quite free from selfishness,—but holiness emulating God, striving to do good for the sake of the good without regard to recompense, and to shun evil because it is evil, aside from all consequences.270

8. The fact is that holiness is a religious term, based upon divine revelation, not a philosophical one resting upon speculative reasoning. It is a postulate of our moral nature that all life is governed by a holy Will to which we must submit willingly, and which makes for the good. How volition and compulsion are with God one and the same, how the good exists in God without the bad, or holiness and moral purpose without unholy or immoral elements, how God can be exactly opposite to all we know of man,—this is a question which philosophy is unable to answer. In fact, holiness is best defined negatively, as the "negation of all that man from his own experience knows to be unholy." These words of the Danish philosopher Rauwenhoff are made still clearer by the following observations: "The strength in the idea of holiness lies exactly in its negative character. There is no comparison of higher or lesser degree possible between man's imperfections and God's perfect goodness. Instead, there is an absolute contrast between mankind which, even in its noblest types, must wrestle with the power of evil, and God, in whom nothing can be imagined which would even suggest the possibility of any moral shortcoming or imperfection."271 As the prophet says, "Thou art too pure of eyes to look complacently upon evil,"272 and according to the Psalmist, "Who shall ascend into the mountain of the Lord, and who shall stand in His holy place? He that hath clean hands and a pure heart."273

9. The idea of holiness became the preëminent feature of Judaism, so that the favorite name for God in Rabbinical literature was "the Holy One, blessed be He," and the acme of all ceremonial and moral laws alike was found in "the Hallowing of His name."274 If the rabbis as followers of the Priestly Code were compelled to lay great stress upon ritual holiness, they yet beheld in it the means of moral purification. They never lost sight of the prophetic principle that moral purity is the object of all human life, for "the holy God is sanctified through righteousness."275

Chapter XVII. God's Wrath and Punishment

1. Scripture speaks frequently of the anger and zeal of God and of His avenging sword and judgment, so as to give the impression that "the Old Testament God is a God of wrath and vengeance." As a matter of fact, these attributes are merely emanations of His holiness, the guide and incentive to moral action in man. The burning fire of the divine holiness aims to awaken the dormant seeds of morality in the human soul and to ripen them into full growth. Whenever we to-day would speak of pangs of conscience, of bitter remorse, Scripture uses figurative language and describes how God's wrath is kindled against the wrongdoing of the people, and how fire blazes forth from His nostrils to consume them in His anger. The nearer man stands to nature, the more tempestuous are the outbursts of his passion, and the more violent is the reaction of his repentance. Yet this very reaction impresses him as though wrought from outside or above by the offended Deity. Thus the divine wrath becomes a means of moral education, exactly as the parents' indignation at the child's offenses is part of his training in morality.

2. Thus the first manifestation of God's holiness is His indignation at falsehood and violence, His hatred of evil and wrongdoing. The longer men persist in sin, the more does He manifest Himself as "the angry God," as a "consuming fire" which destroys evil with holy zeal.276 The husbandman cannot expect the good harvest until he has weeded out the tares from the field; so God, in educating man, begins by purging the soul from all its evil inclinations, and

this zeal is all the more unsparing as the good is finally to triumph in His eternal plan of universal salvation. We must bear in mind that Judaism does not personify evil as a power hostile to God, hence the whole problem is only one of purifying the human soul. Before the sun of God's grace and mercy is to shine, bearing life and healing for all humanity, His wrath and punitive justice must ever burst forth to cleanse the world of its sin. For as long as evil continues unchecked, so long cannot the divine holiness pour forth its all-forbearing goodness and love.

3. On this account the first revelation of God on Sinai was as "a jealous God, who visiteth the sins of the fathers upon the children and the children's children until the third and fourth generation." So the prophets, from Moses to Malachi, speak ever of God's anger, which comes with the fury of nature's unchained forces, to terrify and overwhelm all living beings.277 Thus Scripture considers all the great catastrophes of the hoary past,—flood, earthquakes, and the rain of fire and brimstone that destroys cities—as judgments of the divine anger on sinful generations. Wickedness in general causes His displeasure, but His wrath is provoked especially by violations of the social order, by desecrations of His sanctuary, or attacks on His covenant, and His anger is kindled for the poor and helpless, when they are oppressed and deprived of their rights.278

4. Thus the divine holiness was felt more and more as a moral force, and that which appeared in pre-prophetic times to be an elemental power of the celestial ire became a refining flame, purging men of dross as in a crucible. "I will not execute the fierceness of Mine anger," says the prophet, "for I am God and not man, the Holy One in the midst of thee, and I will not come in fury."279 So sings the Psalmist, "His anger is but for a moment; His favor for a life-time."280 In the same spirit the rabbis interpreted the verse of the Decalogue, "The sin of the fathers is visited upon the children and children's children only if they continue to act as their fathers did, and are themselves haters of God."281

The fact is that Israel in Canaan had become addicted to all the vices of idolatry, and if they were to be trained to moral purity and to loyalty to the God of the Covenant, they must be taught fear and awe before the flame of the divine wrath. Only after that could the prophet address himself to the conscience of the individual, saying:

"Who among us shall dwell with the devouring fire?

Who among us shall dwell with everlasting burnings?

He that walketh righteously, and speaketh uprightly;

He that despiseth the gain of oppressions, that shaketh his hands from holding of bribes,

That stoppeth his ears from hearing of blood, and shutteth his eyes from looking upon evil;

He shall dwell on high; his place of defense shall be the munitions of rocks;

His bread shall be given, his water shall be sure.

Thine eyes shall see the King in His beauty; they shall behold a land stretching afar."282

Here we behold the fiery element of the divine holiness partly depicted as a reality and partly spiritualized. The last of the prophets compares the divine wrath to a melting furnace, which on the Day of Judgment is to consume evildoers as stubble, while to those who fear the Lord He shall appear as the sun of righteousness with healing on its wings.283

5. The idea as expressed by the prophets, then, was that God's anger will visit the wicked, and particularly the ungodly nations of heathendom, and that He shall judge all creatures in fire.284 This was significantly altered under Persian influence, when the Jew began to regard the world to come as promising to the righteous greater bliss than the present one. Then the day of divine wrath meant doom eternal for evil-doers, who were to fall into the fiery depths of Gehenna, "their worm is never to die and their fire never to be quenched."285 This became the prevailing view of the rabbis, of the Apocalyptics and also of the New Testament and the Church literature.286 The Jewish propaganda in the Hellenistic literature, however, combined the fire of Gehenna with the Stoic, or pagan, view of a general world-conflagration, and announced a general doomsday for the heathen world, unless they be converted to the belief in Israel's one and holy God, and ceased violating the fundamental (Noachian) laws of humanity.287

6. A higher view of the punitive anger of God is taken by Beruriah, the noble wife of R. Meir,288—if, indeed, the wife of the saintly Abba Helkiah did not precede her289—in suggesting a different reading of the Biblical text, as to

make it offer the lesson: "not the sinners shall perish from the earth, but the sins." From a more philosophical viewpoint both Juda ha Levi and Maimonides hold that the anger which we ascribe to God is only the transference of the anger which we actually feel at the sight of evildoing. Similarly, when we speak of the consuming fire of hell, we depict the effect which the fear of God must have on our inner life, until the time shall come when we shun evil as ungodly and love the good because it is both good and God-like.290

Chapter XVIII. God's Long-suffering and Mercy

1. In one of the little known apocryphal writings, the Testament of Abraham, a beautiful story is told of the patriarch. Shortly before his death, the archangel Michael drove him along the sky in the heavenly chariot. Looking down upon the earth, he saw companies of thieves and murderers, adulterers, and other evil-doers pursuing their nefarious practices, and in righteous indignation he cried out: "Oh would to God that fire, destruction, and death should instantly befall these criminals!" No sooner had he spoken these words than the doom he pronounced came upon those wicked men. But then spoke the Lord God to the heavenly charioteer Michael: "Stop at once, lest My righteous servant Abraham in his just indignation bring death upon all My creatures, because they are not as righteous as he. He has not learned to restrain his anger."291 Thus, indeed, the wrath kindled at the sight of wrongdoing would consume the sinner at once, were it not for another quality in God, called in Scripture long-suffering. By this He restrains His anger and gives the sinner time to improve his ways. Though every wicked deed provokes Him to immediate punishment, yet He shows compassion upon the feeble mortal. "Even in wrath He remembereth compassion."292 "He hath no delight in the death of the sinner, but that he shall return from his ways and live."293 The divine holiness does not merely overwhelm and consume; its essential aim is the elevation of man, the effort to endow him with a higher life.

2. It is perfectly true that a note of rigor and of profound earnestness runs through the pages of Holy Writ. The prophets, law-givers, and psalmists speak incessantly of how guilt brings doom upon the lands and nations. As the father who is solicitous of the honor of his household punishes unrelentingly every violation of morality within it, so the Holy One of Israel watches zealously over His people's loyalty to His covenant. His glorious name, His holy majesty cannot be violated with immunity from His dreaded wrath. There is nothing of the joyous abandon which was predominant in the Greek nature and in the Olympian gods. The ideal of holiness was presented by the God of Israel, and all the doings of men appeared faulty beside it.

But its power of molding character is shown by Judaism at this very point, in that it does not stop at the condemnation of the sinner. It holds forth the promise of God's forbearance to man in his shortcomings, due to His compassion on the weakness of flesh and blood. He waits for man, erring and stumbling, until by striving and struggling he shall attain a higher state of purity. This is the bright, uplifting side of the Jewish idea of the divine holiness. In this is the innermost nature of God disclosed. In fear and awe of Him who is enthroned on high, "before whom even the angels are not pure," man, conscious of his sinfulness, sinks trembling into the dust before the Judge of the whole earth. But the grace and mercy of the long-suffering Ruler lift him up and imbue him with courage and strength to acquire a new life and new energy. Thus the oppressive burden of guilt is transformed into an uplifting power through the influence of the holy God.

3. The predominance in God of mildness and mercy over punitive anger is expressed most strikingly in the revelation to Moses, when he had entreated God to let him see His ways. The people had provoked God's anger by their faithlessness in the worship of the golden calf, and He had threatened to consume them, when Moses interceded in their behalf. Then the Lord passed by him, and proclaimed: "The Lord, the Lord, God, merciful and gracious, long-suffering and abundant in goodness and truth, keeping mercy unto the thousandth generation, forgiving iniquity and transgression and sin; and that will by no means clear the guilty; visiting the iniquity of the fathers upon the children and upon the children's children, unto the third and unto the fourth generation."294 Such a passage shows clearly the progress in the knowledge of God's nature. For Abraham and the traditions of the patriarchs God was the righteous Judge, punishing the transgressors. He is represented in the same way in the Decalogue on Sinai.295 Was this to be the final word? Was Israel chosen by God as His covenant people, only to encounter the full measure of His just but relentless anger and to be consumed at once for the violation of this covenant? Therefore Moses wrestled with his God. Filled with compassionate love for his people, he is willing to offer his life as their ransom. And should God himself lack this fullness of love and pity, of which even a human being is capable? Then, as from a dark cloud, there flashed suddenly upon him the light of a new revelation; he

became aware of the higher truth, that above the austerity of God's avenging anger prevails the tender forgiveness of His mercy; that beyond the consuming zeal of His punitive justice shines the sun-like splendor of His grace and love. The rabbis find the expression of mercy especially in the name JHVH (i.e. "the One who shall ever be") which is significantly placed here at the head of the divine attributes. Indeed, only He who is the same from everlasting to everlasting, and to whom to-morrow is like yesterday, can show forbearance to erring man, because in whatsoever he has failed yesterday he may make good to-morrow.

4. Like Moses, the master of the prophets, so the prophet Hosea also learned in hard spiritual struggle to know the divine attribute of mercy and lovingkindness. His own wife had proved faithless, and had broken the marital covenant; still his love survived, so that he granted her forgiveness when she was forsaken, and took her back to his home. Then, in his distress at the God-forsaken state of Israel through her faithlessness, he asked himself: "Will God reject forever the nation which He espoused, because it broke the covenant? Will not He also grant forgiveness and mercy?" The divine answer came to him out of the depths of his own compassionate soul. Upon the crown of God's majesty which Amos had beheld all effulgent with justice and righteousness, he placed the most precious gem, reflecting the highest quality of God—His gracious and all-forgiving love.296 Whether the priority in this great truth belongs to Hosea or Moses is a question for historical Bible research to answer, but it is of no consequence to Jewish theology.

5. Certainly Scripture represents God too much after human fashion, when it ascribes to him changes of mood from anger to compassion, or speaks of His repentance.297 But we must bear in mind that the prophets obtained their insight into the ways of God by this very process of transferring their own experience to the Deity. And on the other hand, we are told that "God is not a man that He should lie, neither the son of man that He should repent."298 All these anthropomorphic pictures of God were later avoided by the ancient Biblical translators by means of paraphrase, and by the philosophers by means of allegory.299

6. According to the Midrashic interpretation of the passage from the Pentateuch quoted above, Moses desired to ascertain whether God ruled the world with His justice or with His mercy, and the answer was: "Behold, I shall let My goodness pass before thee. For I owe nothing to any of My creatures, but My actions are prompted only by My grace and good will, through which I give them all that they possess."300 According to Judaism justice and mercy are intertwined in God's government of the world; the former is the pillar of the cosmic structure, and the latter the measuring line. No mortal could stand before God, were justice the only standard; but we subsist on His mercy, which lends us the boons of life without our meriting them. That which is not good in us now is to become good through our effort toward the best. God's grace underlies this possibility.

Accordingly, the divine holiness has two aspects, the overwhelming wrath of His justice and the uplifting grace of His long-suffering. Without justice there could be no fear of God, no moral earnestness; without mercy only condemnation and perdition would remain. As the rabbis tell us, both justice and mercy had their share in the creation of man, for in man both good and bad appear and struggle for supremacy. All generations need the divine grace that they may have time and opportunity for improvement.301

7. Thus this conception of grace is far deeper and worthier of God than is that of Paulinian Christianity; for grace in Paul's sense is arbitrary in action and dependent upon the acceptance of a creed, therefore the very reverse of impartial justice. In Judaism divine grace is not offered as a bait to make men believe, but as an incentive to moral improvement. The God of holiness, who inflicts wounds upon the guilty soul by bitter remorse, offers also healing through His compassion. Justice and mercy are not two separate powers or persons in the Deity, as with the doctrine of the Church; they are the two sides of the same divine power. "I am the Lord before sin was committed, and I am the Lord after sin is committed"—so the rabbis explain the repetition of the name JHVH in the revelation to Moses.302

Chapter XIX. God's Justice

1. The unshakable faith of the Jewish people was ever sustained by the consciousness that its God is a God of justice. The conviction that He will not suffer wrong to go unpunished was read into all the stories of the hoary past. The Babylonian form of these legends in common with all ancient folk-lore ascribes human calamity to blind fate or to the caprice of the gods, but the Biblical narratives assume that evil does not befall men undeserved, and therefore always ascribe ruin or death to human transgression. So the Jewish genius beheld in the destruction of

Sodom and Gomorrah a divine judgment upon the depraved inhabitants, and derived from it a lesson for the household of Abraham that they should "keep the way of the Lord to do righteousness and justice."303 The fundamental principle of Judaism throughout the ages has been the teaching of the patriarch that "the Judge of all the earth cannot act unjustly,"304 even though the varying events of history force the problem of justice upon the attention of Jeremiah,305 the Psalmists,306 the author of the book of Job,307 and the Talmudical sages.308 "Righteousness and justice are the foundations of Thy throne"309—this is the sum and substance of the religious experience of Israel. At the same time man realizes how far from his grasp is the divine justice: "Thy righteousness is like the mighty mountains; Thy judgments are like the great deep."310

2. The Master-builder of the moral world made justice the supporting pillar of the entire creation. "He is The Rock, His work is perfect, for all His ways are just; a God of faithfulness and without iniquity, just and right is He."311 There can be no moral world order without a retributive justice, which leaves no infringement of right unpunished, just as no social order can exist without laws to protect the weak and to enforce general respect. The God of Judaism rules over mankind as Guardian and Vindicator of justice; no wrong escapes His scrutinizing gaze. This fundamental doctrine invested history, of both the individual and the nation, with a moral significance beyond that of any other religious or ethical system.

Whatever practice or sense of justice may exist among the rest of mankind, it is at best a glimpse of that divine righteousness which leads us on and becomes a mighty force compelling us, not only to avoid wrongdoing, but to combat it with all the passion of an indignant soul and eradicate it wherever possible. Though in our daily experience justice may be sadly lacking, we still cling to the moral axiom that God will lead the right to victory and will hurl iniquity into the abyss. As the sages remark in the Midrash: "How could short-sighted and short-lived man venture to assert, 'All His ways are just,' were it not for the divine revelation by which the eyes of Moses were opened, so that he could gaze into the very depths of life?"312 That is, the idea of divine justice is revealed, not in the world as it is, but in the world as it should be, the ideal cosmos which lives in the spirit.

3. It cannot be denied that justice is recognized as a binding force even by peoples on a low cultural plane, and the Deity is generally regarded as the guardian of justice, exactly as in Judaism. This fact is shown by the use of the oath in connection with judicial procedure among many nations. Both Roman jurisprudence and Greek ethics declare justice to be the foundation of the social life. Nevertheless the Jewish ideal of justice cannot be identified with that of the law and the courts. The law is part of the social system of the State, by which the relations of individuals are determined and upheld. The maintenance of this social order, of the status quo, is considered justice by the law, whatever injustice to individuals may result. But the Jewish idea of justice is not reactionary; it owes to the prophets its position as the dominating principle of the world, the peculiar essence of God, and therefore the ultimate ideal of human life. They fought for right with an insistence which vindicated its moral significance forever, and in scathing words of indignation which still burn in the soul they denounced oppression wherever it appeared. The crimes of the mighty against the weak, they held, could not be atoned for by the outward forms of piety. Right and justice are not simply matters for the State and the social order, but belong to God, who defends the cause of the helpless and the homeless, "who executes the judgment of the fatherless and the widow," "who regardeth not persons, nor taketh bribes."313 Iniquity is hateful to Him; it cannot be covered up by pious acts, nor be justified by good ends. "Justice is God's."314 Thus every violation of justice, whether from sordid self-seeking or from tender compassion, is a violation of God's cause; and every vindication of justice, every strengthening of the power of right in society, is a triumph of God.

4. Accordingly, the highest principle of ethics in Judaism, the cardinal point in the government of the world, is not love, but justice. Love has the tendency to undermine the right and to effeminize society. Justice, on the other hand, develops the moral capacity of every man; it aims not merely to avoid wrong, but to promote and develop the right for the sake of the perfect state of morality. True justice cannot remain a passive onlooker when the right or liberty of any human being is curtailed, but strains every effort to prevent violence and oppression. It battles for the right, until it has triumphed over every injustice. This practical conception of right can be traced through all Jewish literature and doctrine; through the laws of Moses, to whom is ascribed the maxim: "Let the right have its way, though it bore holes through the rock",315 through the flaming words of the prophets;316 through the Psalmists, who spoke such words as these: "Thou art not a God who hath pleasure in wickedness; evil shall not sojourn with Thee. The arrogant shall not stand in Thy sight; Thou hatest all workers of iniquity."317

Nor does justice stop with the prohibition of evil. The very arm that strikes down the presumptuous transgressor turns to lift up the meek and endow him with strength. Justice becomes a positive power for the right; it becomes Zedakah, righteousness or true benevolence, and aims to readjust the inequalities of life by kindness and love. It engenders that deeper sense of justice which claims the right of the weak to protection by the arm of the strong.

5. Hence comes the truth of Matthew Arnold's striking summary of Israel's Law and Prophets in his "Literature and Dogma," as "The Power, not ourselves, that maketh for righteousness." Still, when we trace the development of this central thought in the soul of the Jewish people, we find that it arose from a peculiar mythological conception. The God of Sinai had manifested Himself in the devastating elements of nature—fire, storm, and hail; later, the prophetic genius of Israel saw Him as a moral power who destroyed wickedness by these very phenomena in order that right should prevail. At first the covenant-God of Israel hurls the plagues of heaven upon the hostile Egyptians and Canaanites, the oppressors of His people. Afterward the great prophets speak of the Day of JHVH which would come at the end of days, when God will execute His judgment upon the heathen nations by pouring forth all the terrors of nature upon them. The natural forces of destruction are utilized by the Ruler of heaven as means of moral purification. "For by fire will the Lord contend."318

In this process the sense of right became progressively refined, so that God was made the Defender of the cause of the oppressed, and the holiest of duties became the protection of the forsaken and unfortunate. Justice and right were thus lifted out of the civil or forensic sphere into that of divine holiness, and the struggle for the down-trodden became an imperative duty. Judaism finds its strength in the oft-repeated doctrine that the moral welfare of the world rests upon justice. "The King's strength is that he loveth justice," says the Psalmist, and commenting upon this the Midrash says, "Not might, but right forms the foundation of the world's peace."319

6. Social life, therefore, must be built upon the firm foundation of justice, the full recognition of the rights of all individuals and all classes. It can be based neither upon the formal administration of law nor upon the elastic principle of love, which too often tolerates, or even approves certain types of injustice. Judaism has been working through the centuries to realize the ideal of justice to all mankind; therefore the Jew has suffered and waited for the ultimate triumph of the God of justice. God's kingdom of justice is to be established, not in a world to come, but in the world that now is, in the life of men and nations. As the German poet has it, "Die Weltgeschichte ist das Weltgericht" (the history of the world is the world's tribunal of justice).

7. The recognition of God as the righteous Ruler implies a dominion of absolute justice which allows no wrongdoing to remain unpunished and no meritorious act to remain unrewarded. The moral and intellectual maturity of the people, however, must determine how they conceive retribution in the divine judgment. Under the simple conditions of patriarchal life, when common experience seemed to be in harmony with the demands of divine justice, when the evil-doer seemed to meet his fate and the worthy man to enjoy his merited prosperity, reward and punishment could well be expressed by the Bible in terms of national prosperity and calamity. The prophets, impressed by the political and moral decline of their era, announced for both Israel and the other nations a day of judgment to come, when God will manifest Himself as the righteous Ruler of the world. In fact, those great preachers of righteousness announced for all time the truth of a moral government of the world, with terror for the malefactors and the assurance of peace and salvation for the righteous. "He will judge the world with righteousness, and the peoples with equity" becomes a song of joyous confidence and hope on the lips of the Psalmist.320 This final triumph of justice does not depend, as Christian theologians assert, on the mere outward conformity of Israel to the law.321 On the contrary, it offers to the innocent sufferer the hope that "his right shall break forth as light," while "the wicked shall be put to silence in darkness."322 We must admit, indeed, that the Biblical idea of retribution still has too much of the earthly flavor, and often lacks true spirituality. The explanation of this lies in the desire of the expounders of Judaism that this world should be regarded as the battle-ground between the good and the bad, that the victory of the good is to be decided here, and that the idea of justice should not assume the character of other-worldliness.

8. It is true that neither the prophets, such as Jeremiah, nor the sages, such as the authors of Job and Koheleth, actually solved the great enigma which has baffled all nations and ages, the adjustment of merit and destiny by divine righteousness. Yet even a doubter like Job does not despair of his own sense of justice, and wrestles with his God in the effort to obtain a deeper insight. Still the great mass of people are not satisfied with an unfulfilled yearning and seeking. The various religions have gradually transferred the final adjustment of merit and destiny to the hereafter; the rewards and punishments awaiting man after death have been depicted glaringly in colors taken

from this earthly life. It is not surprising that Judaism was influenced by this almost universal view. The mechanical form of the principle of justice demands that "with the same measure one metes out, it shall be meted out to him,"323 and this could not be found either in human justice or in human destiny. Therefore the popular mind naturally turned to the world to come, expecting there that just retribution which is lacking on earth.

Only superior minds could ascend to that higher ethical conception where compensation is no longer expected, but man seeks the good and happiness of others and finds therein his highest satisfaction. As Ben Azzai expresses it, "The reward of virtue is virtue, and the punishment of sin is sin."324 At this point justice merges into divine holiness.

9. The idea of divine justice exerted its uplifting force in one more way in Judaism. The recognition of God as the righteous Judge of the world—Zidduk ha Din325—is to bring consolation and endurance to the afflicted, and to remove from their hearts the bitter sting of despair and doubt. The rabbis called God "the Righteous One of the universe,"326 as if to indicate that God himself is meant by the Scriptural verse, "The righteous is an everlasting foundation of the world."327

Far remote from Judaism, however, is the doctrine that God would consign an otherwise righteous man to eternal doom, because he belongs to another creed or another race than that of the Jew. Wherever the heathens are spoken of as condemned at the last judgment, the presumption based upon centuries of sad experience was that their lives were full of injustice and wickedness. Indeed, milder teachers, whose view became the accepted one, maintained that truly righteous men are found among the heathen, who have therefore as much claim upon eternal salvation as the pious ones of Israel.328

Chapter XX. God's Love and Compassion

1. As justice forms the basis of human morality, with kindness and benevolence as milder elements to mitigate its sternness, so, according to the Jewish view, mercy and love represent the milder side of God, but by no means a higher attribute counteracting His justice. Love can supplement justice, but cannot replace it. The sages say:329 "When the Creator saw that man could not endure, if measured by the standard of strict justice, He joined His attribute of mercy to that of justice, and created man by the combined principle of both." The divine compassion with human frailty, felt by both Moses and Hosea, manifests itself in God's mercy. Were it not for the weakness of the flesh, justice would have sufficed. But the divine plan of salvation demands redeeming love which wins humanity step by step for higher moral ends. The educational value of this love lies in the fact that it is a gift of grace, bestowed on man by the fatherly love of God to ward off the severity of full retribution. His pardon must conduce to a deeper moral earnestness.330 "For with Thee there is forgiveness that Thou mayest be feared."331 R. Akiba says: "The world is judged by the divine attribute of goodness."332

2. As a matter of course, in the Biblical view God's mercy was realized at first only with regard to Israel and was afterward extended gradually to humanity at large. The generation of the flood and the inhabitants of Sodom perished on account of their guilt, and only the righteous were saved. This attitude holds throughout the Bible until the late book of Jonah, with its lesson of God's forgiveness even for the heathen city of Nineveh after due repentance. In the later Psalms the divine attributes of mercy are expanded and applied to all the creatures of God.333 According to the school of Hillel, whenever the good and evil actions of any man are found equal in the scales of justice, God inclines the balances toward the side of mercy.334 Nay more, in the words of Samuel, the Babylonian teacher, God judges the nations by the noblest types they produce.335

The ruling Sadducean priesthood insisted on the rigid enforcement of the law. The party of the pious, the Hasidim, however,—according to the liturgy, the apocryphal and the rabbinical literature,—appealed to the mercy of God in song and prayer, acknowledging their failings in humility, and made kindness and love their special objects in life. Therefore with their ascendancy the divine attributes of mercy and compassion were accentuated. God himself, we are told, was heard praying: "Oh that My attribute of mercy may prevail over My attribute of justice, so that grace alone may be bestowed upon My children on earth."336 And the second word of the Decalogue was so interpreted that God's mercy—which is said to extend "to the thousandth generation"—is five hundred times as powerful as His punitive justice,—which is applied "to the third and fourth generation."337

3. Divine mercy shows itself in the law, where compassion is enjoined on all suffering creatures. Profound sympathy with the oppressed is echoed in the ancient law of the poor who had to give up his garment as a pledge: "When he crieth unto Me, I shall hear, for I am gracious."338 In the old Babylonian code, might was the arbiter of right,339 but the unique genius of the Jew is shown in adapting this same legal material to its impulse of compassion. The cry of the innocent sufferer, of the forsaken and fatherless, rises up to God's throne and secures there his right against the oppressor. Thus in the Mosaic law and throughout Jewish literature God calls himself "the Judge of the widow," "the Father of the fatherless,"340 "a Stronghold to the needy."341 He calls the poor, "My people,"342 and, as the rabbis say, He loves the persecuted, not the persecutors.343

4. Even to dumb beasts God extends His mercy. This Jewish tenderness is an inheritance from the shepherd life of the patriarchs, who were eager to quench the thirst of the animals in their care before they thought of their own comfort.344 This sense of sympathy appears in the Biblical precepts as to the overburdened beast,345 the ox treading the corn,346 and the mother-beast or mother-bird with her young,347 as well as the Talmudic rule first to feed the domestic animals and then sit down to the meal.348 This has remained a characteristic trait of Judaism. Thus, in connection with the verse of the Psalm, "His tender mercies are over all His works,"349 it is related of Rabbi Judah the Saint, the redactor of the Mishnah, that he was afflicted with pain for thirteen years, and gave as reason that he once struck and kicked away a calf which had run to him moaning for protection; he was finally relieved, after he had taught his household to have pity even on the smallest of creatures.350 In fact, Rabban Gamaliel, his grandfather, had taught before him: "Whosoever has compassion on his fellow-creatures, on him God will have compassion."351 The sages often interpret the phrase "To walk in the way of the Lord"—that is, "As the Holy One, blessed be He, is merciful, so be ye also merciful."352

5. Thus the rabbis came to regard love as the innermost part of God's being. God loves mankind, is the highest stage of consciousness of God, but this can be attained only by the closest relation of the human soul to the Most High, after severe trials have softened and humanized the spirit. It is not accidental that Scripture speaks often of God's goodness, mercy, and grace, but seldom mentions His love. Possibly the term ahabah was used at first for sensuous love and therefore was not employed for God so often as the more spiritual hesed, which denotes kind and loyal affection.353 However, Hosea used this term for his own love for his faithless wife, and did not hesitate to apply it also to God's love for His faithless people, which he terms "a love of free will."354 His example is followed by Jeremiah, most tender of the prophets, who gave the classic expression to the everlasting love of God for Israel, His beloved son.355 This divine love, spiritually understood, forms the chief topic of the Deuteronomic addresses.356 In this book God's love appears as that of a father for his son, who lavishes gifts upon him, but also chastises him for his own good.357 The mind opened more and more to regard the trials sent by God as means of ennobling the character,358 and the men of the Talmudic period often speak of the afflictions of the saints as "visitations of the divine love."359

6. The sufferings of Israel in particular were taken to be trials of the divine love.360 God's love for Israel, "His firstborn son,"361 is not partial, but from the outset aims to train him for his world mission. The Song of Moses speaks of the love of the Father for His son "whom He found in the wilderness";362 and this is requited by the bridal love of Israel with which the people "went after God in the wilderness."363 It is this love of God, according to Akiba's interpretation of the Song of Songs, which "all the waters could not quench," "a love as strong as death."364 This love raised up a nation of martyrs without parallel in history, although the followers of the so-called Religion of Love fail to give it the credit it deserves and seem to regard it as a kind of hatred for the rest of mankind.365 Whenever the paternal love of God is truly felt and understood it must include all classes and all souls of men who enter into the relation of children to God. Wherever emphasis is laid upon the special love for Israel, it is based upon the love with which the chosen people cling to the Torah, the word of God, upon the devotion with which they surrender their lives in His cause.366

7. Still, Judaism does not proclaim love, absolute and unrestricted, as the divine principle of life. That is left to the Church, whose history almost to this day records ever so many acts of lovelessness. Love is unworthy of God, unless it is guided by justice. Love of good must be accompanied by hate of evil, or else it lacks the educative power which alone makes it beneficial to man.

God's love manifests itself in human life as an educative power. R. Akiba says that it extends to all created in God's image, although the knowledge of it was vouchsafed to Israel alone.367 This universal love of God is a doctrine of the apocryphal literature as well. "Thou hast mercy upon all ... for Thou lovest all things that are, and hatest nothing which Thou hast made.... But Thou sparest all, for they are Thine, O Lord, Lover of souls," says the Book of Wisdom;368 and when Ezra the Seer laments the calamity that has befallen the people, God replies, "Thinkest thou that thou lovest My creatures more than I?"369

8. Among the mystics divine love was declared to be the highest creative principle. They referred the words of the Song of Songs,—"The midst thereof is paved with love,"370 to the innermost palace of heaven, where stands the throne of God.371 Among the philosophers Crescas considered love the active cosmic principle rather than intellect, the principle of Aristotle, because it is love which is the impulse for creation.372 This conception of divine love received a peculiarly mystic color from Juda Abravanel, a neo-Platonist of the sixteenth century, known as Leo Hebraeus. He says: "God's love must needs unfold His perfection and beauty, and reveal itself in His creatures, and love for these creatures must again elevate an imperfect world to His own perfection. Thus is engendered in man that yearning for love with which he endeavors to emulate the divine perfection."373 Both Crescas and Leo Hebraeus thus gave the keynote for Spinoza's "Intellectual love" as the cosmic principle,374 and this has been echoed even in such works as Schiller's dithyrambs on "Love and Friendship" in his "Philosophic Letters."375 Still this neo-Platonic view has nothing in common with the theological conception of love. In Judaism God is conceived as a loving Father, who purposes to lead man to happiness and salvation. In other words, the divine love is an essentially moral attribute of God, and not a metaphysical one.

9. If we wish to speak of a power that permeates the cosmos and turns the wheel of life, it is far more correct to speak of God's creative goodness.376 According to Scripture, each day's creation bears the divine approval: "It is good."377 Even the evil which man experiences serves a higher purpose, and that purpose makes for the good. Misfortune and death, sorrow and sin, in the great economy of life are all turned into final good. Accordingly, Judaism recognizes this divine goodness not only in every enjoyment of nature's gifts and the favors of fortune, but also in sad and trying experiences, and for all of these it provides special formulas of benediction.378 The same divine goodness sends joy and grief, even though shortsighted man fails to see the majestic Sun of life which shines in unabated splendor above the clouds. Judaism was optimistic through all its experiences just because of this implicit faith in God's goodness. Such faith transforms each woe into a higher welfare, each curse into actual blessing; it leads men and nations from oppression to ever greater freedom, from darkness to ever brighter light, and from error to ever higher truth and righteousness. Divine love may have pity upon human weakness, but it is divine goodness that inspires and quickens human energy. After all, love cannot be the dominant principle of life. Man cannot love all the time, nor can he love all the world; his sense of justice demands that he hate wickedness and falsehood. We must apply the same criterion to God. But, on the other hand, man can and should do good and be good continually and to all men, even to the most unworthy. Therefore God becomes the pattern and ideal of an all-encompassing goodness, which is never exhausted and never reaches an end.

Chapter XXI. God's Truth and Faithfulness

1. In the Hebrew language truth and faithfulness are both derived from the same root; aman, "firmness," is the root idea of emeth, "truth," and emunah, "faithfulness." Man feels insecurity and uncertainty among the varying impressions and emotions which affect his will; therefore he turns to the immovable Rock of life, calls on Him as the Guardian and Witness of truth, and feels confident that He will vindicate every promise made in His sight. He is the God by whom men swear—Elohe amen;379 nay, who swears by Himself, saying, "As true as that I live."380 He is the supreme Power of life, "the God of faithfulness, in whom there is no iniquity."381 The heavens testify to His faithfulness; He is the trustworthy God, whose essence is truth.382

2. Here, too, as with other attributes, the development of the idea may be traced step by step. At first it refers to the God of the covenant with Israel, who made a covenant with the fathers and keeps it with the thousandth generation of their descendants. He shows His mercy to those who love Him and keep His commandments. The idea of God's faithfulness to His covenant is thus extended gradually from the people to the cosmos, and the heavens are called upon to witness to the faithfulness of God throughout the realm of life. Thus in both the Psalms and the liturgy God is praised as the One who is faithful in His word as in His work.383

3. From this conception of faithfulness arose two other ideas which exerted a powerful influence upon the whole spiritual and intellectual life of the Jew. The God of faithfulness created a people of faithfulness as His own, and Israel's God of truth awakened in the nation a passion for truth unrivaled by any other religious or philosophical

system. Like a silver stream running through a valley, the conviction runs through the sacred writings and the liturgy that the promise made of yore to the fathers will be fulfilled to the children. As each past deliverance from distress was considered a verification of the divine faithfulness, so each hope for the future was based upon the same attribute. "He keepeth His faith also to those who sleep in the dust." These words of the second of the Eighteen Benedictions clearly indicate that even the belief in the hereafter rested upon the same fundamental belief.

On the other hand, the same conception formed the keynote of the idea of the divine truthfulness. The primitive age knew nothing of the laws of nature with which we have become familiar through modern science. But the pious soul trusts the God of faithfulness, certain that He who has created the heaven and the earth is true to His own word, and will not allow them to sink back into chaos. One witness to this is the rainbow, which He has set up in the sky as a sign of His covenant.384 The sea and the stars also have a boundary assigned to them which they cannot transgress.385 Thus to the unsophisticated religious soul, with no knowledge of natural science, the world is carried by God's "everlasting arms"386 and His faithfulness becomes token and pledge of the immutability of His will.

4. At this point the intellect grasps an idea of intrinsic and indestructible truth, which has its beginning and its end in God, the Only One. "The gods of the nations are all vanity and deceit, the work of men; Israel's God is the God of truth, the living God and everlasting King."387 With this cry has Judaism challenged the nations of the world since the Babylonian exile. Its own adherents it charged to ponder upon the problems of life and the nature of God, until He would appear before them as the very essence of truth, and all heathenish survivals would vanish as mist. God is truth, and He desires naught but truth, therefore hypocrisy is loathsome to him, even in the service of religion. With this underlying thought Job, the bold but honest doubter, stands above his friends with their affected piety. God is truth—this confession of faith, recited each morning and evening by the Jew, gave his mind the power to soar into the highest realms of thought, and inspired his soul to offer life and all it holds for his faith. "God is the everlasting truth, the unchangeable Being who ever remains the same amid the fluctuations and changes of all other things." This is the fundamental principle upon which Joseph Ibn Zaddik and Abraham Ibn Daud, the predecessors of Maimonides, reared their entire philosophical systems, which were Aristotelian and yet thoroughly Jewish.388

Mystic lore, always so fond of the letters of the alphabet and their hidden meanings, noted that the letters of Emeth—aleph, mem and tav—are the first, the middle, and the last letters of the alphabet, and therefore concluded that God made truth the beginning, the center, and the end of the world.389 Josephus also, no doubt in accordance with the same tradition, declares that God is "the beginning, the center, and the end of all things."390 A corresponding rabbinical saying is: "Truth is the seal of God."391

Chapter XXII. God's Knowledge and Wisdom

1. The attempt to enumerate the attributes of God recalls the story related in the Talmud392 of a disciple who stepped up to the reader's desk to offer prayer, and began to address the Deity with an endless list of attributes. When his vocabulary was almost exhausted, Rabbi Haninah interrupted him with the question, "Hast thou now really finished telling the praise of God?" Mortal man can never know what God really is. As the poet-philosopher says: "Could I ever know Him, I would be He."393 But we want to ascertain what God is to us, and for this very reason we cannot rest with the negative attitude of Maimonides, who relies on the Psalmist's verse, "Silence is praise to Thee."394 We must obtain as clear a conception of the Deity as we possibly can with our limited powers.

To the divine attributes already mentioned we must add another which in a sense is the focus of them all. This is the knowledge and wisdom of God, the omniscience which renders Him all-knowing and all-wise. Through this all the others come into self-consciousness. We ascribe wisdom to the man who sets right aims for his actions and knows the means by which to attain them, that is, who can control his power and knowledge by his will and bend them to his purpose. In the same manner we think of wisdom in view of the marvelous order, design, and unity which we see in the natural and the moral world. But this wisdom must be all-encompassing, comprising time and eternity, directing all the forces and beings of the world toward the goal of ideal perfection.395 It makes no difference where we find this lesson. The Book of Proverbs singles out the tiny ant as an example of wondrous forethought;396 the author of Job dwells on the working together of the powers of earth and heaven to maintain the cosmic life;397 modern science, with its deeper insight into nature, enables us to follow the interaction of the primal chemical and organic forces, and to follow the course of evolution from star-dust and cell to the structure of the human eye or the thought-centers of the brain. But in all these alike our conclusion must be that of the Psalmist: "O Lord, how manifold are Thy works, in wisdom hast Thou made them all."398

2. Accordingly, if we are to speak in human terms, we may consider God's wisdom the element which determines His various motive-powers,—omniscience, omnipotence, and goodness,—to tend toward the realization of His cosmic plan. Or we may call it the active intellect with which God works as Creator, Ordainer, and Ruler of the universe. The Biblical account of creation presupposes this wisdom, as it portrays a logical process, working after a definite plan, proceeding from simpler to more complex forms and culminating in man. Biblical history likewise is based upon the principle of a divinely prearranged plan, which is especially striking in such stories as that of Joseph.399

3. At first the divine wisdom was supposed to rest in part on specially gifted persons, such as Joseph, Solomon, and Bezalel. As Scripture has it, "The Lord giveth wisdom, out of His mouth cometh knowledge and understanding."400 Later the obscure destiny of the nation appears as the design of an all-wise Ruler to the great prophets and especially to Isaiah, the high-soaring eagle among the seers of Israel.401 With the progressive expansion of the world before them, the seers and sages saw a sublime purpose in the history of the nations, and felt more and more the supreme place of the divine wisdom as a manifestation of His greatness. Thus the great seer of the Exile never tires of illumining the world-wide plan of the divine wisdom.402

4. A new development ensued under Babylonian and Persian influence at the time when the monotheism of Israel became definitely universal. The divine wisdom, creative and world-sustaining, became the highest of the divine attributes and was partially hypostatized as an independent cosmic power. In the twenty-eighth chapter of the Book of Job wisdom is depicted as a magic being, far remote from all living beings of earth, beyond the reach of the creatures of the lowest abyss, who aided the Creator with counsel and knowledge in measuring and weighing the foundations of the world. The description seems to be based upon an ancient Babylonian conception—which has parallels elsewhere—of a divine Sybil dwelling beneath the ocean in "the house of wisdom."403 Here, however, the mythological conception is transformed into a symbolic figure. In the eighth chapter of Proverbs the description of divine wisdom is more in accordance with Jewish monotheism; wisdom is "the first of God's creatures," "a master-workman" who assisted Him in founding heaven and earth, a helpmate and playmate of God, and at the same time the instructor of men and counselor of princes, inviting all to share her precious gifts. This conception is found also in the apocryphal literature,—in Ben Sira, the book of Enoch, the Apocalypse of Baruch, and the Hellenistic Book of Wisdom.404

From this period two different currents of thought appeared. The one represented wisdom as an independent being distinct from God, and this finally became merged, under Platonic influence, into the views of neo-Platonism, Gnosticism, and the Christian dogma. The other identified the divine wisdom with the Torah, and therefore it is the Torah which served God as counselor and mediator at the Creation and continues as counselor in the management of the world. This view led back to strict monotheism, so that the cosmology of the rabbis spoke alternately of the divine wisdom and the Torah as the instruments of God at Creation.405

5. The Jewish philosophers of the Middle Ages, such as Saadia, Gabirol, and Jehuda ha Levi, followed the Mohammedan theologians in enumerating God's wisdom among the attributes constituting His essence, together with His omnipotence, His will, and His creative energy. But they would not take wisdom or any other attribute as a separate being, with an existence outside of God, which would either condition Him or admit a division of His nature.406 "God himself is wisdom," says Jehuda ha Levi, referring to the words of Job: "He is wise in heart."407 And Ibn Gabirol sings in his "Crown of Royalty":

"Thou art wise, and the wisdom of Thy fount of life floweth from Thee;

And compared with Thy wisdom man is void of understanding;

Thou art wise, before anything began its existence;

And wisdom has from times of yore been Thy fostered child;

Thou art wise, and out of Thy wisdom didst Thou create the world,

Life the artificer that fashioneth whatsoever delighteth him."408

Chapter XXIII. God's Condescension

1. An attribute of great importance for the theological conception of God, one upon which both Biblical and rabbinical literature laid especial stress, is His condescension and humility. The Psalmist says[409]: "Thy condescension hath made me great," which is interpreted in the Midrash that the Deity stoops to man in order to lift him up to Himself. A familiar saying of R. Johanan is[410]: "Wherever Scripture speaks of the greatness of God, there mention is made also of His condescension. So when the prophet begins, 'Thus saith the High and Lofty One that inhabiteth eternity, whose name is Holy: I dwell in the high and holy place,' he adds the words, 'With him also that is of a contrite and humble spirit.'[411] Or when the Deuteronomist says: 'For the Lord your God, the great God, the mighty and the awful,' he concludes, 'He doth execute justice for the fatherless and widow, and loveth the stranger.'[412] And again the Psalmist: 'Extol Him that rideth upon the skies, whose name is the Lord, a Father of the fatherless and a Judge of the widows.' "[413] "Do you deem it unworthy of God that He should care for the smallest and most insignificant person or thing in the world's household?" asks Mendelssohn in his Morgenstunden. "It certainly does not detract from the dignity of a king to be seen fondling his child as a loving father," and he quotes the verse of the Psalm, "Who is like unto the Lord our God, that is enthroned on high, that looketh down low upon heaven and upon the earth."[414]

2. This truth has a religious depth which no philosophy can set forth. Only the God of Revelation is near to man in his frailty and need, ready to hear his sighs, answer his supplication, count his tears, and relieve his wants when his own power fails. The philosopher must reject as futile every attempt to bring the incomprehensible essence of the Deity within the compass of the human understanding. The religious consciousness, however, demands that we accentuate precisely those attributes of God which bring Him nearest to us. If reason alone would have the decisive voice in this problem, every manifestation of God to man and every reaching out of the soul to Him in prayer would be idle fancy and self-deceit. It is true that the Biblical conception was simple and child-like enough, representing God as descending from the heavens to the earth. Still Judaism does not accept the cold and distant attitude of the philosopher; it teaches that God as a spiritual power does condescend to man, in order that man may realize his kinship with the Most High and rise ever nearer to his Creator. The earth whereon man dwells and the human heart with its longing for heaven, are not bereft of God. Wherever man seeks Him, there He is.

3. Rabbinical Judaism is very far from the attitude assigned to it by Christian theologians,[415] of reducing the Deity to an empty transcendental abstraction and loosening the bond which ties the soul to its Maker. On the contrary, it maintains these very relations with a firmness which betokens its soundness and its profound psychological truth. In this spirit a Talmudic master interprets the Deuteronomic verse: "For what great nation is there that hath God so nigh unto them, as the Lord our God is whensoever we call upon Him?"[416] saying that "each will realize the nearness of God according to his own intellectual and emotional disposition, and thus enter into communion with Him." According to another Haggadist the verse of the Psalm, "The voice of the Lord resoundeth with power,"[417] teaches how God reveals Himself, not with His own overwhelming might, but according to each man's individual power and capacity. The rabbis even make bold to assert that whenever Israel suffers, God suffers with him; as it is written, "I will be with him in trouble."[418]

4. As a matter of fact, all the names which we apply to God in speech or in prayer, even the most sublime and holy ones, are derived from our own sensory experience and cannot be taken literally. They are used only as vehicles to bring home to us the idea that God's nearness is our highest good. Even the material world, which is perceptible to our senses, must undergo a certain inner transformation before it can be termed science or philosophy, and becomes the possession of the mind. It requires still further exertions of the imagination to bring within our grasp the world of the spirit, and above all the loftiest of all conceptions, the very being of God. Yet it is just this Being of all Beings who draws us irresistibly toward Himself, whose nearness we perceive in the very depths of our intellectual and emotional life. Our "soul thirsteth after God, the living God," and behold, He is nigh, He takes possession of us, and we call Him our God.

5. The Haggadists expressed this intimate relation of God to man, and specifically to Israel, by bold and often naïve metaphors. They ascribe to God special moments for wrath and for prayer, a secret chamber where he weeps over the distress of Israel, a prayer-mantle (tallith) and phylacteries which He wears like any of the leaders of the community, and even lustrations which He practices exactly like mortals.[419] But such fanciful and extravagant conceptions were never taken seriously by the rabbis, and only partisan and prejudiced writers, entirely lacking in

a sense of humor, could point to such passages to prove that a theology of the Synagogue carried out a "Judaization of God."420

C. God In Relation To The World

Chapter XXIV. The World and its Master

1. In using the term world or universe we include the totality of all beings at once, and this suggests a stage of knowledge where polytheism is practically overcome. Among the Greeks, Pythagoras is said to have been the first to perceive "a beautiful order of things" in the world, and therefore to call it cosmos.421 Primitive man saw in the world innumerable forces continually struggling with each other for supremacy. Without an ordering mind no order, as we conceive it, can exist. The old Babylonian conception prevalent throughout antiquity divided the world into three realms, the celestial, terrestrial, and the nether world, each of which had its own type of inhabitants and its own ruling divinities. Yet these various divine powers were at war with each other, and ultimately they, too, must submit to a blind fate which men and gods alike could read in the stars or other natural phenomena.

With the first words of the Bible, "In the beginning God created the heavens and the earth," Judaism declared the world to be a unity and God its Creator and Master. Heathenism had always beheld in the world certain blind forces of nature, working without plan or purpose and devoid of any moral aims. But Judaism sees in the world the work of a supreme Intellect who fashioned it according to His will, and who rules in freedom, wisdom, and goodness. "He spoke, and it was; He commanded, and it stood."422 Nature exists only by the will of God; His creative fiat called it into existence, and it ceases to be as soon as it has fulfilled His plan.

2. That which the scientist terms nature—the cosmic life in its eternal process of growth and reproduction—is declared by Judaism to be God's creation. Ancient heathen conceptions deified nature, indeed, but they knew only a cosmogony, that is, a process of birth and growth of the world. In this the gods participate with all other beings, to sink back again at the close of the drama into fiery chaos,—the so-called "twilight of the gods." Here the deity constitutes a part of the world, or the world a part of the deity, and philosophic speculation can at best blend the two into a pantheistic system which has no place for a self-conscious, creative mind and will. In fact, the universe appears as an ever growing and unfolding deity, and the deity as an ever growing and unfolding universe. Modern science more properly assumes a self-imposed limitation; it searches for the laws underlying the action and interaction of natural forces and elements, thus to explain in a mechanistic way the origin and development of all things, but it leaves entirely outside of its domain the whole question of a first cause and a supreme creative mind. It certainly can pass no opinion as to whether or not the entire work of creation was accomplished by the free act of a Creator. Revelation alone can speak with unfaltering accents: "In the beginning God created heaven and earth." However we may understand, or imagine, the beginning of the natural process, the formation of matter and the inception of motion, we see above the confines of space and time the everlasting God, the absolutely free Creator of all things.

3. No definite theological dogma can define the order and process of the genesis of the world; this is rather a scientific than a religious question. The Biblical documents themselves differ widely on this point, whether one compares the stories in the first two chapters of Genesis, or contrasts both of them with the poetical descriptions in Job and the Psalms.423 And these divergent accounts are still less to be reconciled with the results of natural science. In the old Babylonian cosmography, on which the Biblical view is based, the earth, shaped like a disk, was suspended over the waters of the ocean, while above it was the solid vault of heaven like a ceiling. In this the stars were fixed like lamps to light the earth, and hidden chambers to store up the rain. The sciences of astronomy, physics, and geology have abolished these childlike conceptions as well as the story of a six-day creation, where vegetation sprang from the earth even before the sun, moon, and stars appeared in the firmament.

The fact is that the Biblical account is not intended to depreciate or supersede the facts established by natural science, but solely to accentuate those religious truths which the latter disregards.424 These may be summed up in the following three doctrines:

4. First. Nature, with all its immeasurable power and grandeur, its wondrous beauty and harmony, is not independent, but is the work, the workshop, and the working force of the great Master. His spirit alone is the active power; His will must be carried out. It is true that we cannot conceive the universe otherwise than as infinite in time and space, because both time and space are but human modes of apperception. In fact, we cannot think of a Creator without a creation, because any potentiality or capacity without execution would imply imperfection in God. Nevertheless we must conceive of God as the designing and creating intellect of the universe, infinitely transcending its complex mechanism, whose will is expressed involuntarily by each of the created beings. He alone is the living God; He has lent existence and infinite capacity to the beings of the world; and they, in achieving their appointed purpose, according to the poet's metaphor, "weave His living garment." The Psalmist also sings in the same key:

"Of old Thou didst lay the foundations of the earth;

And the heavens are the work of Thy hands;

They shall perish, but Thou shalt endure;

Yea, all of them shall wax old like a garment.

As a vesture shalt Thou change them, and they shall pass away;

But Thou art the selfsame, and Thy years shall have no end."425

5. Second. The numberless beings and forces of the universe comprise a unity, working according to one plan, subserving a common purpose, and pursuing in their development and interaction the aim which God's wisdom assigned them from the beginning. However hostile the various elements may be toward each other, however fierce the universal conflict, "the struggle for existence," still over all the discord prevails a higher concord, and the struggle of nature's forces ends in harmony and peace. "He maketh peace in His high places."426 Even the highest type of heathenism, the Persian, divided the world into mutually hostile principles, light and darkness, good and evil. But Judaism proclaims God as the Creator of both. No force is left out of the universal plan; each contributes its part to the whole. Consequently the very progress of natural science confirms more and more the principle of the divine Unity. The researches of science are ever tending toward the knowledge of universal laws of growth, culminating in a scheme of universal evolution. Hence this supports and confirms Jewish monotheism, which knows no power of evil antagonistic to God.

6. Third. The world is good, since goodness is its creator and its final aim. True enough, nature, bent with "tooth and claw" upon annihilating one or another form of existence, is quite indifferent to man's sense of compassion and justice. Yet in the wise, though inscrutable plan of God she does but serve the good. We see how the lower forms of life ever serve the higher, how the mineral provides food for the vegetable, while the animal derives its food from the vegetable world and from lower types of animals. Thus each becomes a means of vitality for a higher species. So by the continuous upward striving of man the lower passions, with their evil tendencies, work more and more toward the triumph of the good. Man unfolds his God-likeness; he strives to

"Move upward, working out the beast,

And let the ape and tiger die."

7. The Biblical story of Creation expresses the perfect harmony between God's purpose and His work in the words, "And behold, it was good" spoken at the end of each day's Creation, and "behold, it was very good" at the completion of the whole. A world created by God must serve the highest good, while, on the contrary, a world without God would prove to be "the worst of all possible worlds," as Schopenhauer, the philosopher of pessimism, quite correctly concludes from his premises. The world-view of Judaism, which regards the entire economy of life as the realization of the all-encompassing plan of an all-wise Creator, is accordingly an energizing optimism, or, more precisely, meliorism. This view is voiced by the rabbis in many significant utterances, such as the maxim of R. Akiba, "Whatsoever the Merciful One does, is for the good,"427 or that of his teacher, Nahum of Gimzo, "This, too, is for the good."428 His disciple, R. Meir, inferred from the Biblical verse, "God saw all that He had made, and behold, it was very good," that "death, too, is good."429 Others considered that suffering and even sin are included in this verse, because every apparent evil is necessary that we may struggle and overcome it for the final victory of the good.430 As an ancient Midrash says: "God is called a God of faith and faithfulness, because it was His faith in the world that caused Him to bring it into existence."431

Chapter XXV. Creation As the Act of God

1. "Thus shall ye say unto them: The gods that have not made the heavens and the earth, these shall perish from the earth, and from under the heavens. He that hath made the earth by His power, that hath established the world by His wisdom, and hath stretched out the heavens by His understanding ... the Lord God is the true God."432 With this declaration of war against heathenism, the prophet drew the line, once for all, between the uncreated, transcendent God and the created, perishable universe. It is true that Plato spoke of primordial and eternal matter and Aristotle of an eternally rotating celestial sphere, and that even Biblical exegetes, such as Ibn Ezra,433 inferred from the Creation story the existence of primeval chaotic matter. Yet, on the whole, the Jewish idea of God has demanded the assumption that even this primitive matter was created by God, or, as most thinkers have phrased it, that God created the world out of nothing. This doctrine was voiced as early as the Maccabean period in the appeal made by the heroic mother to the youngest of her seven sons.434 In the same spirit R. Gamaliel II scornfully rejects the suggestion of a heretic that God used primeval substances already extant in creating the world.435

2. Of course, thinking people will ever be confronted by the problem how a transcendental God could call into existence a world of matter, creating it within the limits of space and time, without Himself becoming involved in the process. It would seem that He must by the very act subject Himself to the limitations and mutations of the universe. Hence some of the ancient Jewish teachers came under the influence of Babylonian and Egyptian cosmogonies in their later Hellenistic forms, and resorted to the theory of intermediary forces. Some of these adopted the Pythagorean conception of the mysterious power of letters and numbers, which they communicated to the initiated as secret lore, with the result that the suspicion of heresy rested largely upon "those who knew," the so-called Gnostics.

The difficulty of assuming a creation at a fixed period of time was met in many different ways. It is interesting to note that R. Abbahu of Cæsarea in the fourth century offered the explanation: "God caused one world after another to enter into existence, until He produced the one of which He said: 'Behold, this is good.' "436 Still this opinion seems to have been expressed by even earlier sages, as it is adopted by Origen, a Church father of the third century, who admitted his great debt to Jewish teachers.437

The medieval Jewish philosophers evaded the difficulty by the Aristotelian expedient of connecting the concept of time with the motion of the spheres. Thus time was created with the celestial world, and timelessness remained an attribute of the uncreated God.438 Such attempts at harmonization prove the one point of importance to us,—which, indeed, was frankly stated by Maimonides,—that we cannot accept literally the Biblical account of the creation.

The modern world has been lifted bodily out of the Babylonian and so-called Ptolemaic world, with its narrow horizon, through the labors of such men as Copernicus, Galileo, Newton, Lyall, and Darwin. We live in a world immeasurable in terms of either space or time, a world where evolution works through eons of time and an infinite number of stages. Such a world gives rise to concepts of the working of God in nature totally different from those of the seers and sages of former generations, ideas of which those thinkers could not even dream. To the mind of the modern scientist the entire cosmic life, extending over countless millions of years, forming starry worlds without end, is moved by energy arising within. It is a continuous flow of existence, a process of formation and re-formation, which can have no beginning and no end. How is this evolutionist view to be reconciled with the belief in a divine act of creation? This is the problem which modern theology has set itself, perhaps the greatest which it must solve.

Ultimately, however, the problem is no more difficult now than it was to the first man who pondered over the beginnings of life in the childhood of the world. The same answer fits both modes of thought, with only a different process of reasoning. Whether we count the world's creation by days or by millions of years, the truth of the first verse of Genesis remains: "In the beginning God created the heavens and the earth." In our theories the whole complicated world-process is but the working out of simple laws. This leads back as swiftly and far more surely than did the primitive cosmology to an omnipotent and omniscient creative Power, defining at the very outset the aim of the stupendous whole, and carrying its comprehensive plan into reality, step by step. We who are the products of time cannot help applying the relation of time to the work of the Creator; time is so interwoven with our being that a modern evolutionist, Bergson, considers it the fundamental element of reality. Thus it is natural that we should think of God as setting the first atoms and forces of the universe into motion somewhere and somehow, at a given moment. Through this act, we imagine, the order prevailing through an infinitude of space and time was established for the great fabric of life. To earlier thinkers such an act of a supermundane and immutable God appeared as a single act. The idea of prime importance in all this is the free activity of the Creator in contradistinction to the blind necessity of nature, the underlying theory of all pagan or unreligious philosophy.439 The world of God, which is the world of morality, and which leads to man, the image of God, must be based upon the free, purposive creative act of God. Whether such an act was performed once for all or is everlastingly renewed, is a quite secondary matter for religion, however important it may be to philosophy, or however fundamental to science. In our daily morning prayers, which refer to the daily awakening to a life seemingly new, God is proclaimed as "He who reneweth daily the work of creation."440

Chapter XXVI. The Maintenance and Government of the World

1. For our religious consciousness the doctrine of divine maintenance and government of the world is far more important than that of creation. It opposes the view of deism that God withdrew from His creation, indifferent to the destiny of His creatures. He is rather the ever-present Mind and Will in all the events of life. The world which He created is maintained by Him in its continuous activity, the object of His incessant care.

2. Scripture knows nothing of natural law, but presents the changing phenomena of nature as special acts of God and considers the natural forces His messengers carrying out His will. "He opens the windows of heaven to let the rain descend upon the earth."441 "He leads out the hosts of the stars according to their number and calleth them by name."442 He makes the sun rise and set. "He says to the snow: Fall to the earth!"443 and calls to the wind to blow and to the lightning to flash.444 He causes the produce of the earth and the drought which destroys them. "He opens the womb to make beasts and men bring forth their young;" "He shuts up the womb to make them barren."445 "He also provides the food for all His creatures in due season, even for the young ravens when they cry."446 His breath keeps all alive. "He withdraweth their breath, and they perish, and return to their dust. He sendeth forth His spirit, they are created; He reneweth the face of the earth."447 We are told also that God assigns to each being its functions, telling the earth to bring forth fruit,448 the sea not to trespass its boundary,449 the stars and the seas to maintain their order.450 To each one He hath set a measure, a law which they dare not transgress. God's wisdom works in them; they all are subject to His rule.

3. This conclusion betokens an obvious improvement upon the earlier and more childlike view. It recognizes that there is an order in the universe and all under divine supervision. Thus Jeremiah speaks of a covenant of God with heaven and earth, and of the laws which they must obey,451 and in Genesis the rainbow is represented as a sign of the covenant of peace made by God with the whole earth.452 As God "maketh peace in the heavens above,"453 He establishes order in the world. As the various powers of nature are invested with a degree of independence, God's sovereignty manifests itself in the regularity with which they interact and coöperate.454 The lore of the mystics speaks even of an oath which God administered upon His holy Name to the heavens and the stars, the sea and the abyss, that they should never break their designated bounds or disturb the whole order of creation.455

4. Further progress is noted in the liturgy, in such expressions as that "God reneweth daily the work of creation," or "He openeth every morning the gate of heaven to let the sun come out of its chambers in all its splendor" and "at eventide He maketh it return through the portals of the west." Again, "He reneweth His creative power in every phenomenon of nature and in every turn of the season;" "He provideth every living being with its sustenance."456 Indeed, in the view of Judaism the maintenance of the entire household of nature is one continuous act of God which can neither be interrupted nor limited in time. God in His infinite wisdom works forever through the same laws which were in force at the beginning, and which shall continue through all the realms of time and space.

We feeble mortals, of course, see but "the hem of His garment" and hear only "a whisper of His voice." Still from the deeper promptings of our soul we learn that science does not touch the inmost essence of the world when it finds a law of necessity in the realm of nature. The universe is maintained and governed by a moral order. Moral objects are attained by the forces of the elements, "the messengers of God who fulfilled His word."457 Both the hosts of heaven and the creatures of the earth do His bidding; their every act, great or small, is as He has ordered. Yet of them all man alone is made in God's image, and can work self-consciously and freely for a moral purpose. Indeed, as the rabbis express it, he has been called as "the co-worker with God in the work of creation."458

5. The conception of a world-order also had to undergo a long development. The theory of pagan antiquity, echoed in both Biblical and post-Biblical writings, is that the world is definitely limited, with both a beginning and an end. As heaven and earth came into being, so they will wax old and shrink like a garment, while sun, moon, and stars will lose their brightness and fall back into the primal chaos.459 The belief in a cataclysmic ending of the world is a logical corollary of the belief in the birth of the world. In striking contrast, the prophets hold forth the hope of a future regeneration of the world. God will create "a new heaven and a new earth" where all things will arise in new strength and beauty.460

This hope, as all eschatology, was primarily related to the regeneration of the Jewish people. Accordingly, the rabbis speak of two worlds,461 this world and the world to come. They consider the present life only a preliminary of the world to come, in which the divine plan of creation is to be worked out for all humanity through the truths emanating from Israel. This whole conception rested upon a science now superseded, the geocentric view of the universe, which made the earth and especially man the final object of creation. For us only a figurative meaning adheres to the two worlds of the medieval belief, following each other after the lapse of a fixed period of time. On the one hand, we see one infinite fabric of life in this visible world with its millions of suns and planets, among which our earth is only an insignificant speck in the sky. With our limited understanding we endeavor to penetrate more and more into the eternal laws of this illimitable cosmos. On the other hand, we hold that there is a moral and spiritual world which comprises the divine ideals and eternal objects of life. Both are reflected in the mind of man, who enters into the one by his intellect and into the other by his emotions of yearning and awe. At the same time both are the manifestation of God, the Creator and Ruler of all.

Chapter XXVII. Miracles and the Cosmic Order

1. "Who is like unto Thee, O Lord, among the mighty?

Who is like unto Thee, glorious in holiness,

Fearful in praises, doing wonders!"462

Thus sang Israel at the Red Sea in words which are constantly reëchoed in our liturgy. Nothing impresses the religious sense of man so much as unusual phenomena in nature, which seem to interrupt the wonted course of events and thus to reveal the workings of a higher Power. A miracle—that is, a thing "wondered" at, because not understood—is always regarded by Scripture as a "sign"463 or "proof"464 of the power of God, to whom nothing is impossible. The child-like mind of the past knew nothing of fixed or immutable laws of nature. Therefore the question is put in all simplicity: "Is anything too hard for the Lord?"465 "Is the Lord's hand waxed short?"466 "Or should He who created heaven and earth not be able to create something which never was before?"467 Should "He who maketh a man's mouth, or makes him deaf, dumb, seeing or blind,"468 not be able also to open the mouth of the dumb beast or the eyes of the blind? Should not He who killeth and giveth life have the power also to call the dead back to life, if He sees fit? Should not He who openeth the womb for every birth, be able to open it for her who is ninety years old? Or when a whole land is wicked, to shut the wombs of all its inhabitants that they may remain barren? Again, should not He who makes the sun come forth every morning from the gates of the East and enter each night the portals of the West, not be able to change this order once, and cause it to stand still in the midst of its course?469

So long as natural phenomena are considered to be separate acts of the divine will, an unusual event is merely an extraordinary manifestation of this same power, "the finger of God." The people of Biblical times never questioned whether a miracle happened or could happen. Their concern was to see it as the work of the arm of God either for His faithful ones or against His adversaries.

2. With the advance of thought, miracles began to be regarded as interruptions of an established order of creation. The question then arose, why the all-knowing Creator should allow deviations from His own laws. As the future was present to Him at the outset, why did He not make provision in advance for such special cases as He foresaw? This was exactly the remedy which the rabbis furnished. They declared that at Creation God provided for certain extraordinary events, so that a latent force, established for the purpose at the beginning of the world, is responsible for incidents which appeared at the time to be true interferences with the world order. Thus God had made a special covenant, as it were, with the work of creation that at the appointed time the Red Sea should divide before

Israel; that sun and moon should stand still at the bidding of Joshua; that fire should not consume the three youths, Hananel, Mishael, and Azariah; that the sea-monster should spit forth Jonah alive; together with other so-called miracles.470 The same idea occasioned the other Haggadic saying that shortly before the completion of the creation on the evening of the sixth day God placed certain miraculous forces in nature. Through them the earth opened to swallow Korah and his band, the rock in the wilderness gave water for the thirsty multitude, and Balaam's ass spoke like a human being; through them also the rainbow appeared after the flood, the manna rained from heaven, Aaron's rod burst forth with almond blossoms and fruit, and other wondrous events happened in their proper time.471

3. Neither the rabbis nor the medieval Jewish thinkers expressed any doubt of the credibility of the Biblical miracles. The latter, indeed, rationalized miracles as well as other things, and considered some of them imaginary. Saadia accepts all the Biblical miracles except the speaking serpent in Paradise and the speaking ass of Balaam, considering these to be parables rather than actual occurrences.472 In general, both Jewish and Mohammedan theologians assumed that special forces hidden in nature were utilized by the prophets and saints to testify to their divine mission. These powers were attained by their lofty intellects, which lifted them up to the sphere of the Supreme Intellect. All medieval attempts to solve the problem of miracles were based upon this curious combination of Aristotelian cosmology and Mohammedan or Jewish theology.473 True, Maimonides rejects a number of miracles as contrary to natural law, and refers to the rabbinical saying that some of the miraculous events narrated in Scripture were so only in appearance. Still he claims for Moses, as the Mohammedans did for Mohammed, miraculous powers derived from the sphere of the Supreme Intellect. In a lengthy chapter on miracles Albo follows Maimonides,474 while his teacher Crescas considers the Biblical miracles to be direct manifestations of the creative activity of God.475 Gersonides has really two opinions; in his commentary he reduces all miracles to natural processes, but in his philosophical work he adopts the view of Maimonides.476 Jehuda ha Levi alone insisted on the miracles of the Bible as historic evidence of the divine calling of the prophets.477 To all the rest, the miracle is not performed by God but by the divinely endowed man. God himself is no longer conceived of as changing the cosmic order. Both He and the world created by His will remain ever the same. Still, according to this theory, certain privileged men are endowed with special powers by the Supreme Intellect, and by these they can perform miracles.

4. It is evident that in all this the problem of miracles is not solved, nor even correctly stated. Both rabbinical literature and the Bible abound with miracles about certain holy places and holy persons, which they never venture to doubt. But the rabbis were not miracle-workers like the Essenes and their Christian successors.478 On the contrary, they sought to repress the popular credulity and hunger for the miraculous, saying: "The present generation is not worthy to have miracles performed for them, like the former ones;"479 or "The providing of each living soul with its daily food, or the recovery of men from a severe disease is as great a miracle as any of those told in Scripture;"480 or again, "Of how small account is a person for whom the cosmic order must be disturbed!"481 Thus when the wise men of Rome asked the Jewish sages: "If your God is omnipotent, as you claim, why does He not banish from the world the idols, which are so loathsome to Him?" they replied: "Do you really desire God to destroy the sun, moon, and stars, because fools worship them? The world continues its regular course, and idolaters will not go unpunished."482

5. In Judaism neither Biblical nor rabbinical miracles are to be accepted as proof of a doctrinal or practical teaching.483 The Deuteronomic law expressly states that false prophets can perform miracles by which they mislead the multitude.484 We can therefore ascribe no intrinsic religious importance to miracles. The fact is that miracles occur only among people who are ignorant of natural law and thus predisposed to accept marvels. They are the products of human imagination and credulity. They have only a subjective, not an objective value. They are psychological, not physical facts.

The attitude of Maimonides and Albo toward Biblical miracles is especially significant. The former declares in his great Code:485 "Israel's belief in Moses and his law did not rest on miracles, for miracles rather create doubt in the mind of the believer. Faith must rest on its intrinsic truth, and this can never be subverted by miracles, which may be of a deceitful nature." Albo devotes a lengthy chapter to developing this idea still further, undoubtedly referring to the Church; he speaks of miracles wrought by both Biblical and Talmudic heroes, such as Onias the rain-maker, Nicodemus ben Gorion, Hanina ben Dosa, and Phinehas ben Jair, the popular saints.486 In modern times Mendelssohn, when challenged by the Lutheran pastor Lavater either to accept the Christian faith or refute it, attacked especially the basic Christian faith in miracles. He stated boldly that "miracles prove nothing, since every religion bases its claims on them and consequently the truth of one would disprove the convincing proof of the other."487

6. Our entire modern mode of thinking demands the complete recognition of the empire of law throughout the universe, manifesting the all-permeating will of God. The whole cosmic order is one miracle. No room is left for single or exceptional miracles. Only a primitive age could think of God as altering the order of nature which He had fixed, so as to let iron float on water like wood to please one person here,488 or to stop sun, star, or sea in their courses in order to help or harm mankind there.489 It is more important for us to inquire into the law of the mind by which the fact itself may differ from the peculiar form given it by a narrator. With our historical methods unknown to former ages, we cannot accept any story of a miracle without seeking its intrinsic historical accuracy. After all, the miracle as narrated is but a human conception of what, under God's guidance, really happened.

Accordingly, we must leave the final interpretation of the Biblical narratives to the individual, to consider them as historical facts or as figurative presentations of religious ideas. Even now some people will prefer to believe that the Ten Commandments emanated from God Himself in audible tones, as medieval thinkers maintained.490 Some will adopt the old semi-rationalistic explanation that He created a voice for this special purpose. Others will hold it more worthy of God to communicate directly with man, from spirit to spirit, without the use of sensory means; these will therefore take the Biblical description as figurative or mythical. In fact, he who does not cling to the letter of the Scripture will probably regard all the miracles as poetical views of divine Providence, as child-like imagery expressing the ancient view of the eternal goodness and wisdom of God. To us also God is "a Doer of wonders," but we experience His wonderworking powers in ourselves. We see wonders in the acts of human freedom which rises superior to the blind forces of nature. The true miracle consists in the divine power within man which aids him to accomplish all that is great and good.

Chapter XXVIII. Providence and the Moral Government of the World

1. None of the precious truths of Judaism has become more indispensable than the belief in divine Providence, which we see about us in ever new and striking forms. Man would succumb from fear alone, beholding the dangers about him on every side, were he not sustained by a conviction that there is an all-wise Power who rules the world for a sublime purpose. We know that even in direst distress we are guided by a divine hand that directs everything finally toward the good. Wherever we are, we are protected by God, who watches over the destinies of man as "does the eagle who hovers over her young and bears them aloft on her pinions." Each of us is assigned his place in the all-encompassing plan. Such knowledge and such faith as this comprise the greatest comfort and joy which the Jewish religion offers. Both the narratives and the doctrines of Scripture are filled with this idea of Providence working in the history of individuals and nations.491

2. Providence implies first, provision, and second, predestination in accordance with the divine plan for the government of the world. As God's dominion over the visible world appears in the eternal order of the cosmos, so in the moral world, where action arises from freely chosen aims, God is Ruler of a moral government. Thus He directs all the acts of men toward the end which He has set. Judaism is most sharply contrasted with heathenism at this point. Heathenism either deifies nature or merges the deity into nature. Thus there is no place for a God who knows all things and provides for all in advance. Blind fate rules all the forces of life, including the deities themselves. Therefore chance incidents in nature or the positions of the stars are taken as indications of destiny. Hence the belief in oracles and divination, in the observation of flying arrows and floating clouds, of the color and shape of the liver of sacrificial animals, and other signs of heaven and earth which were to hint at the future.492

On the other hand, Judaism sees in all things, not the fortuitous dealings of a blind and relentless fate, but the dispensations of a wise and benign Providence. It knows of no event which is not foreordained by God. It sanctioned the decision by lot493 and the appeal to the oracle (the Urim and Thummim)494 only temporarily, during the Biblical period. But soon it recognized entirely the will of God as the Ruler of destiny, and the people accepted the belief that "the days," "the destinies," and even "the tears" of man are all written in His "book."495 Thus they perceived God as "He who knows from the beginning what will be at the end."496 The prophets, His messengers, could thus foretell His will. They perceive Him as the One who "created the smith that brought forth the weapon for its work, and created the master who uses it for destruction."497 However the foe may rage, he is but "the scourge in the hand of God," like "the axe in the hand of him who fells the tree."498 No device of men or nations can withstand His will, for He turns all their doings to some good purpose and transforms every curse into a blessing.499

3. Naturally this truth was first accepted in limited form, in the life of certain individuals. The history of Joseph and of King David were used as illustrations to show how God protects His own. The experiences of the people confirmed this belief and expanded it to apply to the nation. The wanderings of Israel through the wilderness and its entrance to the promised land were regarded as God's work for His chosen people. The prophets looked still further and saw the destinies of all nations, entering the foreground of history one by one, as the sign of divine Providence, so that finally the entire history of mankind became a great plan of divine salvation, centered upon the truth intrusted to Israel.

Beside this conception of general Providence ruling in history, the idea of special Providence arose in response to human longing. The belief in Providence developed to a full conception of care for the world at large and for each individual in his peculiar destiny, a conviction that divine Providence is concerned with the welfare of each individual, and that the joyous or bitter lot of each man forms a link in the moral government of the world. The first clear statement of this comes from the prophet Jeremiah in his wrestling and sighing: "I know, O Lord, that the way of man is not in himself, it is not in man that walketh to direct his steps."500 Special Providence is discussed still more vividly and definitely in the book of Job. Later on it becomes a specific Pharisaic doctrine, "Everything is foreseen."501 "No man suffers so much as the injury of a finger unless it has been decreed in heaven."502 A divine preordination decides a man's choice of his wife503 and every other important step of his life.

4. This theory of predestination, however, presents a grave difficulty when we consider it in relation to man's morality with its implication of self-determination. While this question of free will is treated fully in another connection,504 we may anticipate the thought at this point. The Jewish conception of divine predestination makes as much allowance as possible for the moral freedom of man. This is shown in Talmudic sayings, such as "Everything is within the power of God except the fear of God,"505 or "Repentance, prayer, and charity avert the evil decree."506 Thus Maimonides expressly states in his Code that the belief in predestination cannot be allowed to influence one's moral or religious character. A man can decide by his own volition whether he shall become as just as Moses or as wicked as Jeroboam.507

5. The service of the New Year brings out significantly the Jewish harmonization between the ideas of God's foreknowledge and man's moral freedom. This festival, in the Bible called the Festival of the Blowing of the Shofar, was transformed under Babylonian influence into the Day of Divine Judgment. But it is still in marked contrast to the Babylonian New Year's Day, when the gods were supposed to go to the House of the Tablets of Destiny in the deep to hear the decisions of fate.508 The Jewish sages taught that on this day God, the Judge of the world, pronounces the destinies of men and nations according to their deserts. They thus replaced the heathen idea of blind fate by that of eternal justice as the formative power of life. Then, moved by a desire to mitigate the rigor of stern justice for the frail and failing mortal, they included also God's long-suffering and mercy. These attributes are thus supposed to intercede, so that the final decision is left in suspense until the Day of Atonement, the great day of pardon. Some Tannaitic teachers509 find it more in accord with their view of God to say that He judges man every day, and even every hour.

Of course, the philosophic mind can take this whole viewpoint in a figurative sense alone. All the more must we recognize that this sublime religious thought of God liberates morality from the various limitations of the ancient pagan conception of Deity and the more recent metaphysical view. In place of these it asserts that there is a moral government of the world, which must be imitated in the moral and religious consciousness of the individual.

6. The belief in a moral government of the world answers another question which the medieval Jewish philosophers and their Mohammedan predecessors endeavored to solve, but without satisfying the religious sentiment, the chief concern of theology. Some of them maintain that God's foreknowledge does not determine human deeds.510 Maimonides and his school, however, say that it is impossible for us to comprehend the knowledge and power of God, and that therefore such a question is outside the sphere of human knowledge. "Know that, just as God has made the elements of fire and air to rise upwards and water and earth to sink downward, so has He made man a free, self-determining being, who acts of his own volition."511 The Mohammedans would often give up human freedom rather than the omniscience and all-determining power of God; but the Jewish thinkers, significantly, with only the possible exception of Crescas,512 laid stress upon the divine nature which man attains through moral freedom, even at the risk of limiting the omniscience of God.

7. The philosophers failed, however, to emphasize sufficiently a point of highest importance for religion, God's paternal care for all His creatures. Indeed, God ceases to be God, if He has not included our every step in His plan of creation, thus surrounding us with paternal love and tender care. Instead of the three blind fates of heathendom who spin and cut the threads of destiny without even knowing why, the divine Father himself sits at the loom of time and apportions the lot of men according to His own wisdom and goodness. Such a belief in divine Providence is ingrained in the soul, and reasoning alone will not suffice to attain it. Therefore even such great thinkers as Maimonides and Gersonides go astray as religious teachers when they follow Aristotelian principles in this very intimate matter. They assume a general Providence aiming for the preservation of the species, but include a special Providence only so far as the recipient of it is endowed with reason and has thus approached the divine Intellect. A Providence of this type, the result of human reasoning, is a mere illusion, as the pious thinker, Hasdai Crescas, clearly shows.513 For the man who prays to God in anxiety or distress this bears nothing but disappointment.

The Aristotelian conception of the world has this great truth, that there is no such thing as chance, that everything is foreseen and provided by the divine wisdom. But religion must hold that the individual is an object of care by God, that "not a sparrow falls into the net without God's will,"514 that "every hair on the head of man is counted and cared for in the heavenly order,"515 and that the most insignificant thing serves its purpose under the guidance of an all-wise God. We use figurative expressions for the divine care, because we cannot grasp it entirely or literally.

8. The Bible in the Song of Moses compares divine Providence to the eagle spreading her protecting wings over her young and bearing them aloft, or urging them to soar along.516 The rabbis elaborate this by referring to the twofold care which the eagle thus bestows, as she watches over those who are still tender and helpless, shielding them from the arrows below by bearing them on her wings, but inspiring the maturer and stronger ones to fly by her side.517 In the same way Providence trains both individuals and generations for their allotted task. A little child requires incessant care on the part of its mother, until it has learned how to eat, walk, speak, and to decide for itself, but the wise parent gradually withdraws his guiding hand so that the growing child may learn self-reliance and self-respect. The divine Father trains man thus through the childhood of humanity. But no sooner does the divine spirit in man awaken to self-consciousness than he is thrown on his own resources to become the master of his own destiny. The divine power which, in the earlier stages, had worked for man, now works with him and within him. In the rabbinic phrase, he is now ready to be a "co-worker with God in the work of creation."518 Only at those grave moments when his own powers fail him, he still feels in the humility of faith that his ancient God is still near, "a very present help in trouble," and that "the Guardian of Israel neither slumbereth nor sleepeth."519

Philosophy cannot tolerate the removal of the dividing line between the transcendent God and finite man. Hence the relation of man's free will and divine foresight cannot be solved by any process of reasoning. But when religion proclaims a moral government of the world, then man, with his moral and spiritual aims, attains a place in Creation akin to the Creator. Of course, so long as he is mentally a child and has no clear purpose, Providence acts for him as it does for the animal with its marvelous instinct. Through His chosen messengers God gives the people bread and water, freedom and victory, instruction and law. The wondrous tales describing the divine protection of Israel in its early life may strike us as out of harmony with the laws of nature, but they are true portrayals of the experience of the people. Whatever happened for their good in those days had to be the work of God; they had not yet wakened to the power hidden in their own soul. Their heroes felt themselves to be divine instruments, roused by His spirit to perform mighty deeds or to behold prophetic visions. It is God who battles through them. It is God who speaks through them. Both their moral and spiritual guidance works from without and above. At this stage of life autonomy is neither felt nor desired. When man awakens to moral self-consciousness and maturity, this inner change impresses him as an outer one; the change in him is interpreted as a change in God. He feels that God has withdrawn behind His eternal laws of nature and morality which work without direct interference, and in his new sense of independence he thinks that he can dispense with the divine protection and forethought. As if mortal man can ever dispense with that Power which has endowed him with his capacity for worthy accomplishment! Thus in times of danger and distress man turns to God for help; thus at every great turning point in the life of an individual or nation the idea of an all-wise Providence imbues him with new hope and new security. And in all these cases the great lesson of providential direction is typified in the history of Israel as related in the Bible.

10. The idea of Providence, indeed, belongs also to certain pagan philosophers, who observed the great purposes of nature which the single creature and the species are both to serve. The Stoics in particular made a study of teleology, the system of purposive ends in nature. Philo adopted much from them in his treatise on Providence.

Later the popular philosophic group among the Mohammedans, the so-called "Brothers of Purity," based their doctrines of God and His relation to the world on a teleological view of nature. In fact, the Jewish philosopher and moralist Bahya ben Pakudah has embodied many of their ideas in his "Duties of the Heart."520

Jewish folklore—preserved in rabbinic literature—has also attempted a popular explanation of the obscure ways of Providence, in strange events of nature as well as the great enigmas of human destiny. Thus the flight of David from Saul affords the lesson of the good purpose which may be served by so insignificant a thing as a spider, or by so dreadful a state as insanity.521 Vast numbers of the Jewish legends and fables deal with adversities which are turned into ultimate good by the working of an all-wise Providence.522

Chapter XXIX. God and the Existence of Evil

1. A leading objection to the belief in divine Providence is the existence in this world of physical and moral evil. All living creatures are exposed to the influence of evil, according to their physical or moral constitutions and the peculiar conditions of their existence. Heathenism accounts for the powers of darkness, pain and death by assuming the existence of forces hostile to the heavenly powers of light and life, or of a primitive principle of evil, the counterpart of the divine beings. But to those who believe in an almighty and all-benign Creator and Ruler of the universe, the question remains: Why do life and the love of life encounter so many hindrances? Why does God's world contain so much pain and bitterness, so much passion and sin? Should not Providence have averted such things? The answer of Judaism has already been stated here, but we need further elaboration of the theme that there is no evil before God, since a good purpose is served even by that which appears bad. In the life of the human body pleasure and pain, the impetus to life and its restraint and inhibition form a necessary contrast, making for health; so, in the moral order of the universe, each being who battles with evil receives new strength for the unfolding of the good. The principle of holiness, which culminates in Israel's holy God, transforms and ennobles every evil. As the Midrash explains, referring to Deut. XI, 26: "If thou but seest that both good and evil are placed in thy hand, no evil will come to thee from above, since thou knowest how to turn it into good."523

2. The conception of evil passed through a development parallel with that of the related conceptions which we have just reviewed. At first every misfortune was considered to be inflicted by divine wrath as a punishment for human misdeeds. Nations and individuals were thought to suffer for some special moral cause; through suffering they were punished for past wrong, warned against its repetition in the future, and urged to repentance and improvement of their conduct. Even death, the fate of all living creatures, was regarded as a punishment which the first pair of human beings brought upon all their descendants through their transgression of the divine command. The Talmudic sages clung to the view of the Paradise legend in the Bible, when they held that every death is due to some sin committed by the individual.524

This view, which was shared by paganism, was accompanied by a higher conception, gradually growing in the thinking mind. As a father does not punish his child in anger, but in order to improve his conduct, so God chastens man in order to purify his moral nature. Good fortune tends to harden the heart; adversity often softens and sweetens it. In the crucible of suffering the gold of the human soul is purified from the dross. The evil strokes of destiny come upon the righteous, not because he deserves them, but because his divine Friend is raising him to still higher tests of virtue. This standpoint, never reached even by the pious sufferer Job, is attained by rabbinic Judaism when it calls the visitations of the righteous "trials of the divine love."525 Thus evil, both physical and spiritual, receives its true valuation in the divine economy. Evil exists only to be overcome by the good. In His paternal goodness God uses it to educate His children for a place in His kingdom.

3. According to the direct words of Scripture good and evil, light and darkness, emanate alike from the Creator. This is accentuated by the great seer of the Exile,526 who protests against the Persian belief in a creative principle of good and a destructive principle of evil. The rabbis, however, ascribe the origin of evil to man; they take as a negation rather than a question the verse in Lam. III, 38: "Do not evil and good come out of the mouth of the Most High?" Thus they refer this to the words of Deuteronomy, "Behold, I have set before you this day life and good, death and evil; choose thou life!"527

Such medieval thinkers as Abraham Ibn Daud and Maimonides did not ascribe to evil any reality at all.528 Evil to them is the negation of good, just as darkness is the negation of light, or poverty of riches. As evil exists only for man, man can overcome it by himself. Before God it has no essential existence. Unfortunately, such metaphysics does not equip man with strength and courage to cope with either pain or sin. The same lack is evident in that modern form of pseudo-science which poses as a religion, Christian Science, which has made propaganda so widely among both Jews and non-Jews. Christian Science declares pain, sickness, and all evil to be merely the "error of mortal mind," which can all be dispelled by faith; such a view neither strengthens the soul for its real struggles nor convinces the mind by an appeal to facts.529

4. Frail mortals as we are, we need the help of the living God. Thus only can we overcome physical evil, knowing that He bears with us, feels with us, and transforms it finally into good. We need it also to overcome moral evil, in the consciousness that He has compassion upon the repentant sinner and gives him courage to follow the right path. The modern philosophers of pessimism had the correct feeling in adopting the Hindu conception, and emphasizing the pain and misery of existence, repeating Job's ancient plaint over the hard destiny of mankind. The shallow optimism of the age would rather conceal the dark side of life and indulge in outbursts of self-sufficiency. Yet if we measure it only by a physical yardstick, life cannot be called a boon. Against shallow optimism we have the testimony of every thorn and sting, every poisonous breath and every destructive element in nature's household, as well as all vice and evil in the world of man. The world does not appear good, unless we measure it by the ideal of divine holiness. If God is the Father watching over the welfare of every mortal, all things are good, because all serve a good purpose in His eternal plan. Every hindrance or pressure engenders new power; every sting acts as a spur to higher things. Short-sighted and short-lived as is man, he forgets too easily that in the sight of God "a thousand years are as a single day," world-epochs like "watches in the night," and that the mills of divine justice grind on, "slowly but exceeding small." But one belief illumines the darkness of destiny, and that is that God stands ever at the helm, steering through every storm and tempest toward His sublime goal. In the moral striving of man we can but realize that our every victory contributes toward the majestic work of God.530

Chapter XXX. God and the Angels

1. Judaism insists with unrelenting severity on the absolute unity and incomparability of God, so that no other being can be placed beside Him. Consequently, every mention of divine beings (Elohim or B'ne Elohim) in either the Bible or post-Biblical literature refers to subordinate beings only. These spirits constitute the celestial court for the King of the World.531 All the forces of the universe are His servants, fulfilling His commands. Hence both the Hebrew and Greek terms for angel, Malak and angelos, mean "messenger." These beings derive their existence from God; some of them are merely temporary, so that without Him they dissolve into nothing. Although Scripture uses the terms, "God of gods" and "King of kings," still we cannot attribute any independent existence to subordinate divine beings. In fact, Maimonides in his sixth article of faith holds that worship of such beings is prohibited as idolatry by the second commandment.532 Thus the unity of God lifts Him above comparison with any other divine being. This is most emphatically expressed in Deuteronomy: "Know this day, and lay it to thy heart, that the Lord He is God in heaven above, and upon the earth beneath; there is none else,"533 and "See now that I, even I, am He, and there is no god with Me; I kill and make alive; I have wounded and I heal, and there is none that can deliver out of My hand."534 The same attitude is found in Isaiah: "I am the Lord that maketh all things, that stretched forth the heavens alone, that spread abroad the earth by Myself" "I am the Lord and there is none else; beside Me there is no god."535 Such conceptions allow no place for angels or spirits.

2. It was certainly not easy for prophet, lawgiver, or sage to dispel the popular belief in divine beings or powers, which primitive Judaism shared with other ancient faiths. No sharp line was drawn at first between God and His accompanying angels, as we may infer from the story of the angels who appeared to Abraham, and the similar incidents of Hagar and Jacob.536 The varying application of the term Elohim to God and to the angels or gods is proof enough of the priority of polytheism, even in Judaism. The trees or springs, formerly seats of the ancient deities, spirits, or demons, were now the places for the appearance of angels, shorn of their independence, looking like fiery or shining human beings. Popular belief, however, perpetuated mythological elements, ascribing to the angels higher wisdom and sometimes sensuality as well. Such a case is the fragment preserved in Genesis telling of the union of sons of God to the daughters of men, causing the generation of giants.537 Obviously the old Babylonian "mountain of the gods," with its food for the gods, became in the Paradise legend the garden of Eden,

the seat of God;538 and the Psalmist still speaks of the "angels' food," which appeared as manna in the wilderness.539 On the whole, the sacred writers were most eager to allot to the angels a very subordinate position in the divine household. They figure usually as hosts of beings, numbered by myriads, wrapped in light or in fleeting clouds. They surround the throne or chariot of God; they comprise His heavenly court or council; they sing His praise and obey His call.

Scripture is quite silent about the creation of these angelic beings, as on most purely speculative questions. At the very beginning of the world God consults them when He is to create man after the image of the celestial beings. For this is the original meaning of Elohim in Gen. I, 26 and 27 and V, 1: "Let us make man in our image, after our likeness"; "And God created man in his own image, in the image of godly beings He created him." This view is echoed in Psalm VIII, verse 6: "Thou hast made him a little lower than godly beings." In Job XXXVIII, 7, both the morning stars and the sons of God, or angels, "shout together in joy" when the Lord laid the foundations of the earth.540

3. In Biblical times—which does not include the book of Daniel, a work of the Maccabean time—the angels and demons were not invested with proper names or special functions. The Biblical system does not even distinguish clearly between good and evil spirits. The goat-like demons of the field popularly worshiped were merely survivals of pagan superstitions.541

In general the angels carry out good or evil designs according to their commands from the Lord of Hosts. They are sent forth to destroy Sodom, to save Lot, and to bring Abraham the good tidings of the birth of a son.542 On one occasion the host of spirits protect the people of God; on another they annihilate hostile powers by pestilence and plagues.543 At one time a multitude appear, led by a celestial chieftain; at another a single angel performs the miracle. In any case the destroying angel is not a demon, but a messenger of the divine will. Originally some of these primitive forces were dreaded or worshiped by the people, but all have been transformed into members of the celestial court and called to bear witness to the dominion of the Omnipotent.

4. The belief in angels served two functions in the development of monotheism. On the one hand, it was a stage in the concentration of the divine forces, beginning with polytheism, continuing through belief in angels, and culminating in the one and only God of heaven and earth. On the other hand, certain sensuous elements in the vision of God by the seers had to be removed in the spiritualization of God, and it was found easiest to transform these into separate beings, related to Deity himself. Thus the fiery appearance of God to the eye or the voice which was manifested to the ear were often personified as angels of God. This very process made possible the purification of the God idea, as the sublime essence of the Deity was divested of physical and temporal elements, and God was conceived more and more as a moral and spiritual personality. Hence in Biblical passages the names of God and of the angel frequently alternate.544 The latter is only a representative of the divine personality—in Scriptural terms, the presence or "face" of God. Therefore the voice of the angel is to be obeyed as that of God himself, because His name is present in His representative. A similar meaning became attached later on to the term Shekinah, the "majesty" of God as beheld in the cloud of fire. This was spoken of in place of God that He might not be lowered into the earthly sphere. For further discussion of this subject, see chapter XXXII, "God and Intermediary Powers." In fact, we note that the post-exilic prophets all received their revelations, not from God, but through a special angel.545 They no longer believed that God might be seen or heard by human powers, and therefore their visions had to be translated into rational thoughts by a mediating angel.

5. Persian influence gave Jewish angelology and demonology a different character. The two realms of the Persian system included vast hosts of beneficent spirits under Ahura-Mazda (Ormuzd) and of demons under the dominion of Angro-mainyus (Ahriman). So in Judaism also different orders of angels arose, headed by archangels who bore special names. The number seven was adopted from the Persians, while both names and order were often changed. All of them, however, were allotted special functions in the divine household. The pagan deities and primitive spirits which still persisted in popular superstition were given a new lease of life. Each force of nature was given a guardian spirit, just as in nature-worship; angels were appointed over fire, water, each herb, each fountain, and every separate function of life. A patron angel was assigned to each of the seventy nations of the world mentioned in the genealogy of Noah.546

Thus the celestial court grew in number and in splendor. A beginning was made with the heavenly chariot-throne of Ezekiel, borne aloft by the four holy living creatures (the hayoth), surrounded by the fiery Cherubim, the winged Seraphim, and the many-eyed Ofanim (wheels).547 This was elaborated by the addition of rows of surrounding angels, called "angels of service," headed by the seven archangels. Of these the chief was Michael, the patron-saint of Israel, and the next Gabriel, who is sometimes even placed first. Raphael and Uriel are regularly mentioned, the other three rarely, and not always by the same names. The Irin of Daniel—known as "the Watchers," but more precisely "the ever-watchful Ones"—are another of the ten classes of angels included. Below these are myriads of inferior angels who serve them. Their classification by rank was a favorite theme of the secret lore of the Essenes, partly preserved for us in the apocalyptic literature and the liturgy. The Essenic saints endeavored to acquire miraculous powers through using the names of certain angels, and thus exorcising the evil spirits.

This secret lore seems to be patterned after the Zoroastrian or Mazdean system. It is noteworthy that the most prominent angelic figure is Metatron, the charioteer of the Merkabah or chariot-throne on high, which is merely another form of Mithras, the Persian god of light, who acts as charioteer for Ahura Mazda.548 Two other angels are mentioned as standing behind the heavenly throne, Akathriel, "the crown-bearer of God," and Sandalphon, "the twin brother" = Synadelphon.

6. A striking contrast exists between the simple habitation in the sky depicted in the prophetic and Mosaic books, and the splendor of the heavenly spheres according to the rabbinical writings. The Oriental courts lent all their grandeur to the majestic throne of God, on which He was exalted above all earthly things. The immense space between was filled in by innumerable gradations of beings leading up to Him. There was no longer a question how far these other beings shared the nature of God; His dominion was absolute. Still a new question, not known to the Bible, arose, as to when the angelic world was created and out of what primordial element. At first a logical answer was given, that the angels emanated from the element of fire. Later the schoolmen, trying to dispose of the angels as possible peers or rivals of the eternal God, ascribed their creation to the second day, when the heaven was made as a vault over the earth, or to the fifth day, when the winged creatures arose.549 On the whole, the rabbis denied every claim of the angels to an independent or an eternal existence. Just because they firmly believed in the existence of angels and even saw them from time to time, they felt bound to declare their secondary rank. Only the archangels were made from an eternal substance, while the others were continually being created anew out of the breath of God or from the "river of fire" which flowed around His throne. Thus even the realm of celestial spirits was merged into the stream of universal life which comes and goes, while God was left alone in matchless sovereignty, above all the fluctuations of time.

On the other hand, the rabbis opposed the Essenic idea of assigning to the angels an intermediary task between God and man, and deprecated as a pagan custom the worship or invocation of angels. "Address your prayer to the Master of life and not to His servants; He will hear you in every trouble," says R. Judan.550 Some of the teachers even declared that any godly son of Israel excels the angels in power. It is certainly significant, as David Neumark has pointed out, that the Mishnah eliminates every reference to the angels.551

7. In spite of this, none of the medieval Jewish philosophers doubted the existence of angels.552 Indeed, there was no reason for them to do so, as they had managed to insert them into their philosophic systems as intermediary beings leading up to the Supreme Intelligence. All that was necessary was to identify the angels of the Bible with the "ideas" of Plato or the "rulers of the spheres," the "separate intelligences" of Aristotle. By this one step the existence of angels as cosmic powers was proved to be a logical necessity. The ten rulers of the spheres even corresponded with the ten orders of angels in the cosmography of the Jewish, Mohammedan, and Christian schoolmen. The only difference between the Aristotelian and the rabbinical views was that the former held the cosmic powers to be eternal; the latter, that they were created.

In both Biblical and rabbinical literature the angels are usually conceived of as purely spiritual powers superior to man. Maimonides, however, following his rationalistic method, declared them to be simply products of the imagination, the hypostases of figurative expressions which were not meant to be taken literally. To him every force and element of nature is an angel or messenger of God. In this way the entire angelology of the Bible, including even Ezekiel's vision of the heavenly chariot (the Merkabah), in becoming a part of the Maimonidean system turns into natural philosophy pure and simple.553 Of course, Saadia, Jehuda ha Levi, and Gabirol do not share this rationalistic view. To them the angels are either cosmic powers of an ethereal substance, endowed with everlasting life, or living beings created by God for special purposes.554

The later Cabbalistic lore extended the realm of the celestial spirits still more, creating new names of angels for its mystical system and its magical practices. Yet in this magic it subordinated the angels to man. In fact, it followed

Saadia largely in this, making man the center and pinnacle of the work of creation, in fact, the very mirror of the Creator.555

8. For our modern viewpoint the existence of angels is a question of psychology rather than of theology. The old Babylonian world has vanished, with its heaven as the dwelling place of God, its earth for man, and its nether world for the shades and demons. The world in which we live knows no above or beneath, no heaven or hell, no host of good and evil spirits moving about to help or hurt man. It sees matter and energy working everywhere after the same immutable laws through an infinitude of space and time, a universe ever evolving new orbs of light, engendering and transforming worlds without number and without end. There is no place in infinite space for a heaven or for a celestial throne. A world of law and of process does not need a living ladder to lead from the earth below to God on high. Though the stars be peopled with souls superior to ours, still they cannot stand nearer to God than does man with his freedom, his moral striving, his visions of the highest and the best. Through man's spiritual nature God, too, is recognized as a Spirit; through man's moral consciousness God is conceived of as the Ruler of a moral world; but this same process at once does away with the need for any other spirits or divine powers beside Him. God alone has become the object of human longing. Man feels akin to His God who is ever near; he learns to know Him ever better. He can dispense with the angelic hosts. As they return to the fiery stream of poetic imagination whence they emerged, nebulous figures of a glorious world that has vanished, man rises above angel and Seraph by his own power to the dignity of a servant, nay, a child of God. Indeed, as the rabbis said, the prophets, sages, and seers are the true messengers of God, the angels who do His service.556

Chapter XXXI. Satan and the Spirits of Evil

1. The great advantage of Judaism over other religious systems lies in its unified view of life, which it regards as a continuous conflict between good and evil influences within man. As man succeeds in overcoming evil and achieving good, he asserts his own moral personality. Outside of man Judaism sees no real contrast between good and evil, since both have emanated from God, the Spirit of goodness. Judaism recognizes no primal power of evil plotting against God and defying Him, such as that of the Persian dualism. Nor does Judaism espouse the dualism of spirit and matter, identifying matter with evil, from which the soul strives to free itself while confined in the prison house of the body. Such a conception is taught by Plato, probably under Oriental influence, and is shared by the Hindu and Christian ascetics who torture themselves in order to suppress bodily desire in their quest of a higher existence. The Jewish conception of the unity of God necessitates the unity of the world, which leaves no place for a cosmic principle of evil. In this Judaism dissents from modern philosophers also, such as John Stuart Mill and even Kant, who speak of a radical evil in nature. No power of evil can exist in independence of God.557 As the Psalmist says: "His kingdom ruleth over all. Bless the Lord, ye angels of His, ye mighty in strength that fulfill His word, hearkening unto the voice of His word."558

This increased the difficulty of the problem of the origin of evil. The answer given by the general Jewish consciousness, expressed by both Biblical and rabbinical writers, is that evil comes from the free will of man, who is endowed with the power of rebelling against the will of God. This idea is symbolized in the story of the fall of man. The serpent, or tempter, represents the evil inclination which arises in man with his first consciousness of freedom. So in Jewish belief Satan, the Adversary, is only an allegorical figure, representing the evil of the world, both physical and moral. He was sent by God to test man for his own good, to develop him morally. He is "the spirit that ever wills evil, but achieves the good," and therefore in the book of Job he actually comes before God's throne as one of the angels.559

2. In tracing the belief in demons we must draw a sharp distinction between popular views and systematic doctrine.560 During the Biblical era the people believed in goat-like spirits roaming the fields and woods, the deserts and ravines, whom they called Seirim—hairy demons, or satyrs,—and to whom they sacrificed in fear and trembling.561 As Ibn Ezra ingeniously pointed out in his commentary, Azazel was originally a desert demon dwelling in the ravines near Jerusalem, to whom a scapegoat was offered at the opening of the year, a rite preserved in the Day of Atonement cult of the Mosaic Code.562 In fact, in ancient Babylon, Syria, and Palestine diseases and accidents were universally ascribed to evil spirits of the wilderness or the nether world. The Bible occasionally mentions these evil spirits as punitive angels sent by God. In the more popular view, which is reflected by apocryphal and rabbinical literature, and which was influenced by both the Babylonian and Persian religions, they appear in increasing numbers and with specific names. Each disease had its peculiar demon. Desolate places,

cemeteries, and the darkness of night were all peopled by superstition with hosts of demons (Shedim), at whose head was Azazel, Samael; Beelzebub, the Philistine god of flies and of illness;563 Belial, king of the nether world;564 or the Persian Ashma Deva (Evil Spirit), under the Hebrew name of Ashmodai or Shemachzai.565 The queen of the demons was Lilith or Iggereth bath Mahlath, "the dancer on the housetops."566

The Essenes seem to have made special studies of both demonology and angelology, believing that they could invoke the good spirits and conjure the evil ones, thus curing various diseases, which they ascribed to possession by demons. While these exorcisms are not so common in the Talmud as they are in the New Testament, there remain many indications that such practices were followed by Jewish saints and believed by the people. Often the rabbis seem to have considered them the work of "unclean spirits," which they endeavored to overcome with the "spirit of holiness," and particularly by the study of the Torah.567

3. This answers implicitly the question of the origin of demons. Obviously the belief in malevolent spirits is incompatible with the existence of an all-benign and all-wise Creator. Accordingly, two alternative explanations are offered in the rabbinical and apocalyptic writings. According to one, the demons are half angelic and half animal beings, sharing intelligence and flight with the angels, sensuality with beasts and with men. Their double nature is ascribed to incompleteness, because they were created last of all beings, and their creation was interrupted by the coming of the Sabbath, putting an end to all creation.568 According to the other view they are the offspring of the "fallen angels," issuing from the union of the angels with the daughters of men as described in Gen. VI, 1 f. These spread the virus of impurity over all the earth, causing carnal desire and every kind of lewdness. The whole world of demons is regarded as alienated from God by the rebellion of the heavenly hosts, as if the fall of man by sin had its prototype in the celestial sphere.569 A rabbinical legend, which corresponds with a Persian myth, ascribes the origin of demons to the intercourse of Adam with Lilith, the night spirit.570 On the other hand, the archangel Samael is said to have cast lascivious glances at the beauty of Eve, and then to have turned into Satan the Tempter.571 The Jewish systems of both angelology and demonology, first worked out in the apocalyptic literature, were further elaborated by the Cabbalah.

Angelology found a conspicuous place in the liturgy in connection with the Kedushah Benediction and likewise in the liturgy and the theology of the Church.572

On the other hand the belief in evil spirits and in Satan, the Evil One, remained rather a matter of popular credulity and never became a positive doctrine of the Synagogue. True, the liturgy contained morning prayers which asked God for protection against the Evil One, and formulas invoking the angels to shield one during the night from evil spirits.573 But the arch-fiend was never invested with power over the soul, depriving man of his perfect freedom and divine sovereignty, as in the Christian Church.

4. In the formation of the idea of the arch-fiend, Satan, we can observe the interworking of several elements. The name Satan in no way indicates a demon. It denotes simply the adversary, the one who offers hindrances. The name was thus applied to the accuser at court.574 In Zechariah and in Job575 Satan appears at the throne of God as the prosecutor, roaming about the earth to espy the transgressions of men, seeking to lure them to their destruction. In the Books of Chronicles576 Satan has become a proper name, meaning the Seducer.

The Serpent in the Paradise story is more completely a demon, although the legend intends rather to account for man's morality, his distinction between good and evil. Satan was then identified with the serpent, who was called by the rabbis Nahash ha Kadmoni, "the primeval Serpent," after the analogy of the serpent-like form of Ahriman. Thus Satan in the person of the serpent became the embodiment of evil, the prime cause of sin and death.577 Possibly a part in this process was played by the Babylonian figure of Tihamat, the dragon of chaos (Tehom in the Hebrew), with whom the god Marduk wrestled for dominion over the world, and who has parallels in the Biblical Rahab and similar mythological figures.

We must not overlook such rabbinical legends as the one about how the poisonous breath of the serpent infected the whole human race, except Israel who has been saved by the law at Sinai.578 Occasionally we hear that the Evil Spirit (Yezer ha Ra) will be slain by God579 or by the Messiah.580 These Haggadic sayings, however, were never accepted as normative for religious belief. On the contrary, they were always in dispute, and many a Talmudic teacher minimized the fiendish character of Satan, who became a stimulus to moral betterment through the trials he imposes.581 Philo, allegorizing the legends, turns the evil angels of the Bible into wicked men.582

5. As to demons in general, the Talmudists never doubted their existence, but endeavored to minimize their importance. They changed the demon Azazel into a geographical term by transposing the letters.583 They explained "the sons of God who came to the daughters of men to give birth to the giants of old" as aristocratic Sethites who intermarried with low-class families of the Cainites.584 As to the rest, the entire belief in demons and ghosts was too deeply rooted in the folk mind to be counteracted by the rabbis. Even lucid thinkers of the Middle Ages were caught by these baneful superstitions, including Jehuda ha Levi, Crescas, and Nahmanides, the mystic.585 Only a small group fought against this offshoot of fear and superstition, among them Saadia, Maimonides and his school, Ibn Ezra, Gersonides, and Juda Ibn Balag. To Maimonides the demons mentioned in Mishnah and Talmud are only figurative expressions for physical plagues. He considers the belief in demons equivalent to a belief in pagan deities. "Many pious Israelites," he says,586 "believe in the reality of demons and witches, thinking that they should not be made the object of worship and regard, for the reason that the Torah has prohibited it. But they fail to see that the Law commands us to banish all these things from sight, because they are but falsehood and deceit, as is the whole idolatry with which they are intrinsically connected."

6. This sound view was disseminated by the rationalistic school in its contest with the Cabbalah, and has exerted a wholesome influence upon modern Judaism. Thus Satan is rejected by Jewish doctrine, while Luther and Calvin, the Reformers of the Christian Church, still believed in him. Milton's "Paradise Lost" placed him in the very foreground of Christian belief, and the leaders of the Protestant Churches, up to the present, accord him a prominent place in their scheme of salvation, as the opponent and counterpart of God. In his work on Christian dogmatics, David Friedrich Strauss observes acutely: "The whole (Christian) idea of the Messiah and his kingdom must necessarily have as its counterpart a kingdom of demons with a personal ruler at its head; without this it is no more possible than the north pole of the magnet would be without a south pole. If Christ has come to destroy the works of the Devil, there would be no need for him to come, unless there were a Devil. On the other hand, if the Devil is to be considered merely the personification of evil, then a Christ who would be only the personification of the ideal, but not a real personality, would suffice equally."587 At present Christian theologians and even philosophers have recourse to Platonic and Buddhist ideas, that evil is implanted in the world from which humanity must free itself, and they thus present Christianity as the religion of redemption par excellence.588 Over against this, Judaism still maintains that there is no radical or primitive evil in the world. No power exists which is intrinsically hostile to God, and from which man must be redeemed. According to the Jewish conception, the goodness and glory of God fill both heaven and earth, while holiness penetrates all of life, bringing matter and flesh within the realm of the divine. Evil is but the contrast of good, as shade is but the contrast of light. Evil can be overcome by each individual, as he realizes his own solemn duty and the divine will. Its only existence is in the field of morality, where it is a test of man's freedom and power. Evil is within man, and against it he is to wage the battles of life, until his victory signalizes the triumph of the divine in his own nature.589

Chapter XXXII. God and the Intermediary Powers

1. In addition to the angels who carried out God's will in the universe, the Biblical and post-Biblical literature recognizes other divine powers which mediate between Him and the world of man. The more a seer or thinker became conscious of the spirituality and transcendency of God, the more he felt the gulf between the infinite Spirit and the world of the senses. In order to bridge this gap, the Deity was replaced by one of His manifestations which could appear and act in a world circumscribed by space and time.590 As we found in prophecy the direct revelation of God giving way to a mediating angel, so either "the Glory" or "the Name" of JHVH takes the place of God himself. That is, instead of God's own being, His reflected radiance or the power invested in His name descends from on high. The rabbis kept the direct revelation of God for the hallowed past or the desired future, but at the same time they needed a suitable term for the presence of God; they therefore coined the word Shekinah—"the divine Condescension" or "Presence"—to be used instead of the Deity himself. Thus the verse of the Psalm:591 "God standeth in the congregation of God," is translated by the Targum, "The divine Presence (Shekinah) resteth upon the congregation of the godly." Instead of the conclusion of the speech to Moses, "Let them make Me a sanctuary, that I may dwell among them,"592 the Targum has, "And I shall let My Presence (Shekinah) dwell among them." Thus in the view of the rabbis Shekinah represents the visible part of the divine majesty, which descends from heaven to earth, and on the radiance of which are fed the spiritual beings, both angels and the souls of the saints.593 God himself was wrapped in light, whose brilliancy no living being, however lofty, could endure; but the Shekinah or reflection of the divine glory might be beheld by the elect either in their lifetime or in the hereafter. In

this way the rabbis solved many contradictory passages of Scripture, some of which speak of God as invisible, while others describe man as beholding Him.594

2. Just as the references to God's appearing to man suggested luminous powers mediating the vision of God, so the passages which represent God as speaking suggest powers mediating the voice. Hence arose the conception of the divine Word, invested with divine powers both physical and spiritual. The first act of God in the Bible is that He spoke, and by this word the world came into being. The Word was thus conceived of as the first created being, an intermediary power between the Spirit of the world and the created world order. The word of God, important in the cosmic order, is still more so in the moral and spiritual worlds. The Word is at times a synonym of divine revelation to the men of the early generations or to Israel, the bearer of the Law. Hence the older Haggadah places beside the Shekinah the divine Word (Hebrew, Maamar; Aramaic, Memra; Greek, Logos) as the intermediary force of revelation.

Contact with the Platonic and Stoic philosophies led gradually to a new development which appears in Philo. The Word or Logos becomes "the first-created Son of God," having a personality independent from God; in fact he is a kind of vice regent of God himself. From this it was but a short step toward considering him a partner and peer of the Almighty, as was done by the Church with its doctrine that the Word became flesh in Christ, the son of God.595 In view of this the rabbinical schools gave up the idea of the personified Word, replacing it with the Torah or the Spirit of God. The older term was retained only in liturgical formulas, such as: "Who created the heavens by His Word," or, "Who by His Word created the twilight and by Wisdom openeth the gates of heaven."596

3. As has been shown above,597 Wisdom is described in the Bible as the first of all created beings, the assistant and counselor of God in the work of creation. Then we see that Ben Sira identifies Wisdom with the Torah.598 Thus the Torah, too, was raised to a cosmic power, the sum and substance of all wisdom. In fact, the Torah, like the Logos of Plato, was regarded as comprising the ideas or prototypes of all things as in a universal plan. The Torah is the divine pattern for the world. In such a connection Torah is far from meaning the Law, as Weber asserts.599 It means rather the heavenly book of instruction which contains all the wisdom of the ages, and which God himself used as guide at the Creation. God is depicted as an architect with His plan drafted before He began the erection of the edifice,—a conception which avoids all danger of deifying the Logos.

4. Several other conceptions, however, do not belong at all to the intermediary powers, where Weber places them.600 This applies to Metatron (identical with the Persian Mithras),601 whom the mystic lore calls the charioteer of the heavenly throne-chariot, represented by the rabbis as the highest of the angels, leader of the heavenly hosts, and vice-regent of God. That no cosmic power was ascribed to him is proved by the very fact of his identification with Enoch, whom the pre-Talmudic Haggadah describes as taken up into heaven and changed into an angel of the highest rank, standing near God's throne.602

5. The only real mediator between God and man is the Spirit of God, which is mentioned in connection with both the creation and divine revelation. In the first chapter of Genesis the Spirit of God is described as hovering over the gloom of chaos like the mother bird over the egg, ready to hatch out the nascent world.603 God breathed His spirit into the body of man, to make him also god-like.604 The prophet likewise is inspired by the spirit of God to see visions and to hear the divine message.605 Thus the spirit of God has two aspects; it is the cosmic principle which imbues primal matter with life; it is a link between the soul of man and God on high. The view of Ezekiel was but one step from this, to conceive the spirit as a personal being, and place him beside God as an angel.

The prophets and psalmists, feeling the spirit of God upon them, considered it an emanation of the Deity. Still, a profounder insight soon disapproved the severance of the Spirit of God from God himself, as if He were not altogether spirit. Therefore the accepted term came to be the Holy Spirit.606 In this form, however, his personality became more distinct and his separate existence more defined. Henceforth he is the messenger of God, performing miracles or causing them, speaking in the place of God, or defending His people Israel. Nay, more, the Holy Spirit is supposed to have dictated the words of Scripture to the sacred writers, and to have inspired the Men of the Great Synagogue in collecting the sacred writings into a canon.607

Moreover, the workings of the Holy Spirit continued long after the completion of the Biblical canon. All the chief institutions of the Synagogue originally claimed that they were prompted by the Holy Spirit, resting upon the leaders of the community. This claim was basic to the authority of tradition and the continuity of the authority of Jewish lore. It seems, however, that certain abuses were caused by miracle-workers who disseminated false doctrines under the alleged inspiration of the Holy Spirit. Therefore the rabbis restricted such claims to ancient times and insisted more strongly than ever upon the preservation of the traditional lore. For a time a substitute was found in the Bath Kol ("Echo" or "Whisper of a heavenly voice"), but this also was soon discredited by the schools.608 Obviously the rabbis desired to avert the deification of either the Holy Spirit or the Word. Sound common sense was their norm for interpreting the truth of the divine revelation. In other words, they relied on God alone as the living force in the development of Judaism.

6. But some sort of mediation was ascribed to several other spiritual forces. First, the Name of God often takes the place of God himself.609 When the name of the Deity was called over some hallowed spot, the worshipers felt that the presence of God also was bound up with the sacred place.610

"My name is in him," says God of the angel whom He sends to lead the people.611 The invocation of the name was believed to have an actual influence upon the Deity. Furthermore, since God is frequently represented as swearing by His own name,612 this ineffable name was invested with magic powers, as if God himself dwelt therein.613 Thus it came to be used as a talisman by the popular saints.614 Indeed, God is described as conjuring the depths of the abyss by His holy name, lest they overflow their boundaries.615 Moreover, the Name, like the Word, or Logos, was regarded as a creative power, so that we are told that before the world was created there were only God and His holy Name.616 Owing to the introduction of Adonai (the Lord) for JHVH, the pronunciation of the Name fell into oblivion and the Name itself became a mystery; therefore its cosmic element also was lost and it dropped into the sphere of mystic and philosophical speculation.

7. Another attribute of God which received some attention, owing to the frequent mention of the omnipotence of God in the Bible, was ha Geburah (the Power). A familiar rabbinic expression is: "We have heard from the mouth of the Power," that is, from the divine omnipotence.617 Two fundamental principles were early perceived in the moral order of the world: the punitive justice and compassion of God. These were taken as the meanings of the two most common Biblical names of God, JHVH and Elohim. Elohim, being occasionally used in dispensing justice,618 was thought to signify God in His capacity as Judge of the whole earth, and hence as the divine Justice. JHVH, on the other hand, meant the divine mercy, as it was used in the revelation of the long-suffering and merciful God to Moses after the sin of Israel before the golden calf.619 Thus both the rabbis and Philo620 often speak of these two attributes, justice and mercy, as though they constituted independent beings, deliberating with God as to what He should do. The Midrash tells in a parable how before the creation of man, Justice, Mercy, Truth, and Peace were called in by God as His counselors to deliberate whether or no man should be created.621

8. One Haggadah concludes from the passage about Creation in Proverbs, that there are three creative powers, Wisdom, Understanding, and Knowledge.622 Another derives from Scripture seven creative principles: Knowledge, Understanding, Might, Grace and Mercy, Justice and Rebuke;623 and seven attributes which do service before God's throne: Wisdom, Judgment and Justice, Grace and Mercy, Truth and Peace.624 By combining these lists of three and seven this was finally enlarged to ten, which became the basis for the entire mystic lore. Thus the Babylonian master Rab enumerates ten creative principles: Wisdom, Understanding, and Knowledge, Might and Power, Rebuke, Justice and Righteousness, Love and Mercy.625 It is hard to say whether the ten attributes of the Haggadah are at all connected with the ten Sefiroth (cosmic forces or circles) of the Cabbalah. These last are hardly the creation of pure monotheism, but rather emanations from the infinite, conceived after the pattern of heathen ideas.626

9. The assumption of all these intermediaries aimed chiefly to spiritualize the conception of God and to elevate Him above all child-like, anthropomorphic views, so that He becomes a free Mind ruling the whole universe. At the same time, it became natural to ascribe material substance to these intermediaries. As they filled the chasm between the supermundane Deity and the world of the senses, they had to share the nature of both matter and mind. Hence the Shekinah and the Holy Spirit are described by both the rabbis and the medieval philosophers as a fine, luminous, or ethereal substance.627 The entire ancient and medieval systems were modeled after the idea of a ladder leading up, step by step, from the lowest to the highest sphere; God, the Most High, being at the same time above the highest rung of the ladder and yet also a part of the whole.

10. Our modern system of thought holds the relation of God to nature and man to be quite different from all this. To our mind God is the only moral and spiritual power of life. He is mirrored in the moral and spiritual as well as intellectual nature of man, and therefore is near to the human conscience, owing to the divine forces within man himself. Not the world without, but the world within leads us to God and tells us what God is. Hence we need no

intermediary beings, and they all evaporate before our mental horizon like mist, pictures of the imagination without objective reality. Ibn Ezra says in the introduction to his commentary on the Bible that the human reason is the true intermediating angel between God and man, and we hold this to be true of both the intellect and the conscience. For the theologian and the student of religion to-day the center of gravity of religion is to be sought in psychology and anthropology. In all his upward striving, his craving and yearning for the highest and the best, in his loftiest aspirations and ideals, man, like Isaiah the prophet, can behold only the hem of God's garment; he seeks God above him, because he feels Him within himself. He must pass, however, through the various stages of growth, until his self-knowledge leads to the knowledge of the God before whom he kneels in awe. Then finally he feels Him as his Father, his Educator in the school of life, the Master of the universal plan in which the individual also has a place in building up the divine kingdom of truth, justice, and holiness on earth. For centuries he groped for God, until he received a Book to serve as "a lamp to his feet and a light to his path," to interpret to him his longing and his craving. Israel's Book of Books must ever be re-read and re-interpreted by Israel, the keeper of the book, through ages yet to come. Well may we say: the mediator between God and the world is man, the son of God; the mediator between God and humanity is Israel, the people of God.

Part II. Man

Chapter XXXIII. Man's Place in Creation

1. The doctrine concerning man is inseparably connected with that about God. Heathenism formed its deities after the image of man; they were merely human beings of a larger growth. Judaism, on the contrary, asserts that God is beyond comparison with mankind; He is a purely spiritual being without form or image, and therefore utterly unlike man. On the other hand, man has a divine nature, as he was made in the image of God, fashioned after His likeness. The highest and deepest in man, his mental, moral, and spiritual life, is the reflection of the divine nature implanted within him, a force capable of ever greater development toward perfection. This unique distinction among all creatures gives man the highest place in all creation.

2. The superiority of the human race is expressed differently in various passages in Scripture. According to the first chapter of Genesis the whole work of creation finds its culmination in man, whose making is introduced by a solemn appeal of God to the hosts of heaven: "Let us make man in our image, after our likeness."628 This declaration proclaimed that man was the completion and the climax of the physical creation, as well as the beginning of a new order of creation, a world of moral aims and purposes, of self-perfection and self-control. In the world of man all life is placed at the service of a higher ideal, after the divine pattern.

The second chapter of Genesis depicts man's creation differently. Here he appears as the first of created beings, leading a life of perfect innocence in the garden of divine bliss. Before him God brings all the newly created beings that he may give them a name and a purpose. But the Serpent enters Paradise as tempter, casting the seed of discord into the hearts of the man and the woman. As they prove too feeble to resist temptation, they can no longer remain in the heavenly garden in their former happy state. Only the memory of Paradise remains, a golden dream to cast hope over the life of struggle and labor into which they enter. The idea of the legend is that man's proper place is not among beings of the earth, but he can reach his lofty destiny only by arduous struggle with the world of the senses and a constant striving toward the divine. The same idea is expressed more directly in the eighth Psalm:

"What is man, that Thou art mindful of him?

And the son of man, that Thou thinkest of him?

Yet Thou hast made him but little lower than the godly beings (Elohim)

And hast crowned him with glory and honor.

Thou madest him to have dominion over the works of Thy hands;

Thou hast put all things under his feet."

3. According to the Haggadists,629 before the fall man excelled even the angels in appearance and wisdom, so that they were ready to prostrate themselves before him. Only when God caused a deep sleep to fall upon man, they recognized his frailty and kinship with other beings of the earth. The idea expressed in this legend resembles the one implied in the legend of Paradise, viz. man has a twofold nature. With his heavenly spirit he can soar freely to the highest realm of thought, above the station of the angels; yet his earthly frame holds him ever near the dust. It is this very contrast that constitutes his greatness, for it makes him a citizen of two worlds, one perishable, the other eternal. He is the highest result of Creation, the pride of the Creator.630 Thus he was appointed God's vice-regent on earth by the words spoken to the first man and woman: "Be fruitful, and multiply, and replenish the earth, and subdue it; and have dominion over the fish of the sea, and over the fowl of the air, and over every living thing that creepeth upon the earth."631 The rabbis add a striking comment upon the word R'du, which is used here for "have dominion" but which may also mean, "go down." They say: "The choice is left in man's own hand. If you maintain your heaven-born dignity, you will have dominion over all things; if not, you will descend to the level of the brute creation."632

4. An ancient Mishnah derives a significant lesson from the story of the creation of man633: "Both the vegetable and animal worlds were created in multitudes. Man alone was created as a single individual in order that he may realize that he constitutes a world in himself, and carries within him the true value of life. Hence each human being

is entitled to say: 'The whole world was created for my sake.' He who saves a single human life is as one who saves a whole world, and he who destroys a single human life is as one who destroys a whole world."

5. While it is man's spiritual side which is the image of God, yet he derives all his powers and faculties from earthly life, just as a tree draws its strength from the soil in which it is rooted. Judaism does not consider the soul the exclusive seat of the divine, as opposed to the body. In fact, Judaism admits no complete dualism of spirit and matter, however striking some aspects of their contrast may be. The whole human personality is divine, just so far as it asserts its freedom and molds its motives toward a divine end. In recognition of this fact Hillel claimed reverence for the human body as well as mind, comparing it to the homage rendered to the statue of a king, for man is made in the image of God, the King of all the world.634 Thus the Greek idea that man is a microcosm, a world in miniature, reflecting the cosmos on a smaller scale, was expressed in the Tannaitic schools as well.635 The stamp of divinity is borne by man in his entire heaven-aspiring nature, as he strives to elevate the very realm of the senses into the sphere of morality and holiness.

6. In this respect the Jewish view parts from that of Plato and the Hindu philosophers. These divide man into a pure celestial soul and an impure earthly body and hold that the physical life is tainted by sin, while the spirit is divine only in so far as it frees itself from its prison house of flesh. Judaism, on the other hand, emphasizes the unified character of man, by which he can bend all his faculties and functions to a godlike mastery over the material world. This appears first in his upright posture and heavenward glance, which proclaim him master over the whole animal world cowering before him in lowly dread. His whole bodily structure corresponds to this, with its constant growth, its wondrous symmetry, and the unique flexibility of the hands, with which he can perform ever new and greater achievements. Above all, we see the nobility of man in his high forehead and receding jaw, which contrast so strikingly with the structure of most animals and even with many of the lower races. Indeed, primitive man could scarcely imagine a nobler pattern by which to model his deity than the figure of a man.

7. In fact, the Biblical verse, "God created man after the image of the divine beings" (elohim), was originally taken literally, in the sense that angels posed as models for the creation of man.636 The phrase was referred to the spiritual, god-like nature of man only when the difference between material and spiritual things became better understood, and man obtained a clearer knowledge of himself. Man grew to feel that his craving for the perfect, whether in the field of truth and right, or of beauty, is the force which lifts him, in spite of all his limitations, into the realm of the divine. His soaring imagination and ceaseless longing for perfection disclose before his eyes a partial vista of the infinite. The human spirit carries mortal man above the confines of time and space into those boundless realms where God resides in lonely majesty.637

Man did not emanate perfect from the hand of the Creator, but ready for an ever greater perfection. Being the last of all created beings, as the Midrash says, he can be put to shame by the smallest insect, which is prior to him. Yet before the beginning of creation a light shone upon his spirit that has illumined his achievements through untold generations.638

8. The resemblance of man to God is attributed also to his free will and self-consciousness, by which he claims moral dignity and mastery over all things.639 Still, all these superior qualities which we call human are not ready-made endowments, free gifts bestowed by God; they are simply potentialities which may be gradually developed. Man must strive to attain the place destined for him in the scheme of creation by the exertion of his own will and the unfolding of the powers that lie within him. The impulse toward self-perfection, which is constantly stimulated by the desire to overcome obstacles and to extend one's power, knowledge, and possessions, forms the kernel of the divine in man. This is the "spirit in man, and the breath of the Almighty, that giveth them understanding."640 Thus the teaching of modern science, of the gradual ascent of man through all the stages of animal life, does not impair the lofty position in creation which Judaism has assigned him. Plant and animal are what they have always been, children of the earth; man with his heaven-aspiring soul is the image of his Creator, a child of God. Giver of name and purpose to all things about him, he ranks above the angels; he "marches on while all the rest stand still."641

Chapter XXXIV. The Dual Nature of Man

1. According to Jewish doctrines, man is formed by a union of two natures: the flesh, which he shares with all the animals, and the spirit, which renders him a child of God. The former is rooted in the earth and is earthward bent;

the latter is a "breath from God" and strives to unfold the divine in man until he attains the divine image. This discord brings a tremendous internal conflict, leading from one historic stage to another, achieving ever higher things, intellectual, moral, and spiritual, until at last the whole earth is to be a divine kingdom, the dwelling-place of truth, goodness, and holiness.

2. According to the Biblical view man consists of flesh (basar) and spirit (ruah). The term flesh is used impartially of all animals, hence the Biblical term "all flesh"642 includes both man and beast. The body becomes a living being by being penetrated with the "breath of life" (ruah hayim), at whose departure the living body turns at once into a lifeless clod. This breath of life is possessed by the animal as well as by man, as both of them breathe the air. Hence in ancient tongues "breath" and "soul" are used as synonyms, as the Hebrew nefesh and neshamah, the Latin anima and spiritus, the Greek pneuma and psyche. A different primitive belief connected the soul with the blood, noting that man or beast dies when the hot life-blood flows out of the body, so that we read in the Bible, "the blood is the soul."643 In this the soul is identified with the life, while the word ruah, denoting the moving force of the air, is used more in the sense of spirit or soul as distinct from the body.

Thus both man and beast possess a soul, nefesh. The soul of man is merely distinguished by its richer endowment, its manifold faculties by which it is enabled to move forward to higher things. Thus the animal soul is bound for all time to its destined place, while the divine spirit in man makes him a free creative personality, self-conscious and god-like. For this reason the creation of man forms a special act in the account in Genesis. Both the plant and animal worlds rose at God's bidding from the soil of mother earth, and the soul of the animal is limited in origin and goal by the earthly sphere. The creation of man inaugurates a new world. God is described as forming the body of man from the dust of the earth and then breathing His spirit into the lifeless frame, endowing it with both life and personality. The whole man, both body and soul, has thus the potentiality of a higher and nobler life.

3. Accordingly Scripture does not have a thorough-going dualism, of a carnal nature which is sinful and a spiritual nature which is pure. We are not told that man is composed of an impure earthly body and a pure heavenly soul, but instead that the whole of man is permeated by the spirit of God. Both body and soul are endowed with the power of continuous self-improvement. In order to see the great superiority of the Jewish view over the heathen one, we need only study the old Babylonian legend preserved by Berosus. In this the deity made man by mixing earth with some of its own life-blood, thus endowing the human soul with higher powers. In the Bible the difference between man and beast does not lie in the blood, although the blood is still thought to be the life. The distinction of man is in the spirit, ruah, which emanates from God and penetrates both body and soul, lifting the whole man into a higher realm and making him a free moral personality.

Still the Bible makes no clear distinction between the three terms, nefesh, neshamah, and ruah.644 Philo first distinguished between three different substances of the soul, but his theory was the Platonic one, for which he simply used the three Biblical names.645 The Jewish philosophers of the Middle Ages, beginning with Saadia, took the same attitude, even though they realized more or less that the division of the soul into three substances has no Scriptural warrant.646 In rabbinical literature this division is scarcely known, and there is little mention of either the animal soul, nefesh, or the vital spark, ruah. Instead the word neshamah is used for the human psyche as the higher spiritual substance, and the contrast to it is not the Biblical basar, flesh, but the Aramaic guph, body.647 This bears a trace of Persian dualism, with its strong contrast between the earthly body and the heavenly soul.

4. In fact, rabbinical Judaism does not recognize any relationship between the soul of the animal and that of man, but claims that man has a special type of existence. The Midrash tells648 that God formed Adam's body so as to reach from earth to heaven, and then caused the soul to enter it. In the same way God implants the soul into the embryo before its birth and while in the womb. Before this the soul had a bird-like existence in an immense celestial cage (guph = columbarium), and when it leaves the body in death, it again takes its flight toward heaven. There its conduct on earth will reap a reward in the garden of eternal bliss or a punishment in the infernal regions. The belief in the preëxistence of the soul was shared by the rabbis with the apocryphal authors and Philo.649

However, rabbinical Judaism never followed Philo so far in the footsteps of Plato as to consider the body or the flesh the source of impurity and sin, or "the prison house of the soul." This view is fundamental in the Paulinian system of other-worldliness. For the rabbis the sensuous desire of the body (yezer) is a tendency toward sin, but never a compulsion. The weakness of the flesh may cause a straying from the right path, but man can turn the desires of the flesh into the service of the good. He can always assert his divine power of freedom by opposing the evil inclination (yezer ha ra) with the good inclination (yezer ha tob) to overcome it.650 In fact, the rabbis are so far from acknowledging the existence of a compulsion of evil in the flesh, that they point to the history of great men as proof that the highest characters have the mightiest passions in their souls, and that their greatness consists in the will by which they have learned to control themselves.651

5. In the light of modern science the whole theory separating body and soul falls to the ground, and the one connecting man more closely with the animal world is revived. In this connection we think of the idea which medieval thinkers adopted from Plato and Aristotle, that there is a substance of souls—nefesh hahiyonith—which forms the basic life-force of men and animals. Physiology and psychology reveal the interaction and dependence of body and soul in the lowest forms of animal life as well as in the higher forms, including man. The beginnings of the human mind must be sought once for all in the animal, just as the origin of the animal reaches back into the plant world. Indeed, Aristotle anticipates the discoveries of modern science, placing the vegetative and animal souls beside the spirit of man. Thus motion and sensibility form the lower boundary-line of the animal kingdom, and self-consciousness and self-determination are the criteria of humanity.

Yet this very self-conscious freedom which forms man's personality, his ego, lifts him into a realm of free action under higher motives, transcending nature's law of necessity, and therefore not falling within the domain of natural science. Dust-born man, notwithstanding his earthly limitations, in spite of his kinship to mollusk and mammal, enters the realm of the divine spirit. In the Midrash the rabbis remark that man shares the nature of both animals and angels.652 Admitting this, we feel that he is tied neither to heaven nor to the earth, but free to lift himself above all creatures or sink below them all.

6. Endowed with this dual nature, man stands in the very center of the universe, and God esteems him "equal in value to the entire creation," as Rabbi Nehemiah says of a single human soul.653 Rabbi Akiba stresses the image of God in humanity when he says: "Beloved is man, for he is created in God's image, and it was a special token of love that he became conscious of it. Beloved is Israel, for they are called the children of God, and it was a special token of love that they became conscious of it."654 The Midrash compares man to God in exquisite manner: "Just as God permeates the world and carries it, unseen yet seeing all, enthroned within as the Only One, the Perfect, and the Pure, yet never to be reached or found out; so the soul penetrates and carries the body, as the one pure and luminous being which sees and holds all things, while itself unseen and unreached."655 The conception of the soul is here divested of every sensory attribute, and portrayed as a divine force within the body. This conception, which was accepted by the medieval philosophers, is thoroughly consistent with our view of the world. The soul it is which mirrors both the material and spiritual worlds and holds them in mutual relation through its own power. It is at the same time swayed upward and downward by its various cravings, heavenly and earthly, and this very tension constitutes the dual nature of the human soul.

Chapter XXXV. The Origin and Destiny of Man

1. Of all created beings man alone possesses the power of self-determination; he assigns his destiny to himself. While he endeavors to find the object of all other things and even of his own existence in the world, he finds his own purpose within himself. Star and stone, plant and beast fulfill their purpose in the whole plan of creation by their existence and varied natures, and are accordingly called "good" as they are. Man, however, realizes that he must accomplish his purpose by his manner of life and the voluntary exertion of his own powers. He is "good" only as far as he fulfills his destiny on earth. He is not good by mere existence, but by his conduct. Not what he is, but what he ought to be gives value to his being. He is good or bad according to the direction of his will and acts by the imperative: "I ought" or "I ought not," which comes to him in his conscience, the voice of God calling to his soul.

2. The problem of human destiny is answered by Judaism with the idea that God is the ideal and pattern of all morality. The answer given, then, is "To walk in the ways of God, to be righteous and just," as He is.656 The prophet Micah expressed it in the familiar words: "It has been told thee, O man, what is good, and what the Lord doth require of thee: Only to do justly, and to love mercy, and to walk humbly with thy God."657 Accordingly the Bible considers men of the older generations the prototypes of moral conduct, "righteous men who walked with God." Such men were Enoch, Noah, and above all Abraham, to whom God said: "I am God Almighty; walk before Me, and be thou whole-hearted. And I will make My covenant between thee and Me."658 The rabbis singled out Abraham as the type of a perfect man on account of his love of righteousness and peace; contrasting him with Adam who

sinned, they beheld him as "the great man among the heroes of the ancient times." They even considered him the type of true humanity, in whom the object of creation was attained.659

3. This moral consciousness, however, which tells man to walk in the ways of God and be perfect, is also the source of shame and remorse. With such an ideal man must feel constantly that he falls short, that he is not what he ought to be. Only the little child, who knows nothing as yet of good and evil, can preserve the joy of life unmarred. Similarly, primitive man, being ignorant of guilt, could pass his days without care or fear. But as soon as he becomes conscious of guilt, discord enters his soul, and he feels as if he had been driven from the presence of God.

This feeling is allegorized in the Paradise legend. The garden of bliss, half earthly, half heavenly, which is elsewhere called the "mountain of God,"660 a place of wondrous trees, beasts, and precious stones, whence the four great rivers flow, is the abode of divine beings. The first man and woman could dwell in it only so long as they lived in harmony with God and His commandments. As soon as the tempter in the shape of the serpent called forth a discord between the divine will and human desire, man could no longer enjoy celestial bliss, but must begin the dreary earthly life, with its burdens and trials.

4. This story of the fall of the first man is an allegorical description of the state of childlike innocence which man must leave behind in order to attain true strength of character. It is based upon a view common to all antiquity of a descent of the race; that is: first came the golden age, when man led a life of ease and pleasure in company with the gods; then an age of silver, another of brass, and finally the iron age, with its toil and bitter woe. Thus did evil deeds and wild passions increase among men. This view fails utterly to recognize the value of labor as a civilizing force making for progress, and it contradicts the modern historical view. The prophets of Israel placed the golden age at the end, not the beginning of history, so that the purpose of mankind was to establish a heavenly kingdom upon the earth. In fact, the fall of man is not referred to anywhere in Scripture and never became a doctrine, or belief, of Judaism. On the contrary, the Hellenistic expounders of the Bible take it for granted that the story is an allegory, and the book of Proverbs understands the tree of life symbolically, in the verse: "She (the Torah) is a tree of life to them that lay hold upon her."661

5. Still the rabbis in Talmud and Midrash accepted the legend in good faith as historical662 and took it literally as did the great English poet:

"The fruit

Of that forbidden tree whose mortal taste

Brought death into the world, and all our woe,

With loss of Eden."

In fact, they even followed the Persian dualism with its evil principle, the primeval serpent, or the Babylonian legend of the sea-monster Tiamat, and regarded the serpent in Paradise as a demon. He was identified with Satan, the arch-fiend, and later with evil in general, the yezer ha ra.663 Thus the belief arose that the poisonous breath of the serpent infected all generations, causing death even of the sinless.664 The apocrypha also held that the envy of Satan brought death into the world.665 This prepared for the dismal church doctrine of original sin, the basis of Paul's teachings, which demanded a blood atonement for curse-laden humanity, and found it after the pagan pattern in the vicarious sacrifice of a dying god.666

Against such perversion of the simple Paradise story the sound common sense of the Jewish people rebelled. While the early Talmudists occasionally mention the poisoning of the human race by the serpent, they find an antidote for the Jewish people in the covenant with Abraham or that of Sinai.667 One cannot, however, discern the least indication of belief in original sin, either as inherent in the human race or inherited by them. Nor does the liturgy express any such idea, especially for the Day of Penitence, when it would certainly be mentioned if the conception found any place in Jewish doctrine. On the contrary, the prevailing thought of Judaism is that of Deuteronomy and Ezekiel,668 that "Each man dies by his own sin," that every soul must bear only the consequences of his own deeds. The rabbis even state that no man dies unless he has brought it upon himself by his own sin, and mention especially certain exceptions to this rule, such as the four saintly men who died without sin,669 or certain children whose death was due to the sin of their parents.670 They could never admit that the whole human race was so corrupted by the sin of the first man that it is still in a state of sinfulness.

6. Of course, the rabbinical schools took literally the Biblical story of the fall of man and laid the chief blame upon woman, who fell a prey to the wiles of the serpent. This is done even by Ben Sira, who says: "With woman came the beginning of sin, and through her we all must die."[671] So the Talmud says that due to woman, man, the crown, light, and life of creation, lost his purity, his luster, and his immortality.[672] The Biblical verse, "They did eat, and the eyes of them both were opened," is interpreted by Rabbi Johanan ben Zakkai and Rabbi Akiba as "They saw the dire consequences of their sin upon all coming generations."[673] The fall of man is treated most elaborately in the same spirit in the two apocalyptic books written after the destruction of the Second Temple, the Apocalypse of Baruch and the IV Book of Esdras.[674] The incompatibility of divine love with the sufferings of man and of the Jewish people on account of the sin of the first man is solved by an appeal to the final Day of Judgment, and the striking remark is added that, after all, "each is his own Adam and is held responsible for his own sin." We cannot deny that these two books contain much that is near the Paulinian view of original sin. It seems, however, that the Jewish teachers were put on their guard by the emphasis of this pessimistic dogma by the nascent Church, and did their best to give a different aspect to the story of the first sin. Thus they say: "If Adam had but shown repentance, and done penance after he committed his sin, he would have been spared the death penalty."[675] Moreover, they actually represent Adam and Eve as patterns of repentant sinners, who underwent severe penance and thus obtained the promise of divine mercy and also of final resurrection.[676] Instead of transmitting the heritage of sin to coming generations, the first man is for them an example of repentance. So do the Haggadists tell us quite characteristically that God merely wanted to test the first man by an insignificant command, so that the first representative of the human race should show whether he was worthy to enter eternal life in his mortal garb, as did Enoch and Elijah. As he could not stand the test, he forfeited the marks of divine rank, his celestial radiance, his gigantic size, and his power to overcome death.[677] Obviously the Biblical story was embellished with material from the Persian legend of the fall of Yima or Djemshid, the first man, from superhuman greatness because of his sin,[678] but it was always related frankly as a legend, and could never influence the Jewish conception of the fall of man.

7. Judaism rejects completely the belief in hereditary sin and the corruption of the flesh. The Biblical verse, "God made man upright; but they have sought out many inventions,"[679] is explained in the Midrash: "Upright and just as is God, He made man after His likeness in order that he might strive after righteousness, and unfold ever more his god-like nature, but men in their dissensions have marred the divine image."[680] With reference to another verse in Ecclesiastes:[681] "The dust returneth unto the earth as it was, and the spirit returneth unto God who gave it," the rabbis teach "Pure as the soul is when entering upon its earthly career, so can man return it to his Maker."[682] Therefore the pious Jew begins his daily prayers with the words: "My God, the soul which Thou hast given me is pure."[683] The life-long battle with sin begins only at the age when sensual desire, "the evil inclination," awakens in youth; then the state of primitive innocence makes way for the sterner contest for manly virtue and strength of character.

8. In fact, the whole Paradise story could never be made the basis for a dogma. The historicity of the serpent is denied by Saadia;[684] the rabbis transfer Paradise with the tree of life to heaven as a reward for the future;[685] and both Nahmanides the mystic and Maimonides the philosopher give it an allegorical meaning.[686] On the other hand, the Haggadic teachers perceived the simple truth that a life of indolence in Paradise would incapacitate man for his cultural task, and that the toils and struggles inflicted on man as a curse are in reality a blessing. Therefore they laid special stress on the Biblical statement: "He put man into the garden of Eden to dress it and to keep it."[687] The following parable is especially suggestive: "When Adam heard the stern sentence passed: 'Thou shalt eat the herb of the field,' he burst into tears, and said: 'Am I and my ass to eat out of the same manger?' Then came another sentence from God to reassure him, 'In the sweat of thy face shalt thou eat bread,' and forthwith he became aware that man shall attain a higher dignity by dint of labor."[688] Indeed, labor transforms the wilderness into a garden and the earth into a habitation worthy of the son of God. The "book of the generations of man" which begins with Adam is accordingly not the history of man's descent, but of his continuous ascent, of ever higher achievements and aspirations; it is not a record of the fall of man, but of his rise from age to age. According to the Midrash[689] God opened before Adam the book with the deeds and names of the leading spirits of all the coming generations, showing him the latent powers of the human intellect and soul. The phrase, "the fall of man," can mean, in fact, only the inner experience of the individual, who does fall from his original idea of purity and divine nobility into transgression and sin. It cannot refer to mankind as a whole, for the human race has never experienced a fall, nor is it affected by original or hereditary sin.

Chapter XXXVI. God's Spirit in Man

1. Man is placed in an animal world of dull feelings, of blind and crude cravings. Yet his clear understanding, his self-conscious will and his aspirations forward and upward lead him into a higher world where he obtains insight into the order and unity of all things. By the spirit of God he is able to understand material things and grasp them in their relations; thus he can apply all his knowledge and creative imagination to construct a world of ideals. But this world, in all its truth, beauty and goodness, is still limited and finite, a feeble shadow of the infinite world of God. As the Bible says: "The spirit of man is the lamp of the Lord, searching all the inward parts."690 "It is a spirit in man, and the breath of the Almighty, that giveth them understanding."691

2. According to the Biblical conception, the spirit of God endows men with all their differing capacities; it gives to one man wisdom by which he penetrates into the causes of existence and orders facts into a scientific system; to another the seeing eye by which he captures the secret of beauty and creates works of art; and to a third the genius to perceive the ways of God, the laws of virtue, that he may become a teacher of ethical truth. In other words, the spirit of God is "the spirit of wisdom and understanding, the spirit of counsel and might, the spirit of knowledge and the fear of the Lord."692 It works upon the scientific interest of the investigator, the imagination of the artist and poet, the ethical and social sense of the prophet, teacher, statesman, and lawgiver. Thus their high and holy vision of the divine is brought home to the people and implanted within them under the inspiration of God. In commenting upon the Biblical verse, "Wisdom and might are His ... He giveth wisdom to the wise, and knowledge to them that know understanding,"693 the sages wisely remark, "God carefully selects those who possess wisdom for His gift of wisdom." Even as a musical instrument must be attuned for the finer notes that it may have a clear, resonant tone, so the human soul must be made especially susceptible to the gifts of the spirit in order to be capable of unfolding them. Thus the Talmud records an interesting dialogue on this very passage between a Roman matron familiar with the Scripture, and Rabbi Jose ben Halafta. She asked sarcastically, "Would it not have been more generous of your God to have given wisdom to those that are unwise than to those that already possess it?" Thereupon the Jewish master replied, "If you were to lend a precious ornament, would you not lend it to one who was able to make use of it? So God gives the treasure of wisdom to the wise, who know how to appreciate and develop it, not to the unwise, who do not know its value."694

3. Thus the diverse gifts of the divine spirit are distributed differently among the various classes and tribes of men, according to their capacity and the corresponding task which is assigned them by Providence. The divine spark is set aglow in each human soul, sometimes feebly, sometimes brightly, but it blazes high only in the privileged personality or group. The mutual relationship between God and man is recognized by the Synagogue in the Eighteen Benedictions, where the one directly following the three praises of God is devoted to wisdom and knowledge: "Thou favorest man with knowledge, and teachest mortals understanding. So favor us with knowledge, understanding, and discernment from Thee. Blessed art Thou, O Lord, gracious Giver of knowledge."695 This petition, remarks Jehuda ha Levi,696 deserves its position as first among these prayers, because wisdom brings us nearer to God. It is also noteworthy that the Synagogue prescribes a special benediction at the sight of a renowned sage, even if he is not a Jew, reading, "Praised be He who has imparted of His wisdom to flesh and blood."697

4. Maimonides holds that in the same degree as a man studies the works of God in nature, he will be filled with longing for direct knowledge of God and true love of Him.698 "Not only religion, but also the sciences emanate from God, both being the outcome of the wisdom which God imparts to all nations,"—thus wrote a sixteenth-century rabbi, Loewe ben Bezalel of Prague, known usually as "the eminent Rabbi Loewe."699 The men of the Talmud also accord the palm in certain types of knowledge to heathen sages, and did not hesitate to ascribe to some heathens the highest knowledge of God in their time.700 As a mystic of the thirteenth century, Isaac ben Latif, says: "That faith is the most perfect which perceives truth most fully, since God is the source of all truth."701 Of the two heads of the Babylonian academies, Rab and Samuel, one asserted that Moses through his prophetic genius reached forty-nine of the fifty degrees of the divine understanding (as the fiftieth is reserved for God alone), while the other claimed the same distinction for King Solomon as the result of his wisdom.702

5. Thus the spirit of God creates in man both consciously and unconsciously a world of ideas, which proves him a being of a higher order in creation. This impulse may work actively, searching, investigating, and creating, or passively as an instrument of a higher power. At first it is a dim, uncertain groping of the spirit; then the mind acquires greater lucidity by which it illumines the dark world; and, as one question calls for the other and one

thought suggests another, the world of ideas opens up as a well-connected whole. Thus man creates by slow steps his languages, the arts and sciences, ethics, law and all the religions with their varying practices and doctrines. At times this spirit bursts forth with greater vehemence in great men, geniuses who lift the race with one stroke to a higher level. Such men may say, in the words of David, the holy singer: "The spirit of the Lord spoke by me, and His word was upon my tongue."703 They may repeat the experience of Eliphaz the friend of Job:

"Now a word was secretly brought to me,

And mine ear received a whisper thereof.

In thoughts from the visions of the night,

When deep sleep falleth on men,

Fear came upon me, and trembling,

And all my bones were made to shake.

Then a spirit passed before my face,

That made the hair of my flesh to stand up.

It stood still, but I could not discern the appearance thereof;

A form was before mine eyes;

I heard a still voice."704

In such manner men of former ages received a religious revelation, a divine message.

6. The divine spirit always selects as its instruments individuals with special endowments. Still, insight into history shows that these men must needs have grown from the very heart of their own people and their own age, in order that they might hold a lofty position among them and command attention for their message. However far the people or the age may be from the man chosen by God, the multitude must feel at least that the divine spirit speaks through him, or works within him. Or, if not his own time, then a later generation must respond to his message, lest it be lost entirely to the world.

The rabbis, who knew nothing of laws of development for the human mind, assumed that the first man, made by God Himself, must have known every branch of knowledge and skill, that the spirit of God must have been most vigorous in him.705 They therefore believed in a primeval revelation, coeval with the first man. Our age, with its tremendous emphasis on the historical view, sees the divine spirit manifested most clearly in the very development and growth of all life, social, intellectual, moral and spiritual, proceeding steadily toward the highest of all goals. With this emphasis, however, on process, we must lay stress equally on the origin, on the divine impulse or initiative in this historical development, the spirit which gives direction and value to the whole.

Chapter XXXVII. Free Will and Moral Responsibility

1. Judaism has ever emphasized the freedom of the will as one of its chief doctrines. The dignity and greatness of man depends largely upon his freedom, his power of self-determination. He differs from the lower animals in his independence of instinct as the dictator of his actions. He acts from free choice and conscious design, and is able to change his mind at any moment, at any new evidence or even through whim. He is therefore responsible for his every act or omission, even for his every intention. This alone renders him a moral being, a child of God; thus the moral sense rests upon freedom of the will.706

2. The idea of moral freedom is expressed as early as the first pages of the Bible, in the words which God spoke to Cain while he was planning the murder of his brother Abel: "Whether or not, thou offerest an acceptable gift," (New Bible translation: "If thou doest well, shall it not be lifted up? and if thou doest not well,") "sin coucheth at the door; and unto thee is its desire, but thou mayest rule over it."707 Here, without any reference to the sin of Adam in the first generation, the man of the second generation is told that he is free to choose between good and evil, that he alone is responsible before God for what he does or omits to do. This certainly indicates that the moral freedom of man is not impaired by hereditary sin, or by any evil power outside of man himself. This principle is established in

the words of Moses spoken in the name of God: "I have set before thee life and death, the blessing and the curse; therefore choose life, that thou mayest live, thou and thy seed."708 In like manner Jeremiah proclaims in God's name: "Behold I set before you the way of life and the way of death."709

3. From these passages and many similar ones the sages derived their oft-repeated idea that man stands ever at the parting of the ways, to choose either the good or the evil path.710 Thus the words spoken by God to the angels when Adam and Eve were to be expelled from Paradise: "Behold, the man is become as one of us, to know good and evil," are interpreted by R. Akiba: "He was given the choice to go the way of life or the way of death, but he chose the way of death by eating of the forbidden fruit."711 R. Akiba emphasizes the principle of the freedom of the will again in the terse saying: "All things are foreseen (by God), but free will is granted (to man)."712

4. At the first encounter of Judaism with those philosophical schools of Hellas which denied the freedom of the human will, the Jewish teachers insisted strongly on this principle. The first reference is found in Ben Sira, who refutes the arguments of the Determinists that God could make man sin, and then goes on: "God created man at the beginning, endowing him with the power of self-determination, saying to him: If thou but willest, thou canst observe My commandments; to practice faithfulness is a matter of free will.... As when fire and water are put before thee, so that thou mayest reach forth thy hand to that which thou desirest, so are life and death placed before man, and whatever he chooses of his own desire will be given to him."713 The Book of Enoch voices this truth also in the forceful sentences: "Sin has not been sent upon the earth (from above), but men have produced it out of themselves; therefore they who commit sin are condemned."714 We read similar sentiments in the Psalms of Solomon, a Pharisean work of the first pre-Christian century:715 "Our actions are the outcome of the free choice and power of our own soul; to practice justice or injustice lies in the work of our own hands."

The Apocalypse of Ezra is especially instructive in the great stress which it lays on freedom, in connection with its chief theme, the sinfulness of the children of Adam. "This is the condition of the contest which man who is born on earth must wage, that, if he be conquered by the evil inclination, he must suffer that of which thou hast spoken (the tortures of hell), but if he be victorious, he shall receive (the reward) which I (the angel) have mentioned. For this is the way whereof Moses spoke when he lived, saying unto the people, 'Choose life, that thou mayest live!'... For all who knew Me not in life when they received My benefits, who despised My law when they yet had freedom, and did not heed the door of repentance while it was still open before them, but disregarded it, after death they shall come to know it!"716

5. Hellenistic Judaism also, particularly Philo,717 considered the truly divine in man to be his free will, which distinguishes him from the beast. Yet Hellenistic naturalism could not grasp the fact that man's power to do evil in opposition to God, the Source of the good, is the greatest reminder of his moral responsibility. Josephus likewise mentions frequently as a characteristic teaching of the Pharisees that man's free will determines his acts without any compulsion of destiny.718 Only we must not accept too easily the words of this Jewish historian, who wrote for his Roman masters and, therefore, represented the Jewish parties as so many philosophical schools after the Greek pattern. The Pharisean doctrine is presented most tersely in the Talmudic maxim: "Everything is in the hands of God except the fear of God."719 Like the quotation from R. Akiba above, this contains the great truth that man's destiny is determined by Providence, but his character depends upon his own free decision. This idea recurs frequently in such Talmudic sayings as these: "The wicked are in the power of their desires; the righteous have their desires in their own power;"720 "The eye, the ear, and the nostrils are not in man's power, but the mouth, the hand, and the feet are."721 That is, the impressions we receive from the world without us come involuntarily, but our acts, our steps, and our words arise from our own volition.

6. A deeper insight into the problem of free will is offered in two other Talmudic sayings; the one is: "Whosoever desires to pollute himself with sin will find all the gates open before him, and whosoever desires to attain the highest purity will find all the forces of goodness ready to help him."722 The other reads: "It can be proved by the Torah, the Prophets, and the other sacred writings that man is led along the road which he wishes to follow."723

As a matter of fact, no person is absolutely free, for innumerable influences affect his decisions, consciously and unconsciously. For this reason many thinkers, both ancient and modern, consider freedom a delusion and hold to determinism, the doctrine that man acts always under the compulsion of external and internal forces. In opposition to this theory is one incontestable fact, our own inner sense of freedom which tells us at every step that we have acted, and at every decision that we have decided. Man can maintain his own power of self-determination against all influences from without and within; his will is the final arbiter over every impulse and every pressure.

Moreover, as we penetrate more deeply into the working of the mind, we see that a long series of our own voluntary acts has occasioned much that we consider external, that the very pressure of the past on our thoughts, feelings and habits, which leaves so little weight for the decision of the moment, is really only our past will influencing our present will. That is, the will may determine itself, but it does not do so arbitrarily; its action is along the lines of its own character. We have the power to receive the influence of either the noble or the ignoble series of impressions, and thus to yield either to the lofty or the low impulses of the soul.

In this way the rabbis interpret various expressions of Scripture which would seem to limit man's freedom, as where God induces man to good or evil acts, or hardens the heart of Pharaoh so that he will not let the Israelites go, until the plagues had been fulfilled upon him and his people.724 They understand in such an instance that a man's heart has a prevailing inclination toward right or wrong, the expression of his character, and that God encouraged this inclination along the evil course; thus the freedom of the human will was kept intact.

7. The doctrine of man's free will presents another difficulty from the side of divine omniscience. For if God knows in advance what is to happen, then man's acts are determined by this very foreknowledge; he is no longer free, and his moral responsibility becomes an idle dream. In order to escape this dilemma, the Mohammedan theologians were compelled to limit either the divine omniscience or human freedom, and most of them resorted to the latter method. It is characteristic of Judaism that its great thinkers, from Saadia to Maimonides and Gersonides,725 dared not alter the doctrine of man's free will and moral responsibility, but even preferred to limit the divine omniscience. Hisdai Crescas is the only one to restrict human freedom in favor of the foreknowledge of God.726

8. The insistence of Judaism on unrestricted freedom of will for each individual entirely excludes hereditary sin. This is shown in the traditional explanation of the verse of the Decalogue: "Visiting the iniquity of the fathers upon the children unto the third and fourth generation of them that hate Me."727 According to the rabbis the words "of them that hate Me" do not refer to the fathers, according to the plain meaning of the passage, but to the children and children's children. These are to be punished only when they hate God and follow the evil example of their fathers.728 Despite example and hereditary disposition, the descendants of evildoers can lead a virtuous life, and their punishment comes only when they fail to resist the evil influences of their parental household. To illustrate the Biblical words, "Who can bring a clean thing out of an unclean?"729 the rabbis single out Abraham, the son of Terah, Hezekiah, the son of Ahaz, and Josiah, the son of Manasseh.730 Man, being made in God's image, determines his own character by his own free choice; by his will he can raise or lower himself in the scale of being.

9. The fundamental character of the doctrine of free will for Judaism is shown by Maimonides, who devotes a special chapter of his Code to it,731 and calls it the pillar of Israel's faith and morality, since through it alone man manifests his god-like sovereignty. For should his freedom be limited by any kind of predestination, he would be deprived of his moral responsibility, which constitutes his real greatness. In endeavoring to reconcile God's omnipotence and omniscience with man's freedom, Maimonides says that God wants man to erect a kingdom of morality without interference from above; moreover, God's knowledge is different in kind from that of man, and thus is not an infringement upon man's freedom, as the human type of knowledge would be. However, Abraham ben David of Posquieres blames Maimonides for proposing questions which he could not answer satisfactorily in the Code, which is intended for non-philosophical readers. The fact is that this is only another of the problems insoluble to human reasoning; the freedom of the will must remain for all time a postulate of moral responsibility, and therefore of religion.

Chapter XXXVIII. The Meaning of Sin

1. Sin is a religious conception. It does not signify a breach of law or morality, or of popular custom and sacred usage, but an offense against God, provoking His punishment. As long as the deity is merely dreaded as an external power, not adored as a moral power ruling life from within for a holy purpose, sin, too, is considered a purely formal offense. The deity demands to be worshiped by certain rites and may be propitiated by other formal acts.732 For Judaism, however, sin is a straying from the path of God, an offense against the divine order of holiness. Thus it signifies an abuse of the freedom granted man as his most precious boon. Therefore sin has a twofold character; formally it is an offense against the majesty of God, whose laws are broken; essentially it is a severance of the soul's inner relations to God, an estrangement from Him.

2. Scripture has three different terms for sin, which do not differ greatly in point of language, but indicate three stages of thought. First is het or hataah, which connotes any straying from the right path, whether caused by levity, carelessness, or design, and may even include wrongs committed unwittingly, shegagah. Second is avon, a crookedness or perversion of the straight order of the law. Third is pesha, a wicked act committed presumptuously in defiance of God and His law. As a matter of course, the conception of sin was deepened by degrees, as the prophets, psalmists and moralists grew to think of God as the pattern of the highest moral perfection, as the Holy One before whom an evil act or thought cannot abide.

The rabbis usually employed the term aberah, that is, a transgression of a divine commandment. In contrast to this they used mitzwah, a divine command, which denotes also the whole range of duty, including the desire and intention of the human soul. From this point of view every evil design or impulse, every thought and act contrary to God's law, becomes a sin.

3. Sin arises from the weakness of the flesh, the desire of the heart, and accordingly in the first instance from an error of judgment. The Bible frequently speaks of sin as "folly."[733] A rabbinical saying brings out this same idea: "No one sins unless the spirit of folly has entered into him to deceive him."[734] A sinful imagination lures one to sin; the repetition of the forbidden act lowers the barrier of the commandment, until the trespass is hardened into "callous" and "stubborn" disregard, and finally into "reckless defiance" and "insolent godlessness." Such a process is graphically expressed by the various terms used in the Bible. According to the rabbinical figure, "sin appears at first as thin as a spider's web, but grows stronger and stronger, until it becomes like a wagon-rope to bind a man." Or, "sin comes at first as a passer-by to tarry for a moment, then as a visitor to stay, finally as the master of the house to claim possession." Therefore it is incumbent upon us to "guard" the heart, and not "to go astray following after our eyes and our heart."[735]

4. According to the doctrine of Judaism no one is sinful by nature. No person sins by an inner compulsion. But as man has a nature of flesh, which is sensuous and selfish, each person is inclined to sin and none is perfectly free from it. "Who can say: I have made my heart clean, I am pure from any sin?"[736] This is the voice of the Bible and of all human experience; "For there is not a righteous man upon earth, that doeth good, and sinneth not."[737] The expression occurs repeatedly in Job: "Shall mortal man be just before God? Shall a man be pure before his Maker?"[738] Even Moses is represented in numerous passages as showing human foibles and failings.[739] In fact, "the greater the personality, the more severely will God call him to account for the smallest trespass, for God desires to be 'sanctified' by His righteous ones."[740] The Midrash tells us that no one is to be called holy, until death has put an end to his struggle with the ever-lurking tempter within, and he lies in the earth with the victor's crown of peace upon his brow.[741] When we read the stern sentence: "Behold, He putteth no trust in His holy ones,"[742] the rabbis refer us to the patriarchs, each of whom had his faults.[743] Measured by the Pattern of all holiness, no human being is free from blemish.

5. In connection with the God-idea, the conception of sin grew from crude beginnings to the higher meaning given it by Judaism. The ancient Babylonians used the same terminology as the Bible for sin and sin-offering, but their view, like that of other Semites, was far more external.[744] If one was afflicted with disease or misfortune, the inference was that he had neglected the ritual of some deity and must appease the angered one with a sacrificial offering. Any irregularity in the cult was an offense against the deity. This became more moralized with the higher God-idea; the god became the guardian of moral principles; and the calamities, even of the nation, were then ascribed to the divine wrath on account of moral lapses. The same process may be observed in the views of ancient Israel. Here, too, during the dominance of the priestly view the gravest possible offense was one against the cult, a culpable act entailing the death penalty—asham, or "doom" of the offender. We shudder at the thought that the least violation of the hierarchical rules for the sanctuary or even for the burning of incense should meet the penalty of death. Yet such is the plain statement of the Mosaic law and such was the actual practice of the people.[745]

The more the prophetic conception of the moral nature of the Deity permeated the Jewish religion, the more the term sin came to mean an offense against the holiness of God, the Guardian of morality. Hence the great prophets upbraided the people for their moral, not their ceremonial failings. They attacked scathingly transgressions of the laws of righteousness and purity, the true sins against God, because these originate in dullness of heart, unbridled passion, and overbearing pride, all so hateful to Him. The only ritual offenses emphasized as sins against God are idolatry, violation of the name of God and of the Sabbath, for these express the sanctity of life.[746] Except for these points, the prophets and psalmists insisted only on righteous conduct and integrity of soul, and repudiated entirely the ritualism of the priesthood and the formalism of the cult.747 This view is anticipated by Samuel, the master of the prophetic schools, when he says:

"Behold, to obey is better than sacrifice,

And to hearken than the fat of rams.

For rebellion is as the sin of witchcraft,

And stubbornness is as idolatry and teraphim."748

As soon as we realize that obedience to God's will means right conduct and purity of soul, we see in sin the desecration of the divine image in man, the violation of his heavenly patent of nobility.

6. Sin, then, is in its essence unfaithfulness to God and to our own god-like nature. We see this thought expressed in Job:749

"If thou hast sinned, what doest thou against Him?

And if thy transgressions be multiplied, what doest thou unto Him?

If thou be righteous, what givest thou unto Him?

Or what receiveth He of thy hand?

Thy wickedness concerneth a man as thou art;

And thy righteousness a son of man."

Thus the source of sin is the human heart, the origin of all our thinking and planning. We know sin chiefly as consciousness of guilt. Man's conscience accuses him and compels him to confess, "Against Thee, Thee only, have I sinned."750 Not only the deed itself, but even more the will which caused it, is condemned by conscience. Such self-accusation constantly proves anew that there is no place for original sin through the fall of Adam. "I could have controlled my evil desire, if I had but earnestly willed it," said King David, according to the Talmud.751

7. Sin engenders a feeling of disunion with God through the consciousness of guilt which accompanies it. It erects a "wall of separation" between man and his Maker, depriving him of peace and security.752 Guilt causes pain, which overwhelms him, until he has made atonement and obtained pardon before God. This is no imaginary feeling, easily overcome and capable of being suppressed by the sinner with impunity. Instead, he must pay the full penalty for his sin, lest it lead him to the very abyss of evil, to physical and moral death. Sin in the individual becomes a sense of self-condemnation, the consciousness of the divine anger. Hence the Hebrew term avon, sin, is often synonymous with punishment,753 and asham, guilt, often signifies the atonement for the guilt, and sometimes doom and perdition as a consequence of guilt.754 Undoubtedly this still contains a remnant of the old Semitic idea that an awful divine visitation may come upon an entire household or community because of a criminal or sacrilegious act committed, consciously or unconsciously, by one of its members. Such a fate can be averted only by an atoning sacrifice. This accords with the rather strange fact that the Priestly Code prescribes certain guilt offerings for sins committed unwittingly, which are called asham.755

8. But even these unintentional sins can be avoided by the constant exercise of caution, so that their commission implies a certain degree of guilt, which demands a measure of repentance. Thus the Psalmist says: "Who can discern errors? Clear Thou me from hidden faults."756 He thus implies that we feel responsible in a certain sense for all our sins, including those which we commit unknowingly. The rabbis dwell especially on the idea that we are never altogether free from sinful thoughts. For this reason, they tell us, the two burnt offerings were brought to the altar each morning and evening, to atone for the sinful thoughts of the people during the preceding day or night.757

9. At any rate, Judaism recognizes no sin which does not arise from the individual conscience or moral personality. The condemnation of a whole generation or race in consequence of the sin of a single individual is an essentially heathen idea, which was overcome by Judaism in the course of time through the prophetic teaching of the divine justice and man's moral responsibility. This sentiment was voiced by Moses and Aaron after the rebellion of Korah in the words: "O God, the God of the spirits of all flesh, shall one man sin, and wilt Thou be wroth with all the congregation?"758 In commenting upon this, the Midrash says: "A human king may make war upon a whole

province, because it contains rebels who have caused sedition, and so the innocent must suffer together with the guilty; but it does not behoove God, the Ruler of the spirits, who looks into the hearts of men, to punish the guiltless together with the guilty."759 The Christian view of universal guilt as a consequence of Adam's sin, the dogma of original sin, is actually a relapse from the Jewish stage to the heathen doctrine from which the Jewish religion freed itself.

10. According to the Biblical view sin contaminates man, so that he cannot stand in the presence of God. The holiness of Him who is "of eyes too pure to behold evil"760 becomes to the sinner "a devouring fire."761 Even the lofty prophet Isaiah realizes his own human limitations at the sublime vision of the God of holiness enthroned on high, while the angelic choruses chant their thrice holy. In humility and contrition he cries out: "Woe is me, for I am undone! Because I am a man of unclean lips, and I dwell in the midst of a people of unclean lips; For mine eyes have seen the King, the Lord of hosts."762 The prophet must undergo atonement in order to be prepared for his high prophetic task. One of the Seraphs purges him of his sins by touching his lips with a live coal taken from the altar of God.

Under the influence of Persian dualism, rabbinical Judaism considers sin a pollution which puts man under the power of unclean spirits.763 In the later Cabbalah this idea is elaborated until the world of sin is considered a cosmic power of impurity, opposed to the realm of right, working evil ever since the fall of Adam.764 Still, however close this may come to the Christian dogma, it never becomes identical with it; the recognition is always preserved of man's power to extricate himself from the realm of impurity and to elevate himself into the realm of purity by his own repentance. Sin never becomes a demoniacal power depriving man of his divine dignity of self-determination and condemning him to eternal damnation. It ever remains merely a going astray from the right path, a stumbling from which man may rise again to his heavenly height, exerting his own powers as the son of God.

Chapter XXXIX. Repentance Or the Return To God

1. The brightest gem among the teachings of Judaism is its doctrine of repentance or, in its own characteristic term, the return of the wayward sinner to God.765 Man, full of remorse at having fallen away from the divine Fountainhead of purity, conscious of deserving a sentence of condemnation from the eternal Judge, would be less happy than the unreasoning brute which cannot sin at all. Religion restores him by the power to rise from his shame and guilt, to return to God in repentance, as the penitent son returns to his father. Whether we regard sin as estrangement from God or as a disturbance of the divine order, it has a detrimental effect on both body and soul, and leads inevitably to death. On this point the Bible affords many historical illustrations and doctrinal teachings.766 If man had no way to escape from sin, then he would be the most unfortunate of creatures, in spite of his god-like nature. Therefore the merciful God opens the gate of repentance for the sinner, saying as through His prophets of old: "I have no pleasure in the death of the wicked, but that the wicked turn from his way and live."767

2. The great value of the gift of divine grace, by which the sinner may repent and return to God with a new spirit, appears in the following rabbinical saying: "Wisdom was asked, 'What shall be the sinner's punishment?' and answered, 'Evil pursues sinners';768 then Prophecy was asked, and answered, 'The soul that sinneth, it shall die';769 the Torah, or legal code, was consulted, and its answer was: 'He shall bring a sin-offering, and the priest shall make atonement for him, and he shall be forgiven.'770 Finally God Himself was asked, and He answered:771 'Good and upright is the Lord; therefore doth He instruct sinners in the way.' "772 The Jewish idea of atonement by the sinner's return to God excludes every kind of mediatorship. Neither the priesthood nor sacrifice is necessary to secure the divine grace; man need only find the way to God by his own efforts. "Seek ye Me, and live,"773 says God to His erring children.

3. Teshubah, which means return, is an idea peculiar to Judaism, created by the prophets of Israel, and arising directly from the simple Jewish conception of sin. Since sin is a deviation from the path of salvation, a "straying" into the road of perdition and death, the erring can return with heart and soul, end his ways, and thus change his entire being. This is not properly expressed by the term repentance, which denotes only regret for the wrong, but not the inner transformation. Nor is Teshubah to be rendered by either penitence or penance. The former indicates a sort of bodily self-castigation, the latter some other kind of penalty undergone in order to expiate sin. Such external forms of asceticism were prescribed and practiced by many tribes and some of the historical religions. The

Jewish prophets, however, opposed them bitterly, demanding an inner change, a transformation of soul, renewing both heart and spirit.

"Let the wicked forsake his way,

And the man of iniquity his thoughts;

And let him return unto the Lord, and He will have compassion upon him,

And to our God, for He will abundantly pardon."[774]

Judaism considers sin merely moral aberration, not utter corruption, and believes in the capability of the very worst of sinners to improve his ways; therefore it waits ever for his regeneration. This is truly a return to God, the restoration of the divine image which has been disfigured and corrupted by sin.

4. The doctrine of Teshubah, or the return of the sinner, has a specially instructive history, as this most precious and unique conception of Judaism is little understood or appreciated by Christian theologians. Often without intentional bias, these are so under the influence of the Paulinian dogma that they see no redemption for man corrupted by sin, except by his belief in a superhuman act of atonement. It is certainly significant that the legal code, which is of priestly origin, does not mention repentance or the sinner's return. It prescribes various types of sin-offerings, speaks of reparation for wrong inflicted, of penalties for crime, and of confession for sins, but it does not state how the soul can be purged of sin, so that man can regain his former state of purity. This great gap is filled by the prophetic books and the Psalms. The book of Deuteronomy alone, written under prophetic influence, alludes to repentance, in connection with the time when Israel would be taken captive from its land as punishment for its violation of the law. There we read: "Thou shalt return unto the Lord thy God, ... with all thy heart, and all thy soul, then the Lord thy God will turn thy captivity, and have compassion upon thee."[775]

Amos, the prophet of stern justice, has not yet reached the idea of averting the divine wrath by the return of the sinner.[776] Hosea, the prophet of divine mercy and loving-kindness, in his deep compassion for the unfaithful and backsliding people, became the preacher of repentance as the condition for attaining the divine pardon.

"Return, O Israel, unto the Lord thy God;

For thou hast stumbled in thine iniquity.

Take with you words (of repentance),

And return unto the Lord;

Say unto Him, "Forgive all iniquity,

And accept that which is good;

So will we render for bullocks the offering of our lips.' "[777]

The appeal of Jeremiah is still more vigorous:

"Return, thou backsliding Israel, saith the Lord....

Only acknowledge thine iniquity, that thou hast transgressed against the Lord thy God....

Break up for you a fallow ground, and sow not among thorns....

O Jerusalem, wash thy heart from wickedness, that thou mayest be saved;

How long shall thy baleful thoughts lodge within thee?...

Return ye now every one from his evil way, and amend your ways and your doings."[778]

Ezekiel, while emphasizing the guilt of the individual, preached repentance still more insistently. "Return ye, and turn yourselves from all your transgressions; so shall they not be a stumbling-block of iniquity to you. Cast away from you all your transgressions, wherein ye have transgressed; and make you a new heart and a new spirit; for why will ye die, O house of Israel? For I have no pleasure in the death of him that dieth, saith the Lord God; wherefore turn yourselves, and live."779 The same appeal recurs after the exile in the last prophets, Zechariah780 and Malachi.781 The latter says: "Return unto Me, and I shall return unto you." Likewise the penitential sermon written in a time of great distress, which is ascribed to the prophet Joel, contains the appeal:

"Turn ye unto Me with all your heart,

And with fasting, and with weeping, and with lamentation;

And rend your heart, and not your garments,

And turn unto the Lord your God;

For He is gracious and compassionate,

Long-suffering, and abundant in mercy,

And repenteth Him of the evil."782

This prophetic view, which demands contrition and craving for God instead of external modes of atonement, is expressed in the penitential Psalms as well,783 especially in Psalm LI. The idea is expanded further in the parable of the prophet Jonah, which conveys the lesson that even a heathen nation like the people of Nineveh can avert the impending judgment of God by true repentance.784 From this point of view the whole conception took on a larger aspect, and the entire history of mankind was seen in a new light. The Jewish sages realized that God punishes man only when the expected change of mind and heart fails to come.785

5. The Jewish plan of divine salvation presents a striking contrast to that of the Church, for it is built upon the presumption that all sinners can find their way back to God and godliness, if they but earnestly so desire. Even before God created the world, He determined to offer man the possibility of Teshubah, so that, in the midst of the continual struggle with the allurements of the senses, the repentant sinner can ever change heart and mind and return to God.786 Without such a possibility the world of man could not endure; thus, because no man can stand before the divine tribunal of stern justice, the paternal arm of a merciful God is extended to receive the penitent. This sublime truth is constantly reiterated in the Talmud and in the liturgy, especially of the great Day of Atonement.787 Not only does God's long-suffering give the sinner time to repent; His paternal love urges him to return. Thus the Haggadists purposely represent almost all the sinners mentioned in the Bible as models of sincere repentance. First of all comes King David, who is considered such a pattern of repentance, as the author of the fifty-first Psalm, that he would not have been allowed to sin so grievously, if he had not been providentially appointed as the shining example of the penitent's return to God.788 Then there is King Manasseh, the most wicked among all the kings of Judah and Israel, who had committed the most abominable sins of idolatrous worship. Referring to the story told of him in Chronicles, it is said that God responded to his tearful prayers and incessant supplications by opening a rift under His throne of mercy and receiving his petition for pardon. Thus all mankind might see that none can be so wicked that he will not find the door of repentance open, if he but seek it sincerely and persistently.789 Likewise Adam and Cain, Reuben and Judah, Korah, Jeroboam, Ahab, Josiah, and Jechoniah are described in Talmud, Midrash, and the apocalyptic literature as penitent sinners who obtained at last the coveted pardon.790 The optimistic spirit of Judaism cannot tolerate the idea that mortal man is hopelessly lost under the burden of his sins, or that he need ever lose faith in himself. No one can sink so low that he cannot find his way back to his heavenly Father by untiring self-discipline. As the Talmud says, nothing can finally withstand the power of sincere repentance: "It reaches up to the very seat of God;" "upon it rests the welfare of the world."791

6. The rabbis follow up the idea first announced in the book of Jonah, that the saving power of repentance applies to the heathen world as well. Thus they show how God constantly offered time and opportunity to the heathens for repentance. For example, when the generation of the flood, the builders of the Tower of Babel, and the people of Sodom and Gomorrah were to be punished, God waited to give them time for Repentance and improvement of their ways.792 Noah, Enoch, and Abraham are represented as monitors of their contemporaries, warning them, like the prophets, to repent in time lest they meet their doom.793 Thus the whole Hellenistic literature of propaganda, especially the Sibylline books, echoes the warning and the hope that the heathen should repent of their grievous sins and return to God, whom they had deserted in idolatry, so that they might escape the impending doom of the last judgment day. According to one Haggadist,794 even the Messiah will appear first as a preacher of repentance, admonishing the heathen nations to be converted to the true God and repent before Him, lest they fall

into perdition. Indeed, it is said that even Pharaoh and the Egyptians were warned and given time for repentance before their fate overtook them.

7. Accordingly, the principle of repentance is a universal human one, and by no means exclusively national, as the Christian theologians represent it.795 The sages thus describe Adam as the type of the penitent sinner, who is granted pardon by God. The "sign" of Cain also was to be a sign for all sinners, assuring them they might all obtain forgiveness and salvation, if they would but return to God.796 In fact, the prophetic appeal to Israel for repentance, vain at the time, effected the regeneration of the people during the Exile and gave rise to Judaism and its institutions. In the same way, the appeal to the heathen world by the Hellenistic propaganda and the Essene preachers of repentance did not induce the nations at once to prepare for the coming of the Messianic kingdom, but finally led to the rise of the Christian religion, and, through certain intermediaries, of the Mohammedan as well.

However, the long-cherished hope for a universal conversion of the heathen world, voiced in the preachments and the prayers of the "pious ones," gave way to a reaction. The rise of antinomian sects in Judaism occasioned the dropping of this pious hope, and only certain individual conversions were dwelt on as shining exceptions.797 The heathen world in general was not regarded as disposed to repent, and so its ultimate fate was the doom of Gehenna. Experience seemed to confirm the stern view, which rabbinical interpretation could find in Scripture also, that "Even at the very gate of the nether world wicked men shall not return."798 The growing violence of the oppressors and the increasing number of the maligners of Judaism darkened the hope for a universal conversion of humanity to the pure faith of Israel and its law of righteousness. On the contrary, a certain satisfaction was felt by the Jew in the thought that these enemies of Judaism should not be allowed to repent and obtain salvation in the hereafter.799

8. The idea of repentance was applied all the more intensely in Jewish life, and a still more prominent place was accorded it in Jewish literature. The rabbis have numberless sayings800 in the Talmud and also in the Haggadic and ethical writings concerning the power and value of repentance. In passages such as these we see how profoundly Judaism dealt with the failings and shortcomings of man. The term asa teshubah, do repentance, implies no mere external act of penitence, as Christian theologians often assert. On the contrary, the chief stress is always laid on the feeling of remorse and on the change of heart which contrition and self-accusation bring. Yet even these would not be sufficient to cast off the oppressive consciousness of guilt, unless the contrite heart were reassured by God that He forgives the penitent son of man with paternal grace and love. In other words, religion demands a special means of atonement, that is, at-one-ment with God, to restore the broken relation of man to his Maker. The true spiritual power of Judaism appears in this, that it gradually liberates the kernel of the atonement idea from its priestly shell. The Jew realizes, as does the adherent of no other religion, that even in sin he is a child of God and certain of His paternal love. This is brought home especially on the Day of Atonement, which will be treated in a later chapter.

9. At all events, the blotting out of man's sins with their punishment remains ever an act of grace by God.801 In compassion for man's frailty He has ordained repentance as the means of salvation, and promised pardon to the penitent. This truth is brought out in the liturgy for the Day of Atonement, as well as in the Apocalyptic Prayer of Manasseh. At the same time, Judaism awards the palm of victory to him who has wrestled with sin and conquered it by his own will. Thus the rabbis boldly assert: "Those who have sinned and repented rank higher in the world to come than the righteous who have never sinned," which is paralleled in the New Testament: "There is more joy in heaven over one sinner who repenteth than over ninety and nine righteous persons, who need no repentance."802 No intermediary power from without secures the divine grace and pardon for the repentant sinner, but his own inner transformation alone.

Chapter XL. Man, the Child of God

1. The belief that God hears our prayers and pardons our sins rests upon the assumption of a mutual relation between man and God. This belief is insusceptible of proof, but rests entirely upon our religious feelings and is rooted purely in our emotional life. We apply to the relation between man and God the finest feelings known in human life, the devotion and love of parents for their children and the affection and trust the child entertains for its parents. Thus we are led to the conviction that earth-born man has a Helper enthroned in the heavens above, who hearkens when he implores Him for aid. In his innermost heart man feels that he has a special claim on the divine

protection. In the words of Job,803 he knows that his Redeemer liveth. He need not perish in misery. Unlike the brute creation and the hosts of stars, which know nothing of their Maker, man feels akin to the God who lives within him; he is His image, His child. He cannot be deprived of His paternal love and favor. This truly human emotion is nowhere expressed so clearly as in Judaism. "Ye are the children of the Lord your God."804 "Have we not all one Father? Hath not one God created us?"805 "Like as a father hath compassion on his children, so hath the Lord compassion upon them that fear Him."806

2. Still, this simple idea of man's filial relation to God and God's paternal love for man did not begin in its beautiful final form. For a long time the Jew seems to have avoided the term "Father" for God, because it was used by the heathen for their deities as physical progenitors, and did not refer to the moral relation between the Deity and mankind. Thus worshipers of wooden idols would, according to Scripture, "say to a stock, Thou art my father."807 Hosea was the first to call the people of Israel "children of the living God,"808 if they would but improve their ways and enter into right relations with Him. Jeremiah also hopes for the time when Israel would invoke the Lord, saying, "Thou art my Father," and in return God would prove a true father to him.809 However, Scripture calls God a Father only in referring to the people as a whole.810 The "pious ones" established a closer relation between God and the individual by means of prayer, so that through them the epithets, "Father," "Our Father," and "Our Father in heaven" came into general use. Hence, the liturgy frequently uses the invocation, "Our Father, Our King!" We owe to Rabbi Akiba the significant saying, in opposition to the Paulinian dogma, "Blessed are ye, O Israelites! Before whom do you purify yourselves (from your sins)? And who is it that purifies you? Your Father in heaven."811 Previously Rabbi Eliezer ben Hyrcanos dwelt on the moral degeneration of his age, which betokened the end of time, and exclaimed: "In whom, then, shall we find support? In our Father who is in heaven."812 The appellative "Father in heaven" was the stereotyped term used by the "pious ones" during the century preceding and the one following the rise of Christianity, as a glance at the literature of the period indicates.813

3. It is instructive to follow the history of this term. In Scripture God is represented as speaking to David, "I will be to him for a father, and he shall be to Me for a son,"814 or "He shall call unto Me: Thou art my Father, … I also will appoint him first-born."815 So in the apocryphal writings God speaks both to Israel and to individual saints: "I shall be to them a Father, and they shall be My children."816 Elsewhere it is said of the righteous, "He calls God his Father," and "he shall be counted among the sons of God."817 We read concerning the Messiah: "When all wrongdoing will be removed from the midst of the people, he shall know that all are sons of God."818 Obviously only righteousness or personal merit entitles a man to be called a son of God. In fact, we are expressly told of Onias, the great Essene saint, that his intimate relation with God emboldened him to converse with the Master of the Universe as a son would speak with his father.819 According to the Mishnah the older generation of "pious ones" used to spend "an hour in silent devotion before offering their daily prayer, in order to concentrate heart and soul upon their communion with their Father in heaven."820 Thus it is said of congregational prayer that through it "Israel lifts his eyes to his Father in heaven."821 In this way prayer took the place of the altar, of which R. Johanan ben Zakkai said that it established peace between Israel and his Father in heaven.822 Afterwards the question was discussed by Rabbi Meir and Rabbi Jehuda whether even sin-laden Israel had a right to be called "children of God." Rabbi Meir pointed to Hosea as proof that the backsliders also remain "children of the living God."823

4. In the Hellenistic literature, with its dominating idea of universal monotheism, God is frequently invoked or spoken of as the Father of mankind. The implication is that each person who invokes God as Father enters into filial relation with Him. Thus what was first applied to Israel in particular was now broadened to include mankind in general, and consequently all men were considered "children of the living God." The words of God to Pharaoh, speaking of Israel as His "first-born son,"824 were taken as proof that all the nations of the earth are sons of God and He the universal Father. Israel is the first-born among the sons of God, because his patriarchs, prophets, and psalmists first recognized Him as the universal Father and Ruler. From this point of view Judaism declared love for fellow-men and regard for the dignity of humanity to be fundamental principles of ethics. "As God is kind and merciful toward His creation, be thou also kind and merciful toward all fellow-creatures," is the oft-repeated teaching of the rabbis.825 Likewise, "Whoever takes pity on his fellow-beings, on him God in heaven will also take pity."826 Love of humanity has so permeated the nature of the Jew that the rabbis assert: "He who has pity on his fellow-men has the blood of Abraham in his veins."827 This bold remark casts light upon the strange dictum: "Ye Israelites are called by the name of man, but the heathen are not."828 The Jewish teachers were so deeply impressed with man's inhumanity to man, so common among the heathen nations, and the immorality of the lives

by which these desecrated God's image, that they insisted that the laws of humanity alone make for divine dignity in man.

5. Rabbi Akiba probably referred to the Paulinian dogma that Jesus, the crucified Messiah, is the only son of God, in his well-known saying: "Beloved is man, for he is created in God's image, and it was a special token of love that he became conscious of it. Beloved is Israel, for they are called the children of God, and it was a special token of love that they became conscious of it."829 Here he claims the glory of being a son of God for Israel, but not for all men. Still, as soon as the likeness of man to God is taken in a spiritual sense, then it is implied that all men have the same capacity for being a son of God which is claimed for Israel. This is unquestionably the view of Judaism when it considers the Torah as entrusted to Israel to bring light and blessing to all the families of men. Rabbi Meir, the disciple of Rabbi Akiba, said: "The Scriptural words, 'The statutes and ordinances which man shall do and live thereby,' and similar expressions indicate that the final aim of Judaism is not attained by the Aaronide, nor the Levite, nor even the Israelite, but by mankind."830 Such a saying expresses clearly and emphatically that God's fatherly love extends to all men as His children.

6. According to the religious consciousness of modern Israel man is made in God's image, and is thus a child of God. Consequently Jew and non-Jew, saint and sinner have the same claim upon God's paternal love and mercy. There is no distinction in favor of Israel except as he lives a higher and more god-like life. Even those who have fallen away from God and have committed crime and sin remain God's children. If they send up their penitent cry to the throne of God, "Pardon us, O Father, for we have sinned! Forgive us, O King, for we have done evil!"; their prayer is heard by the heavenly Father exactly like that of the pious son of Israel.

Chapter XLI. Prayer and Sacrifice

1. The gap between man and the sublime Master of the universe is vast, but not absolute. The thoughts of God are high above our thoughts, and the ways of God above our ways, baffling our reason when we endeavor to solve the vexatious problems of destiny, of merit and demerit, of retribution and atonement. Yet religion offers a wondrous medium to bring the heart of man into close communion with Him who is enthroned above the heavens, one that overleaps all distances, removes all barriers, and blends all dissonances into one great harmony, and that is— Prayer. As the child must relieve itself of its troubles and sorrows upon the bosom of its mother or father in order to turn its pain into gladness, so men at all times seek to approach the Deity, confiding to Him all their fears and longings in order to obtain peace of heart. Prayer, communion between the human soul and the Creator, is the glorious privilege enjoyed by man alone among all creatures, as he alone is the child of God. It voices the longing of the human heart for its Father in heaven. As the Psalmist has it, "My soul thirsteth for God, for the living God."831

2. However, both language, the means of intercourse between man and man, and prayer, the means of intercourse between man and God, show traces of a slow development lasting for thousands of years, until the loftiest thoughts and sublimest emotions could be expressed. The real efficacy of prayer could not be truly appreciated, until the prophetic spirit triumphed over the priestly element in Judaism. In the history of speech the language of signs preceded that of sounds, and images gradually ripened into abstract thoughts. Similarly, primitive man approaches his God with many kinds of gifts and sacrificial rites to express his sentiments. He acts out or depicts what he expects from the Deity, whether rain, fertility of the soil, or the extermination of his foes. He shares with his God his food and drink, to obtain His friendship and protection in time of trouble, and sacrifices the dearest of his possessions to assuage His wrath or obtain His favor.

3. In the lowest stage of culture man needed no mediator in his intercourse with the Deity, who appeared to him in the phenomena of nature as well as in the fetish, totem, and the like. But soon he rose to a higher stage of thought, and the Deity withdrew before him to the celestial heights, filling him with awe and fear; then rose a class of men who claimed the privilege to approach the Deity and influence Him by certain secret practices. Henceforth these acted as mediators between the mass of the people and the Deity. In the first place, these were the magicians, medicine-men, and similar persons, who were credited with the power to conjure up the hidden forces of nature, considered either divine or demoniac. After these arose the priests, distinguished from the people by special dress and diet, who established in the various tribes temples, altars, and cults, under their own control. Then there were the saints, pious penitents or Nazarites, who led an ascetic life secluded from the masses, hoping thus to obtain higher powers over the will of the Deity. All these entertained more or less clearly the notion that they stood in

closer relation to the Deity than the common people, whom they then excluded from the sanctuary and all access to the Deity.

The Mosaic cult, in the so-called Priestly Code, was founded upon this stage of religious life, forming a hierarchical institution like those of other ancient nations. It differed from them, however, in one essential point. The prime element in the cult of other nations was magic, consisting of oracle, incantation and divination, but this was entirely contrary to the principles of the Jewish faith. On the other hand, all the rites and ceremonies handed down from remote antiquity were placed in the service of Israel's holy God, in order to train His people into the highest moral purity. The patriarchs and prophets, who are depicted in Scripture as approaching God in prayer and hearing His voice in reply, come under the category of saints or elect ones, above the mass of the people.

4. Foreign as the entire idea of sacrifice is to our mode of religious thought, to antiquity it appeared as the only means of intercourse with the Deity. "In every place offerings are presented unto My name, even pure oblations,"832 says the prophet Malachi in the name of Israel's God. Even from a higher point of view the underlying idea seems to be of a simple offering laid upon the altar. Such were the meal-offering (minha);833 the burnt offering (olah), which sends its pillar of smoke up toward heaven, symbolizing the idea of self-sacrifice; while the various sin-offerings (hattath or asham) expressed the desire to propitiate an offended Deity. However, since the sacrificial cult was always dominated by the priesthood in Israel as well as other nations, the lawgiver made no essential changes in the traditional practice and terminology. Thus it was left to the consciousness of the people to find a deeper spiritual meaning in the sacrifices instead of stating one directly. The want was supplied only by the later Haggadists who tried to create a symbolism of the sacrificial cult. The laying on of hands by the individual who brought the offering, seems to have been a genuine symbolic expression of self-surrender. In the case of sin-offerings the Mosaic cult added a higher meaning by ordering a preceding confession of sin. Here, indeed, the individual entered into personal communion with God through his prayer for pardon, even though the priest performed the act of expiation for him.

5. The great prophets of Israel alone recognized that the entire sacrificial system was out of harmony with the true spirit of Judaism and led to all sorts of abuses, above all to a misconception of the worship of God, which requires the uplifting of the heart. In impassioned language, therefore, they hurled words of scathing denunciation against the practice and principle of ritualism: "I hate, I despise your feasts, and I will take no delight in your solemn assemblies.

Yea, though ye offer Me burnt-offerings and your meal-offerings, I will not accept them; Neither will I regard the peace-offerings of your fat beasts.

Take thou away from Me the noise of thy songs; and let Me not hear the melody of thy psalteries.

But let justice well up as waters, and righteousness as a mighty stream."834

Thus speaks Amos in the name of the Lord. And Hosea:

"For I desire mercy, and not sacrifice, and the knowledge of God rather than burnt-offerings."835

Isaiah spoke in a similar vein:

"To what purpose is the multitude of your sacrifices unto Me? saith the Lord; I am full of the burnt-offerings of rams, and the fat of fed beasts; and I delight not in the blood of bullocks, or of lambs, or of he-goats....

Bring me no more vain oblations; it is an offering of abomination unto Me; new moon and sabbath, the holding of convocations—I cannot endure iniquity along with the solemn assembly....

And when ye spread forth your hands, I will hide Mine eyes from you; yea, when ye make many prayers, I will not hear; your hands are full of blood.

Wash you, make you clean, put away the evil of your doings From before Mine eyes, cease to do evil; learn to do well; seek justice, relieve the oppressed, judge the fatherless, plead for the widow."836

Most striking of all are the words of Jeremiah, spoken in the name of the Lord of hosts, the God of Israel: "Add your burnt-offerings unto your sacrifices, and eat ye flesh. For I spoke not unto your fathers, nor commanded them in the day that I brought them out of the land of Egypt, concerning burnt-offerings and sacrifices, but this thing I commanded them, saying; 'Hearken unto My voice, and I will be your God, and ye shall be My people; and walk ye in all the way that I command you, that it may be well with you.' "837

6. However, the mere rejection of the sacrificial cult was quite negative, and did not satisfy the normal need for communion with God. Therefore the various codes established a sort of compromise between the prophetic ideal and the priestly practice, in which the ideal was by no means supreme. Sometimes the prophetic spirit stirred the soul of inspired psalmists, and their lips echoed forth again the divine revelation:

"Hear, O My people, and I will speak; O Israel, and I will testify against thee: God, thy God, am I. I will not reprove thee for thy sacrifices; and thy burnt-offerings are continually before Me. I will take no bullock out of thy house, nor he-goats out of thy folds. For every beast of the forest is Mine, and the cattle upon a thousand hills.... Do I eat the flesh of bulls, or drink the blood of goats?"838 Another psalmist says: "Sacrifice and meal-offering thou hast no delight in; Mine ears hast Thou opened; burnt-offering and sin-offering hast Thou not required."839

Still, the sacrificial cult was too deeply rooted in the life of the people to be disturbed by the voice of the prophets or the words of a few psalmists. It was connected with the Temple, and the Temple was the center of the social life of the nation. The few faint voices of protest went practically unheeded. The priestly pomp of sacrifice could only be displaced by the more elevating and more spiritual devotion of the entire congregation in prayer, and this process demanded a new environment, and a group of men with entirely new ideas.

7. The need of a deeper devotion through prayer was not felt until the Exile. There altar and priesthood were no more, but the words of the prophets and the songs of the Levites remained to kindle the people's longing for God with a new zeal. Until then prayer was rare and for special occasions. Hannah's prayer at Shiloh filled even the high priest with amazement.840 The prophets alone interceded in behalf of the people, because the ordinary man was not considered sufficiently clean from sin to approach the Deity in prayer. But on foreign soil, where sacrifices could not be offered to the God of Israel, the harp of David resounded with solemn songs expressing the national longing toward God. The most touching psalms of penitence and thanksgiving date from the exile. A select class of devout men, called the godly or pious ones, Hasidim or Anavim,841 assembled by the rivers of Babylon for regular prayer, turning their faces toward Jerusalem, that the God of Israel might answer them from His ancient seat.842 Thus the great seer of the exile voiced the hope for "a house of prayer for all peoples" to stand in the very place where the sacrifices were offered to God.843 The congregation of Hasidim elaborated a liturgy under the Persian influence, in which prayer was the chief element, and the secondary part, the instruction from the Torah and the monitions of the prophets. The Synagogue, the house of meeting for the people, spread all over the world, and by its light of truth and glow of fervor it soon eclipsed the Temple, with all its worldly pomp. In fact, the priesthood of the Temple were finally compelled to make concessions to the lay movement of the Hasidim. They added a prayer service, morning and evening, to the daily sacrifices, and opened the Hall of Hewn Stones, the meeting place of the High Court of Justice, as a Synagogue in charge of the priests.844

8. In this manner the ancient sacrificial cult, thus long monopolized by the priesthood, was gradually superseded by congregational prayer which was no longer confined to a certain time or class, and justly called by the rabbis "a service of the heart."845 Moreover, the Temple itself lost much of its hold upon the hearts of the people, owing to the more spiritual character of the Synagogue. Thus the torch of the Roman soldiery which turned the Temple into a heap of ashes broke only the national bond, but left the religious bond of the Synagogue unbroken. True, the hope for the restoration of the Temple with the priestly sacrifices was not relinquished, and officially the daily prayers were considered only a "temporary substitute" for the divinely ordained sacrificial cult.846

Nevertheless, the deeper religious consciousness of the people felt that the celestial gate of divine mercy opens only to prayer, which emanates from the innermost depths of the soul. Accordingly, some of the Haggadists try to prove from Scripture that prayer ranks above sacrifice,847 while others even identify worship with prayer.848 They represent God as appearing to Moses in the guise of one who leads the congregation in prayer, His face covered by the prayer-shawl (tallith), in order to teach man for all time the mode and power of prayer.849 Still these remain isolated expressions of an underlying sentiment; on the whole, the rabbis regarded the Mosaic legislation, with its emphasis on sacrifice, far too highly to accord prayer any but a secondary place, either accompanying sacrifice or as its substitute.850

9. Through many centuries, then, the belief in the divine origin of the sacrificial cult remained, even though it could no longer be carried out. The liturgy contained prayers for the speedy restoration of the Temple and the sacrifices,

which were preserved by tradition, and nowhere was even an echo heard of the bold words of Jeremiah denying the divine character of the sacrifices,851 even though the idea of the restoration of the old cult must have been repugnant to thinkers. The sages of former ages could only resort to a compromise or an allegorical interpretation. It is noteworthy that the Haggadist Rabbi Levi considered the sacrifices a concession of God to the people, who were disposed to idolatry, in order to win them gradually for the pure monotheistic ideal.852 This view was adopted by the Church Fathers, and later by Maimonides and other medieval thinkers. On the other hand, an allegorical meaning was assigned to the sacrifices by Philo and Jehuda ha Levi, as well as by Samson Raphael Hirsch in modern times.853

Reform Judaism, recognizing the results of Biblical research and the law of religious progress, adopted the prophetic view of the sacrifices. Accordingly, the sacrificial cult of the Mosaic code has no validity for the liberal movement, and all reference to it has been eliminated from the reform liturgy. In this, however, the connection with the past was by no means severed. The main part of the service remains the same, although much of the character and many of the details have been changed.854 Only the allusions to the Temple worship and the sacrifices were eliminated, and the entire form of the service was made more solemn and inspiring "by combining ancient time-honored formulas with modern prayers and meditations in the vernacular and in the spirit of the age." The morning and evening services retained their places, while the additional festal service (mussaf) was abrogated, because it stood for the additional festal sacrifice. As to the voluntary element in the old sacrificial system, the peace, sin, and thank-offerings, this is replaced in the reform ritual, as in the traditional practice, by private devotions for special occasions, to be selected by the individual.

The traditional Jewish prayer has certainly a wondrous force. It remains a source of inspiration from which the religious consciousness will ever draw new strength and vitality. It echoes the voice of Israel singing the song of redemption by the Red Sea: "This is My God, and I will glorify Him; My father's God, and I will exalt Him."855 Consequently our liturgy must ever respond to a double demand; it must throb with the spirit of continuity with our great past, to make us feel one with our fathers of yore; and it must express clearly and fully our own views and needs, our convictions and our hopes.

Chapter XLII. The Nature and Purpose of Prayer

1. Prayer is the expression of man's longing and yearning for God in times of dire need and of overflowing joy, an outflow of the emotions of the soul in its dependence on God, the ever-present Helper, the eternal Source of its existence. Springing from the deepest necessity of human weakness, the expression of a momentary wish, prayer is felt to be the proud prerogative of man as the child of God, and at last it becomes adoration of the Most High, whose wisdom and whose paternal love and goodness inspire man with confidence and love.

2. Every prayer is offered on the presumption that it will be heard by God on high. "O Thou that hearest prayer, unto Thee doth all flesh come," sings the Psalmist.856 No doubt of the efficacy of prayer can arise in the devout spirit. There can be only the question whether, and how far, the Deity can allow its decrees to be influenced by human wishes. Childlike faith anticipates divine interference in the natural order at any time, because it has not yet attained the conception of a moral order in the universe and, therefore, expects from prayer also miraculous effects on life. As the Deity can suddenly send or withhold rain or drought, barrenness or birth, life or death, so the inference is that the man of God can do the same with his prayer. This is the point of view of the Biblical and Talmudic periods, as well as of the entire ancient world. It seems almost childish to our religious consciousness when, according to Talmudic tradition, the high priest petitioned God in the Sanctuary on the Day of Atonement for a year rich in rain and blessed with sunshine and with dew, and at the same time expressed the entreaty that the prayers of travelers for dry or cool weather should find no hearing.857 That the prayers of the pious may alter God's decree is not doubted for a moment by the rabbis; only they insist that God has taken into account beforehand the efficacy of this prayer in deciding the fate of the pious, in order that they may petition for that which He actually plans to do. "God longs for the prayer of the pious"; for that reason, they say, the Mothers of Israel were afflicted with barrenness, until the prayers of the Patriarchs had accomplished the transformation in their constitutions.858 On the other hand, the rabbis warn against excessive pondering over prayer and its efficacy, as through it that childlike faith would be weakened, which is the basis of all prayer.859

3. According to the rabbinic viewpoint, prayer has the power to reverse every heavenly decree, inasmuch as it appeals from the punitive justice of God, which has decided thus, to His attributes of grace and mercy, which can at any time effect a change. When the prophet Isaiah came to King Hezekiah with the message: "Set thine house in order, for thou shalt die," he replied, "Finish thy message and go; I have received the tradition from my royal ancestor David that, even when the sword already touches the neck, man shall not desist from an appeal to the divine mercy."860 Nay more, the rabbis believed that God Himself prays, saying, "Oh, that My mercy shall prevail over My justice!"861 Only after the divine judgment has been executed prayer becomes vain. In general, the entire Talmudic period ascribed miraculous power to prayer, especially the prayers of the pious, like the popular saint Onias or Hanina ben Dosa.862 In many such cases the invocation of God was combined with the use of the sacred name, the tetragrammaton, to which magical powers were ascribed.863

4. The two attributes of God, Justice and Mercy, correspond to the double nature of mankind, as the sinful man, who deserves punishment, is called to account by the former, while the righteous man may appeal to the latter. Accordingly, the efficacy of prayer could be so explained that, before it can influence the decision of God, it demands the reformation of man. While the unregenerate man meets an evil destiny, the reformed man has become a different being, and hence instead of justice mercy will control his fate. Albo pleads for this view of prayer, when he cites the Talmudic incident about R. Meir. It is said that R. Meir interceded for the people of Mimla, who all seemed to have been doomed to die on attaining manhood because they inherited the curse of the priestly family of Eli.864 But he also recommended to them that they should devote their lives to worthy deeds, as it is said in the Proverbs:865 "The hoary head is a crown of glory, it is found in the way of righteousness."866

Other thinkers ascribe to prayer the power to change the fate determined by the stars, because it exalts man into a higher sphere of godliness, exactly like the spirit of prophecy. Of course, this conception is connected with the belief in astrology, which swayed even clear thinkers like Ibn Ezra.867

5. According to our modern thinking there can be no question of any influence upon a Deity exalted above time and space, omniscient, unchangeable in will and action, by the prayer of mortals. Prayer can exert power only over the relation of man to God, not over God Himself. This indicates the nature and purpose of prayer. Man often feels lonely and forlorn in a world which overpowers him, to which he feels superior, and yet which he cannot master. Therefore he longs for that unseen Spirit of the universe, with whom alone he feels himself akin, and in whom alone he finds peace and bliss amid life's struggle and unrest. This longing is both expressed and satisfied in prayer. Following the natural impulse of his soul, man must pour out before his God all his desires and sighs, all the emotions of grief and delight which sway his heart, in order that he may find rest, like a child at its mother's bosom. Therefore the childlike mind believes that God can be induced to come down from His heavenly heights to offer help, and that He can be moved and influenced in human fashion. The truth is that every genuine prayer lifts man up toward God, satisfies the desire for His hallowing presence, unlocks the heavenly gate of mercy and bliss, and bestows upon man the beatific and liberating sense of being a child of God. The intellect may question the effect of prayer upon the physical, mental, or social constitution of man, or may declare prayer to be pious self-deception. The religious spirit experiences in prayer the soaring up of the soul toward union with God in consecrated moments of our mortal pilgrimage. This is no deception. The man who prays receives from the Godhead, toward whom he fervently lifts himself, the power to defy fate, to conquer sin, misery, and death. "The Lord is nigh to all them that call upon Him, to all that call upon Him in truth."868

6. To pray, then, is to look up to God and to pour out before Him one's wishes, thoughts, sorrows, and joys. Certainly the All-knowing does not require to be told by us what we desire or what we need. "For there is not a word in my tongue, but lo, O Lord, Thou knowest it altogether."869 But we mortals merely aspire toward Him who bears the world on His eternal arms, to express in His presence our agony and our jubilation, because we are certain of His paternal sympathy. When we praise and extol Him for the happiness and the many pleasures which He has granted us, He becomes the Partaker and Protector of our fortune, just as He is our sympathetic Helper when we cry out to Him under the burden of sin or grief, in the anxiety of danger or of guilt. Every genuine prayer realizes deeply the truth of the words, "Cast thy burden upon the Lord, and He will sustain thee."870

7. Self-expression before God in prayer has thus a double effect; it strengthens faith in God's love and kindness, as well as in His all-wise and all-bountiful prescience. But it also chastens the desires and feelings of man, teaching him to banish from his heart all thoughts of self-seeking and sin, and to raise himself toward the purity and the freedom of the divine will and demand. The essence of every prayer of supplication is that one should be in unison

with the divine will, to sum up all the wishes of the heart in the one phrase, "Do that which is good in Thine own eyes, O Lord."871 On the other hand, only the prayer which avoids impure thoughts and motives can venture to approach a holy God, as the sages infer from the words of Job, "There is no violence in my hands, and my prayer is pure."872

8. Every prayer, teach the sages, should begin with the praise of God's greatness, wisdom, and goodness, in order that man should learn submission and implicit confidence before he proffers his requests.873 While looking up to the divine Ideal of holiness and perfection, he will strive to emulate Him, and seek to grow ever nearer to the holy and the perfect. But only when he prays with and for others, that is, in public worship, will he realize that he is a member of a greater whole, for then he prays only for that which advances the welfare of all. "He who prays with the community," say the rabbis, "will have his prayer granted."874

Another saying of theirs is that he who prays should have his face directed to the sanctuary, and when he stands on its sacred precincts, he should turn his face toward the Holy of Holies.875 By this they meant that the attitude of the suppliant should ever be toward the highest, making the soul soar up to the Highest and Holiest in reverent awe and adoration, transforming the worshiper into a new character, pure from all dross.

9. Therefore prayer offered with the community upon the sanctified ground of the house of God exerts a specially powerful influence upon the individual. In the silent chamber the oppressed spirit may find calm and composure in prayer; but the pure atmosphere of heavenly freedom and bliss is attained with overwhelming might only by the united worship of hundreds of devout adorers, which rings out like the roaring of majestic billows: "The Lord is in His holy temple; let all the earth keep silence before Him."876 The familiar strains from days of yore touch the deep, long-silent chords of the heart, and awaken dormant sentiments and repressed thoughts, endowing the soul with new wings, to lift itself up toward God, the Father, from whom it had felt itself alienated. In the ardor of communal worship the traditional words of the prayer-book obtain invigorating power; the heart is newly strengthened; the covenant with heaven sealed anew. To such communal prayer, which springs from the heart, the rabbis refer the Biblical words, "to serve Him with the whole heart."877 The synagogal worship exerts an ennobling influence upon the spirit of the individual as well as that of the community. For after all the main object is that the soul which aspires toward God may learn to find God. "Seek ye the Lord while He may be found; call ye upon Him while He is near."878 No man is so poor as he who calls in agony: "O God!" and to whom neither the heaven above nor the heart within answers, "Behold, God is here." Nor is any man so rich with all his possessions as he who realizes, like the Psalmist, that "the nearness of God is the true good," and imbued with this thought exclaims, "Whom have I in heaven but Thee? And beside Thee I desire none upon earth."879

Chapter XLIII. Death and the Future Life

1. The vision of man is directed upwards and forwards; he will not resign himself to decay in the dust like the beast. As he bears in his breast the consciousness of a higher divine world, he is equally confident of his own continuity after death. He cannot and will not believe that with the giving up of his last living breath his being would become dust like that of the animal; or that his soul, which has hitherto accomplished and planned so much, should now suddenly cease altogether to exist. The longing for a future life, however expressed, has filled him and buoyed him up since the very beginning of history. Even the most primitive tribe does not allow its dead to lie and rot like the carcasses of the beast, but lays them to rest in the grave with all their possessions, in the expectation that somewhere and somehow, under, over or beyond the earth, they will continue their lives, even in a better form than before.

This longing for immortality implanted in the human soul is so represented in the legend of Paradise that the tree whose fruit bestowed upon the celestial beings the gift of eternal life—like the Greek ambrosia, "the food of the gods"—was originally intended for mankind also in the divine "Garden of Bliss." But after man fell through sin, all access to it was denied him, in order that he might not stretch out his hand for it and thereby attain that immortality which was vouchsafed only to divine beings.880 According to his original destiny, therefore, man should live forever; and, just as legend allows those divinely elected, like Enoch and Elijah,881 to ascend to heaven alive, so at a later period prophecy predicts a time when God will annihilate death forever.882 Accordingly, through the power of his divine soul man possesses a claim to immortality, to eternal life with God, the "Fountain of life."

2. It was just this keen longing for an energetic life on earth, this mighty yearning to "walk before God in the land of the living,"883 which made it more difficult for Judaism to brighten the "valley of the shadow of death" and to elevate the vague notion of a shadowy existence in the hereafter into a special religious teaching. Until long after the Exile the Jewish people shared the view of the entire ancient world,—both the Semitic nations, such as the Babylonians and Phœnicians, and the Aryans, such as the Greeks and Romans,—that the dead continue to exist in the shadowy realm of the nether world (Sheol), the land of no return (Beliyaal),884 of eternal silence (Dumah), and oblivion (Neshiyah),885 a dull, ghostly existence without clear consciousness and without any awakening to a better life. We must, however, not overlook the fact that even in these most primitive conceptions a certain imperishability is ascribed to man as marking his superiority over the animal world, which is altogether abandoned to decay. Hence the belief in the existence of the shades, the Refaim in Sheol.886 But throughout the Biblical period no ethical idea yet permeated this conception, and no attempt was made to transform the nether world into a place of divine judgment, of recompense for the good and evil deeds accomplished on earth,887 as did the Babylonians and Egyptians. Both the prophets and the Mosaic code persist in applying their promises and threats, in fact, their entire view of retribution, to this world, nor do they indicate by a single word the belief in a judgment or a weighing of actions in the world to come.

3. Whether the Mosaic-prophetic writings be regarded from the standpoint of traditional faith or of historical criticism, the limitation of their teaching and exhortation to the present life can be considered narrowness only by biased expounders of the "Old Testament." The Israelitish lawgiver could not have been altogether ignorant of the Egyptian or the Babylonian conceptions of the future world. Obviously Israel's prophets and lawgivers deliberately avoided giving any definite expression to the common belief in a future life after death, especially as the Canaanitish magicians and necromancers used this popular belief to carry on their superstitious practices, so dangerous to all moral progress.888 The great task which prophetic Judaism set itself was to place the entire life of men and nations in the service of the God of justice and holiness; there was thus no motive to extend the dominion of JHVH, the God of life, to the underworld, the playground of the forces of fear and superstition. As late as the author of the book of Job and of the earlier Psalms, Sheol was known as the despot of the nether world with its demoniacal forms, as the "king of terrors" who extends his scepter over the dead.889 Only gradually does the thought find expression in the Psalms that the Omnipotent Ruler of heaven could also rescue the soul out of the power of Sheol,890 and that His omnipresence included likewise the nether world.891 In this trustful spirit the Hasidic Psalmist expressed the hope: "Thou wilt not abandon my soul to Sheol, neither wilt Thou suffer Thy godly one to see the pit. Thou makest me to know the path of life; in Thy presence is fulness of joy; in Thy right hand bliss forevermore."892

4. Biblical Judaism evinced such a powerful impetus toward a complete and blissful life with God, that the center and purpose of existence could not be transferred to the hereafter, as in other systems of belief, but was found in the desire to work out the life here on earth to its fullest possible development. Virtue and wisdom, righteousness and piety, signify and secure true life; vice and folly, iniquity and sin, lead to death and annihilation. This is the ever recurring burden of the popular as well as of the prophetic and priestly wisdom of Israel.893 In the song of thanks of King Hezekiah after his recovery, the Jewish soul expresses itself, when he says:894 "I said, I shall not see the Lord, even the Lord in the land of the living.... But Thou hast delivered my soul from the pit of corruption. For the nether world cannot praise Thee; death cannot celebrate Thee. The living, the living, he shall praise Thee, as I do this day. The father to the children shall make known Thy truth." Therefore the author of the seventy-third Psalm, ennobled by trials, finds sufficient comfort and happiness in the presence of God that he can spurn all earthly treasures.895 Job, too, in his affliction longed for death as release from all earthly pain and sorrow, but not to bring him a state of rest and peace like the Nirvana of the Indian beggar-monk, or an outlook into a better world to come. Such an awakening to a new life seems to him unthinkable,—although many commentators have often endeavored to read such a hope into certain of his expressions.896 Instead, his belief in God as the Ruler of the infinite world, with His lofty moral purpose far outreaching all human wisdom, lent him courage and power for further effort and persistent striving on earth. Since to this suffering hero, impelled to deeds by his own energy, life is a continuous battle, a hereafter as a "world of reward and punishment" can hardly solve the great enigma of human existence in a satisfactory manner for him. The wise ones—says a Talmudic maxim—find rest neither in this world nor in the world to come, but "they shall ascend from strength to strength, until they appear before God on Zion."897

5. In the course of time, however, the question of existence after death demanded more and more a satisfactory answer. Under the severe political and social oppression that came upon the Jewish people, the pious ones failed to

see a just equation of man's doings and his destiny in this life. The bitter disappointment which they experienced made them look to the God of justice for a future, when virtue would receive its due reward and vice its befitting punishment. The community of the pious especially awaited in vain the realization of the great messianic hope with which the prophetic words of comfort had filled their hearts. They had willingly offered up their lives for the truth of Judaism, and the God of faithfulness could not deceive them. Surely the shadowy realm of the nether world could not be the end of all. So the voice of promise came to them from the book of Isaiah, where these encouraging and comforting words were inserted by a later hand: "Thy dead shall live; thy (My) dead bodies shall arise. Awake and sing, ye that dwell in the dust, for Thy dew is as the dew of herbs, and the earth shall cast forth the shades."898 Even before this time the God of Israel had been praised as "He who killeth and maketh alive, who bringeth down to Sheol, and bringeth up."899 So was also the miraculous power of restoring the dead to life ascribed to the prophets.900 Furthermore, the vision of the prophet Ezekiel concerning the dry bones which arose to new life, in which he beheld the divine revelation of the approaching event of the restoration of the Jewish nation,901 shows how familiar the idea of resurrection must have been to the people. Hence the minds of the Jewish people were sufficiently prepared to adopt the Persian belief in the resurrection of the dead.

6. This, however, led to a tremendous process of transformation in Judaism with a wide chasm between Mosaism and Rabbinism, or, more accurately, between the Sadducees, who adhered to the letter of the law, and the Pharisees, who embodied the progressive spirit of the people. On the one hand, Jesus ben Sira, who at the close of his book speaks with great admiration of the high-priest Simon the Just as his contemporary, knew as yet nothing of a future life, and like Koheleth saw the end of all human existence in the dismal realm of the nether world. Yet at the same time, the Hasidim or pious ones and their successors, the Pharisees, were developing after the Persian pattern the thought of a divine judgment day after death, when the just were to awaken to eternal life, and the evil-doers to shame and everlasting contempt.902 This advanced moral view, frequently overlooked, transformed the ancient Semitic Sheol from the realm of shades to a place of punishment for sinners, and thus invested it with an ethical purpose.903 After this the various Biblical names for the nether world became the various divisions of hell.904 Indeed, the Psalmists and the Proverbs had announced to the wicked their destruction in Sheol, and on the other hand held out for the godly the hope of deliverance from Sheol and a beatific sight of God in the land of the living. Thus the transition was prepared for the new world-conception. All the promises and threats of the law and the prophets, when they did not receive fulfillment in this world, appeared now to point forward to the world to come. Moreover, the Pharisees in their disputes with the Sadducees made use of every reference, however slight, to the future life,—even of such passages as those which speak of the Patriarchs as receiving the promise of possessing the Holy Land, as if they were still alive,—as proofs of the continued life of the dead, or of their resurrection.905 Thus it came about that the leading authorities of rabbinic Judaism were in the position to declare in the Mishnah: "He who says that the belief in the resurrection of the dead is not founded on the Torah (and therefore does not accept it) shall have no share in the world to come."906

7. The founders of the liturgy of the Synagogue, in opposition to the Sadducees, formulated therefore the belief in resurrection in the second of the "Eighteen (or Seven) Benedictions" of the daily prayer in the following words: "Thou, O Lord, art mighty forever. Thou revivest the dead. Thou art mighty to save. Thou sustainest the living with loving-kindness, revivest the dead with great mercy, supportest the falling, healest the sick, loosest the bound, and keepest Thy faith to them that sleep in the dust. (This refers to the Patriarchs, to whom God has promised the land of the future.) Who is like unto Thee, O Lord of mighty acts, and who resembleth Thee, O King, who killest and bringest to life, and causest salvation to spring forth? Yea, faithful art Thou to revive the dead. Blessed art Thou, O Lord, who revivest the dead." In this prayer dating from the age of the Maccabees907 the Jewish consciousness of two thousand years found a twofold hope,—the national and the universally human. The national hope, which combined the belief in the restoration of the kingdom of David and of the sacrificial cult with the resurrection of the dead in the Holy Land, can be understood only in connection with a historic view of Israel's place in the world, and is treated in the third part of this book. The purely human hope for the continuity or the renewal of life rests on two fundamental problems which must be examined more closely in the next two chapters. The one belongs to the province of psychology and considers the question: What is the eternal divine element in man? The other goes more deeply into the religious and moral nature of man and considers the question: Where and how does divine retribution—reward or punishment—take place in human life? To both of these questions our modern view, with its special aim toward a unified grasp of the totality of life, requires a special answer. This can be neither that of rabbinic Judaism, which rests upon Persian dualism, nor that of medieval philosophy, which was under the Platonic-Aristotelian influence.

Chapter XLIV. The Immortal Soul of Man

1. The idea of immortality has been found in Scripture in a rather obscure and probably corrupt passage,908 "In the way of righteousness is life, and in the pathway thereof there is no death." In the same spirit Aquila, the Bible translator, who belonged to the school of R. Eliezer and R. Joshua, renders the equally obscure passage from the Psalms,909 "He will lead us to immortality," reading al maveth, the Al with Alef, for al muth, the Al with Ayin. There is more solid foundation for the view that the verse, "God created man in His own image" implies that there is an imperishable divine essence in man. In fact, that which distinguishes man from the animal as well as from the rest of creation, both the starry worlds above and the manifold forms of life on earth about him, is his self-conscious personality, his ego, through which he feels himself akin with God, the great world-ruling I Am. This self-conscious part of man, which lends to his every manifestation its value and purpose, can no more disappear into nothingness than can God, who called into existence this world with all its phenomena, who set it in motion and directs it. Whatever thought the crudest of men may have of his ego, his self,910 or however the most learned scholar may explain the marvelous action and interaction of physical and psychical or spiritual forces which culminates in his own self-conscious personality, it appears certain that this ego cannot cease to be with the cessation of the bodily functions. There is in us something divine, immortal, and the only question is wherein it may be found.

2. The creation of man which is described in the Bible in the words, "God formed man of the dust of the ground, and breathed into his nostrils the breath of life, and man became a living soul"911 corresponds to the child-like conceptions of a primitive people. On the other hand, Scripture speaks of death in parallel terms, "The dust returneth to the earth as it was, and the spirit (Ruah, the life-giving breath) returneth unto God who gave it."912

The conception that the soul enters into man as the breath of life and leaves him at his death, flying toward heaven like a bird,913 is quite as ancient and as universal as the other, that the soul descends into the nether world as a shadowy image of the body, there to continue a dull existence. The two are related to one another, and in the Bible, as well as in the literature of other peoples, they have given rise to diverse definitions of the soul. This was the point of departure for the development of the conception of immortality in one or the other direction, according to whether the body was considered a part of the personality which somehow survives after death, or only the spiritual substance of the soul was thought to live on in celestial regions as something divine. The former led to the theory of the resurrection of the body and its reunion with the soul; the latter to the belief in a future life for the soul, after it had been separated or released from the body.

3. When once the soul was felt to be a "lamp of the Lord," filling the body with light when man is awake,914 it was easy to imagine that the soul had escaped and temporarily returned to God in sleep. This induced the teachers of the Synagogue to prescribe a morning prayer of thanks which reads, "Blessed art Thou, O God, who restorest the souls unto dead bodies."915 The conception underlying this prayer throws light upon the entire belief in resurrection. Death to the pious is only a prolonged sleep. On that account the prophet in the passage from Isaiah already referred to, as well as the Hasidic author of the Book of Daniel,916 could express the hope that "those who sleep in the dust shall awake." As at every awakening from sleep in the morning, so at the great awakening in the future, the souls which have departed in death shall return again to their bodies. These bodies could then hardly be conceived of as subject to decomposition, and the picture in Ezekiel's vision of resurrection917 had to be accepted as fact. Still R. Simeon b. Yohai in the especially instructive thirty-fourth chapter of Pirke de R. Eliezer assumes the complete disintegration of the body, in order to render the miracle of resurrection so much the greater. Later still arose the legend of an indestructible bone of the spinal column, called Luz, which was to form the nucleus for the revival of the whole body.918 The name Luz, which denotes an almond tree and is the name given in the Bible to a city also,919 seemed to point to a connection with two legends, a fabulous city into which death could not enter,920 and the tree of resurrection in the Osiris cycle.921

4. Still, no clear, consistent view of the soul prevailed as yet in the rabbinic age. The popular belief, influenced by Persian notions, was that the soul lingers near the body for a certain time after it has relinquished it, either from three to seven days or for an entire year.922 Furthermore it was said that after death the souls hovered between heaven and earth in the form of ghosts, able to overhear the secrets of the future decreed above and to betray them to human beings below. In fact, the rabbis of the Talmud, especially the Hasidim, never hesitated to accept these ghost stories.923 Some sages of the Talmudic period taught that the souls of the righteous ascend to heaven, there to dwell under the throne of the divine majesty, awaiting the time of the renewal of the world, while the souls of

the godless hovered over the horizon of the earth as restless demoniacal spirits, finally to succumb to the fate of annihilation, after they had been cast down into the fiery pit of Gehenna or Sheol.924 Of course, this view, which prevails in both the Talmud and the New Testament, according to which the souls of the wicked are to be consumed in the fire of Gehenna, is inconsistent with the conception of the purely spiritual nature of the soul.

Nevertheless at this same epoch we find the higher idea expressed that the soul is an invisible, god-like essence, pervading the body as a spiritual force and differing from it in nature in much the same way as God is differentiated from the world.925 "Thou wishest to know where God dwells, who is as high as are the heavens above the earth; tell me then where dwells thy soul, which is so near," replied R. Gamaliel to a heathen.926 The prevailing view of the schools is that God implants the soul in the embryo while in the mother's womb, together with all the spiritual potentialities which make it human. In fact, R. Simlai, the third-century Haggadist, advances the Platonic conception of the preëxistence of the soul, as a being of the highest intelligence, which sees before birth all things throughout the world, but forgets all at birth, so that all subsequent learning is only a recollection.927 In Hellenistic Judaism especially the doctrine seems to have been general of the preëxistence of the soul, or of the creation of all human souls simultaneously with the creation of the world.928 Of course, the soul which emanates from a higher world must be eternal.

5. The first clear idea of the nature of the soul came with the philosophically trained thinkers, who were dependent either on Plato, main founder of the doctrine of the immortality of the soul, or on Aristotle, who ascribes immortality only to the creative spirit of God, the supreme Intelligence as a cosmic power. The nearest approach to Plato was Philo,929 who saw in the three Biblical names for the soul, nefesh, ruah, and neshama, the three souls of the Platonic system,—the sensuous soul, which has its seat in the abdomen; the courageous or emotional soul, situated in the breast; and the intellectual soul, which dwells in the brain and contains the imperishable divine nature. This last is kept in its physical environment as in a prison or a grave, and ever yearns for liberation and reunion with God. The soul of the righteous enters the world of angels after death; that of the wicked the world of demons.

Saadia, who was under the influence of Aristotle interpreted from the neo-Platonic viewpoint, did not share the Platonic dualism of matter and spirit, nor did he divide the soul into three parts, seated in various parts of the human body. He finds the soul to be a spiritual substance created simultaneously with the body, and uniting the three forces of the soul distinguished in Scripture into one inseparable whole, the seat of which is in the heart,—wherefore soul and heart are often synonymous in the Bible. This indivisible substance possesses a luminous nature like that of the spheres, but is simpler, finer, and purer than they, and endowed with the power of thought. It was created by God out of the primal ether from which He made the angels, simultaneously with the body and within it. By this union it was qualified to display that moral activity prescribed for it in the divine teaching, the neglect of which would defile and tarnish it. According to Saadia some kind of material substance adheres to the soul as well as to the angels, and on that account he does not hesitate to accept the Talmudic expressions about the abode of the soul after death, or the last judgment which is to take place as soon as the appointed number of souls shall have made their entrance into their earthly bodies, when the souls of the righteous will have their angelic nature recognized, and those of the wicked will have their lower character revealed. However, Saadia combats with so much greater fervor the Hindu teaching of metempsychosis, which had been adopted by Plato and Pythagoras.930

Bahya connects his theory with the three souls of Plato, and likewise ascribes to the soul an ethereal essence.931 He holds that its destiny is to raise itself to the order of the angels through self-purification, and finally to return to God as the divine Source of light. To this end the intellectual soul, which has its being from the primal light, must overcome the lower sensuous soul which leads to sin.

6. The conception that the soul is a substance derived from the luminous primal matter, like the heavenly spheres and the angels, was now persistently retained by the Jewish thinkers, who explained thereby its immortality. In adopting the Aristotelian theory that the soul is the form-principle of the body, the Platonic doctrine of its preexistence was gradually relinquished, and its existence ascribed to a creative act of God at the birth of the child or at its conception. But Jehuda ha-Levi, the most pious of all the philosophers, emphasized vigorously the indivisibility of the soul, its incorporeality and its reality apart from the condition of the body, and—in opposition to the Aristotelian free-thinkers, who expected the human soul to be absorbed into the divine soul, the active intellect,—he declared the immortality of the individual a fundamental article of faith.932

Now some of the Jewish thinkers, following Jehuda ha Levi, Ibn Daud, and others, though Aristotelians, shrank from the logical conclusion of denying all individuality to the soul, and attributed to it rather a process of purification, which ends with the elevation of the soul-essence to angelic rank and thus guarantees its immortality. Not so Maimonides, who accepted with inexorable earnestness the Aristotelian idea of form as the perfection of matter. The essence of the human soul is, for him, that force or potentiality which qualifies it for the highest development of the intellect, and is alone capable of grasping the divine. Yet it can acquire a part in the creative World-spirit only in the same degree as it unfolds this potentiality to share the divine intellect, whose seat is the highest sphere of the universe. By dint of this acquired intelligence it can live on as an independent intellect, in the image of God, and thus attain beatitude in the contemplation of Divinity.933

7. Naturally the view of Maimonides, that a certain measure of immortality is granted only to the wise,—though they must be morally perfect as well,—aroused great opposition. Hasdai Crescas proves its untenableness by asking, "Why shall the wise alone share in immortality? Furthermore, how can something that came into existence in the course of human life suddenly acquire eternal duration? Or how can there be any bliss in the knowledge of God where there is no personality, no self-conscious ego to enjoy it?" Therefore Crescas ascribed to the soul an indestructible spiritual essence whose perfection is attained, not by mere intellect or knowledge, but by love of God manifested in a religious and moral life, and which is thereby made to share in eternal bliss.934

8. All these various thinkers find the future life either expressed or suggested in the Scriptures as a truth based upon reason. This is especially the conception of Abraham ibn Daud, who, contrary to his Aristotelian successor Maimonides, sees in self-consciousness, by which the soul differentiates itself from the body as a personality, the proof that it cannot be subject to dissolution with the body.935

Besides the philosophic doctrine of the immortality of the soul, however, the traditional belief in the resurrection of the body demanded some consideration on the part of these philosophers. Saadia defends the latter with all his might, endeavoring to reconcile the two as best he can.936 All the rest leave us in doubt whether resurrection is to be understood literally or symbolically. Maimonides especially involves himself in difficulties, inasmuch as in his commentary on the Mishna he considers the resurrection of the dead an unalterable article of faith, whereas in his Code937 and in the Moreh he speaks only of immortality; and again before the end of his life he wrote, obviously in self-defense, a work which seems to favor bodily resurrection, yet without clarifying his conceptions at any time.938 The belief in resurrection had taken too deep a root in the Jewish consciousness and had been too firmly established through the liturgy of the Synagogue for any philosopher to touch it without injuring the very foundations of faith.

Moreover, beside external caution a certain inner need seems to have impelled toward the acceptance of resurrection. As soon as one thinks of the soul as existing or continuing to live in an incorporeal state, one is involuntarily led toward the belief in the soul's preëxistence or even in the possibility of metempsychosis. Thus it seemed more reasonable to believe in a new formation of the human body together with a new creation of the world. Therewith came the disposition to assign to the soul in the future world a body of finer substance, like that assumed by the mystic Nahmanides,939 in order to assure to the new humanity a wondrous duration of life like that of Elijah.

9. While the popular philosopher Albo rightly declares that the nature of the soul is as far beyond all human understanding as is the nature of God,940 the mystics sought all the more to penetrate its secrets. The Cabbalah also divides the soul into three different substances according to the three Biblical names, assigning their origins to the three different spheres of the universe, and reiterating the Platonic theory of the preexistence of the soul and its future transmigration. This division into three parts provided scope for all types of theories concerning the soul in its sensuous, its moral, and its intellectual nature. Fundamentally the Cabbalah considered the soul an emanation from the divine intellect with a luminous character just like the philosophers. But in the Platonic view of the ascending order of creation, which forms the basis of the Cabbalah, this mundane life is an abyss of moral degradation, so that the soul yearns toward the primal Source of light, finally to find freedom and bliss with God.941 Thus the later Cabbalah returned to the teachings of Philo, the Jewish Plato, for whom death was only the stripping off of the earthly frame in order to enter the pure and luminous world of God.

10. With Moses Mendelssohn, who in his Phædon tried to translate Plato's proof of immortality into modern terms, a new attitude toward the nature and destiny of the soul arose in Judaism among both the philosophers and the educated laity. Mendelssohn not only endeavored to prove the immortality of the soul through its indivisibility and

incorporeality, as all the neo-Platonists and Jewish philosophers had done before him; he also attempted to show from the harmonious plan which pervades and controls all of God's creation, that the soul may enter a sphere of existence greater in extent and content than the little span of earthly life which it relinquishes. The progress of the soul toward its highest unfolding, unsatisfied in this life, demands a future growth in the direction of god-like perfection.942 At this point the philosopher enters the province of faith, and thus furnishes for all time the cardinal point of the belief in immortality. The divine spirit in man, which is evinced in the self-conscious, morally active personality, bears within itself the proof and promise of its future life. Moreover, this corresponds with the belief in God as One who rules the world for the eternal purposes and aims of perfection, who cannot deceive the hope of the human heart for a continued living and striving onward and forward, without thereby impairing His own perfection. For we all close our lives without having attained the goal of moral and spiritual perfection toward which we strive; and therefore our very nature demands a world where we may reach the higher degree of perfection for which we long. In this sense we may interpret the Psalmist's verse: "I shall be satisfied, when I awake, with (beholding) Thy likeness."943 That is: our spirit, when no longer bound to the earth, shall behold the divine glory,—a vision which transcends our powers of thought.

11. In the light of modern investigation, body and soul are seen to be indissolubly bound together by a reciprocal relation which either benefits or impedes them both. Wherein the spiritual bond exists that renders both the physical organs with their muscular and nervous systems and the magnetic or electric currents which set them in motion subservient to the will of the intellect; what the mind actually is, into whose deepest recesses science is casting its search-light to illumine its processes,—these are problems which will probably remain ever incapable of solution by human knowledge, and will therefore always afford new food for the imagination. Yet it is just in periods like ours, when the belief in God is weakening, that the human spirit is especially solicitous to guard itself against the thought of the complete annihilation of its god-like self-conscious personality. This gives rise to the superstitious effort to spy out the soul by sensory means and to find ways of seeing or hearing the spirits of the dead,—a tendency which is as dangerous to the spiritual and moral welfare of humanity as was the ancient practice of necromancy.944 It is therefore all the more important to base the belief in immortality solely on the God-likeness of the human soul, which is the mirror of Divinity. Just as one postulate of faith holds that God, the Creator of the world, rules in accordance with a moral order, so another is the immortality of the human soul, which, amidst yearning and groping, beholds God. The question where, and how, this self-same ego is to continue, will be left for the power of the imagination to answer ever anew.

12. Certainly it is both comforting and convenient to imagine the dead who are laid to rest in the earth as being asleep and to await their reawakening. As the fructifying rain awakens to a new life the seeds within the soil, so that they rise from the depths arrayed in new raiment, so, when touched by the heavenly dew of life, will those who linger in the grave arise to a new existence, clad in new bodies. This is the belief which inspired the pious founders of the synagogal liturgy even before the period of the Maccabees, when they expressed their praise of God's power in that He would send the fertilizing rain upon the vegetation of the earth, and likewise in due time the revivifying dew upon the sleeping world of man. Both appeared to the sages of that age to be evidences of the same wonder-working power of God. Whoever, therefore, still sees God's greatness, as they did, revealed through miracles, that is, through interruptions of the natural order of life, may cling to the traditional belief in resurrection, so comforting in ancient times. On the other hand, he who recognizes the unchangeable will of an all-wise, all-ruling God in the immutable laws of nature must find it impossible to praise God according to the traditional formula as the "Reviver of the dead," but will avail himself instead of the expression used in the Union Prayer Book after the pattern of Einhorn, "He who has implanted within us immortal life."945

Chapter XLV. Divine Retribution: Reward and Punishment

1. The feeling of equity is deeply rooted in human nature, demanding reparation for every wanton wrong and yielding recognition to every benevolent act. In fact, upon this universal principle is based all justice and to a certain extent all morality. Judaism of every age compresses this demand of the religious and moral nature of man into the doctrine: God rewards the good and punishes the evil. This doctrine, which is the eleventh of Maimonides' articles of faith, constitutes the underlying presumption of all the Biblical narratives as well as of the prophetic threats and warnings and those of the Mosaic law, in so far as earthly success and prosperity were regarded as the rewards of God and earthly misfortune and misery as His punishments. In the same degree, however, as experience

contradicted this doctrine, and as examples multiplied of wicked persons revelling in prosperity and innocent ones laboring under adversity and woe, it became necessary to defer the divine retribution more and more to the future—at first to a future on earth and later to one in the world to come, until finally it developed into a pure spiritual conception in full accord with a higher ethical view of life.

2. As long as in the primitive process of law the family or the clan was held responsible for the crime of the individual, ancient Israel also adhered to the idea that "God visits the sins of the fathers upon the third and fourth generation," as Jeremiah still did946 in full accord with the second commandment. It was in a far later stage that the rabbis interpreted the words "of those who hate Me" in the sense of individual responsibility.947 Only in accordance with the Deuteronomic law which says: "The fathers shall not be put to death for the children, neither shall the children be put to death for the fathers; every man shall be put to death for his own sin,"948 did the religious consciousness rebel against the thought that a later generation should suffer for the sins of its ancestors, and hence the popular adage arose, "The fathers have eaten sour grapes, and the teeth of the children are set on edge."949 It is the prophet Ezekiel who refutes once and for all the idea of a guilt transmitted to children and consequently of hereditary sin and punishment, insisting on the doctrine that personal responsibility alone determines divine retribution.950 But here a new element affects divine retribution. God's long-suffering and mercy do not desire the immediate punishment, the death of the sinner. He should be given time to return to a better mode of life.951

But the great enigma of human destiny, which vexes the author of the seventy-third Psalm and that of the book of Job, still presses for a better solution. It is true that the popular belief and popular legends which are preserved in post-Biblical writings as well, insisted on a justice which requites "measure for measure."952 Still insight into actual life does not confirm the teaching of the popular philosophy that the "righteous will be requited in the earth" and that "evil pursueth sinners."953 The unshakeable belief in the justice of God had to find another solution for life's antinomies, and was forced to reach out for another world in which the divine righteousness would find its complete realization.

3. Biblical Judaism with few exceptions recognized only the present world and the subterranean world of shadows, a view preserved in its essentials by Ben Sira and the Sadducees, who were subsequently declared heretics. In contrast to them Pharisaic or Rabbinic Judaism teaches a resurrection after death for a life of eternal bliss or eternal torment, according as the divine judgment finds one righteous and another wicked. We may leave aside the consideration that the first impulse toward a Jewish belief in resurrection came from the non-fulfillment of the national hope, wherefore it was always bound up with the soil of the Holy Land, as will be seen in Chapter LIV. The fact remains that the divine judgment to follow upon resurrection was consistently regarded as a great world-judgment, which was to decide the future lot of all men and spirits. It must be noted also that the apocalyptic and midrashic literature often identifies the pious with the God-fearing Israelites as those who shall arise to eternal life, while the wicked are identified with the idolatrous heathen, who are condemned to eternal death, or, as it is frequently expressed, to a second death.954

4. Exactly as the old Persian Mazdaism expected the resurrection of all, both good and bad, the believers in Ahura Mazda as well as the rest of humanity, so the apocalyptic writers prior to the Talmudic period describe resurrection as universal: "In those days the earth will give back those who have been entrusted to her, and the nether-world will release that which it has received," according to Enoch LI, 1. Similarly fourth Esdras remarks: "And after seven days of silence for all creatures, the new order of the world shall be raised up, and mortality itself shall perish; and the earth shall restore those that are asleep in her; and so shall the dust give back those that dwell in silence; and the chambers shall deliver those souls that were committed unto them. The Most High shall appear on the throne of judgment, and shall say: Judgment only shall remain, truth shall stand, and faith shall wax strong. The good deeds shall be of force, and wicked deeds shall no longer sleep. The lake of torment shall be revealed, and opposite to it the place of joy; the furnace of Gehinnom will be visible, and opposite to it the bliss of Paradise. Then the Most High will speak to the heathen nations, who have awakened: behold now Him whom ye have denied, whom ye have not served, whose command ye have abhorred. Gaze now here and there,—here bliss and rest, there fire and torment."955

The rabbinic form of the doctrine of resurrection is quite unambiguous: "Those born into the world are destined to die; the dead, to live again; and those who enter the world to come, to be judged."956 And wherever the rabbinic or apocalyptic literature mentions the share of the pious, or of Israel, in eternal life, this implies that, while these enter the world to come, the evil-doers or idolaters shall enter hell for eternal death; the understanding being that there is a universal resurrection for the world-judgment.

5. The whole system of eschatology in connection with resurrection arose undoubtedly from the Persian doctrine, according to which death together with all that is evil and unclean is created by Ahriman, the evil principle, and will suffer annihilation with him, as soon as the good principle, Ahura Mazda, has achieved the final victory. Then Soshiosh "the Savior," the descendant of Zoroaster, will begin his kingdom of eternal life for the righteous, coincident with the awakening of the dead.957 Pharisaic Judaism, however, gave the hope of resurrection a deeper moral and religious meaning. The proofs, or rather analogies from nature, of the seeds springing from the earth in a new form, of men awakening from sleep in the morning, or of the original creation, are shared by the rabbis and the New Testament writers with the Persians. On the other hand, proofs based on the prophetic hope for the future are purely national. So also are those proofs based on the Biblical passage that the God of the fathers had sworn to the Patriarchs to give them the Promised Land.958 Likewise the reference to the wondrous resurrections related in the history of Elijah and Elisha offers no proof of a universal resurrection. A striking point and one which deepens the idea of retribution is the simile of the Lame and the Blind959 employed by Jehuda ha Nasi in a dialogue with the Emperor Antoninus. The latter had said that at the last judgment both soul and body might deny all guilt. The body may say: "The soul alone has sinned, for since it has parted from me, I have lain motionless as a stone." And the soul, on its part, may reply: "It must be the body that sinned, for since I have parted from it I soar about in the air free as a bird." To this Jehuda ha Nasi answered: "A king once possessed a garden with splendid fig-trees, and appointed as watchmen in it a blind man and a lame man. Then the lame man spoke to the blind man, 'I see fine figs up there; take me upon your shoulders, and I shall pick them, and we can enjoy them together.' They did so, and when the king entered the garden, the figs were gone. But when they were held to account for it, the lame man said, 'How could I have taken them, since I cannot walk?' And the blind man said, 'And I cannot see.' Then the king had the lame man placed upon the shoulders of the blind man and judged them both together. In like manner will God treat the body and the soul, as it is said:960 'He calleth to the heavens above—that is, the heavenly element, the soul—and to the earth beneath—the earthly body—and places them together before His throne of judgment.'"

6. It cannot be denied that the idea that the soul and body, having committed good or evil deeds together in this life, should receive in common their reward or punishment in the world to come, satisfied the Jewish sense of justice better than the conception developed by Hellenistic Judaism (after the Platonic and, in the last resort, the Egyptian view) that the soul alone should partake of eternal bliss or torment. Nevertheless the philosophically trained Jewish thinkers of Alexandria could not bring themselves to accept a bodily resurrection, and therefore emphasized so much more strongly the great day of judgment and the reward and punishment of the soul in the world to come. Still we find much inconsistency among various authors, sometimes even in the same work, in the conception of future bliss for the good and torture for the wicked. These varied according to the more sensuous or more spiritual view taken of the soul and the celestial world, and according to the literal or figurative interpretation of the Biblical allusions to "fire," "worms," and the like in the punishment of evil-doers, and of the delights awaiting the righteous in the future.961

On this point free play was allowed to the imagination of the people and the fancy of the Haggadists. Still, throughout, the solemn thought found its echo that mortal man must give account to the inexorable Judge of the living and the dead for the life just completed, in order to be ushered, according to his deserts, into the portals of the celestial Paradise or of hell.962 This led to the view that this whole mundane life is but like a wayfarers' inn for the life to come, or the vestibule of the palace (more precisely the "banquet-hall") of the future.963

7. A further development of the principle of justice in application to future retribution led not merely to such a depiction of the tortures of hell and the delights of heaven that the maxim: "measure for measure," so often deviated from in this life, could find complete realization in the world to come. An intermediate stage also was devised for those whose merit or guilt would enroll them neither among the righteous for eternal bliss, nor among the wicked for eternal punishment. While the stern teachers of the school of Shammai insisted that these mediocre ones must undergo a twelve-month process of purification in the fires of Gehenna, the milder school of Hillel maintained that the divine mercy would grant them admission into Paradise even without the fires of purgatory964, either through the merit of the patriarchs965 or owing to the deserts of a son who has been trained to reverence for God, as is indicated by the legend concerning the Kaddish prayer.966 In any case, the teaching of Hillel concerning the all-sufficing mercy of God swept aside the old hopeless conception that eternal suffering in

hell awaits the average man, which was adhered to by the Christian church in connection with its dogma of the atoning blood of Christ. Likewise, in the dispute of schools as to whether or not the bliss of eternal life would be accorded also to the righteous among the heathen, the more humane view of Joshua ben Hananiah prevailed over the gloomier one of the Shammaite Eliezer ben Hyrcanos, and therefore the doctrine became generally accepted, "The righteous of all nations shall have a share in the world to come."967

8. The apocalyptic writers, who largely influenced the New Testament, and also the Haggadists refer with fond interest to the banquet of the pious in the world to come, where they would be served with heavenly manna as bread, with wine preserved from the days of the creation, and with the flesh of the Leviathan or the fruit of the Tree of Life.968 On the other hand they elaborated the tortures of the evil-doers in hell which are to afford a pleasing sight to the pious in heaven, just as the torments of the sinners are aggravated by the sight of the righteous enjoying all delights.969 But at the same time we meet with a more refined and spiritual conception of future reward and punishment among the disciples of R. Jehuda ha Nasi, in the Babylonian Rab, and the Palestinian R. Johanan and his pupil Simeon ben Lakish. "In the future world," says Rab, "there are no sensual enjoyments nor passions, but the righteous sit at the table of God with wreaths upon their heads (like the Greek sages at a symposium!), feeding on the radiance of the divine majesty, as did the chosen ones of Israel on the heights of Sinai."970 R. Johanan teaches, "All the promises held forth in Scripture in definite form as reward for the future, refer to the Messianic era, whereas in regard to the bliss awaiting the pious in the world to come, the words of Isaiah hold good: 'No eye hath seen it, O God, beside Thee.'"971 Simeon ben Lakish even went so far as to say, "There is neither hell nor paradise. Instead, God sends out the sun in its full strength from its encasement, and the wicked are consumed by its heat, while the pious find delight and healing in its beams."972

However, the popular imagination demanded more perceptible pictures of heaven and hell, if fear of punishment was to deter men from sin, and hope of reward to lead them to virtue. The description of the modes of reward and punishment for the future in the Koran is the outcome of mingled Persian and Jewish popular conceptions, and its crass sensuousness exerted in turn a decisive influence upon the entire Gaonic period,973 leaving its mark upon even so clear a thinker as Saadia. Not only does he admit into his philosophic work all the crude and conflicting descriptions of the future world, but he also argues for the eternity of the punishments of hell and of the delights of heaven as logical necessities, because only such could sufficiently deter or allure mankind, and a righteous God must certainly carry out His threats and promises.974

9. The entire Jewish philosophy or theology of the Middle Ages remained under the influence of the traditional belief in resurrection. Even Maimonides, whose purely spiritual conception of the soul and of salvation is utterly irreconcilable with the belief in bodily resurrection, and who accordingly dwells instead, in both his Moreh and his Code, on the future world of spirits, with explicit emphasis on their incorporeality, did not have the courage to break altogether with the traditional belief in resurrection. In his apologetic treatise on resurrection he even attempts to present it as a miraculous act of God beyond the grasp of the intellect. He omits, however, to specify what purpose this miracle may serve, since in the Maimonidean system reward and punishment would be administered in the world of spirits in a much purer and more satisfactory manner.975 The same standpoint is taken also by Jehuda ha Levi as well as by Crescas and Albo.976 If then resurrection be a miracle, it falls outside the scope of philosophic speculation and becomes a matter of faith; accordingly the mystics from Nahmanides down to Manasseh ben Israel associated with it the grossest conceptions.977

10. The actual view of Maimonides concerning future retribution is expressed clearly and unambiguously in both his early product, the commentary on the Mishna, and in the ripest fruit of his life work, the Mishneh Torah, where he says "Not immortality, but the power to win eternal life through the knowledge and the love of God is implanted in the human soul. If it has the ability to free itself from the bondage of the senses and by means of the knowledge of God to lift itself to the highest morality and the purest thinking, then it has attained divine bliss, true immortality, and it enters the realm of the eternal Spirit together with the angels. If it sinks into the sensuousness of earthly existence, then it is cut off from eternal life; it suffers annihilation like the beast. In reality this life eternal is not the future, but is already potentially present and invariably at hand in the spirit of man himself, with its constant striving toward the highest. When the rabbis speak of paradise and hell, describing vividly the delights of the one and the torments of the other, these are only metaphors for the agony of sin and the happiness of virtue. True piety serves God neither from fear of punishment nor from desire for reward, as servants obey their master, but from pure love of God and truth. Thus the saying of Ben Azai is verified, 'The reward of a good deed is the good deed itself.'978 Only children need bribes and threats to be trained to morality. Thus religion trains mankind. The

people who cannot penetrate into the kernel need the shell, the external means of threats and promises."979 These splendid words of the great thinker require supplementing or modification in only one direction, and that has been afforded by the keenest critic among Jewish philosophers, Hasdai Crescas. Too deeply enmeshed in the Aristotelian system, Maimonides found the happiness and immortality of man solely in the acquired intellectual power which becomes part of the divine intellect, and the mere knowledge of God is to him tantamount to the blissful enjoyment of the pious in the radiance of God's majesty. Consequently those who strive and soar heavenward through their moral conduct and noble aspirations, without at the same time being thinkers, receive no reward. Against this Aristotelian one-sidedness Crescas emphasizes God's love and goodness for which the righteous yearn, and in whose pursuit man finds perfection and happiness. Not for the sake of attaining bliss shall we love God and practice virtue and truth, but to love God and practice virtue is itself true bliss. This is the nearness of God referred to by the Psalmist and declared to be man's highest good.980 There is no need of any other reward than this, and there is no greater punishment than to be deprived of this boon forever.981

11. In the face of these two great thinkers, to whom Spinoza owes the fundamental ideas of his ethics,982 the question considered by Albo, whether the eternal duration of the tortures of hell is reconcilable with the divine mercy,983 a question which still plays an important rôle in Christian theology, and which was probably suggested to Albo through his disputations with representatives of the Church,—is for us superfluous and superseded. Our modern conceptions of time and space admit neither a place or a world-period for the reward and punishment of souls, nor the intolerable conception of eternal joy without useful action and eternal agony without any moral purpose. Modern man knows that he bears heaven and hell within his own bosom. Indeed, so much more difficult is the life of duty which knows of no other reward than happiness through harmony with God, the Father of the immortal soul, and of no other punishment than the soul's distress at its inner discord with the primal Source and the divine Ideal of all morality. All the more powerfully is modern man controlled by the thought that the universe permits no stagnation, no barren enjoyment or barren suffering, but that every death marks the transition to a higher goal for greater accomplishment. This yearning of the soul finds expression in the Talmudic maxim, "The righteous find rest neither in this world, nor in the world to come, as it is said, 'They go from strength to strength, until they appear before God on Zion.' "984

Chapter XLVI. The Individual and the Race

1. In every system of belief the object of divine care and guidance is the individual. His soul and his conscience raise him up, especially according to the Jewish doctrine, to the divine image, to Godchildship. His freedom and moral responsibility are the patent of nobility for his divine nature; his ego, controlling external forces and carrying out its own designs, vouches for his immortality. Nevertheless the spirit of the Biblical language indicates rightly that the individual is only a son of man,—ben adam,—that is, a segment or member of the human race, but not the perfect typical exemplification of the whole of mankind. From the social organism he receives what he is, what he has, and what he ought to do, both his nature and his destiny; and only in association with the community and under the guidance of the highest ideal of humanity can he attain true perfection. Only mankind as a whole, in its coöperation, as it extends over the vast expanse of the earth, and in its succession which reaches through the centuries of the world's history, can bring to full development the divine image in man, his moral and religious nature with all its varied potentialities. It is man collectively who in the first chapter of Genesis receives the command to subject the earth with all its creatures to his cultural purposes.985 In whatever stage of culture we meet man, his modes of thought and speech, his customs and moral views, even his spiritual faculties are the result of a long historic process of development, the product of an extremely complicated past, as well as the basis of a future which expands in all directions. The ancients expressed this in their suggestive way, remarking in connection with the verse of the Psalm, "Thine eyes did see mine unformed substance, and in Thy book they were all written,"986 that at the creation of the first man God recorded the succession of races with their sages, seers and leaders until the end of time.987 And when the Haggadists say that in creating man God took dust from every part of the world, so that he would be everywhere at home,988 again they were thinking of mankind. Similarly in the passage from the Psalms, "Thou hast hemmed me in behind and before," they explain that God made the first man with two faces, one looking forward and the other backward, that is, with a Janus head; and thus they regard man in his relation to the past and the future, in his historic continuity.989 As both physically and spiritually he is the heir of innumerable ancestors who have transmitted to him with their blood all their idiosyncrasies and capacities in a peculiar combination, so will he transmit both consciously and unconsciously the inherited

possessions of mankind to future generations for continued growth or for degeneration. He forms but a link in the great chain of history, whose goal is the perfected ideal of humanity, the completed idea of man. This was the underlying thought of Ben Azzai in his dispute with R. Akiba, who held that the principal maxim of Jewish teaching is "Thou shalt love thy neighbor as thyself." In opposition to this Ben Azzai presented as the most important lesson of the Bible the verse which says, "This is the book of the generations of man; in the day that God created man, in the likeness of God made He him."990 The godlikeness of man develops more and more through the evolution of the human race. This is the basic force for all human love and all human worth.

2. This social bond existing between the individual and the race imposes upon him in accordance with his occupation certain duties in the same degree as it confers benefits. Ben Zoma, a colleague of Ben Azzai, expressed this as follows: When he saw great crowds of people together, he exclaimed, "Praised be Thou who hast created all these to serve me." In explanation of this blessing he said, "How hard the first man in his loneliness must have toiled, until he could eat a morsel of bread or wear a garment, but I find everything prepared. The various workmen, from the farmer to the miller and the baker, from the weaver to the tailor, all labor for me. Can I then be ungrateful and be oblivious of my duty?"991 In the same sense he interprets the last verse in Koheleth, "This is the end of the matter; fear God and keep His commandments, for this is the whole duty of man." That is to say, all mankind toils for him who does so. Thus does human life rest upon a reciprocal relation, upon mutual duty.992

3. Man is a social being who must strike root in many spheres of life in order that the variegated blossoms and fruits of his spiritual and emotional nature may sprout forth. The more richly the communal life is specialized into professions and occupations, the more does the province of the individual expand, and the more difficult it is for him to attain perfection on all sides. According to his faculties and predisposition he must always develop one or the other side of human endeavor and pursue now the beautiful, now the good, now the true and now the useful, if as the image of God he is to emulate the Ideal of all existence, the Pattern of all creation. Consequently he may reflect some radiance of the divine glory in his character and achievements, whether as moral hero, as sage and thinker, as statesman and battler for freedom, as artist, or as the discoverer of new forces and new worlds; and yet the full splendor of God's greatness is mirrored only by mankind as a whole through its ceaseless common action and interaction. Therefore Judaism deprecates every attempt to present a single individual, be he ever so noble or wise, as the ideal of all human perfection, as a perfect man, free from fault or blemish. "There is none holy as the Lord, for there is none beside Thee," says Scripture.993 Instead of extolling any single mortal as the type or ideal of perfection, our sages rather say with reference to the lofty characters of the Bible: "There is no generation which cannot show a man with the love for righteousness of an Abraham, or the nobility of spirit of a Moses, or the love for truth of a Samuel."994 That is to say, every age creates its own heroes, who reflect the majesty of God in their own way.

4. As man is the keystone of all creation, so he is called upon to take his full share in the progress of the race. "He who formed the earth created it not a waste; He formed it to be inhabited," says the prophet.995 True humanity has its seat, not in the life of the recluse, but in the family circle, amid mutual love and loyalty between husband and wife, between parents and children. The sages, with their keen insight into the spirit of the Scripture, point to the fact that it is man and wife together who first receive the name of "man," because only the mutual helpfulness and influence, the care and toil for one another draw forth the treasures of the soul, and create relations which warrant permanency and give promise of a future.996

5. Still the family circle itself is only a segment of the nation, which creates speech and custom, and assigns to each person his share in the common activity of the various classes of men. Only within the social bond of the nation or tribe is the interdependence of all brought home to the consciousness of the individual, together with all the common moral obligations and religious yearnings. Through the few elect ones of the nation or tribe, God's voice is heard as to what is right in both custom and law, and through them the individual is roused to a sense of duty. It is society which enables the human mind to triumph over physical necessity by ever new discoveries of tools and means of life, thus to attain freedom and prosperity, and, through meditation over the continually expanding realm of God's world, to build up the various systems of science and of art.

6. But the single nation also is too dependent upon the conditions of its historic past, of its land and its racial characteristics, to bring the divine image to its full development in a perfect man. Humanity as a whole comes to its own, to true self-consciousness, only through the reciprocal contact of race with race, through the coöperation of

the various circles and classes of life which extend beyond the narrow limits of nationality and have in view common interests and aims, whether in the pursuit of truth, in the achievement of good, or in the creation of the useful and the beautiful. Only when the various nations and groups of men learn to regard themselves as members of one great family, will the life of the individual find its true value in relation to the idea and the ideal of humanity. Then only will the unity and harmony of the entire cosmic life find its reflection in the blending of the factors and forces of human society.

7. Judaism has evolved the idea of the unity of mankind as a corollary of its ethical monotheism. Therefore the Bible begins the history of the world with the creation of Adam and Eve, the one human pair. The covenant which God concluded after the flood with Noah, the father of the new mankind, has its corresponding goal at the end of time in the divine covenant which is to include all tribes of men in one great brotherhood; and so also the dispersion of man through the confusion of tongues at the building of the Tower of Babel has its counterpart in the rallying of all nations at the end of time for the worship of the One and Only God in a pure tongue and a united spirit on Zion's heights.997 Whatever the civilizations of Greece and Rome and the Stoic philosophy have achieved for the idea of humanity, Judaism has offered in its prophetic hope for a Messianic future the guiding idea for the progress of man in history, thus giving him the impulse to ceaseless efforts toward the highest of all aims for the realization of which all nations and classes, all systems of faith and thought, must labor together for millenniums to come.

Chapter XLVII. The Moral Elements of Civilization

1. Because Judaism sees the attainment of human perfection only when the divine in man has reached complete development through the unimpeded activity of all his spiritual, moral, and social forces, it insists upon the full recognition of all branches of human society as instruments of man's elevation, either individually or collectively. It deprecates the idea that any force or faculty of human life be regarded as unholy and therefore be suppressed. It thus rejects on principle monastic renunciation and isolation, pointing to the Scriptural verse, "He who formed the earth created it not a waste; He formed it to be inhabited.998"

2. Accordingly Judaism regards the establishment of family life through marriage as a duty obligatory on mankind, and sees in the entrance into the marital relation an act of life's supreme consecration. In contrast to the celibacy sanctioned by the Church and approved by the rabbis only under certain conditions, and exceptionally for their holy exercises by the Essenes, the Tannaite R. Eliezer pronounces the man who through bachelorhood shirks the duty of rearing children to be guilty of murder against the human race. Another calls him a despoiler of the divine image. Another rabbi says that such a one renounces his privilege of true humanity, in so far as only in the married state can happiness, blessing, and peace be attained.999 It is significant as to the spirit of Judaism that, while other religions regard the celibacy of the priests and saints as signs of highest sanctity, the Jewish law expressly commands that the high priest shall not be allowed to observe the solemn rites of the Day of Atonement if unmarried.1000 Love for the wife, the keeper and guardian of the home, must attune his heart to tenderness and sympathy, if he is to plead for the people before the Holy God. He can make intercession for the household of Israel only if he himself has founded a family, in which are practiced faithfulness and modesty, love and regard for the life-companion, all the domestic virtues inherited from the past.

3. Another moral factor for human development is industry, which secures to the individual his independence and his dignity when he engages in creative labor after the divine pattern, and which rewards him with comfort and the joy of life. This also is so highly valued by Judaism that industrial activity, which unlocks from the earth ever new treasures to enrich human life, is enjoined upon all, even those pursuing more spiritual vocations. "Seest thou a man diligent in his business? He shall stand before kings."1001 "When thou eatest the labor of thy hands, happy art thou and it shall be well with thee."1002 In commenting on this last verse, the sages say: "This means that thou wilt be doubly blessed; happy art thou in this world, and it shall be well with thee in the world to come."1003 Again they say, "No labor, however humble, is dishonoring,"1004 also: "Idleness, even amid great wealth, leads to the wasting of the intellect."1005 Moreover it is said, "Whoever neglects to train his son to a trade, rears him to become a robber."1006 True, there were some among the pious who themselves abstained from participation in industry, and therefore proclaimed, in the same tenor as the Sermon on the Mount, "Behold the beasts of the field and the birds of heaven, they sow not and reap not, and their heavenly Father cares for them."1007 But these

formed an exception, while the majority of Jewish teachers extolled the real blessing of labor and its efficacy in ennobling heart and spirit.1008

4. Neither does Judaism begrudge man the joy of life which is the fruit of industry, nor rob it of its moral value. On the contrary, that ascetic spirit which encourages self-mortification and rigid renunciation of all pleasure is declared sinful.1009 Instead, we are told that in the world to come man shall have to give account for every enjoyment offered him in this life, whether he used it gratefully or rejected it in ingratitude.1010 Abstinence is declared to be praiseworthy only in curbing wild desires and passions. For the rest, true piety lies in the consecration of every gift of God, every pleasure of life which He has offered, and using it in His service, so that the seal of holiness shall be imprinted even upon the satisfaction of the most sensuous desires.

5. Judaism, then, lays special emphasis upon sociability as advancing all that is good and noble in man. The life of the recluse, according to its teaching, is of little use to the world at large and hence of no moral value. Only in association with one's fellow-men does life find incentive and opportunity for worthy work. "Either a life among friends or death" is a Talmudic proverb.1011 Unselfish friendship like that of David and Jonathan is lauded and pointed out for imitation.1012 Through it man learns to step beyond the narrow boundaries of his ego, and in caring for others he will purify and exalt his own soul, until at last its love will include all mankind.

6. "Iron sharpeneth iron; so a man sharpeneth the countenance of his friend," says the book of Proverbs,1013 and the sages derive from this verse the doctrine that learning does not thrive in solitude.1014 A single log does not nourish the flame; to keep up the fire one must throw in one piece of wood after the other. This applies also to learning; it lacks in vigor, if it is not communicated to others. Wisdom calls to her votaries on the highways, in order that the stream of knowledge may overflow for many. For both the culture of the intellect and the ennobling of the soul it is necessary that man should step out of the narrow limits of self and come into touch with a larger world. Only in devotion to his fellows is man made to realize his own godlike nature. In the same measure as he honors God's image in others, in foe as well as in friend, in the most lowly servant as well in the most noble master, man increases his own dignity. This is the fundamental thought of morality as expressed in Job, especially in the beautiful thirty-first chapter, and as embodied in Abraham,1015 and later reflected in various Talmudic sayings about the dignity of man.1016 Everywhere man's relation to society becomes a test of his own worth. The idea of interdependence and reciprocal duty among all members of the human family forms the outstanding characteristic of Jewish ethics. For it is far more concerned in the welfare of society than in that of the individual, and demands that those endowed with fortune should care for the unfortunate, the strong for the weak, and those blessed with vision for the blind. As God Himself is Father to the fatherless, Judge of the widows, and Protector of the oppressed, so should man be. "Works of benevolence form the beginning and the end of the Torah," points out R. Simlai.1017

7. It is in the life of the nation that the individual first realizes that he is only a part of a greater whole. The nation to which he belongs is the mother who nourishes him with her spirit, teaches him to speak and to think, and equips him with all the means to take part in the achievements and tasks of humanity. In fact, the State, which guarantees to all its citizens safety, order and opportunity under the law, and which arranges the relations of the various groups and classes of society that they may advance one another and thus promote the welfare and progress of all, is human society in miniature. Here the citizen first learns obedience to the law which is binding upon all alike, then respect and reverence for the authority embodied in the guardians of the law who administer justice "which is God's," and hence also loyalty and devotion to the whole, together with reciprocal obligation and helpfulness among the separate members and classes of society. The words of Jeremiah to his exiled brethren, "Seek ye the peace of the city whither I have caused you to be carried away captive, and pray unto the Lord for it, for in the peace thereof shall ye have peace,"1018 became the guiding maxim of Jewry when torn from its native soil. It impressed upon them, once for all, the deeply rooted virtues of loyalty and love for the country in which they dwelt. To pray for the welfare of the State and its ruler, under whose dominion all citizens were protected, and so in modern times for its legislative and administrative authorities, has become a sacred duty of the Jewish religious community. To sacrifice one's life willingly, if need be, for the welfare of the country in which he lived, was a demand of loyalty which the Jew has never disregarded. "The law of the State is as the law of God"1019 taught Samuel the Babylonian, and another sage of Babylon said, "The government on earth is to be regarded as an image of God's government in heaven."1020

8. But, after all, the community of the State or the nation is too confined in its cultural work by its special interests and particular tasks ever to reach the universal ideal of man, that is, a perfected humanity. Where the interests of

one State or nation come into conflict with those of another, far too often the result is enmity and murderous warfare. Therefore there must be a higher power to quench the brands of war whenever they flare up, to cultivate every motive leading toward peace and harmony among nations, to impel men toward a higher righteousness and to obviate all conflict of interests, because in place of selfishness it implants in the heart the self-forgetfulness of love. Religion is the power which trains peoples as well as individuals toward the conception of one humanity, in the same measure as it points to the one and only God, Ruler over all the contending motives of men, the Source and Shield of all righteousness, truth, and love, the Father of mankind as the only foundation upon which the grand edifice of human civilization must ultimately rest. Thus it teaches us to regard the common life and endeavor of peoples and societies as one household of divine goodness. Every system of belief, every religious denomination which transcends the limits of the national consciousness with a view to the broader conception of mankind, and binds the national groups and interests into a higher unity to include and influence all the depths and heights of the human spirit, paves the way toward the attainment of the mighty goal. In the same sense the united efforts of the various classes and societies or States for the common advance of culture, prosperity, national welfare and international commerce, as well as of science and art, tend unceasingly toward that full realization of the idea of humanity which constitutes the brotherhood of man.

9. Not yet has any religious body, however great and remarkable its accomplishments may have been, nor any of the religious, scientific, or national organizations, much as they have achieved, performed the sublime task which the prophets of Israel foretold as the goal of history. Each one has drawn to itself only a portion of mankind, and promised it success or redemption and bliss, while the rest have been excluded and denied both temporal and eternal happiness. Each one has singled out one side of human nature in order to link to it the entire absolute truth, but at the same time has underestimated or cast aside all other sides of human life, and thereby blocked the road to complete truth, which can never be presented in final form, nor ever be the exclusive possession of one portion of humanity. Judaism, which is neither a religious nor a national system solely, but aims to be a covenant with God uniting all peoples, lays claim to no exclusive truth, and makes its appeal to no single group of mankind. The Messianic hope, which aims to unite all races and classes of men into a bond of brotherhood, has become an impelling force in the history of the world, and both Christianity and Islam, in so far as they owe their existence to this hope and to the adoption of Jewish teachings, constitute parts of the history of Judaism. Between these world-religions with their wide domains of civilization stands the little Jewish people as a cosmopolitan element. It points to an ideal future, with a humanity truly united in God, when, through ceaseless progress in the pursuit of ever more perfect ideals, truth, justice, and peace will triumph,—to the realization of the kingdom of God.

Part III. Israel And The Kingdom Of God

Chapter XLVIII. The Election of Israel

1. The central point of Jewish theology and the key to an understanding of the nature of Judaism is the doctrine, "God chose Israel as His people." The election of Israel as the chosen people of God, or, what amounts to the same, as the nation whose special task and historic mission it is to be the bearer of the most lofty truths of religion among mankind, forms the basis and the chief condition of revelation. Before God proclaimed the Ten Words of the Covenant on Sinai, He addressed the people through His chosen messenger, Moses, saying: "Ye have seen what I did unto the Egyptians, and how I bore you on eagles' wings, and brought you unto Myself. Now therefore, if ye will hearken unto My voice, indeed, and keep My covenant, then ye shall be Mine own treasure from among all peoples, for all the earth is Mine; and ye shall be unto Me a kingdom of priests, and a holy nation."1021

2. The fact of Israel's election by God as His peculiar nation is repeated in Deuteronomy, with the special declaration that God had found delight in them as the smallest of the peoples, on account of the love and the faith He had sworn to the Patriarchs.1022 It is accentuated in the Synagogal liturgy, especially in the prayer for holy days which begins with the words: "Thou hast chosen us from all peoples; Thou hast loved us and found pleasure in us and hast exalted us above all tongues; Thou hast sanctified us by Thy commandments and brought us near unto Thy service, O King, and hast called us by Thy great and holy name."1023 Inasmuch as the election of Israel is connected with the deliverance of the people from Egypt, the whole relation of the Jewish nation to its God assumes from the outset an essentially different character from that of other nations to their deities. The God of Israel is not inseparably connected with His people by mere natural bonds, as is the case with every other ancient divinity. He is not a national God in the ordinary sense. He has chosen Israel freely of His own accord. "When Israel was a child, then I loved him, and out of Egypt I called My son," says God through Hosea,1024 and thus prefers to call Himself "thy God from the land of Egypt." This election from love is echoed also in Jeremiah, who said, "Israel is the Lord's hallowed portion, His first-fruits of the increase."1025 The moral relation between God and Israel is most clearly characterized, however, by Amos, in the words: "You only have I known of all the families of the earth; therefore I will visit upon you all your iniquities."1026 Here is stated in explicit terms that the God of history selected Israel as an instrument for His plan of salvation, in the expectation that he would remain faithful to His will.

3. The real purpose of the election and mission of Israel was announced by the great prophet of the Exile when he called Israel the "servant of the Lord," who has been formed from his mother's bosom and delivered from every other bondage, in order that he may declare the praise of God among the peoples, and be a harbinger of light and a bond of union among the nations, the witness of God, the proclaimer of His truth and righteousness throughout the world.1027 The entire history of Israel as far back as the Patriarchs was reconstructed in this light, and we find the election of Abraham also similarly described in the Psalms1028 and in the liturgy. Indeed, in every morning prayer for the past two thousand years the Jewish people have offered thanks to God for the divine teaching that has been intrusted to their care, and praised Him "who has chosen Israel in love."1029

4. The belief in the election of Israel rests on the conviction that the Jewish people has a certain superiority over other peoples in being especially qualified to be the messenger and champion of religious truth. In one sense this prerogative takes into account every people which has contributed something unique to any department of human power or knowledge, and therein has served others as pattern and guide. From the broader standpoint, all great historic peoples appear as though appointed by divine providence for their special cultural tasks, in which others can at most emulate them without achieving their greatness. Yet we cannot speak in quite the same way of the election of the Greeks or Romans or of the nations of remote antiquity for mastery in art and science, or for skill in jurisprudence and statecraft. The fact is that these nations were never fully conscious that they had a historic or providential destiny to influence mankind in this special direction. Israel alone was self-conscious, realizing its task as harbinger and defender of its religious truth as soon as it had entered into its possession. Its election, therefore, does not imply presumption, but rather a grave duty and responsibility. As the great seer of the Captivity had already declared, to be the servant of the Lord is to undergo the destiny of suffering, to be "the man of sorrow," from whose bruises comes healing unto all mankind.1030

5. Accordingly the election of Israel cannot be regarded as a single divine act, concluded at one moment of revelation, or even during the Biblical period. It must instead be considered a divine call persisting through all ages and encompassing all lands, a continuous activity of the spirit which has ever summoned for itself new heralds and heroes to testify to truth, justice, and sublime faith, with an unparalleled scorn for death, and to work for their dissemination by words and deeds and by their whole life. Judaism differs from all other religions in that it is neither the creation of one great moral teacher and preacher of truth, nor seeks to typify the moral and spiritual sublimity which it aims to develop in a single person, who is then lifted up into the realm of the superhuman. Judaism counts its prophets, its sages, and its martyrs by generations; it is still demonstrating its power to reshape and regenerate religion as a vital force. Moreover, Judaism does not separate religion from life, so as to regard only a segment of the common life and the national existence as holy. The entire people, the entire life, must bear the stamp of holiness and be filled with priestly consecration. Whether this lofty aim can ever be completely attained is a question not to be decided by short-sighted humanity, but only by God, the Ruler of history. It is sufficient that the life of the individual as well as that of the people should aspire toward this ideal.

6. Of course, the election of Israel presupposes an inner calling, a special capacity of soul and tendency of intellect which fit it for the divine task. The people which has given mankind its greatest prophets and psalmists, its boldest thinkers and its noblest martyrs, which has brought to fruition the three great world-religions, the Church, the Mosque, and—mother of them both—the Synagogue, must be the religious people par excellence. It must have within itself enough of the heavenly spark of truth and of the impetus of the religious genius as to be able and eager, whenever and wherever the opportunity is favorable, to direct the spiritual flight of humanity toward the highest and holiest. In fact, the soul of the Jewish people reveals a peculiar mingling of characteristics, a union of contrasts, which makes it especially fit for its providential mission in history. Together with the marked individuality of each person we find a common spirit highly sensitive to every encroachment. Here there is a tenacious adherence to what is old and traditional, and there an eager assimilation of what is new and strange. On the one hand, a materialistic self-interest; on the other, an idealism soaring to the stars.1031 The sages of the Tannaitic period already remarked that Israel has been intrusted with the law which it is to defend and to disseminate, just because it is the boldest and most obstinate of nations.1032 On the other hand, the three special characteristics of the Jewish people according to the Talmud are its chastity and purity of life, its benevolence and its active love for humanity.1033 A heathen scoffer calls Israel "a people of generous impulses which promised at Sinai to do what God would command, even before it had hearkened to the commandments."1034 "Gentle and shy as a dove, it is also willing like the dove to stretch out its neck for the sacrifice, for love of its heavenly Father," says the Haggadist.1035 And yet R. Johanan remarks that Israel, called to be the bearer of light to the world, must be pressed like the olive before it will yield its precious oil.1036 Every individual in Israel possesses the requisite qualities for a holy priest-people, according to a Midrash of the Tannaitic period, and hence we read in Deuteronomy, "The Lord hath chosen thee to be His own treasure out of all peoples that are upon the face of the earth."1037

7. All these and similar sayings disprove completely the idea that the election of Israel was an arbitrary act of God. It is due rather to hereditary virtues and to tendencies of mind and spirit which equip Israel for his calling. To this must be added the important fact that God educated the people for its task through the Law, which was to make it conscious of its priestly sanctity and keep it ever active in mind and heart. The election of Israel is emphasized in Deuteronomy especially in connection with the prohibition of marriage with idolaters and with the prohibition of unclean animals, which also originated in the priestly laws.1038 The underlying idea is that the mission of Israel to battle for the Most High imperatively demands separation from the heathen peoples, and on the other hand, that its priestly calling necessitates an especial abstinence. And as has the law in its development and realization for thousands of years, so has also God's wise guidance trained Israel in the course of history so as to render him at times the unyielding preserver and defender and at other times the bold champion and protagonist of the highest truth and justice, according as the outlook and the mental horizon of the period were narrow or broad.

8. It is true that the thought of Israel's calling and mission in world-history first became clear when its prophets and sages attained a view of great world-movements from the lofty watch-tower of the centuries, so that they could take cognizance of the varying relations of Judaism to the civilized peoples around. The summons of the Jewish people to be heralds of truth and workers for peace is first mentioned in Isaiah and Micah,1039 while only in the great movement of nations under Cyrus did the seer of the Exile recognize the peculiar mission of Israel in the history of the world. If in gloomy periods the outlook became dark, still the hope for the fulfillment of this mission

was never entirely lost. In fact, the contact of the Jewish people with Greek culture after Alexander the Great gave new power and fresh impetus to the conception of Israel's mission,1040 as the rich Hellenistic literature and the vision of Daniel in chapter VII testify. In fact, Abraham, the ancestor of the Jewish people, became for the earliest Haggadists a wandering missionary and a great preacher of the unity of God, and his picture was the pattern for both Paul and Mohammed.1041 The election of Israel is clearly and unequivocally expressed by Rabbi Eleazar ben Pedath in the words, "God sent Israel among the heathen nations that they may win a rich harvest of proselytes, for, as God said through Hosea, 'I will sow her unto Me in the land,' so He wishes from this seed to reap a bountiful and world-wide harvest."1042

9. In the Middle Ages, when the historical viewpoint and the idea of human progress were both lacking, the belief in the mission of Israel was confined to the Messianic hope. Both Jehuda ha Levi and Maimonides, however, regard Christianity and Islam as preparatory steps for the Messiah, who is to unify the world through the knowledge of God.1043 "The work of the Messiah is the fruit, of which Israel will be universally acknowledged as the root," says the Jewish sage in the Cuzari. Therefore he rightly accepts the election of Israel as a fundamental doctrine of belief. Modern times, however, with their awakened historical sense and their idea of progress, have again placed in the foreground the belief in the election and mission of Israel. The founders of reform Judaism have cast this ancient doctrine in a new form. On the one hand, they have reinterpreted the Messianic hope in the prophetic spirit, as the realization of the highest ideals of a united humanity. On the other, they have rejected the entire theory that Israel was exiled from his ancient land because of his sins, and that he is eventually to return there and to restore the sacrificial cult in the Temple at Jerusalem. Therefore the whole view concerning Israel's future had to undergo a transformation.1044 The historic mission of Israel as priest of humanity and champion of truth assumed a higher meaning, and his peculiar position in history and in the Law necessarily received a different interpretation from that of Talmudic Judaism or that of the Church. As individuals, indeed, many Jews have taken part in the achievements and efforts of all civilized peoples; the Jewish people as such has accomplished great things in only one field, the field of religion. The following chapters will consider more closely how Judaism has taken up and carried out this sacred mission.

Chapter XLIX. The Kingdom of God and the Mission of Israel

1. The hope of Judaism for the future is comprised in the phrase, "the kingdom of God,"—malkuth shaddai or malkuth Shamayim,—which means the sovereign rule of God. From ancient times the liturgy of the Synagogue concludes regularly with the solemn Alenu, in which God is addressed as the "King of kings of kings"—king of kings being the Persian title for the ruler of the whole Empire—and directly after this the hope is expressed that "we may speedily behold the glory of Thy might, when Thou wilt remove the abominations from the earth, and the idols will be utterly cut off; when the world will be perfected under the kingdom of the Almighty, and all the children of flesh will call upon Thy name; when Thou wilt turn unto Thyself all the wicked of the earth. Let all the inhabitants of the earth perceive and know that unto Thee every knee must bend, and every tongue give homage. Let them all accept the yoke of Thy kingdom, and do Thou reign over them speedily, and forever and ever."1045 At the close of the Torah lesson in the house of learning the assembly regularly recited the blessing, "Praised be Thy name! May Thy kingdom soon come!"—afterwards known as the Kaddish,1046 and reëchoed in the so-called "Lord's Prayer" of the Church. The words of the prophet, "The Lord shall be King over all the earth; in that day shall the Lord be One, and His name One,"1047 voiced for all ages this ideal of the future, and thus gave a goal and a purpose to the history of the world and at the same time centered it in Israel, the chosen people of God.

2. The establishment of the kingdom of the One and Only God throughput the entire world constitutes the divine plan of salvation toward which, according to Jewish teaching, the efforts of all the ages are tending. This "Kingdom of God" is not, however, a kingdom of heaven in the world to come, which men are to enter only after death, and then only if redeemed from sin by accepting the belief in a supernatural Savior as their Messiah, as is taught by the Church. Judaism points to God's Kingdom on earth as the goal and hope of mankind, to a world in which all men and nations shall turn away from idolatry and wickedness, falsehood and violence, and become united in their recognition of the sovereignty of God, the Holy One, as proclaimed by Israel, His servant and herald, the Messiah of the nations. It is not the hope of bliss in a future life (which is the leading motive of Christianity), but the building up of the divine kingdom of truth, justice, and peace among men by Israel's teaching and practice.1048 In this sense God speaks through the mouth of the prophet, "I will also give thee for a light of the nations, that My

salvation may be unto the end of the earth."1049 "All the ends of the earth shall see the salvation of our God."1050 "The remnant of Jacob shall be in the midst of many peoples, as dew from the Lord, as showers upon the grass."1051

3. Clearly, the idea of a world-kingdom of God arose only as the result of the gradual development of the Jewish God-consciousness. It was necessary at first that the prophetic idea of God's kingship, the theocracy in Israel, should triumph over the monarchical view and absorb it. The patriarchal life of the shepherd was certainly not favorable to a monarchical rule. "I will not rule over you, neither shall my son rule over you, the Lord shall rule over you," said Gideon in refusing the title of king which the people had offered him.1052 According to one tradition Samuel blamed the people for desiring a king and thereby rejecting the divine kingship.1053 "I give thee a king in Mine anger," says God through Hosea.1054 The more the monarchy, with its exclusively worldly and materialistic aims, came into conflict with the demands of the prophets and their religious truth, the higher rose the prophetic hope for the dawning of a day when God alone would rule in absolute sovereignty over the entire world. Now, in the kingdom of the Ten Tribes, with its frequently changing dynasties, the old patriarchal conception was dominant, while in the kingdom of Judah, which remained loyal to the house of David, the monarchical idea developed. Isaiah, living in Jerusalem and favorably disposed towards the monarchy, prophesied that a shoot from the house of David, endowed with marvelous spiritual powers, should come forth, occupying the throne in the place of God, and through his victories would plant righteousness and the knowledge of God everywhere upon earth, and establish throughout the world a wonderful reign of peace.1055 Upon this royal "shoot" of David1056 rested the Messianic hope during the Exile, and amidst the disappointments of the time this vision became all the more idealized. In contrast to this the great prophet of the Exile announced the establishment of the absolute dominion of God as the true "King of Israel"1057 over all the earth by the nucleus of Israel, "the servant of God," who would become conscious of his great historic mission in the world and be willing to offer his very life in its cause. In all this the prophet makes no reference to the royal house of David, but makes bold to confer the title of the "anointed of God"—that is, Messiah—upon Cyrus, the king of Persia, as the one who was to usher in the new era.1058 Subsequently these two divergent hopes for the future run parallel in the Psalms and the liturgy as well as in the apocryphal and rabbinic literature.

4. While the Messianic aspirations as such bore rather a political and national character in Judaism (as will be explained in Chapter LIII), yet the religious hope for a universal kingdom of God took root even more deeply in the heart of the Jewish people. It created the conception of Israel's mission and also the literature and activity of the Hellenistic propaganda, and it gave a new impetus to the making of proselytes among the heathen, to which both Christianity and Islam owe their existence. The words of Isaiah, repeated later by Habakkuk, "The earth will be full of the knowledge of the Lord, as the waters cover the sea,"1059 became now an article of faith. While in earlier times the rule of Israel's God, JHVH, was attached to Zion, from whose holy mount He ruled as invisible King,1060 later on we find Zechariah proclaiming Him who was enthroned in heaven as having dominion over the entire earth,1061 and the Psalter summons all nations to acknowledge, adore, and extol Him as King of the world.1062 Nay, at the very time when Judah lay humbled to the ground, the prophet exclaimed, "Who would not fear Thee, O King of the nations? for it befitteth Thee; forasmuch as among all the wise men of the nations, and in all their royalty there is none like unto Thee."1063 Israel's great hope for the future is expressed most completely and in most sublime language in the New Year liturgy: "O Lord our God, impose Thine awe upon all Thy works, and let Thy dread be upon all that Thou hast created, that they may all form one single band to do Thy will with a perfect heart.... Our God and God of our fathers, reveal Thyself in Thy splendor as King over all the inhabitants of the world, that every handiwork of Thine may know that Thou hast made it, and every creature may acknowledge that Thou hast created it, and whatsoever hath breath in its nostrils may say: the Lord God of Israel is King, and His dominion ruleth over all."1064

5. In the earlier period, then, the rule of JHVH seems to have been confined to Israel as the people of His covenant. During the Second Temple Jerusalem was called the "city of the great King"1065 and the constitution was considered by Josephus to have been a theocracy, that is, a government by God.1066 Indeed, the entire Mosaic code has as its main purpose to make Israel a "kingdom of priests," over which JHVH, the God of the covenant, was alone to rule as King. The chief object of the strict nationalists, in opposition to the cosmopolitanism of the Hellenists, was that this government of God, in its intimate association with the Holy Land and the Holy People, should be maintained unchanged for all the future. Thus the book of Daniel predicts the speedy downfall of the fourth world-kingdom and the establishment of the kingdom of God through Israel, "the people of the saints of the Most High;

their kingdom is an everlasting kingdom."1067 Naturally, such a purely nationalistic conception of the rulership of God does not admit the thought of a mission or its corollary, the conversion of the heathen.1068 These appear among the liberal school of Hillel in their opposition to the more rigorous Shammaites and the party of the Zealots.1069 It is, therefore, quite consistent that the modern nationalists should again dispute the mission of Israel.

6. As soon as Jewish monotheism had once been conceived by the Jewish mind as the universal truth, the idea of the mission of Israel as a bearer of light and a witness of God for the nations, as enunciated by Deutero-Isaiah, became ever more firmly established. Many Psalms exhort the people to make known the wondrous doings of God among the nations, so that the heathen world might at last acknowledge the One and Only God.1070 Nay, Israel is even called God's anointed and prophet,1071 and in one Psalm we find Zion, the city of God, elevated to be the religious metropolis of the world.1072 The book of Jonah is simply a refutation of the narrow nationalistic conception of Judaism; it holds forth the hope of the conversion of the heathen to the true knowledge of God. In the same spirit Ruth the Moabitess became the type of the heathen who are eager to "take refuge under the wings of God's majesty."1073 The author of the book of Job no longer knows of a national God; to him God is the highest ideal of morality as it lives and grows in the human heart. The wisdom literature also teaches a God of humanity. Under His wings Shem and Japheth, the teaching of the Jew and the wisdom of the Greek, can join hands; the religious truth of the one and the philosophic truth of the other may harmoniously blend.

7. Thus a new impulse was given to Jewish proselytism in Alexandria, and the earlier history of Israel, especially the pre-Israelite epoch with its simple human types, was read in a new light. Enoch1074 and Noah1075 became preachers of penitence, heralds of the pure monotheism from which the heathen world had departed. Abraham especially, the progenitor of Israel, was looked upon as a prototype of the wandering missionary people, converting the heathen.1076 Wherever he journeyed, his teaching and his example of true benevolence won souls for the Lord proclaimed by him as the "God of the heaven and the earth."1077 In this sense of missionary activity were now interpreted the words, "Be thou a blessing ... and in thy seed shall all the nations of the earth be blessed."1078 This was no longer understood in the original sense, that Abraham by his prosperity should be an example of a blessed man, to be pointed out in blessing others; the words were given the higher meaning that Abraham with his descendants should become a source of blessing for mankind through his teachings and his conduct, so that all the families of men should attain blessing and salvation by following his doctrine and example. Thus the idea of the Jewish mission was connected with Abraham, the "father of a multitude of nations,"1079 and this was later on adopted by Paul and Mohammed in establishing the Church and the Mosque.

8. In contradistinction, then, to the political concept of the kingdom of God, which Ezekiel still hoped to see established by the exercise of external power,1080 the idea assumed now a purely spiritual meaning. This kingdom of God is accepted by the pious Jew every morning through his confession of the divine Unity in the Shema. Abraham had anticipated this, say the rabbis, when he swore by the God of heaven and earth, and so also had Israel in accepting the Torah at Sinai and at the Red Sea.1081 In fact, the kingdom of God began, we are told, with the first man, since, when he adored God freely as King of the world, every living creature acknowledged Him also. But only when Israel as a people proclaimed God's dominion at the Red Sea, was the throne of God and His kingdom on earth established for eternity.1082 And when Ezekiel says: "With a mighty hand will I be King over you," they explain this to mean that the people chosen as the servant of God will be continually constrained anew by the prophets to recognize His kingdom.1083 Yea, the closing words of the Song at the Red Sea, "The Lord shall reign for ever and ever" were taken to imply that all the nations would in the end recognize only Israel's One God as King of the world.1084 As a matter of fact, the rabbinical view is that every proselyte, in "taking upon himself the yoke of the sovereignty of God," enters that divine Kingdom which at the end of time will embrace all men and nations.1085 In the book of Tobit and the Sibylline Oracles also we find this universalistic conception of the Messianic age expressed.1086

9. Accordingly, proselytism found open and solemn recognition both before and after the time of the Maccabees, as we see in the Psalms,—especially those which speak of proselytes in the term, "they that fear the Lord,"1087 and also in the ancient synagogal liturgy, where the "proselytes of righteousness" are especially mentioned.1088 The school of Hillel followed precisely this course. Matters changed, however, under the Roman dominion, which was contrasted to the dominion of God especially from the time of Herod, when the belief became current that "only when the one is destroyed, will the other arise."1089 Particularly after the Christian Church had become identified with Rome, all missionary endeavors by the Jews were considered dangerous and were therefore discouraged as

much as possible. In their place arose the hope for a miraculous intervention of God. In Hellenistic circles the Messiah was believed to be the future founder of the kingdom of God,1090 which assumed more and more of an other-worldly nature, such as the Church developed for it later on.

10. The more the harsh oppression of the times forced the Jew to isolate himself and to spend his life in studying and practicing the law,—which was tantamount to "placing himself under the kingdom of God,"1091 the more he lost sight of his sublime mission for the world at large. Only individual thinkers, such as Jehuda ha Levi and Maimonides, kept a vision of the world-mission of Israel, when they called Jesus and Mohammed, as founders of Christianity and Islam, messengers of God to the idolatrous nations, divinely appointed to bring them nearer to Israel's truth,1092 or when they pointed forward to the time when all peoples will recognize in the truth their common mother and in God the Father of all mankind.1093 A most instructive Midrash on Zechariah IX, 9 gives the keynote of this belief. "At that time God as the King of Zion will speak to the righteous of all times, and say to them, 'Dear as the words of My teaching are to Me, yet have ye erred in that ye have followed only My Torah, and have not waited for My world-kingdom. I swear to you that I shall remember for good him who has waited for My kingdom, as it is said, Wait ye for Me until the day that I rise up as a witness.'"1094

On the other hand, it was owing to the sad consequences of the missionary endeavors of the Church that the idea of the mission of Judaism was given a different direction. Not conversion, but conviction by teaching and example, is the historic task of Judaism, whose maxim is expressed in the verse of Zechariah, "Not by might, nor by power, but by My spirit, saith the Lord of hosts."1095 It is not the creed, but the deed, which tells. Not the confession, but conduct, with the moral principles which govern it, counts. Such a view is implied in the well-known teaching of Joshua ben Hananiah, "The righteous of all nations will have a share in the world of eternal bliss."1096 Judaism does not deny salvation to those professing other religions, which would tend to undermine the foundation of their spiritual life. Standing upon the high watchtower of time, it rather strives ever to clarify and strengthen the universal longing for truth and righteousness which lies at the heart of all religion, and is thus to become a bond of union, an all-illuminating light for the world. To quote the beautiful words of Leopold Stein in his Schrift des Lebens:1097 "Judaism, while recognizing the historic justification of all systems of thought and faith, does not cherish the ambition to become the Church Universal in the usual sense of the term, but aims rather to be the focus, or mirror, of religious unity for all the rest. 'The people from of old,' as the prophet called them, are to accompany mankind in its progress through the ages and the continents, until it reaches the goal of the kingdom of God on earth, the 'new heaven and new earth' of the prophetic vision."1098 The thought of the Jewish mission is most adequately expressed in the Neilah service of the Union Prayer Book, based upon the Einhorn Prayerbook, which reads as follows:1099 "Endow us, our Guardian, with strength and patience for our holy mission. Grant that all the children of Thy people may recognize the goal of our changeful career, so that they may exemplify by their zeal and love for mankind the truth of Israel's watchword: One humanity on earth, even as there is but One God in heaven. Enlighten all that call themselves by Thy name with the knowledge that the sanctuary of wood and stone, which erst crowned Zion's hill, was but a gate through which Israel should step out into the world, to reconcile all mankind unto Thee!"

Chapter L. The Priest-people and its Law of Holiness

1. The checkered, stormy, and yet triumphant march of the Jewish people through the ages remains the great enigma of history for all those who do not believe in a divine plan of salvation to be consummated through Israel. The idea of Israel's mission alone throws light on its law and its destiny. Even before God had revealed to the people at Mt. Sinai the Ten Commandments, the foundation of all religion and morality, and there concluded with them a covenant for all time, He spoke: "Ye shall be unto Me a kingdom of priests and a holy nation," thus consecrating them to be a priest-people among the nations, and enjoining them to a life of especial holiness. Possessing as a heritage from the Patriarchs the germ of a higher religious consciousness, in distinction from all other peoples, they were to make the cultivation, development, and promotion of the highest religious truth their life-task, and thus to become the people of God. At first they were to establish in the Holy Land a theocratic government, a State in which God alone was the Ruler, while they lived in priestly isolation from all the nations around. Thus they prepared themselves for the time when, scattered over all the earth, they might again work as the priest-people through the ages for the upbuilding of the universal kingdom of God. This was Israel's destiny

from the very first, as expressed by the great seer of the Exile when he beheld Israel wandering forth among the nations, "Ye shall be named the priests of the Lord; men shall call you the ministers of our God."1100

2. Among all religions the priest is considered especially holy as the mediator between God and man, and in his appearance as well as in his mode of life he must observe special forms of purity and holiness. He alone may approach the Godhead, ascertain its will, and administer the sacrificial cult in the sanctuary. He must represent the Divinity in its relation to the people, embody it in his outward life, enjoy nothing which it abhors, and touch nothing which could render him impure. These priestly rules exist among all the nations of antiquity in striking similarity, and indicate a common origin in the prehistoric period, during which the entire cult developed through a priestly caste, beginning with simple, primitive conceptions and transmitted in ever more elaborate form from father to son. It goes without saying that the priests of the original Hebrew race, which migrated from Babylonia, retained the ancient customs and rules. They must also have adopted many other things from neighboring peoples. During the entire period of the first temple, the priests—despite all prophetic warnings—preferred the heathen cult with its vainglorious pomp to the simple worship of the patriarchal times. As everywhere else, the priesthood of Israel, and later of Judæa as well, thought only of its own interests, of the retention of its ancient prerogatives, unmindful of the higher calling to which it had been chosen, to serve the God of truth and justice, to exemplify true holiness, to stand for moral rather than ceremonial purity. Yet the sacerdotal institutions were indispensable so long as the people required a sanctuary where the Deity should dwell, and where the sacrificial cult should be administered. Every trespass by a layman on the sanctuary reserved for the priests was considered sacrilege and called for divine punishment. It was thus necessary to deepen the popular notion of holiness and of the reverence due the sanctuary, before these could be elevated into the realm of spirituality and morality. The priesthood had to be won for the service of the loftier religious ideas, so that it might gradually educate the people in general for its sublime priestly mission. This conception underlies both the Mosaic law and its rabbinical interpretation.

3. Through Biblical and post-Biblical literature and history there runs a twofold tendency, one anti-sacerdotal,—emanating from the prophets and later the Hasideans or Pharisees,—the other a mediating tendency, favorable to the priesthood. The ritualistic piety of the priests was bitterly assailed by the prophets as being subversive of all morality, and later on the Saducean hierarchy also constituted a threat to the moral and spiritual welfare of the people. Before even the revelation at Sinai was to take place, we read that warning was given to the priests "not to break through" and stand above the people.1101

On the other hand, the law demands of the Aaronites a peculiar degree of holiness, since "they offer the bread of their God upon the altar."1102 Their blood must be kept pure by the avoidance of improper marriages. Everything unclean or polluting must be kept far from them.1103 The law, following a tradition which probably arose in ancient Babylon, prescribed minutely their mode of admission into the divine service, their vestments and their conditions of life, the ritual of sacrifice and of purity; and every violation of these laws, every trespass by a layman, was declared to be punishable with death.1104 The sanctuary contains no room for the nation of priests; no layman durst venture to cross its threshold. Even in the legal system of the rabbis the ancient rights and privileges of the priesthood, dating from the time when they possessed no property, remained inviolate, and their precedence in everything was undisputed.1105

The glaring contrast between the idea of a universal priesthood of the people and the institution of the Aaronites is explained by a deeper insight into history. The success of the reformation under Josiah on the basis of the Deuteronomic code rested in the last analysis on the fact that the priests of the house of Zadok at Jerusalem were placed in the service of the higher prophetic teaching by being rendered the guardians, executors, and later, in conjunction with the Levites, the teachers of the Law, as it was presented in the book of the law of Moses, soon afterward completed. The priesthood, deprived of everything that might remind one of the former idolatry and heathenish practices, was, in its purer and holier character, to lead the priest-people to true moral holiness through its connection with the sanctuary and its ancient cult. Still the impulse for the moral rebirth of the nation, for the establishment of a priest-people, did not emanate from the Temple priesthood, nor even from the sacred soil of Palestine; but from the Synagogue, which began in the Exile, under the influence of the prophetic word and the Levitical song, in the form of public worship by the congregation of the pious. Here arose a generation of godly men, a class of singularly devout ones, living in priestly holiness, who consecrated their lives to the practice of the law, and whom the exile seer had designated as the true Israel, the servant of the Lord, and these formed the nucleus of the renewed Israel.

4. That which the prophet Ezekiel had attempted in his proposed constitution1106 was accomplished in a far more thorough manner by the Holiness Code, which emanated from his school and became the central portion of the Mosaic books, and by the so-called Priestly Code, which followed later. The object was to bring about the sanctification of the entire people upon the holy soil of the national land, through institutions embodying the ideal of the holiness of God in the life and cult of the people. Circumcision, idealized by the prophetic author of Deuteronomy,1107 was to be made the sign of the covenant to mark as holy the progeny of Abraham;1108 strict laws of marriage were to put an end to all heathenish unchastity; the Sabbath rest was to consecrate the labors of the week, the Sabbatical month and year the produce of the soil.1109 The prohibition of unclean foods, heretofore reserved, as among other nations, for the priests and other consecrated persons, was now applied to the whole community in order that Israel should learn "to set itself apart from all other nations as a holy people."1110 Even their apparel was to proclaim the priestly holiness of the people by a blue fringe at the border of the garments.1111

Whereas from the time of Ezra to Simon the Just priestly rulers endeavored to promote the work of educating the people for holiness, the pious men from among the people made still greater efforts to assert the claim of holiness for the entire Jewish people as a priest-nation.1112 The repasts of these pious fellowships should be in no way inferior in sanctity to those of the priests in the Temple. New ceremonies of sanctification were to open and close the Sabbaths and festivals. Symbols of priestly consecration should adorn forehead and arm in the form of the phylacteries (tefillin), and should be placed at the entrance of every house in the so-called mezuzzah. "God has given unto all an heritage (the Torah), the kingdom, the priesthood, and the sanctuary"1113—this became the leitmotif for the Pharisaic school, who constantly enlarged the domain of piety so that it should include the whole of life. Whoever did not belong to this circle of the pious was regarded with scorn as one of the lower class (am ha-aretz).

5. The chief effort of the pious, the founders of the Judaism of the Synagogue, was to keep the Jewish people from the demoralizing influences of pagan nature-worship, represented first by Semitic and later by Greek culture. The leaders of the Pharisees "built a fence about the law"1114 extending the prohibition of mingling with the heathen nations so as also to prohibit eating with them and participating in their feasts and social gatherings,—not for the preservation of the Jewish race merely, as Christian theologians maintain, but for the sake of keeping its inner life intact and pure.1115 "God surrounded us with brazen walls, hedged us in with laws of purity in regard to food and drink and physical contact, yea, even to that which we see and hear, in order that we should be pure in body and soul, free from absurd beliefs, not polluted by contact with others or through association with the wicked; for most of the peoples defile themselves with their sexual practices, and whole lands pride themselves upon it. But we hold ourselves aloof from all this"—so spoke Eleazar the priest to King Ptolemy Philadelphus, according to the Letter of Aristeas, thus giving expression to the sentiment most deeply rooted in the souls of the pious of that period.1116 They strove to build up a nation of whom the Tannaim could say, "Whoever possesses no sense of shame and chastity, of him it is certain that his ancestors did not stand at Sinai."1117

Naturally enough, the Greek and Roman people took offense at this aloofness and separation from every contact with the outer world, and explained it as due to a spirit of hostility to mankind. Even up to the present it has been the lot of Jewry and Judaism to be misunderstood by the world at large, to be the object of either its hate or its pity. The world disregards the magnificence of the plan by which an entire people were to be reared as a priest-nation, as citizens of a kingdom of God, among whom, in the course of centuries, the seed of prophetic truth was to germinate and sprout forth for the salvation of humanity. If, in complete contrast to heathen immorality, the Jew in his life, his thinking, and his will was governed by the strictest moral discipline; if, in spite of the most cruel persecutions and the most insidious temptations, the Jewish people remained steadfast to its pure belief in God and its traditional standards of chastity, exhibiting a loyalty which amazed the nations and the religious sects about, but was neither understood nor followed by them, this was mainly due to the hallowing influences of the priestly laws. They steeled the people for the fulfillment of their duty and shielded them against all hostile powers both within and without. The very burden of the law, so bitterly denounced by Christianity since the time of Paul, lent Judaism its dignity at all times, protecting it from the assaults of the tempter; and that which seemed to the outsider a heavy load was to the Jew a source of pride in the consciousness of his divine election.1118

6. But most significant in the character and development of Judaism is the fact that all the leading ideas and motives which emanated from the priesthood of the Jewish people were concentrated in one single focus, the hallowing of the name of God. Two terms expressed this idea in both a negative and a positive form, the warning

against "Hillul ha Shem"—profanation of the name of God—and the duty of "Kiddush ha Shem"—sanctification of God's name. These exerted a marvelous power in curbing the passions and self-indulgence of the Jew and in spurring him on to the greatest possible self-sacrifice and to an unparalleled willingness to undergo suffering and martyrdom for the cause. These terms are derived from the Biblical verse, "Ye shall not profane My holy name, but I will be hallowed among the children of Israel; I am the Lord who halloweth you."1119 This verse forms the concluding sentence of the precepts for the Aaronitic priesthood and warns them as the guardians of the sanctuary to do nothing which might in the popular estimation degrade them or the divine cause intrusted to them. When, however, during the Maccabean wars, the little band of the pious proved themselves to be the true priesthood in their Opposition to the faithless Aaronites, offering their very lives as a sacrifice for the preservation of the true faith in God, the Scriptural word received a new and higher meaning. It came to signify the obligation of the entire priest-people to consecrate the name of God by the sacrifice of their lives, and also their duty to guard against its profanation by any offensive act. In connection with this Scriptural passage the sages represent God as saying, "I have brought you out of Egypt only on the condition that you are ready to sacrifice your lives, if need be, to consecrate My name."1120 From that period it became a duty and even a law of Judaism, as Maimonides shows in his Code, for each person in life and in death to bear witness to His God.1121 "Ye are My witnesses, saith the Lord, and I am God"1122—and witnesses being in the Greek version martyrs, the word afterward received the meaning of "blood-witnesses."—This passage of the prophet is commented on by Simeon ben Johai, one of the great teachers who suffered under Hadrian's persecution, in the following words, "If ye become My witnesses, then am I your Lord, God of the world; but if ye do not witness to Me, I cease to be, as it were, the Lord, God of all the world."1123 That is to say, it is the martyrdom of the pious which glorifies God's name before all the world. Or, as Felix Perles says so beautifully, "As every good and noble man must ever bear in mind that the dignity of humanity is intrusted to his hand, so should each earnest adherent of the Jewish faith remember that the glory of God is intrusted to his care."1124 The Jewish people has fulfilled this priestly task through a martyrdom of over two thousand years and has scornfully resisted every demand to abandon its faith in God, not consenting to do so even in appearance. Surely historians or philosophers who can ridicule or commiserate such resistance betray a hatred which blinds their sense of justice. As a matter of fact, it was the consciousness of the Jewish people of its priestly mission that has made it a pattern of loyalty for all time.

7. Moreover, the fear of profaning the divine name became the highest incentive to, and safeguard of the morality of the Jew. Every misdeed toward a non-Jew is considered by the teachers of Judaism a double sin, yea, sometimes, an unpardonable one, because it gives a false impression of the moral standard of Judaism and infringes upon the honor of God as well as that of man. The disciples of Rabbi Simeon ben Shetach once bought an ass for him from an Arab, and to their joy found a precious stone in its collar. "Did the seller know of this gem?" asked the master. On being answered in the negative, he called out angrily, "Do you consider me a barbarian? Return the Arab his precious stone immediately!" And when the heathen received it back, he cried out, "Praised be the God of Simeon ben Shetach!"1125 Thus the conscientious Jew honors his God by his conduct, says the Talmud, referring to this and many similar examples. Such lessons of the Jew's responsibility for the recognition of the high moral purity of his religion have ever constituted a high barrier against immoral acts.

The words, "Be ye holy, for I the Lord your God am holy" form significantly the introduction to the chapter on the love of man, the nineteenth chapter of Leviticus, placed at the very center of the entire Priestly Code. "Your self-sanctification sanctifies Me, as it were," says God to Israel, according to the interpretation of this verse by the sages.1126 In contrast to heathendom, which deifies nature with its appeal to the senses, Judaism teaches that holiness is a moral quality, as it means the curbing of the senses. And in order to prevent Israel, the bearer of this ideal of holiness, from sinking into the mire of heathen wantonness and lust, the separation of the Jew from the heathen world, whether in his domestic or social life, was a necessity and became the rule and maxim of his life for that period. All the many prohibitions and commands had for their object the purification of the people in order to render the highest moral purity a hereditary virtue among them, according to the rabbis.1127

8. It is true that the accumulation of "law upon law, prohibition upon prohibition" by the rabbis had eventually the same injurious effect which it had exerted upon the priests in the Temple. The formal law, "the precepts learned by rote," became the important factor, while their purpose was lost to sight. The shell smothered the kernel, and blind obedience to the letter of the law came to be regarded as true piety. It cannot be denied that adherence to the mere form, which was transmitted from the Temple practice to the legalism of the Pharisees and the later rabbinic

schools with their casuistry, impaired and tarnished the lofty prophetic ideal of holiness. It almost seems as if the clarion notes of such sublime passages as that of the Psalmist,

"Who shall ascend into the mountain of the Lord,

And who shall stand in His holy place?

He that hath clean hands and a pure heart;

Who hath not taken My name in vain, and hath not sworn deceitfully,"1128

no longer found its full resonance in the heart of Judaism. In the practice of external acts of piety religion became petrified and the spirit took flight. That which is of secondary importance became of primary consideration. This is the fundamental error into which the practice and the development of the Law in Judaism lapsed, and to which no careful observer can or dares close his eyes. Undoubtedly the Law, as it embraced the whole of life in its power, sharpened the Jewish sense of duty, and served the Jew as an iron wall of defense against temptations, aberrations, and enticements of the centuries. As soon as the modern Jew, however, undertook to free himself from the tutelage of a blind acceptance of authority and inquired after the purpose of all the restrictions which the Law laid upon him, his ancient loyalty to the same collapsed and the pillars of Judaism seemed to be shaken. Then the leaders of Reform, imbued with the prophetic spirit, felt it to be their imperative duty to search out the fundamental ideas of the priestly law of holiness, and, accordingly, they learned how to separate the kernel from the shell. In opposition to the orthodox tendency to worship the letter, they insisted on the fact that Israel's separation from the world—which it is ultimately to win for the divine truth—cannot itself be its end and aim, and that blind obedience to the law does not constitute true piety. Only the fundamental idea, that Israel as the "first-born" among the nations has been elected as a priest-people, must remain our imperishable truth, a truth to which the centuries of history bear witness by showing that it has given its life-blood as a ransom for humanity, and is ever bringing new sacrifices for its cause.

Only because it has kept itself distinct as a priest-people among the nations could it carry out its great task in history; and only if it remains conscious of its priestly calling and therefore maintains itself as the people of God, can it fulfill its mission. Not until the end of time, when all of God's children will have entered the kingdom of God, may Israel, the high-priest among the nations, renounce his priesthood.

Chapter LI. Israel, the People of the Law, and its World Mission

1. Judaism differs from all the ancient religions chiefly in its intrusting its truth to the whole people instead of a special priesthood. The law which "Moses commanded us is an inheritance of the Congregation of Jacob,"1129 is the Scriptural lesson impressed upon every Jew in early childhood. As soon as the Torah passed from the care of the priests into that of the whole nation, the people of the book became the priest-nation, and set forth to conquer the world by its religious truth. This aim was expressed by all the prophets beginning with Moses, who said: "Would that all the Lord's people were prophets, that the Lord would put His spirit upon them."1130 The prophetic ideal was that "they shall all know Me (God), from the least of them unto the greatest of them,"1131 and that "all thy (Zion's) children shall be taught of the Lord."1132 After the people came to realize that the Law was "their wisdom and understanding in the sight of the peoples,"1133 they soon felt the hope that one day "the isles shall wait for His teaching,"1134 and confidently expected the time when "many peoples shall go and say, Come ye, and let us go up to the mountain of the Lord, to the house of the God of Jacob; and He will teach us of His ways, and we will walk in His paths, for out of Zion shall go forth the law, and the word of the Lord from Jerusalem."1135 Once liberated from the dominance of the priesthood, religion became the instrument of universal instruction, the factor of general spiritual and moral advancement. In addition it endowed humanity with an educational ideal, destined to regenerate its moral life far more deeply than Greek culture could ever do. The object was to elevate all classes of the people by the living word of God, by the reading and expounding of the Scripture for the dissemination of its truth among the masses.

2. Those who define Judaism as a religion of law completely misunderstand its nature and its historic forces. This is done by all those Christian theologians who endeavor to prove the extraordinary assertion of the apostle Paul that the Jewish people was providentially destined to produce the Old Testament law and become enmeshed in it, like the silkworm in its cocoon, finally to dry up and perish, leaving its prophetic truth for the Church. This fateful

misconception of Judaism is based upon a false interpretation of the word Torah, which denotes moral and spiritual instruction as often as law, and thus includes all kinds of religious teaching and knowledge together with its primary meaning, the written and the oral codes.1136 In fact, in post-Biblical times it comprised the entire religion, as subject of both instruction and scientific investigation. True, law is fundamental in Jewish history; Israel accepted the divine covenant on the basis of the Sinaitic code; the reforms of King Josiah were founded on the Deuteronomic law;1137 and the restoration of the Judean commonwealth was based upon the completed Mosaic code brought from Babylon by Ezra the Scribe.1138 This book of law, with its further development and interpretation, remained the normative factor for Judaism for all time. Still, from the very beginning the Law of the covenant contained a certain element which distinguished it from all the priestly and political codes of antiquity. Beside the traditional juridical and ritualistic statutes, which betray a Babylonian origin, it contains laws and doctrines of kindness toward the poor and helpless, the enemy and the slave, even toward the dumb beast, in striking contrast to the spirit of cruelty and violence in the Babylonian law.1139 In the name of the all-seeing, all-ruling God it appeals to the sympathy of man. These exhortations to tenderness increase in later codes of law under the prophetic influence, until finally the rabbis extended them as far as possible. They held that every negligence which leads to the loss of life or property by the neighbor, every neglect of a domestic animal, even every act of deceit by which one attempts to "steal" the good opinion of one's fellow-men, is a violation of the law.1140 Hence Rabbi Simlai, the Haggadist, said that from beginning to end the Law is but a system of teachings of human love,1141 while another sage tried to prove from the books of Moses that God implanted mercy, modesty, and benevolence in the souls of Israel as hereditary virtues.1142 In the same spirit Rabbi Meir described the law of Israel as the law of humanity, supporting his statement by a number of biblical passages.1143

3. But, as light by its very nature illumines its surroundings, so the Torah in the possession of the Jewish people was certain to become the light of mankind. First of all, the book of Law itself insists that the father shall teach the word of God to his children, using many signs and ceremonies that they may meditate on the works of God and walk in the path of virtue, and that the divine commands should be "in the mouth and in the heart of all to do them."1144 It was made incumbent upon the high priest or king to read the Law at least once every seven years to the whole people assembled in the holy city for the autumnal festival,—men, women, children, and the sojourners in the gates,—so that it should become their common property.1145 This precept probably gave rise to the triennial and later the annual system of Torah reading on the Sabbath. But in addition to the book of Law the prophetic words of consolation were read to the people, a custom which originated in the Babylonian exile, and was continued under the name of Haftarah ("dismissal" of the congregation).1146 The seer of the exile refers to these prophetic words of comfort which were offered to the people on the Sabbath as well as other feasts and fasts: "Attend unto Me, O My people, and give ear unto Me, O My nation, for instruction (Torah) shall go forth from Me, and My right on a sudden for a light of the people.... Hearken unto Me, ye that know righteousness, the people in whose heart is My law; fear ye not the taunt of men, neither be ye dismayed at their revilings. For the moth shall eat them up like a garment, and the worm shall eat them like wool; but My favor shall be forever, and My salvation unto all generations."1147 Moved by such stirring ideals, Synagogues arose in Jewish settlements all over the globe, and the book of the Law, in its vernacular versions, Greek and Aramaic, together with the words of the prophets, became the general source of instruction. In the words of the Psalms, it became "the testimony of the Lord, making wise the simple," "rejoicing the heart," "enlightening the eyes," "more to be desired than gold."1148 Nay more, the study of the Law became the duty of every man, and he who failed to live up to the precepts of the devotees of the Law, the Pharisean fellowships, was scorned as belonging to the lower class, am haaretz. Every morning the pious Jew, first thanking God for the light of day, followed this up by thanking Him for the Torah, which illumines the path of life. "The welfare of society rests upon the study of the Law, divine service and organized charity," was a saying of Simon the Just, a high priest of the beginning of the third pre-Christian century.1149 Thus learning and teaching became leading occupations for the Jew, and the two main departments of Jewish literature, correspondingly, are Torah and Talmud, that is, the written Law and its exposition. Indeed, the highest title which the rabbis could find for Moses was simply "Moses our Teacher." Nay, God Himself was frequently represented as a venerable Master, teaching the Law in awful majesty.1150

4. Later under the successive influence of Babylonian and Greek culture, the wisdom literature was added to the Prophets and the Psalms, giving to the whole Torah a universal scope, like that claimed for Greek philosophy. The Jewish love of learning led to an ever greater longing for truth by adding the wisdom of other cultured nations to its own store of knowledge. This motive for universalism became all the stronger, as the faith became more centered in the sublime conception of God as Master of all the world. As the God of Israel appeared the primal

source of all truth, so the revealed word of God was considered the very embodiment of divine wisdom.1151 In fact, the men of hoary antiquity described in the opening chapters of Genesis were actually credited with being the instructors of the Greeks and other nations.1152 We read a strange story by a pupil of Aristotle that the great sage admired a Jew, whom he happened to meet, as both wise and pious, so that the little Jewish nation was often considered, like the wise men of India, to be a sect of philosophers.1153 Indeed, Judaism became a matter of curiosity to the pagan world on account of the Synagogue, which attracted them as a unique center of religious devotion and instruction, and especially because of the Bible, which was read and expounded in its Greek garb from Sabbath to Sabbath. The Jewish people raised themselves to be a nation of thinkers, and largely through association with Greek thought. For example, in the Greek translation of the Scriptures all anthropomorphic expressions are avoided. As the personal name of Israel's God of the covenant, JHVH, was replaced by the name Adonai, "the Lord,"1154 the universality of the Jewish God became still more evident. Thus the pagan world could find God in the Scriptures to be the living God who dwells in the heart and is sought by all mankind. The Jew became the herald of the One God of the universe, his Bible a book of universal instruction. Many of the heathen, without merging themselves into the community of the covenant people and without accepting all its particularistic customs, rallied around its central standard as simple theists, "worshipers of God," or "they who fear the Lord," according to the terminology of the Psalms.1155

5. An old rabbinical legend, which is reflected in the New Testament miracle of Pentecost, relates that the Ten Words of Sinai were uttered in seventy tongues of fire to reach the known seventy nations of the earth.1156 We are told that when the people entered Canaan, the words of the Law were engraved in seventy languages on the stones of the altar at Mount Ebal.1157 That is, the law of Sinai was intended to provide the foundation for all human society. One Haggadist even asserts that the heathen nations all refused to accept the Law, and if Israel also had rejected it, the world would have returned to chaos.1158 Israel was, so to speak, forced by divine Providence to accept the Law on behalf of the entire race. Hillel, under the Romanized reign of Herod, was fully conscious of this world-mission when he said: "Love your fellow creatures and lead them to the study of the Law."1159

6. The outlook for the Jewish people, however, became darker and darker through its struggle with Rome. The fanatical Zealots entirely opposed the spreading of the knowledge of the Torah among those who did not belong to the household of Israel.1160 Then the Church sent forth her missionaries to convert the pagan world by constant concessions to its polytheistic views and practices. The seed sown by Hellenistic Judaism yielded a rich harvest for the Church, even though it was won at the sacrifice of pure Jewish monotheism. The Ten Words of Sinai, the Mosaic laws of marriage, the poor laws, and other Biblical statutes became the cornerstone of civilization, but in a different guise; the heritage of Judaism was transplanted to the Christian and Mohammedan world in a new garb and under a new name. Henceforth the Jew, dispersed, isolated, and afflicted, had to struggle to preserve his faith in its pristine purity. The very danger besetting the study of the Law during the Hadrianic persecutions, which followed the Bar Kochba revolt, increased his zeal and courage. "Devoid of the Torah, our vital element, we are surely threatened with death," said Rabbi Akiba, applying to himself the fable of the fox and the fishes, as he defied the Roman edict.1161 The fear lest the Torah should be forgotten, stimulated the teachers and their disciples ever anew to its pursuit. The Torah was regarded as the bond and pledge of God's nearness; hence the many rabbinical sayings concerning its value in the eyes of God, which are frequently couched in poetic and extravagant language.1162 The underlying idea of them all is that Israel could dispense with its State and its Temple, but not with its storehouse of divine truth, from which it constantly derives new life and new youth.

7. One important question, however, remains, which must be answered: Has the Jewish people, shut up for centuries by the ramparts of Talmudic Judaism, actually renounced its world mission? In transmitting part of its inheritance to its two daughter-religions, has Judaism lost its claim to be a world-religion? The Congregation of Israel, according to the Midrash, answers this question in the words of the Shulamite in the Song of Songs: "I sleep, but my heart waketh."1163 During the sad period of the Middle Ages, Judaism in its relation to the outer world slept a long winter-sleep, now in one land and now in another, but its inner life always manifested a splendid activity of mind and soul, exerting a mighty influence upon the history of the world. It was declared dead by the ruling Church, and yet it constantly filled her with alarm by the truths it uttered. The Jewish people was given over to destruction and persecution a thousand times, but all the floods of hatred and violence could not quench its flame. Its marvelous endurance constituted the strongest possible protest against the creed of the Church, which claimed to possess an exclusive truth and the only means of salvation. To suffer and die as martyrs by thousands and tens of thousands, at the stake and under the torture of bloodthirsty mobs, testifying to the One Only God of

Israel and humanity, was, to say the least, as heroic a mission as to convert the heathen. Indeed, the Jew, in reciting the Shema each morning in the house of God, renewed daily his zeal and faith, by which he was encouraged to sacrifice himself for his sacred heritage.

8. But the cultivation of the Torah, obligatory upon every Jew, effected more even than the preservation of monotheism. Alongside of the Church, which did its best to suppress free thought, Islam provided a culture which encouraged study and investigation, and this brought the leading spirits in Judaism to a profounder grasp of their own literary treasures. Bold truth-seekers arose under the Mohammedan sway who had the courage to break the chains of belief in the letter of the Scripture, and to claim the right of the human reason to give an opinion on the highest questions of religion. The leading authorities of the Synagogue followed a different course from that of the Church, which had brought the Deity into the sphere of the senses, divided the one God into three persons, and induced the people to worship the image of Mary and her God-child rather than God the Father. They insisted on the absolute unity and spirituality of God, eliminated all the human attributes ascribed to Him in Scripture, and strove to attain the loftiest and purest possible conception of His being. It took a mighty effort for the people of the Law to reëxamine the entire mass of tradition in order to harmonize philosophy and religion, and invest the divine revelation with the highest spiritual character. This mental activity exerted a great influence upon the whole course of thought of subsequent centuries and even upon modern philosophy. Again Israel became conscious of his mission of light. Jewish thinkers, often combining rabbi, physician, and astronomer in one person, carried the torch of science and free investigation, directly or indirectly, into the cell of many a Christian monk, rousing the dull spirit of the Middle Ages and bringing new intellectual nurture to the Church, else she might have starved in her mental poverty.

The Jews of Spain became the teachers of Christian Europe. The forerunners of the Protestant Reformation sat at the feet of Jewish masters. Jewish students of the Hebrew language, scientifically trained, opened up the simple meaning of the Scriptural word, so long hidden by traditional interpretation. The Lutheran and the English translations of the Bible were due to their efforts, and thus also the rise of Protestantism, which inaugurated the modern era. Yet this intellectual revival, this wonderful activity of various thinkers among medieval Jewry, required a soil susceptible to such seeds, an atmosphere favorable to this intense search for truth. This existed only in the Jewish people, since the universal study of the Torah brought it about that "all the children of Israel had light in their dwellings" even while dense darkness covered the nations of the medieval world.

9. We must not underrate the cultural mission of the Jewish people, with its striking contrast to the New Testament point of view, which created monasteries and the celibate ideal, and thus discouraged industry, commerce, and scientific inquiry. Dispersed as they were, the Jewish people cultivated both commerce and science, and thus for centuries were the real bearers of culture, the intermediaries between East and West. While the Church divided mankind into heirs of heaven and hell, thus sowing discord and hatred, the little group of Jews maintained their ideal of an undivided humanity. But even their industrial and commercial activity had more than a mere economic significance. Forced upon the Jew by external pressure, it was favored by Jewish teaching as a means of promoting spiritual life. Not poverty and beggary, but wealth begotten by honest toil has the sanction of Judaism in accordance with the saying "Where there is no flour for bread, there can be no support for the study of the Torah."1164 Moreover, the rabbis interpreted the verse, "Rejoice, O Zebulun, in thy going out, and thou, Issachar, in thy tents,"1165 as meaning that Zebulun, the seafarer, shared the profit of his commerce with Issachar, who taught the law in the tents of the Torah, that he, in turn, might share his brother's spiritual reward. Indeed, the Jew used his gains won by trade in the service of the promotion of learning, and thus his entire industry assumed a higher character. Our modern civilization, with its higher values of life, owes much to the cultural activity of the medieval Jew, which many leaders of the ruling Church still ignore completely. It is true that the hard struggle for their very existence kept the people unconscious of their cultural mission, and only now that they have attained the higher historical point of view can they exclaim with Joseph their ancestor: "As for you, ye meant evil against me; but God meant it for good, to bring it to pass, as it is this day, to save much people alive."1166 The fact is that Jewish commerce has been an important cosmopolitan factor in the past, and is still working, to a certain extent, in the same direction.1167

10. New and great tasks have been assigned by divine Providence to the Jew of modern times, who is a full citizen in the cultural, social, and political life of the various nations. These tasks are most holy to him as Jew, the bearer of a great mission to the world, which is embodied in his heritage, the Torah. However splendid may have been his achievements in the fields of industry and commerce, of literature and art, his own peculiar possession is the Torah

alone, the religious truth for which he fought and suffered all these centuries past; this must forever remain the central thought, the aim of all his striving.1168 Every achievement of the Jewish people, every attainment in power, knowledge, or skill, must lead toward the completion of the divine kingdom of truth and justice; that for which the Jew laid the foundation at the beginning of his history is still leading forward the entire social life of man to render it a divine household of love and peace. In order that it may carry out the world mission mapped out by its great seers of yore, the Jewish people must guard against absorption by the multitude of nations as much as against isolation from them. It must preserve its identity without going back into a separation rooted in self-adulation and clannishness. Instead, the great goal of Israel will be reached only by patient endurance and perseverance, confidently awaiting the fulfillment in God's own time of the glorious prophecy that all the nations shall be led up to the mountain of the Lord by the priest-people, there to worship God in truth and righteousness. The Law is to go forth from Zion and the word of the Lord from Jerusalem, as a spiritual, not a geographical center. This vision forms the highest pinnacle of human aspiration, rising higher and higher before the mind, as man ascends from one stage of culture to another, striving ever for perfection, for the sublimest ideal of life. This is characteristically expressed by the Midrash, which refers to the Messianic vision: "And it shall come to pass in the end of days, that the mountain of the Lord's house shall be established as the top of the mountains, and shall be exalted above the hills."1169 "One great mountain of the earth will be piled upon the other, and Mount Zion will be placed upon the top as the culminating point of all human ascents." Taken in a figurative sense, in which alone the saying is acceptable, this means that all the heights of the various ideals will finally merge into the loftiest of all ideals, when Israel's one holy God will be acknowledged as the One for whom all hearts yearn, whom all minds seek as the Ideal of all ideals.

Chapter LII. Israel, the Servant of the Lord, Martyr and Messiah Of the Nations

1. "If there are ranks in suffering, Israel takes precedence. If the duration of sorrows and the patience with which they are borne, ennoble, the Jews are among the aristocracy of every land. If a literature is called rich which contains a few classic tragedies, what shall we say to a national tragedy lasting for fifteen hundred years, in which the poets and the actors are also the heroes?" With these classic words Leopold Zunz introduces the history of sufferings which have occasioned the hundreds of plaintive and penitential songs of the Synagogue described in his book, Die Synagogale Poesie des Mittelalters. They are the cries of a nation of martyrs, resounding through the whole Jewish liturgy, and appearing already in many of the Psalms: "Thou hast given us like sheep to be eaten; and hast scattered us among the nations. Thou makest us a taunt to our neighbors, a scorn and a derision to them that are round about us. All this is come upon us, yet have we not forgotten Thee, neither have we been false to Thy covenant: Nay, for Thy sake are we killed all the day; we are accounted as sheep for the slaughter. Awake, why sleepest Thou, O Lord? Arouse Thyself, cast not off forever. Wherefore hidest Thou Thy face, and forgettest our affliction and our oppression?"1170 Thus the congregation of Israel laments; and what is the answer of Heaven?

2. The Bible contains two answers: the first by Ezekiel, priest and prophet; the other by the great unknown seer of the Exile whose words of comfort are given in the latter part of Isaiah. Ezekiel gave a stern and direct answer: "The nations shall know that the house of Israel went into captivity because of their iniquity, because they broke faith with Me, and I hid My face from them; so I gave them into the hand of their adversaries, and they fell all of them by the sword. According to their uncleanness and according to their transgressions did I unto them; and I hid My face from them. Therefore thus saith the Lord God: Now will I bring back the captivity of Jacob, and have compassion upon the whole house of Israel; and I will be jealous for My holy name. And they shall bear their shame, and all their breach of faith which they committed against Me."1171 These words are echoed in the harrowing admonitory chapter of Leviticus, which, however, closes with words of comfort: "And they shall confess their iniquity ... if then perchance their uncircumcised heart be humbled, and they then be paid the punishment of their iniquity; then will I remember My covenant with Jacob, and also My covenant with Isaac, and also My covenant with Abraham will I remember; and I will remember the land."1172 This view of divine justice as external and punitive was basic to the Synagogue liturgy and the entire rabbinic system. The priestly idea of atonement, that sin could be wiped out by sacrifice, made a profound impression, not only upon individual sinners, but also upon the nation. Hence it was applied especially to the people in exile when they could not bring sacrifices to their God. Still, one means of atonement remained, the exile itself, which could lead the people to repentance and finally to God's forgiveness.1173 Thus the people retained a hope of return from their captivity. They were assured by their prophetic monitors that the faithful community of the Lord would again be received in favor by the God of

faithfulness. They even built their hope upon the portions of the Law, which was read to assembled worshipers that they might know and observe it on their return to the land of their fathers. Israel could say with the Psalmist: "Unless Thy law had been my delight, I should then have perished in mine affliction."1174 According to a Palestinian Haggadist, "Israel would never have persevered so long, had not the Torah, the marriage contract of Israel with its God, pledged to it a glorious future on the holy soil."1175 Wait patiently for God's mercy, which in His own time will rebuild Israel's State and Temple!—this is the keynote of all the prayers and songs of the Synagogue.

3. But the great seer of the exile, whose anonymity lends still greater impressiveness to his words of comfort, stood on a higher historical plane than that of Ezekiel the priest. He witnessed the transformation of the entire political world of his time through the victory of Cyrus the Mede over the Babylonian empire, and thus was able to attain a profounder grasp of the destiny of his own nation. Hence he was not satisfied with the view of Ezekiel. The latter had applied the popular saying, "The fathers have eaten sour grapes, and the children's teeth are set on edge,"1176 to refute the belief that an individual was punished for the sins of his fathers; but he failed to extend this doctrine to the whole nation. Whatever sins were committed by the generation who were exiled, their children ought not to suffer for them "in double measure."1177 Moreover, the realm of love has a higher law than atonement through retribution. Love brings its sacrifice without asking why. By willing sacrifice of self it serves its higher purpose. He who struggles and suffers silently for the good and true is God's servant, who cannot perish. He attains a higher glory, transcending the fate of mortality. This is the new revelation that came to the seer, as he pondered on the destiny of Israel in exile, illumining for him that dark enigma of his people's tragic history.

The problem of suffering, especially that of the servant of God, or the pious, occupied the Jewish mind ever since the days of Jeremiah and especially during the exile. The author of the book of Job elaborated this into a great theodicy, speaking of Job also as the "servant of the Lord."1178 Whatever pattern our exilic seer employed, beside the chapters about the Servant of the Lord,1179 whatever tragic fate of some great contemporary the plaintive song in the fifty-second and fifty-third chapters referred to (some point to Jeremiah, others to Zerubabel),1180 or whether the poet had in mind only the tragic fate of Israel, as many modern exegetes think; in any case he conceived the unique and pathetic picture of Israel as the suffering Servant of the Lord, who is at last to be exalted:1181

"Behold, My servant shall prosper, he shall be exalted and lifted up, and shall be very high. According as many were appalled at thee—so marred was his visage unlike that of a man, and his form unlike that of the sons of men—so shall he startle many nations; kings shall shut their mouths because of him; for that which had not been told them they shall see, and that which they had not heard shall they perceive. Who would have believed our report? And to whom hath the arm of the Lord been revealed? For he shot up right forth as a sapling, and as a root out of a dry ground; he had no form nor comeliness, that we should look upon him, nor beauty that we should delight in him. He was despised and forsaken of men, a man of pains, and acquainted with disease, and as one from whom men hide their face; he was despised, and we esteemed him not. Surely our diseases he did bear, and our pains he carried; whereas we did esteem him stricken, smitten of God and afflicted. But he was wounded because of our transgressions, he was crushed because of our iniquities; the chastisement of our welfare was upon him, and with his stripes we were healed. All we, like sheep, did go astray, we turned every one to his own way; and the Lord hath made to light on him the iniquity of us all. He was oppressed, though he humbled himself, and opened not his mouth; as a lamb that is led to the slaughter, and as a sheep that before her shearers is dumb; yea, he opened not his mouth. By oppression and judgment he was taken away, and with his generation who did reason? For he was cut off out of the land of the living, for the transgression of my people to whom the stroke was due. And they made his grave with the wicked, and with the rich his tomb; although he had done no violence, neither was any deceit in his mouth. Yet it pleased the Lord to crush him by disease; to see if his soul would offer itself in restitution, that he might see his seed, prolong his days, and that the purpose of the Lord might prosper by his hand. Of the travail of his soul he shall see to the full, even My servant, who by his knowledge did justify the Righteous One to the many, and their iniquities he did bear. Therefore will I divide him a portion among the great, and he shall divide his soul with the mighty; because he bared his soul unto death, and was numbered with the transgressors; yet he bore the sin of many, and made intercession for the transgressors."

4. Whatever be the historical background of this great elegy, our seer uses it to portray Israel as the tragic hero of the world's history. His prophetic genius possessed a unique insight into the character and destiny of his people, seeing Israel as a man of woe and grief, chosen by Providence to undergo unheard-of trials for a great cause, by

which, at the last, he is to be exalted. Bent and disfigured by his burden of misery and shame, shunned and abhorred as one laden with sin, he suffers for no guilt of his own. He is called to testify to his God among all the peoples, and is thus the Servant of the Lord, the atoning sacrifice for the sins of mankind, from whose bruises healing is to come to all the nations,—an inimitable picture of a self-sacrificing hero, whose death means life to the world and glory to God, and who will at last live forever with the Lord whom he has served so steadfastly. Our seer mentions in earlier passages the Servant of the Lord who "gave his back to the smiters, and his cheeks to them that plucked off the hair; and hid not his face from shame and spitting."1182 Yet "he shall set his face like a flint," so that "he shall not fail nor be crushed, till he have set the right in the earth; and the isles shall wait for his teaching."1183 Still more directly, he says: "And He said unto Me, 'Thou art My servant, Israel, in whom I will be glorified.' ... It is too light a thing that thou shouldest be My servant to raise up the tribes of Jacob and to restore the offspring of Israel; I will also give thee for a light of the nations, that My salvation may be unto the end of the earth. Thus saith the Lord, the Redeemer of Israel, his Holy One, to him who is despised of men, to him who is abhorred of nations, to a servant of rulers: kings shall see and arise, princes, and they shall prostrate themselves; because of the Lord that is faithful, even the Holy One of Israel, who hath chosen thee."1184

5. It was, however, no easy matter for men reared in the old view to reach the lofty conception of a suffering hero. Even the dramatic figure of Job seemed to lack the right solution. Job protests his guiltlessness, defies the dark power of fate, and even challenges divine justice, but God himself announces at the end that no man can grasp the essence of His plan for the world. A later and more naïve writer, who added the conclusion of the book, reversed Job's destiny and compensated him by a double share of what he had lost in both wealth and family.1185 As if the great problem of suffering could be solved by such external means! Neither would the problem of the great tragedy of Israel, the martyr-priest of the centuries, the Job of the nations, ever find its solution in a national restoration. A mere political rebirth could never compensate for the thousandfold death and untold woe of the Jew for his God and his faith! But the people at large could not grasp such a conception as is that of Deutero-Isaiah's of the mission of Israel to be the suffering servant of the Lord, the witness of God—which is "martyr" in the Greek version,—the redeemer of the nations. They were eager to return to Palestine, to rebuild State and Temple under the leadership of the heir to the throne of David. But when their hope had failed that Zerubbabel would prove to be the "shoot of Jesse,"1186 the prophetic elegy was referred to the Messiah, and the belief gained ground that he would have to suffer before he would triumph.1187 Thus many a pseudo-Messiah fell a victim to the tyranny of Rome in both Judæa and Samaria,—for the Samaritans also hoped for a Messiah, a redeemer of the type of Moses.1188 Finally a belief arose that there would be two Messiahs, one of the house of Joseph, that is, the tribe of Ephraim, who would fall before the sword of the enemy,1189 and the other of the house of David, who was to conquer the heathen nations and establish his throne forever.1190

The Church referred the pathetic figure of the man of sorrow to her crucified Messiah or Christ. Yet he who was to be a world-savior bore through his followers damnation to his own kinsmen, and thus was rendered the chief cause of the persecution of the martyr-race of Israel.

6. We learn, however, from Origen, a Church father of the third century, that Jewish scholars, in a controversy with him, expressed the view that the Servant of the Lord refers to the Jewish people, which, dispersed among the nations and universally despised, would finally obtain the ascendancy over them, so that many of the heathen would espouse the Jewish faith.1191 Most of the medieval Jewish exegetes, including Rashi, who usually follows the traditional view, refer the chapter likewise to the Jewish people. As a matter of fact, the earlier chapters which speak of the Servant of the Lord can have no other meaning, while many points in the description of the suffering hero, especially the reference to his seed after his death, do not fit the Nazarene at all. Hence all independent Christian scholars to-day have abandoned the tradition of the Church, and admit that Israel alone is declared by the prophet to be the one singled out by God to atone for the sins of the nations, to arouse all humanity to a deeper spiritual vision, and finally to triumph over all the heathen world.1192

7. Thus the strange history of the martyr people is put in the right light and the great tragedy of Israel explained. Israel is the champion of the Lord, chosen to battle and suffer for the supreme values of mankind, for freedom and justice, truth and humanity; the man of woe and grief, whose blood is to fertilize the soil with the seeds of righteousness and love for mankind. From the days of Pharaoh to the present day, every oppressor of the Jews has become the means of bringing greater liberty to a wider circle; for the God of Israel, the Hater of bondage, has been appealed to in behalf of freedom in the old world and the new. Every hardship that made life unbearable to the Jew became a road to humanity's triumph over barbarism. All the injustice and malice which hurled their bitter shafts

against Israel, the Pariah of the nations, led ultimately to the greater victory of right and love. So all the dark waves of hatred and fanaticism that beat against the Jewish people served only to impress the truth of monotheism, coupled with sincere love of God and man, more deeply upon all hearts and to consign hypocrisy and falsehood to eternal contempt. Such is the belief confidently held by the people of God, and ever confirmed anew by the history of the ages. "He is near that justifieth me; who will contend with me? let us stand up together; who is mine adversary? let him come near to me. Behold, the Lord God will help me; who is he that shall condemn me?"1193 Thus speaks the Servant of the Lord, certain that he will finally triumph, because he defends God's cause, and is bound indissolubly to Him.1194 Indeed, God says of him: "Surely, he that toucheth you toucheth the apple of Mine (his) eye."1195

8. The great importance which the rabbis attached to Israel's martyrdom is shown by the following remarks in connection with the laws of sacrifice: "Behold, how the Torah selects for the sacrificial altar only such animals as belong to the pursued, not the pursuers: the ox which is pursued by the lion; the lamb which is pursued by the wolf; the goat which is pursued by the panther, but none of those which feed on prey. In like manner God chose for His own the persecuted ones: Abel, who was persecuted by his brother Cain; Noah, who was derided by the generation of the flood; Abraham, who had to flee before the tyrant Nimrod; and Isaac, Jacob, and Joseph, who met with unkindness from their own brothers. In the same way God has chosen Israel from among the seventy nations, as the lamb hunted, as it were, by seventy wolves, that it should bear His law to mankind."1196 This idea is expressed also in the Haggadic saying: "Those shall be privileged to see the majesty of God in full splendor who meet humiliation, but do not humiliate others; who bear insult, but do not inflict it on others; and who endure a life of martyrdom in pure love of God."1197

Indeed, the medieval Jew accepted his sad lot in this spirit of resignation. But the modern Jew is in a different situation. In the mighty effort of our age for higher truth, broader love and larger justice, he beholds the nearing of the prophetic goal of a united humanity, based on the belief in God, the King and Father of all. Accordingly, modern Judaism proclaims more insistently than ever that the Jewish people is the Servant of the Lord, the suffering Messiah of the nations, who offered his life as an atoning sacrifice for humanity and furnished his blood as the cement with which to build the divine kingdom of truth and justice. Indeed, the cosmopolitan spirit of the Jew is the one element needed for the universality of culture. On the other hand, the world at large is to-day learning more and more to regard the superb loyalty of the Jew to his ancestral faith with greater fairness and admiration and to accord larger appreciation to him and his religion. Once the flood of hatred, dissension, and prejudice that brought such untold havoc shall have disappeared from the earth; once religion emerges from the nebulous atmosphere of other-worldliness, and directs its longing for God toward a life of godliness on earth in the spirit of the ancient prophets, then the historic mission of the Jew will also be better understood. Israel, the hunted dove, which found no resting-place for the sole of its foot during the flood of sin and persecution, will then appear with the olive-branch of peace for all humanity, to open the hearts of men that all may enter the covenant with the universal Father. Then, and not till then, will the shame of those thousands of years be rolled away, when the world will recognize that not a Jew, but the Jew has been the suffering Messiah, and that he was sent forth to be the savior of the nations.

Chapter LIII. The Messianic Hope

1. Recent investigators have brought to light many a vision of an era of heavenly bliss brought about by some powerful ruler, voiced in hoary antiquity by seer or singer in addressing the royal masters of Babylon or Egypt.1198 But no word in the entire vocabulary of ancient poetry or prose can so touch the deeper chords of the heart, and so voice the highest hopes of mankind, as does the name Messiah ("God's anointed"). From a simple title for any of the kings of Israel, it grew in meaning until it comprised the highest hopes of the nation. The Jewish vision of the future was not the twilight of the gods, which meant the end of the world with its deities, but the dawn of a new world, bright with the knowledge of God and blessed by the brotherhood of man. This, the Messianic ideal, is the creation of the prophetic genius of Israel, and in turn it influenced man's conception of God, lifting Him out of the national bounds, and making Him the God of humanity, Ruler of history. Israel's Messianic hope has become the motive power of civilization. In the time of deepest national humiliation it gave the prophets their power to surmount the present and soar to heights of vision; through it the Jewish people attained their strength to resist oppression, buoyed up by perfect confidence and sublime hope. At the same time its magic luster captivated the

non-Jewish nations, spurring them on to mighty deeds. Thus it has actually conquered the whole world of man. With every step in culture it points forward to higher aims, still unattained; it promises to lead mankind, united in God, the Only One, to truth and justice, righteousness and love. As the banner of Israel, the Messiah of the nations, it is destined to become the lode-star of all nations and all religions. This is the kernel of the Jewish doctrine concerning the Messiah.

2. This Messianic hope, on closer analysis, reveals two elements, both of prophetic origin: one national, the other religious and universal. The latter is the logical outcome of the monotheism of the great exilic seer, who based his stirring pictures of the glorious future of Israel upon the all-encompassing knowledge of God possessed by the Chosen People. The classic expression of this hope appears in Isaiah II, 1-4, and Micah IV, 1-14: "And it shall come to pass in the end of days, that the mountain of the Lord's house shall be established as the top of the mountains, and shall be exalted above the hills; and all nations shall flow unto it. And many peoples shall go and say: 'Come ye and let us go up to the mountain of the Lord, to the house of the God of Jacob; and He will teach us of His ways, and we will walk in His paths,' for out of Zion shall go forth the law, and the word of the Lord from Jerusalem. And He shall judge between the nations, and shall decide for many peoples; and they shall beat their swords into ploughshares, and their spears into pruning-hooks; nation shall not lift up sword against nation, neither shall they learn war any more." We note, indeed, that no reference to the Messiah or a king of the house of David appears either in this passage or any of the prophecies of Deutero-Isaiah. Justice and peace for all humanity are expected through the reign of God alone. The specific Messianic character of this prophecy took shape only in its association with the older national hope, voiced by the prophet Isaiah.

3. The real Messianic hope involved the reëstablishment of the throne of David, and was expressed most perfectly in the words of Isaiah: "And there shall come forth a shoot out of the stock of Jesse, and a twig shall grow forth out of his roots. And the spirit of the Lord shall rest upon him, the spirit of wisdom and understanding, the spirit of counsel and might, the spirit of knowledge and of the fear of the Lord. And his delight shall be in the fear of the Lord; and he shall not judge after the sight of his eyes, neither decide after the hearing of his ears; but with righteousness shall he judge the poor, and decide with equity for the meek of the land; and he shall smite the land with the rod of his mouth, and with the breath of his lips shall he slay the wicked. And righteousness shall be the girdle of his loins, and faithfulness the girdle of his reins. And the wolf shall dwell with the lamb, and the leopard shall lie down with the kid; and the calf and the young lion and the fatling together; and a little child shall lead them.... They shall not hurt nor destroy in all My holy mountain; for the earth shall be full of the knowledge of the Lord, as the waters cover the sea."1199

This pattern of the ideal ruler may have been modeled after some ancient Babylonian formula for the adoration of kings, as has been asserted of late; and the same may be true of the mystic titles given by Isaiah to the royal heir: "Wonderful counselor, divine hero, father of spoil, prince of peace."1200 When the little kingdom of Judæa fell, the prospect of a realization of the great prophetic vision seemed gone forever. Therefore the exiles in Babylon fastened their hopes so much more firmly on the "Shoot," particularly on Zerubabel ("the seed born in Babylon"), the object of the fondest hopes of the later prophets.1201 When he, too, disappointed their expectations, probably due to Persian interference, they transferred the advent of the Messiah more and more into the realm of miracle, and popular fancy dwelt fondly on his appearance as God's champion against the hosts of heathendom (Gog and Magog).1202

4. The conception of the priest-prophet Ezekiel is very significant in this connection; for him the kingdom of Israel's God could only be established by the restoration of the throne of David, the servant of the Lord, and by the utter destruction of the hosts of heathendom, who were hostile to both God and Israel. In accordance with this hope the author of the second Psalm presents a dramatic picture of the Messiah triumphing over the heathen nations, a picture which became typical for all the future. "Why are the nations in an uproar? And why do the peoples mutter in vain? The kings of the earth stand up, and the rulers take counsel together against the Lord, and against His anointed: 'Let us break their bands asunder, and cast away their cords from us.' He that sitteth in heaven laugheth, the Lord hath them in derision. Then will He speak unto them in His wrath, and affright them in His sore displeasure: 'Truly it is I that have established My king upon Zion, My holy mountain.' I will tell of the decree: The Lord said unto me: 'Thou art My son, this day have I begotten thee. Ask of Me, and I will give the nations for thine inheritance, and the ends of the earth for thy possession. Thou shalt break them with a rod of iron; thou shalt dash them in pieces like a potter's vessel.'" Henceforth the conception of the Messiah alternated between Isaiah's prince of peace and the world-conqueror of the Psalmist.1203 The name Messiah does not occur in Scripture in the

absolute form, but always occurs in the construct with JHVH or a pronoun, signifying "the Anointed of the Lord." Accordingly, it expresses the relation of the Anointed to God, his sovereign, in striking contrast to the heathen kings who themselves claimed adoration as gods. The very name Messiah excludes the possibility of deification. The term Messiah was used with the article only in much later times, ha Meshiah, or in the Aramaic, Meshiha, from which we derive the name, Messiah.

5. In the course of time, however, as the people waited in vain for a redeemer, the expected Messiah was lifted more and more into the realm of the ideal. The belief took hold especially in the inner circle of the pious (Hasidim) that the Messiah was hidden somewhere, protected by God, to appear miraculously after having vanquished the hostile powers. The Essenes, the representatives of the secret lore, developed this conception in the Apocalyptic writings, thus giving the Messiah a certain cosmic or supernatural character. They probably modeled their thoughts upon the Zoroastrian system, where Soshiosh, the world savior, would appear in the last millennium as the messenger of Ormuzd to destroy forever the kingdom of evil and establish the dominion of the good.1204 Thus, when Isaiah says of the Messiah that "by the breath of his mouth he shall slay the wicked," this is referred to the principle of evil, Satan or Belial, who was sometimes actually identified with the Persian Ahriman.1205 Moreover, after the Persian system, the whole process of history was divided into six millenniums of strife between the principle of good and evil, represented by the Torah and the ungodliness of the world, and a seventh millennium, the kingdom of God or the Messianic age. The dates of these were calculated upon the basis of the book of Daniel, with its four world-kingdoms and mysterious numbers.1206

6. The Biblical passages which refer to "the end of days" were also connected with the advent of the Messianic age, and the so-called eschatological writings speak of fixed periods following one another. In accordance with certain prophetic hints, they expected first the "birth-throes"1207 or "vestiges" of the Messianic age, a great physical and moral crisis with the turmoil of nature, plagues, and moral degeneracy. Before the Messiah would suddenly appear from his hiding place, the prophet Elijah was to return from heaven, whither he had ascended in a fiery chariot. But, while he had lived in implacable wrath against idolaters, he was now to come as a messenger of peace, reconciling the hearts of Israel with God and with one another, preparing the way to repentance, and thus to the redemption and reunion of Israel.1208 The next stage is the gathering together of Israel from all corners of the earth to the holy land under the leadership of the Messiah, summoned by the blast of the heavenly trumpet.1209 Then begins that gigantic warfare on the holy soil between the hosts of Israel and the vast forces of heathendom led by the half-mystic powers of Gog and Magog, a conflict which, according to Ezekiel, is to last for seven years and to end with the annihilation of the powers of evil. Before the real Messiah, the son of David, appears in victory, another Messiah of the tribe of Ephraim is to fall in battle, according to a belief dating from the second century and possibly connected with the Bar Kochba war.1210 In another tradition, probably older, the true Messiah himself is to suffer and die.1211 At all events, he must destroy Rome, the fourth world-kingdom. But he is also to slay the arch-fiend Ahriman, afterwards known as Armillus. Moreover, he will redeem the dead from Sheol, as he possesses the key to open all the graves of the holy land, and thus all the sons of Israel will partake in the glory of his kingdom. Then at last the city of Jerusalem will arise in splendor, built of gold and precious stones, the marvel of the world, and in its midst the Temple, a structure of surpassing magnificence. The holy vessels of the tabernacle, hidden for ages in the wilderness, will appear, and the nations will offer the wealth of the whole earth as their tribute to the Messiah. All will practice righteousness and piety, and will be rewarded by bliss and numerous posterity.1212

Opinions differ widely as to the duration of the Messianic age. They range from forty to four hundred years, and again from three generations to a full millennium.1213 This difference is partly caused by the distinction between the national hope, with the temporary welfare of the people of Israel, and the religious hope concerning the divine kingdom, which is to last forever. A very late rabbinic belief holds that the Messiah will be able to give a new law and even to abrogate Mosaic prohibitions.1214

7. At any rate, no complete system of eschatology existed during the Talmudic age, as the views of the various apocalyptic writers were influenced by the changing events of the time and the new environments, with their constant influence upon popular belief. A certain uniformity, indeed, existed in the fundamental ideas. The Messianic hope in its national character includes always the reunion of all Israel under a victorious ruler of the house of David, who shall destroy all hostile powers and bring an era of supreme prosperity and happiness as well as of peace and good-will among men. The Haggadists indulged also in dreams of the marvelous fertility of the soil of Palestine in the Messianic time,1215 and of the resurrection of the dead in the holy land. But in Judaism such

views could never become dogmas, as they did in the Church, even though they were common in both the older and younger Haggadah. These national expectations were expressed in the liturgy by the Eighteen Benedictions, composed by the founders of the Synagogue, the so-called Men of the Great Synagogue; here the prayers for "the gathering of the dispersed" and the "destruction of the kingdom of Insolence" precede those for the "rebuilding of Jerusalem and the restoration of the throne of David." But the mystic speculations on the origin, activity, and sojourn of the Messiah, which were a favorite theme of the apocalyptic writers and the Haggadists during the pre-Christian and the first Christian centuries, gave way to a more sober mode of thought, in the disappointment that followed the collapse of the great Messianic movements. On the one hand, the Church deified its Messiah and thus relapsed into paganism; on the other, Bar Kochba, "the son of the star," whom the leading Jewish masters of the law actually considered the Messiah who would free them from Rome, proved to be a "star of ill-luck" to the Jewish people.1216 "Like one who wanders in the dark night, now and then kindling a light to brighten up his path, only to have it again and again extinguished by the wind, until at last he resolves to wait patiently for the break of day when he will no longer require a light," so were the people of Israel with their would-be deliverers, who appeared from time to time to delude their hopes, until they exclaimed at last: "In Thy light alone, O Lord, we behold light."1217 Samuel the Babylonian, of the third century, in opposition to the Messianic visionaries of his time, declared: "The Messianic age differs from the present in nothing except that Israel will throw off the yoke of the nations and regain its political independence."1218 Another sage said: "May the curse of heaven fall upon those who calculate the date of the advent of the Messiah and thus create political and social unrest among the people!"1219 A third declared: "The Messiah will appear when nobody expects him."1220 Most remarkable of all is the bold utterance of Rabbi Hillel of the fourth century, a lineal descendant of the great master Hillel and the originator of the present Jewish calendar system. In all likelihood many of his contemporaries were busy calculating the advent of the Messianic time according to the number of Jubilees in the world-eras, whereupon he said: "Israel need not await the advent of the Messiah, as Isaiah's prophecy was fulfilled by the appearance of King Hezekiah."1221

8. Throughout the Middle Ages, when the political or national hopes rose high, we find various Messianic movements in both East and West revived by religious aspirations. But Maimonides, the great rationalist, in his commentary on the Mishnah and in his Code, formulated a Messianic belief which was quite free from mystical and supernatural elements. His twelfth article of faith declares that "the Jew, unless he wishes to forfeit his claim to eternal life by denial of his faith, must, in acceptance of the teachings of Moses and the prophets down to Malachi, believe that the Messiah will issue forth from the house of David in the person of a descendant of Solomon, the only legitimate king; and he shall far excel all rulers in history by his reign, glorious in justice and peace. Neither impatience nor deceptive calculation of the time of the advent of the Messiah should shatter this belief. Still, notwithstanding the majesty and wisdom of the Messiah, he must be regarded as a mortal being like any other and only as the restorer of the Davidic dynasty. He will die and leave a son as his successor, who will in his turn die and leave the throne to his heir. Nor will there be any material change in the order of things in the whole system of nature and human life; accordingly Isaiah's picture of the living together of lamb and wolf cannot be taken literally, nor any of the Haggadic sayings with reference to the Messianic time. We are only to believe in the coming of Elijah as a messenger of peace and the forerunner of the Messiah, and also in the great decisive battle with the hosts of heathendom embodied in Gog and Magog, through whose defeat the dominion of the Messiah will be permanently established." "The Messianic kingdom itself," continues Maimonides with reference to the utterance of Samuel quoted above, "is to bring the Jewish nation its political independence, but not the subjection of all the heathen nations, nor merely material prosperity and sensual pleasure, but an era of general affluence and peace, enabling the Jewish people to devote their lives without care or anxiety to the study of the Torah and universal wisdom, so that by their teachings they may lead all mankind to the knowledge of God and make them also share in the eternal bliss of the world to come."1222

9. Against this rationalized hope for the Messiah, which merges the national expectation into the universal hope for the kingdom of God, strong objections were raised by Abraham ben David of Posquieres, the mystic, a fierce opponent of Maimonides, who referred to various Biblical and Talmudical passages in contradiction to this view.1223 On the other hand, Joseph Albo, the popular philosopher, who was trained by his public debates against the representatives of the Church, emphasized especially the rational character of the Jewish theology, and declared that the Messianic hope cannot be counted among the fundamental doctrines of Judaism, or else Rabbi Hillel could never have rejected it so boldly.1224

On this point we must consider the fine observation of Rashi that Hillel denied only a personal Messiah, but not the coming of a Messianic age, assuming that God himself will redeem Israel and be acknowledged everywhere as Ruler of the world. As a matter of fact, too much difference of opinion existed among the Tanaim and Amoraim on the personality of the Messiah and the duration of his reign to admit of a definite article of faith on the question. The expected Messiah, the heir of the Davidic throne, naturally embodied the national hope of the Jewish people in their dispersion, when all looked to Palestine as their land and to Jerusalem as their political center and rallying point in days to come. Traditional Judaism, awaiting the restoration of the Mosaic sacrificial cult as the condition for the return of the Shekinah to Zion, was bound to persist in its belief in a personal Messiah who would restore the Temple and its service.

10. A complete change in the religious aspiration of the Jew was brought about by the transformation of his political status and hopes in the nineteenth century. The new era witnessed his admission in many lands to full citizenship on an equality with his fellow-citizens of other faiths. He was no longer distinguished from them in his manner of speech and dress, nor in his mode of education and thought; he therefore necessarily identified himself completely with the nation whose language and literature had nurtured his mind, and whose political and social destinies he shared with true patriotic fervor. He stood apart from the rest only by virtue of his religion, the great spiritual heritage of his hoary past. Consequently the hope voiced in the Synagogal liturgy for a return to Palestine, the formation of a Jewish State under a king of the house of David, and the restoration of the sacrificial cult, no longer expressed the views of the Jew in Western civilization. The prayer for the rebuilding of Jerusalem and the restoration of the Temple with its priestly cult could no longer voice his religious hope. Thus the leaders of Reform Judaism in the middle of the nineteenth century declared themselves unanimously opposed to retaining the belief in a personal Messiah and the political restoration of Israel, either in doctrine or in their liturgy.1225 They accentuated all the more strongly Israel's hope for a Messianic age, a time of universal knowledge of God and love of man, so intimately interwoven with the religious mission of the Jewish people. Harking back to the suffering Servant of the Lord in Deutero-Isaiah, they transferred the title of Messiah to the Jewish nation. Reform Judaism has thus accepted the belief that Israel, the suffering Messiah of the centuries, shall at the end of days become the triumphant Messiah of the nations.1226

11. This view taken by reform Judaism is the logical outcome of the political and social emancipation of the Jew in western Europe and America. Naturally, it had no appeal to the Jew in the Eastern lands, where he was kept apart by mental training, social habits and the discrimination of the law, so that he regarded himself as a member of a different nationality in every sense. Palestine remained the object of his hope and longing in both his social and religious life. When modern ideas of life began to transform the religious views and habits in many a quarter, and terrible persecutions again aroused the longing of the unfortunate sufferers for a return to the land of their fathers, the term Zionism was coined, and the movement rapidly spread. It expressed the purely national aims of the Jewish people, disregarding the religious aspirations always heretofore connected with the Messianic hope. This term has since become the watchword of all those who hope for a political restoration of the Jewish people on Palestinian soil, as well as of others whose longings are of a more cultural nature. Both regard the Jewish people as a nation like any other, denying to it the specific character of a priest-people and a holy nation with a religious mission for humanity, which has been assigned to it at the very beginning of its history and has served to preserve it through the centuries. On this account Zionism, whether political or cultural, can have no place in Jewish theology. Quite different is the attitude of religious Zionism which emphasizes the ancient hopes and longings for the restoration of the Jewish Temple and State in connection with the nationalistic movement.

12. Political Zionism owes its origin to the wave of Anti-Semitism which rose as a counter-movement to the emancipation of the Jew, that alienated many of the household of Israel from their religion. Thus it has the merit of awakening many Jews upon whom the ancestral faith had lost its hold to a sense of love and loyalty to the Jewish past. In many it has aroused a laudable zeal for the study of Jewish history and literature, which should bring them a deeper insight into, and closer identification with, the historic character of Israel, the suffering Messiah of the nations, and thus in time transform the national Jew into a religious Jew. The study of Israel's mighty past will, it is hoped, bring to them the conviction that the power, the hope and the refuge of Israel is in its God, and not in any territorial possession. We require a regeneration, not of the nation, but of the faith of Israel, which is its soul.

Chapter LIV. Resurrection, a National Hope

1. The Jewish belief in resurrection is intimately bound up with the hope for the restoration of the Israelitish nation on its own soil, and consequently rather national; indeed, originally purely local and territorial.1227 True, the rabbis justified their belief in resurrection by such Scriptural verses as: "I kill and I make alive"1228 and "The Lord killeth, and maketh alive; He bringeth down to the grave, and bringeth up."1229 Founded on such passages, the belief would have to include all men, and could be confined neither to the Jewish people nor to the land of Judea. However, we find no trace of such a belief in the entire Bible save for two late post-exilic passages1230 which are in fact apocalyptic, being based upon earlier prophecies, and themselves, in turn, basic to the later dogma of the Pharisees.

2. The picture of a resurrection was first drawn by the prophet Hosea, who applied it to Israel. In his distress over the destiny of his people he says: "Come, and let us return unto the Lord; for He hath torn, and He will heal us, He hath smitten, and He will bind us up. After two days will He revive us, on the third day He will raise us up, that we may live in His presence."1231 Ezekiel's vision of the dry bones which rose to a new life under the mighty sway of the spirit of God,1232 gave more definite shape to the picture, although in the form of allegory. As the prophet himself says, he aimed to describe the resurrection of Judah and Israel from their grave of exile. The obscure Messianic prophecy in Isaiah, chapters XXIV to XXVII, strikes a new note. First the author deals with the terrible slaughter which God will inflict upon the heathen, after which "He will swallow up death forever; and the Lord God will wipe away tears from off all faces; and the reproach of His people will He take away from off all the earth."1233 Finally, when the oppressors of Israel are completely annihilated, exclaims the seer: "Thy dead shall live, thy dead bodies shall arise—awake and sing, ye that dwell in the dust—for thy dew is a fructifying dew, and the earth shall bring to life the shades."1234 Daniel speaks in a similar vein: "And many of them that sleep in the dust of the earth shall awake, some to everlasting life, and some to reproaches and everlasting abhorrence."1235

3. In this hope for resurrection at the end of days the leading thought is that the prophecies which have been unfulfilled during the lifetime of the pious, and particularly the martyrs, shall be realized in the world to come.1236 In the oldest apocalyptic writings this life of the future is still conceived as earthly bliss, inasmuch as the writers think only of the Messianic time of national glory, depicted in such glowing colors by the prophets. Unbounded richness of the soil and numerous offspring, abundant treasures brought by remote nations and their rulers, peace and happiness far and wide—such are the characteristics of the Messianic age. In order that the dead may share in all this, it is to be preceded by the resurrection and the great Day of Judgment in the valley of Jehoshaphat or Gehinnom (Gehenna), where the righteous are to be singled out to participate in the realm of the Messiah.1237 As a national prospect the Messianic hope was based upon the passage in Deutero-Isaiah: "Thy people also shall be all righteous, they shall inherit the land forever."1238 Consequently an ancient Mishnah taught that "All Israel shall have a share in the world to come."1239 In fact, the term "inherit the land" was used as late as the Mishnah to express the idea of sharing in the future life; so also in the New Testament, where the resurrection was expected before the coming of the kingdom of the Messiah.1240

4. The logical assumption was, accordingly, that only the dead of the holy land should enjoy the resurrection. The prophetic verses were cited: "I will set glory in the land of the living,"1241 and "He that giveth breath to the people upon it, and spirit to them that walk therein,"1242 and were interpreted in the sense that God would restore the breath of life only to those buried in the holy land.1243 Likewise the verse of the Psalmist, "I shall walk before the Lord in the land of the living," was referred to Palestine, as the land where the dead shall awaken to a new life.1244 Hence the rabbis held the strange belief that when the great heavenly trumpet is sounded to summon all the tribes of Israel from the ends of the earth to the holy land,1245 those who have been buried outside of Palestine must pass through cavities under the earth, until they reach the soil where the miracle of the resurrection will be performed.1246 It has, therefore, become a custom of the pious among the Orthodox to this very day, in case they could not bury the dead in Palestine, to put dust of the holy land beneath their head, that they might arise wherever they were buried.

5. We may take it for granted that this naïve conception of the resurrection could not be permanent, and so was modified to include a double resurrection: the first, national, to usher in the Messianic kingdom, and the other, universal, to usher in the everlasting life of the future. The former offered scant room for the heathen world, at best only for those who had actually joined the ranks of Judaism; the latter, however, included the last judgment for all

souls and thus opened the way for the salvation of the righteous among the nations as well as the people of Israel. At this point the conception of resurrection led to higher and more spiritual ideas, as has been shown in Chapter XLIII.

6. However, the belief in the resurrection of the body, though expressed in the ancient liturgy, is in such utter contradiction to our entire attitude toward both science and religion, that it may be considered obsolete for the modern Jew. Orthodoxy, which clings to it in formal loyalty to tradition, regards it as a miracle which God will perform in the future, exactly like the many Biblical miracles which defy reason.

7. The Zionist movement has given many Jews a new attitude toward the national resurrection of Israel. The nationalists expect the Jewish nation to awaken from a sleep of eighteen hundred years to new greatness in its ancient home, not as a religious, but as a political body, and in renouncing all allegiance to the priestly mission of Israel and its ancestral faith they are as remote from genuine Orthodoxy as from Reform Judaism. They assert that the soul of the Jewish people requires a national body rooted in its ancient soil in order that it may fulfill its appointed task among the nations; they even go so far as to declare all the achievements brought about by the assimilation of the culture of the surrounding nations to be a deterioration of the genuine character of the Jewish nation. The fact is that, as in nature there is nowhere a resurrection of the dead but an ever renewed regeneration of life, so is the history of the Jew and of Judaism a continuous process of regeneration manifested at every great turning-point of history, when the ideas and cultural elements of a new civilization exert their powerful influence on life and thought. There never was, nor will be an exclusively Jewish culture. It is the wondrous power of assimilation of the Jew which ever created and fashioned his culture anew. That which constitutes the peculiarity of the Jew and his life force is his religion fostered through the ages, preserved amidst the most antagonistic influences and hostile environments, and ever rejuvenated by its unique universalistic spirit when revived by contact with kindred movements. To maintain and propagate this, his religion in all lands and amidst all civilizations, is the task assigned to him by Providence, until God's Kingdom has been established all over the globe.

Chapter LV. Israel and the Heathen Nations

1. As there is but one Creator and Ruler of the universe, so there is before Him but one humanity. All the nations are under His guidance, while Israel, His chosen people, points to the kingdom of God which is to embrace them all. Israel was called the "first-born son" of God1247 at the very moment of his election, implying that all the sons of men are His children. All of them are links in the divine plan of salvation. In the same sense God spoke through Isaiah: "Blessed be Egypt, My people, and Assyria the work of My hands, and Israel Mine inheritance."1248 As the first page of Scripture assigns a common origin to them all in the first man, so, the prophets tell us, at the end of time they shall all be filled with longing for the one God and form with Israel one community on earth, a great brotherhood of man serving the common Father above.1249 Still, the actual world began, not with the unity, but with the wide diversity and dispersion of mankind. The idea of the unity of man came as a corollary to the kindred conception of the unity of God, after a long historical process.

Just as the creation of the world opens with the separation of light from darkness, so the process of the spiritual and moral development of mankind begins, according to the divine plan of salvation, with the separation of Israel from the heathen nations.1250 The sharper the contrast became between the spiritual God of Israel and the crude sensual gods of heathendom, the wider grew the chasm between Judaism and heathenism, between Israel and the nations. As light is opposed to darkness, so Israel's truth stood opposed to the idolatry of the nations, until Christianity and Islam, its daughter-religions, arose between the two extremes. Henceforth Israel waits with still more confidence for the age whose dawning will bring the full knowledge of God to all mankind, leading the world from the night of error and discord to the noon-day brightness of truth and unity, when a universal monotheism will make all humanity one.

2. Nothing was more remote from ancient Israel than the hatred of the stranger or hostility to other nations, so often attributed to it.1251 In the time of the patriarchs and under the monarchy, the Hebrews fostered a spirit of friendly intercourse with their neighbors, which was often confirmed by peaceful alliances.1252 Of course, during war time the spirit of hostility had full sway, particularly as ancient warfare imposed a relentless ban upon both booty and human life among the vanquished. But even then the kings of Israel were called compassionate also toward their enemies when compared with other rulers.1253 Indeed, the code of Israel is distinguished from all

other codes of antiquity by mildness and tender compassion. On the other hand, the God of justice, revealed through Amos, Isaiah, Jeremiah, and Habakkuk, punishes Israel and the nations impartially on account of their moral transgressions.1254 He avenges acts of treachery, even when committed against pagan tyrants. "Shall not the Judge of all the earth do justly?"1255 Such is the recurrent thought that governs Israel, demanding the same standard of judgment for Israelite and stranger.

3. The simple sense of justice inherent in the Jewish people admits so little difference between our own God-consciousness and that of others, that Scripture represents the Philistine King Abimelech as receiving a warning from Abraham's God JHVH.1256 As the Bible holds up Job, the Bedouin Sheik, as the pattern of a blameless servant of God and true lover of mankind,1257 so the Talmud cites the Philistine Dama ben Nethina as an example of filial piety.1258 Altogether, the merits of the heathen receive their full measure of appreciation throughout Jewish literature,1259 even though a narrow dissenting view occurs now and then.1260

4. Still from the very beginning a tendency to relentless harshness existed in one direction, when the pure worship of Israel's one and only God was endangered. The early Book of the Covenant forbade every alliance with idolatrous nations,1261 and the Deuteronomic Code made this more stringent by prohibiting intermarriage and even the toleration of idolaters in the land, lest they seduce the people of God to turn away from Him.1262 The Pharisean leaders, the founders of Rabbinism, went still further by placing an interdict upon eating with the heathen or using food and wine prepared by them, thus aiming at a complete separation from the non-Jewish world.1263

The contrast between Judaism and heathenism was further heightened by the view of the prophets and psalmists, showing that the great nations were the very embodiment of idolatrous iniquity, murderous violence and sexual impurity, a world of arrogance and pride, defying God and doomed to perdition, because they opposed the kingdom of God proclaimed by Israel.1264 Henceforth the term "the nations" (goyim) was taken by the religious as meaning the wicked ones, who would not be able to stand the divine judgment in the future life, but would go down to Sheol, or Gehenna, to fall a prey to everlasting corruption, to the fire that is never quenched.1265

5. Yet such a wholesale condemnation could not long be maintained; it was too strongly contradicted in principle by the prophets and Psalmists, and quite as much by the apocalyptic writers and Haggadists of later times. The book of Jonah testifies that Israel's God sent His prophet to the heathen of Nineveh to exhort them to repentance, that they might obtain forgiveness and salvation like repentant Israel.1266 Heathenism is doomed to perish, not the heathen; they are to acknowledge the heavenly Judge in their very punishments and return to Him. Such is the conclusion of all the exhortations of the prophets predicting punishment to the nations. Moreover, those heathen who escape the doom of the world-powers are to proclaim the mighty deeds of the Lord to the utmost lands. Nay, according to the grand vision of the exilic seer, among the many nations that shall assemble at the end of days to worship the Lord in Zion, select ones will be admitted to the priesthood with the sons of Aaron.1267 The name Hadrak, understood as "he who bringeth back," suggested itself to the rabbis as a title of the Messiah, the converter of the heathen nations.1268 So in both the Talmud and the Sibylline books1269 Noah is represented as a preacher of repentance to the nations before the flood, and accordingly the latter book adjures the Hellenic world to repent of their sinful lives before they would be overwhelmed by the flood of fire at the great judgment day. In the same spirit the Haggadists tell that God sent Balaam, Job, and other pious men as prophets of the heathen to teach them the way of repentance.1270 And the rabbis actually say that, if the heathen nations had not refused the Torah when the Lord offered it to them at Sinai, it would have been the common property of all mankind.1271

6. The leading minds of Judaism felt only pity for the blind obstinacy of the great mass of heathen, who worshiped the creatures instead of the Creator, or the stars of heaven instead of Him who is enthroned above the skies. They regarded heathenism either as evidence of spiritual want and weakness, or as the result of destiny. Indeed, the words of the Deuteronomist sound like an echo of Babylonian fatalism when he asserts that God himself assigned to the nations the worship of the stars as their inheritance.1272 Later the opinion gained ground that the heathen deities were real demons, holding dominion over the nations and leading them astray.1273 The exilic seer attacked idolatry most vigorously as folly and falsehood, and thus the note of derision and irony is struck by Deutero-Isaiah, the Psalms, and in many of the propaganda writings of the Hellenistic age, in their references to heathenism.

On the other hand, it is very significant that the Palestinian sages and their successors condemned heathenism as a moral plague, conducing to depravity, lewdness, and bloodshed. They regarded the powers of the world, especially Edom (Rome), as being under the dominion of the Evil One, and therefore doomed to perish in the flames of

Gehenna. As they rejected the Ten Commandments out of love for bloodshed, lust, and robbery, so, according to the Haggadists, they will be unable to withstand the last judgment and will suffer eternal punishment. Since their one desire was to enjoy the life of this world, their lot in the future will be Gehenna; while the gates of the Garden of Eden will be open for Israel, the people oppressed and sorely tried, yet ever faithful to the covenant of Abraham.1274 Of course, this view implied both comfort and vengeance, but we must not forget that the harsh statements contained in the Talmud owe their origin to bitter distress and cannot be considered Jewish doctrines, as unfriendly critics frequently do.1275

7. As has been shown above, the dominant view of the Synagogue is that eternal salvation belongs to the righteous among the nations as well as those of Israel. In this sense, Psalm IX, 18, is understood to the effect that "all those heathens who have forgotten God will go down to the nether world."1276 One of the sages expresses a still broader view: "When judging the nations, God determines their standard by their best representatives."1277 Many rabbis held the belief that circumcision secured for the Jew a place in "Abraham's bosom" while the uncircumcised are consigned to Gehenna, thus assigning to circumcision a corresponding place to that of baptism in the Christian Church. This belief seems to be based upon a passage in Ezekiel, where the prophet speaks of the arelim, or "uncircumcised," as dwelling in the nether world.1278 But a number of passages in the Talmud, especially in the Tosefta,1279 show that circumcision was not believed to have the power to save a sinner from Gehenna, On the other hand, we have the great teaching of R. Johanan ben Zakkai in opposing his disciple Eliezer ben Hyrcanus, telling that the sacrifices which atoned for the sins of Israel are paralleled by deeds of benevolence, which can atone for the sins of the heathen.1280 Both the Talmud and Philo state that the seventy bullocks which were offered up during the seven days of the Feast of Tabernacles were brought by Israel as sacrifices for the seventy nations of the world.1281

8. Where no cause existed to fear the influence of idolatry, friendly relations with non-Jews were always recommended and cultivated. A non-Jew who devotes his life to the study and practice of the law, said Rabbi Meir, is equal to the high priest; for Scripture says: "The laws which, if a man do, he shall live by them," implying that pure humanity is the one essential required by God.1282 Indeed, Rabbi Meir enjoyed a close friendship with Œnomaos of Gadara,1283 a heathen philosopher spoken of admiringly in Talmudic sources and placed on a par with Balaam as noble representatives of heathendom. Obviously this good opinion was held, because both spoke favorably of Judaism, whose "synagogues and schoolhouses formed the strongest bulwark against the attacks of Jew-haters." Other friendships which were described in popular legends and held up as examples for emulation are those between Jehuda ha Nasi and the Emperor Antoninus (Severus)1284 and that of Samuel of Babylonia with Ablat, a Persian sage.1285

9. The Mosaic and Talmudic law prescribed quite different treatment for those heathen who persisted in idolatrous practices and refused to observe the laws of humanity, called the seven Noahitic laws, as will be explained more fully in the next chapter. No toleration could be granted them within the ancient jurisdiction; "Thou shall show them no mercy" was the phrase of the law for the seven tribes of Canaan, and this was applied to all idolaters.1286 Hence Maimonides lays down the rule in his Code that "wherever and whenever the Mosaic law is in force, the people must be compelled to abjure heathenism and accept the seven laws of Noah in the name of God, or else they are doomed to die."1287

On the other hand, in the very same Code, Maimonides writes in the spirit of Rabbi Meir: "Not only the Jewish tribe is sanctified by the highest degree of human holiness, but every human being, without difference of birth, in whom is the spirit of love and the power of knowledge to devote his life exclusively to the service of God and the dissemination of His knowledge, and who, walking uprightly before Him, has cast off the yoke of the many earthly desires pursued by the rest of men. God is his portion and his eternal inheritance, and God will provide for his needs, as He did for the priest and the Levite of yore."1288

10. To be sure, a statement of this nature presents a different judgment of heathenism from that of the ancient national law. But the historical and comparative study of religions has caused us to entertain altogether different views of the various heathen religions, both those representing primitive stages of childlike imagination and superstition, and those more developed faiths which inculcate genuine ideals of a more or less lofty character. Certainly the laws of Deuteronomy, written when the nation had dwindled down to the little kingdom of Judæa, and those further expounded in the Mishnah enjoining the most rigorous intolerance toward every vestige of paganism, had only a theoretical value for the powerless Jewish nation; while both the Church and the rulers of

Islam were largely guided by them in practical measures. The higher view of Judaism was expressed by the last of the prophets: " 'For from the rising of the sun even unto the going down of the same My name is great among the nations; and in every place offerings are presented unto My name, even pure oblations, for My name is great among the nations,' saith the Lord of hosts."1289 The fact is that heathenism seeks the God whom Israel by its revelation has found. In this spirit both Philo and Josephus took the Scriptural passage, "Thou shalt not curse God," taking the Hebrew Elohim in the plural sense, "the gods"; thus they said a Jew must not offend the religious sense of the heathen by scorn or ridicule, however careful he must be to avoid the imitation of their practices and superstitions.1290

As a matter of fact, the Code of Law aimed to separate Israel and the nations in order to avoid the crude worship of idols, animals and stars practiced by the heathen of antiquity. It was not framed for masters like Socrates, Buddha, and Confucius, with their lofty moral views and their claims upon humanity. The God who revealed himself to Abraham, Job, Enoch, and Balaam, as well as to Moses and Isaiah, spoke to them also, and the wise ones of Israel have ever hearkened to their inspiring lessons. Their words are echoed in Jewish literature together with Solomon's words of wisdom. Plato, Plotinus, and Aristotle received the most friendly hospitality from the rabbinic philosophers and mystic writers of Jewry, and so Buddhist sayings and views penetrated into Jewish ethics and popular teachings. Both the Jew and his literature are cosmopolitan, and Judaism never withholds its appreciation of the merits of the heathen world.1291

11. We must especially emphasize one claim of the Jewish people above other nations which the rabbis call zekuth aboth, "the merit of the fathers," and which we may term "hereditary virtue." The election of Israel, in spite of its own lack of merit, is declared in Deuteronomy and elsewhere to be due to the merit of the fathers, with whom God concluded His covenant in love.1292 The promise is often repeated that God will ever remember His covenant with the fathers and not let the people perish, even though their sins were great; therefore the rabbis assumed that the patriarchs had accumulated a store of merit by their virtues which would redound before God to the benefit of their descendants, supplementing their own weaknesses.1293 This merit or righteousness of the fathers formed a prominent part of the hope and prayer, nay, of the whole theological system of the Jewish people. They regarded the patriarchs and all the great leaders of the past as patterns of loyalty and love for God, so that, according to the Midrash, Israel might say in the words of the Shulamite: "Black am I" considering my own merit, "but comely" when considering the merit of the fathers.1294 Whether this store of merit would ever be exhausted is a matter of controversy among the rabbis. Some referred to God's own words that He will ever remember His covenant with the fathers; others pointed to the verse in Deutero-Isaiah: "For the mountains may depart, and the hills be removed; but My kindness shall not depart from thee, neither shall My covenant of peace be removed," which they interpreted symbolically to mean: when the merit of the patriarchs and matriarchs of Israel is exhausted, God's mercy and compassion for Israel will be there never to depart.1295 Translated into our own mode of thinking, this merit of the fathers claimed for Israel signifies the unique treasure of a spiritual inheritance which belongs to the Jew. This inheritance of thousands of years provides such rare examples and such high inspiration that it incites to the highest virtue, the firmest loyalty, and the greatest love for truth and justice. Judaism, knowing no such thing as original sin, points with pride instead to hereditary virtue, deriving an inexhaustible source of blessing from its historical continuity of four thousand years.

Chapter LVI. The Stranger and the Proselyte

1. Among all the laws of the Mosaic Code, that which has no parallel in any other ancient code is the one enjoining justice, kindness and love toward the stranger. The Book of the Covenant teaches: "And a stranger shalt thou not wrong, neither shalt thou oppress him; for ye were strangers in the land of Egypt,"1296 and "A stranger shalt thou not oppress; for ye know the heart of a stranger, seeing ye were strangers in the land of Egypt." The Deuteronomic writer lays special stress on the fact that Israel's God, "who regardeth not persons nor taketh bribes, doth execute justice for the fatherless and the widow, and loveth the stranger, in giving him food and raiment." He then concludes: "Love ye therefore the stranger; for ye were strangers in the land of Egypt."1297 The Priestly Code goes still further, granting the stranger the same legal protection as the native.1298

2. We would, however, misunderstand the spirit of all antiquity, including ancient Israel, if we consider this as an expression of universal love for mankind and the recognition of every human being as fellow-man and brother. Throughout antiquity and during the semi-civilized Middle Ages, a stranger was an enemy unless he became a

guest. If he sought protection at the family hearth or (in the Orient) under the tent of a Sheik, he thereby entered into a tutelary relation with both the clan or tribe and its deity. After entering into such a relation, temporary or permanent, he became, in the term which the Mosaic law uses in common with the general Semitic custom, a Ger or Toshab, "sojourner" or "settler," entitled to full protection.1299 This relation of dependency on the community is occasionally expressed by the term: "thy stranger that is within thy gates."1300 Such protection implied, in turn, that the Ger or protegé owed an obligation to the tribe or community which shielded him. He stood under the protection of the tribal god, frequently assumed his name, and thus dared not violate the law of the land or of its deity, lest he forfeit his claim to protection.

3. In accordance with this, the oft-repeated Mosaic command for benevolence toward the stranger, which placed him on the same footing with the needy and helpless, imposed certain religious obligations upon him. He was enjoined, like the Israelite, not to violate the sanctity of the Sabbath by labor, nor to provoke God's anger by idolatrous practices, and, according to the Priestly Code, to avoid the eating of blood and the contracting of incestuous marriages as well as the transgression of the laws for Passover and the Day of Atonement. Naturally, in criminal cases such as blasphemy he was subject to the death-penalty just like the native.1301 Still, the Ger was not admitted as a citizen, and in the Mosaic system of law he was always a tolerated or protected alien, unless he underwent went the rite of circumcision and thus joined the Israelitish community.1302

4. With the transformation of the Israelitish State into the Jewish community—in other words, with the change of the people from a political to a religious status,—this relation to the non-Jew underwent a decided change. As the contrast to the heathen became more marked, the Ger assumed a new position. As he pledged himself to abandon all vestiges of idolatry and to conform to certain principles of the Jewish law, he entered into closer relations with the people. Accordingly, he adopted certain parts of the Mosaic code or the entire law, and thus became either a partial or a complete member of the religious community of Israel. In either case he was regarded as a follower of the God of the Covenant. In spite of the exclusive spirit which was dominant in the period following Ezra, two forces favored the extending of the boundaries of Judaism beyond the confines of the nation. On the one hand, the Babylonian Exile had visualized and partially realized the prophecy of Jeremiah: "Unto Thee shall the nations come from the ends of the earth, and shall say: 'Our fathers have inherited naught but lies, vanity and things wherein there is no profit.' "1303 For example, Zechariah announced a time when "many peoples and mighty nations shall come to seek the Lord of Hosts in Jerusalem and to entreat the favor of the Lord," and "Ten men shall take hold, out of all the languages of nations, shall even take hold of the skirt of him that is a Jew, saying, 'We will go with you, for we have heard that God is with you.' "1304 Another prophet said at the time of the overthrow of Babylon: "For the Lord will have compassion on Jacob, and will yet choose Israel, and set them in their own land, and the stranger (Ger, or proselyte) shall join himself with them, and they shall cleave to the house of Jacob."1305 The Psalmists especially refer to the heathen who shall join Israel,1306 so that Ger now becomes the regular term for proselyte.1307

In addition to this inward religious desire we must consider the social and political impulse. The handful of Judæans who had returned from Babylonia were so surrounded by heathen tribes that, while the Samaritans had attracted the less desirable groups, they were glad to welcome the influx of such as promised to become true worshipers of God. The chief problem was how to provide a legal form for these to "come over," proselyte being the Greek term for "him who comes over." By such a form they could enter the community while accepting certain religious obligations. In fact, such obligations had been stated before in the Priestly Code, which admitted into the political community as "sojourners" or "indwellers" those who pledged themselves to abstain from idolatry, blasphemy, incest, the eating of blood or of flesh from living animals, and from all violence against human life and property. They were debarred only from marriage into the religious community, "the congregation of the Lord." Henceforth Ger and Ger Toshab became juridical terms, the social and legal designation of those proselytes who had abjured heathenism and joined the monotheistic ranks of Judaism as "worshipers of God."

5. Thus the first great step in the progress of Judaism from a national system of law to a universal religion was made in Judæa. The next step was to recognize the idea of the revelation of God to the "god-fearing men" of the primeval ages, as described in the Mosaic books, and thus to open the gates of the national religion for heathen who had become "God-fearing men" or "worshipers of the Lord." Thus the Psalms, after enumerating the customary two or three classes, "the house of Israel," "of Aaron," and "of Levi," often add the "God-fearing" proselyte.1308 The Synagogue was especially attractive to the heathen who sought religious truth because of its elevating devotion and its public instruction in the Scripture, translated into Greek, the language of the cultured

world. This sponsored a new system for propagating the Jewish faith. The so-called Propaganda literature of Alexandria laid its chief stress upon the ethical laws of Judaism, not seeking to submit the non-Jew to the observance of the entire Mosaic law or to subject him to the rite of circumcision. The Jewish merchants, coming into contact with non-Jews in their travels on land and sea, endeavored especially to present their religious tenets in terms of a broad, universal religion. As a universal faith forms the background of the entire Wisdom literature, particularly the book of Job, a simple monotheism could be founded upon a divine revelation to mankind in general, corresponding to the one to Noah and his sons after the flood. The laws connected with this covenant, called the Noahitic laws, were general humanitarian precepts. We find these enumerated in the Talmud as six, seven, and occasionally ten. Sometimes we read of thirty such laws to be accepted by the heathen, probably founded upon the nineteenth chapter of Leviticus, at one time central in Jewish ethics.1309 At any rate, the observance of the so-called Noahitic laws was demanded of all worshipers of the one God of Israel.

Strange to say, however, this extensive propaganda of the Alexandrian Jews during the two or three pre-Christian centuries left few traces in the history and literature of Palestinian Judaism. Two reasons seem at hand; the growth of the Paulinian Church, which absorbed the missionary activity of the Synagogue, and the effort of Talmudic Judaism to obliterate the old missionary tradition. To judge from occasional references in Josephus and the New Testament, as well as many inscriptions all over the lands of the Mediterranean,1310 the number of heathen converts to the Synagogue was very large and caused attacks on Judaism in both Rome and Alexandria. Josephus tells us that Jews and proselytes in all lands sent sacrificial gifts to Jerusalem in such abundance as to excite the avarice of the Romans.1311 The Midrash preserves a highly interesting passage which casts light on the earlier significance of the winning of heathen converts, reading as follows: "When it is said in Zephaniah II, 5: 'Woe to the inhabitants of the sea-coast, the nation of Kerethites'; this means that the inhabitants of the various pagan lands would be doomed to undergo Kareth, 'perdition,' save for the one God-fearing proselyte, who is won over to Judaism each year and set up to save the heathen world."1312 In other words, the merit of the one proselyte whose conversion awakens the hope for the winning of the entire heathen world to pure monotheism, is an atoning power for all. Such was the teaching of the Pharisees, whom the gospel of Matthew brands as hypocrites because of their zeal in making proselytes.

6. This kind of proselytism was encouraged only by Alexandrian or Hellenistic Judaism. In Palestine, however, the social system of the nation was quite unfavorable to the simple "God-worshiper," who remained merely a tolerated alien, even though protected, and never really entered the national body. Legally he was termed Ger Toshab, "settler," which meant semi-proselyte. The type of this class was Naaman, the Syrian general who was instructed by Elijah to bathe in the Jordan to cure his leprosy, and then became a worshiper of the God of Israel.1313 Similarly, whatever the real origin of the proselyte's bath may have been, a baptismal bath was prescribed for the proselyte to wash off the stain of idolatry.1314 He was regarded as one who had "fled from his former master" (in heaven) to find refuge with the only God;1315 therefore he was legally entitled to shelter, support, and religious instruction from the authorities.1316 Certain places were assigned where he was to receive protection and provision for his needs, but he was not allowed to settle in Jerusalem, where only full proselytes were received as citizens.1317 According to Philo, special hospices were fitted out for the reception of semi-proselytes.1318

7. In order to enjoy full citizenship and equal rights, the proselyte had to undergo both the baptismal bath and the rite of circumcision, thus accepting all the laws of the Mosaic Code equally with the Israelite born. Beside this, he had to bring a special proselyte's sacrifice as a testimony to his belief in the God of Israel. In distinction from the Ger Toshab, or semi-proselyte, he was then called Ger ha Zedek or Ger Zedek. This name, usually translated as "proselyte of righteousness," obviously possesses a deeper historical meaning. The Psalmist voices a pure ethical monotheism in his query: "O Lord, who shall be a guest (Ger, sojourner) in thy tent?" which he answers: "He that walketh uprightly and worketh righteousness and speaketh truth in his heart."1319 But the legal view of the priestly authorities was that only the man who offers a "sacrifice of righteousness" and pledges himself to observe all the laws binding upon Israel might become a "guest" in the Temple on Zion, an adopted citizen of Jerusalem, the "city of righteousness."1320 In illustration of this view a striking interpretation to a Deuteronomic verse is preserved: "They shall call people unto the mountain, there shall they offer sacrifices of righteousness: that is, the heathen nations with their kings who come to Jerusalem for commerce with the Jewish people shall be so fascinated by its pure monotheistic worship and its simple diet, that they will espouse the Jewish faith and bring sacrifices to the God of Israel as proselytes."1321

The prominence of the full proselyte in the early Synagogue appears in the ancient benediction for the righteous leaders and Hasidim, the Soferim and Synedrion, the ruling authorities of the Jewish nation, where special mention is made of "the Proselytes of (the) Righteousness."1322 These full proselytes pushed aside the half-proselytes, so that, while both are mentioned in the earlier classification, only the latter are considered by the later Haggadah.1323 With the dissolution of the Jewish State no juridical basis remained for the Ger Toshab, the "protected stranger." R. Simeon ben Eleazar expressed this in the statement: "With the cessation of the Jubilee year there was no longer any place for the Ger Toshab in Judæa."1324 We read in Josephus that no proselytes were accepted in his time unless they submitted to the Abrahamitic rite and became full proselytes.1325

However, as Josephus tells us, a strong desire to espouse the Jewish faith existed among the pagan women of neighboring countries, especially of Syria.1326 The same situation existed in Rome according to the rabbinical sources, Josephus, Roman writers, and many tomb inscriptions.1327 Conspicuous among these proselytes was Queen Helen of Adiabene, who won lasting fame by her generous gifts to the Jewish people in time of famine and to the Temple at Jerusalem; her son Menobaz, at the advice of a Jewish teacher, underwent the rite of circumcision in order to rise from a mere God-worshiper to a full proselyte.1328 The Midrash1329 enumerates nine heathen women of the Bible who became God-worshipers: Hagar; Asenath, the wife of Joseph, whose conversion is described in a little known but very instructive Apocryphal book by that name;1330 Zipporah, the wife of Moses; Shifra and Puah, the Egyptian midwives;1331 Pharaoh's daughter, the foster-mother of Moses, whom the rabbis identified with Bithia (Bath Yah, "Daughter of the Lord");1332 Rahab, whom the Midrash represents as the wife of Joshua and ancestress of many prophets;1333 Ruth and Jael. Philo adds Tamar, the daughter-in-law of Judah, as a type of a proselyte.1334

8. Beside the term Ger, with its derivatives, which gave legal standing to the proselyte, the religious genius of Judaism found another term which illustrated far better the idea of conversion to Judaism. The words of Boaz to Ruth: "Be thy reward complete from the Lord thy God of Israel, under whose wings thou art come to take refuge,"1335 were applied by the Pharisean leaders to all who joined the faith as Ruth did. So it became a technical term for converts to Judaism, "to come, or be brought, under the wings of the divine majesty" (Shekinah).1336 Philo frequently expresses the idea that the proselyte who renounces heathenism and places himself under the protection of Israel's God, stands in filial relation to Him exactly like the born Israelite.1337 Therefore Hillel devoted his life to missionary activity, endeavoring "to bring the soul of many a heathen under the wings of the Shekinah." But in this he was merely following the rabbinic ideal of Abraham,1338 and of Jethro, of whom the Midrash says: "After having been won to the monotheistic faith by Moses, he returned to his land to bring his countrymen, the Kenites, under the wings of the Shekinah."1339 The proselyte's bath in living water was to constitute a rebirth of the former heathen, poetically expressed in the Halakic rule: "A convert is like a newborn creature."1340 The Paulinian idea that baptism creates a new Adam in place of the old is but an adaptation of the Pharisaic view. Some ancient teachers therefore declared the proselyte's bath more important than circumcision, since it forms the sole initiatory rite for female proselytes, as it was with the wives of the patriarchs.1341

9. The school of Hillel followed in the footsteps of Hellenistic Judaism in accentuating the ethical element in the law;1342 so naturally it encouraged proselytism as well. The Midrash preserves the following Mishnah, handed down by Simeon ben Gamaliel, but not contained in our Mishnaic Code: "If a Ger desires to espouse the Jewish faith, we extend to him the hand of welcome in order to bring him under the wings of the Shekinah."1343 Both the Midrash and the early Church literature reveal traces of a Jewish treatise on proselytes, containing rules for admission into the two grades, which was written in the spirit of the Hellenistic propaganda, but was afterward rewritten and adopted by the Christian Church. The school of Shammai in its rigorous legalism opposed proselytism in general, and its chief representative, Eliezer ben Hyrcanos, distrusted proselytes altogether.1344 On the other hand, the followers of Hillel were decidedly in favor of converting the heathen and were probably responsible for many Haggadic passages extolling the proselytes. Thus the verse of Deutero-Isaiah: "One shall say, 'I am the Lord's,' and another shall call himself by the name of Jacob; and another shall subscribe with his hand unto the Lord, and surname himself by the name of Israel" is peculiarly applied in the Midrash. The first half, we are told, denotes two classes of Israelites, those who are without blemish, and those who have sinned and repented; the second half includes the two classes of proselytes, those who have become full Jews (Gere ha Zedek) and those who are merely worshippers of God (Yir'e Shamayim). A later Haggadic version characteristically omits the last, recognizing only the full converts (Gere Emeth) as proselytes.1345 The following parable in the spirit of the Essenes illustrates their viewpoint. In commenting upon the verse from the Psalms: "The Lord keepeth the

strangers," the story is told: A king possessed a flock of sheep and goats and noted that a deer joined them, accompanying them to their pasture and returning with them. So he said to the herdsmen: "Take good care of this deer of mine which has left the free and broad desert to go in and out with my flock, and do not let it suffer hunger or thirst." Likewise God takes special delight in the proselytes who leave their own nation, giving up their fellowship with the great multitude in order to worship Him as the One and Only God, together with the little people of Israel.1346 Similarly the Biblical verse concerning wisdom: "I love them that love me, and those that seek me earnestly shall find me"1347 is referred to the proselytes, "who give up their entire past from pure love of God, and place their lives under the sheltering wings of the divine majesty." All these Midrashic passages and many others are but feeble echoes of the conceptions of the Hellenistic propaganda, which were so ably set forth by Philo and the Book of Asenath. Indeed, Judaism must have exerted a powerful influence upon the cultured world of Hellas and Rome in those days, as is evidenced both in the Hellenistic writings of the Jew and in the Greek and Roman writers themselves. Their very defamation of Judaism unwittingly gives testimony to the danger to which Judaism exposed the pagan conception of life, and to the hold it took upon many of the heathen.1348

10. The reaction against this missionary movement took place in Judea. The enforced conversion of the Idumeans to Judaism by John Hyrcanus benefited neither the nation nor the faith of the Jew, and turned the school of Shammai, which belonged to the party of the Zealots, entirely against the whole system of proselytism. On the whole, bitter experience taught the Jews distrust of conversions due to fear, such as those of the Samaritans who feared the lions that killed the inhabitants, or to political and social advantage, like those under David and Solomon, or in the days of Mordecai and Esther, or still later under John Hyrcanus.1349 Instead, all stress was laid upon religious conviction and loyalty to the law. In fact, Josephus mentions many proselytes who in his time fell away from Judaism,1350 who may perhaps have been converts to Christianity. The later Halakah, fixed under the influence of the Hadrianic persecution and quoted in the Talmud as Baraitha, prescribes the following mode of admission for the time after the destruction of the Temple, omitting significantly much that was used in the preceding period:1351 "If a person desires to join Judaism as a proselyte, let him first learn of the sad lot of the Jewish people and their martyrdom, so as to be dissuaded from joining. If, however, he persists in his intention, let him be instructed in a number of laws, both prohibitory and mandatory, easy and hard to observe, and be informed also as to the punishment for their disobedience and the reward for fulfillment. After he has then declared his willingness to accept the belief in God and to adhere to His law, he must submit to the rite of circumcision in the presence of two members of the Pharisean community, take the baptismal bath, and is then fully admitted into the Jewish fold." It is instructive to compare this Halakic rule with the manual for proselytes preserved by the Church under the name of "The Two Ways," but in a revised form.1352 The mode of admission in the Halakah seems modeled superficially after the more elaborate one of the earlier code, where the Shema as the Jewish creed and the Ten Commandments, possibly with the addition of the eighteenth and nineteenth chapters of Leviticus and the twenty-seventh chapter of Deuteronomy, seem to have formed the basis for the instruction and the solemn oath of the proselyte.

11. As long as the Jewish people possessed a flourishing world-wide commerce, unhampered by the power of the Church, they were still joined by numerous proselytes in the various lands and enjoyed general confidence. Indeed, many prominent members of the Roman nobility became zealous adherents of Judaism, such as Aquilas, the translator of the Bible, and Clemens Flavius, the senator of the Imperial house,1353 and many prominent Jewish masters were said to be descendants of illustrious proselytes.1354 All this changed as soon as the Christian Church girded herself with "the sword of Esau." From that time on proselytism became a peril and a source of evil to the Jew. The sages no longer took pride in the prophetic promise that "the stranger will join himself to Israel," nor did they find in the words "and they shall cleave to the house of Jacob" an allusion to the prediction that some of these proselytes would be added "to the priesthood of the Lord," as some earlier teachers had interpreted the passage.1355 R. Helbo of the fourth century, on the contrary, explained that proselytes have become a plague like "leprosy" for the house of Jacob, taking the Hebrew nispehu as an allusion to the word Sappahat, "leprosy."1356 Henceforth all attempts at proselytism were deprecated and discouraged, while uncircumcised proselytes,—probably meaning the persecuting Christians—were relegated to Gehinnom.1357

12. This view was not shared by all contemporaries, however. R. Abbahu of Cæsarea, who had many an interesting and bitter dispute with his Christian fellow-citizens,1358 was broad-minded enough to declare the proselytes to be genuine worshipers of God.1359 Joshua ben Hanania encouraged the proselyte Aquilas and prognosticated great success for proselytes in general as teachers of both the Haggada and Halakah. So other Haggadists urged special

love and compassion for the half-proselyte,1360 and entertained a special hope of the Messianic age that many heathen should turn to God in sincerity of heart.1361 At all events, it was considered a great sin to reproach a convert with his idolatrous past.1362 Indeed, the phrase, "they that fear the Lord," used so often in the Psalms, is referred by the Haggadists to the proselytes; true, the chief stress is laid upon the full proselytes, the Gere Zedek, but a foremost place in the world to come is still reserved for God-worshipers like the Emperor Antoninus.1363 Thus Psalm CXXVIII, which speaks of the "God-fearing man," was applied to the proselyte, to whom were therefore promised temporal bliss and eternal salvation, rejoicing in the Law, in deeds of love and bounteous blessing from Zion.1364 While the Halakah remained antagonistic to proselytism on account of its narrow adherence to the spirit of the Priestly Code, the Haggadah exhibits a broader view. Resonant with the spirit of prophecy, it beckons to all men to come and seek shelter under the wings of the one and only God, in order to disseminate light and love all over the world.

13. Modern Judaism, quickened anew with the spirit of the ancient seers of Israel, cannot remain bound by a later and altogether too rigid Halakah. At the very beginning of the Talmudic period stands Hillel, the liberal sage and master of the law, who, like Abraham of old, extended the hand of fellowship to all who wished to know God and His law; he actually pushed aside the national bounds to make way for a faith of love for God and the fellow man. For this is the significance of his answer to the Roman scoffer who wanted to hear the law expounded while he was standing on one foot: "Whatever is hateful to thee, do not do to thy fellow man! That is the law; all the rest is only commentary."1365 Thus the leaders of progressive Judaism also have stepped out of the dark prison walls of the Talmudic Ghetto and reasserted the humanitarian principles of the founders of the Synagogue, who welcomed the proselytes into Israel and introduced special blessings for them into the liturgy. They declare again, with the author of Psalm LXXXVII, that Zion, the "city of God," should be, not a national center of Israel, but the metropolis of humanity, because Judaism is destined to be a universal religion.1366

Not that Judaism is to follow the proselytizing methods of the Church, which aims to capture souls by wholesale conversion without due regard for the attitude or conviction of the individual. But we can no longer afford to shut the gate to those who wish to enter, impelled by conviction or other motives having a religious bearing, even though they do not conform to the Talmudic law.1367 This attitude guided the leaders of American Reform Judaism at the rabbinical conference under the presidency of Isaac M. Wise, when they considered the admission of proselytes at the present time. In their decision they followed the maxim of the prophet of yore: "Open the gates (of Judaism) that a righteous nation may enter that keepeth the faith."1368

14. It is interesting to observe how Philo of Alexandria contrasts those who join the Jewish faith with those who have become apostates. The former, he says, become at once prudent, temperate, modest, gentle, kind, human, reverential, just, magnanimous, lovers of truth, and superior to the temptations of wealth and pleasure, whereas the latter are intemperate, unchaste, unjust, irreverent, low-minded, quarrelsome, accustomed to falsehood and perjury, and ready to sell their freedom for sensual pleasures of all kinds.1369 In the times of Hellenic culture apostasy made its appearance among the upper classes of the Jews. As the higher-minded among the heathen world were drawn towards the sublime monotheistic faith of the Jew, so the pleasure-seeking and worldly-minded among the Jews were attracted by the allurements of Greek culture to become faithless to the God of Israel, break away from the law, and violate the covenant. Especially under Syrian rule, apostasy became a real danger to the Jewish community, and many measures had to be decided upon to avert it. The desertion of the ancestral faith was looked upon as rebellion and treason against God and Israel.1370 With the rise of the Christian Church to power and influence the number of apostates increased, and with it also the danger to the small community of the Jews in the various lands. In the same measure as the Church made a meritorious practice of the conversion of the Jews, whether by persuasive means or by force and persecution, the authorities of Judaism had to provide the Jew with spiritual weapons of self-defense in the shape of polemical and apologetic writings,1371 and to warn him against too close a contact with the apostate, which was too often fraught with peril for the whole community. As a number of these apostates became actual maligners of the Jews under the Roman empire, a special malediction against sectarians, the so-called Birkat ha-Minim, was inserted in the Eighteen Benedictions under the direction of Gamaliel II.1372 "Those who have emanated from my own midst hurt me most," says the Synagogue, referring to herself the words of the Sulamite in the Song of Songs.1373 While every other offender from among the Jewish people is declared to be "brother," notwithstanding his sin,1374 the apostate was declared to be one from whom no free-will offering was to be accepted,1375 and to whom the gates of repentance and the gates of salvation are forever closed.1376 The feeling of bitterness against him grew in intensity, as throughout Jewish history he often

played the despicable rôle of an accuser of his former coreligionists and betrayer of their faith. The modern Jew also, though he sympathizes with every liberal movement among men and respects every honest opinion, however radically different from his own, cannot but behold in the attitude of him who deserts the small yet heroic band of defenders of his ancient faith and joins the great and powerful majority around him, a disloyalty and weakness of character unworthy of a son of Abraham, the faithful. Since the beginning of the new era in the time of Mendelssohn, apostasy has made great inroads upon the numerical and intellectual strength of Judaism, especially among the upper classes. It is no longer, however, of an aggressive character, but rather a result of the lack of Jewish self-respect and religious sentiment, against which measures tending to a revival of the Jewish spirit are being taken more and more. The Jews are called by the rabbis "the faithful sons of the faithful." The apostate must be made to feel that he is of a lower type, since he has become a deserter from the army of the battlers for the Lord, the Only One God of Israel.

Chapter LVII. Christianity and Mohammedanism, the Daughter-Religions Of Judaism

1. "It shall come to pass on that day that living waters shall go out from Jerusalem; half of them toward the eastern sea and half of them toward the western sea.... And the Lord shall be King over all the earth; in that day shall the Lord be One, and His name one."1377 These prophetic words of Zechariah may be applied to the two great world-religions which emanated from Judaism and won fully half of the human race, as it exists at present, for the God of Abraham. Though they have incorporated many non-Jewish elements in their systems, they have spread the fundamental truths of the Jewish faith and Jewish ethics to every part of the earth. Christianity in the West and Islam in the East have aided in leading mankind ever nearer to the pure monotheistic truth. Consciously or unconsciously, both found their guiding motive in the Messianic hope of the prophets of Israel and based their moral systems on the ethics of the Hebrew Scriptures. The leading spirits of Judaism recognized this, declaring both the Christian and Mohammedan religions to be agencies of Divine Providence, intrusted with the historical mission of coöperating in the building up of the Messianic Kingdom, thus preparing for the ultimate triumph of pure monotheism in the hearts and lives of all men and nations of the world. These views, voiced by Jehuda ha Levi, Maimonides, and Nahmanides,1378 were reiterated by many enlightened rabbis of later times. These point out that both the Christian and Mohammedan nations believe in the same God and His revelation to man, in the unity of the human race, and in the future life; that they have spread the knowledge of God by a sacred literature based upon our Scripture; that they have retained the divine commandments essentially as they are phrased in our Decalogue; and have practically taught men to fulfill the Noahitic laws of humanity.1379 On account of the last fact the medieval Jewish authorities considered Christians to be half-proselytes,1380 while the Mohammedans, being pure monotheists, were always still closer to Judaism.

2. In general, however, rabbinic Judaism was not in a position to judge Christianity impartially, as it never learned to know primitive Christianity as presented in the New Testament. We see no indication in either the oldest Talmudic sources or Josephus that the movement made any more impression in Galilee or Jerusalem than the other Messianic agitations of the time. All that we learn concerning Jesus from the rabbis of the second century and later is that magic arts were practiced by him and his disciples who exorcised by his name; and, still worse, that the sect named after him was suspected of moral aberrations like a few Gnostic sects, known by the collective name of Minim, "sectarians."1381 As a matter of fact, the early Church was chiefly recruited from the Essenes and distinguished itself little from the rest of the Synagogue. Its members, who are called Judæo-Christians, continued to observe the Jewish law and changed their attitude to it only gradually.1382 Matters took a different turn under the influence of Paul, the apostle to the heathen, who emphasized the antinomian spirit; the Judæo-Christian sects were then pushed aside, hostility to Judaism became prominent, and the Church strove more and more for a rapprochement with Rome.1383 Then the rabbis awoke to the serious danger to Judaism from these heretics, Minim, when after the tragic downfall of the Jewish nation they grew to world-power as allies of the Roman Empire. Thus Isaac Nappaha, a Haggadist of the fourth century, declared: "The turning point for the advent of the Messiah, the son of David, will not come until the whole (Roman) Empire has been converted to Christianity (Minuth)."1384 This is supplemented by the Babylonian Rabbah, who plays with a Biblical phrase, saying: "Not until the whole (Roman) world has turned to the Son (of God)."1385 Henceforth Christian Rome was termed Edom, like pagan Rome from the days of Herod the Idumean. In fact, her imperial edicts showed the fratricidal hatred of Esau, with hardly a trace of the professed religion of love. No wonder the Haggadists identified Rome with the

Biblical "Boar of the forest," and waited impatiently for the time when she would have to give up her rule as the fourth world-empire to the people of God, ushering in the Messianic era.1386

3. Meanwhile the relapse of Christianity from monotheism became more steady and more apparent. The One God of the Jew was pushed into the background by the "Son of Man"; and the Virgin-Mother with her divine child became adored like the Queen of Heaven of pagan times, showing similarity especially to Isis, the Egyptian mother-goddess, with Horus, the young son-god, on her lap. The pagan deities of the various lands were transformed into saints of the Church and worshiped by means of images, in order to win the pagan masses for the Christian faith. The original pure and absolute monotheism and the stern conception of holiness were thus turned into their very opposites by the hierarchy and monasticism of the Church. How, then, could the Jewish people recognize the crucified Christ as one of their own? One whose preaching seemed to bring them only damnation and death instead of salvation and life, even while speaking in the name of Israel's God after the manner of the prophets of yore? How could they see in the strange doctrines of the Church any resemblance to their own system of faith, especially as the very doctrines which repelled them were those most emphasized by Christianity? Maimonides considered the adherents of the Roman Church to be idolaters,1387 a view which was modified by the Jewish authorities in the West, as they became better acquainted with Christian doctrines.1388

4. The world-empire of the Church was subsequently divided between Rome, which the Jewish writers called Edom,1389 and Byzantium, which they named Yavan, but neither showed any real advance in religious views and ideals. On the contrary, they both persecuted with fire and sword the little people who were faithful to their ancient monotheism, and suppressed what remained of learning and science. As the Church had the great task of disciplining wild and semi-barbarous races, there was little room left for learning or for high ideals. At this time a rigorous avenger of the persecuted spirit of pure monotheism arose among the sons of Ishmael in the desert of Arabia in the person of Mohammed, a camel-driver of Mecca, a man of mighty passions and void of learning, but imbued with the fire of the ancient prophets of Israel. He felt summoned by Allah, the God of Abraham, to wage war against the idolatry of his nation and restore the pure faith of antiquity. He kindled a flame in the hearts of his countrymen which did not cease, until they had proclaimed the unity of God throughout the Orient, had put to flight the trinitarian dogma of the Church in both Asia and Africa, and extended their domain as far as the Spanish peninsula. He offered the Jews inducements to recognize him as the last, "the seal," of the prophets, by promising to adopt some of their religious practices; but when they refused, he showed himself fanatical and revengeful, a genuine son of the Bedouins, unrelenting in his wrath and ending his career as a cruel, sensuous despot of the true Oriental type. Nevertheless, he created a religion which led to a remarkable advancement of intellectual and spiritual culture, and in which Judaism found a valuable incentive to similar endeavors. Thus Ishmael proved a better heir to Abraham than was Esau, the hostile brother of Jacob.1390

5. The important, yet delicate question, which of the three religions is the best, the Mohammedan, Christian or Jewish, was answered most cleverly by Lessing in his Nathan the Wise, by adapting the parable of the three rings, taken from Boccaccio. His conclusion is that the best religion is the one which induces men best to promote the welfare of their fellow men.1391 But the question itself is much older; it was discussed at the court of the Kaliphs in Bagdad as early as the tenth century, where the adherents of every religion there represented expressed their opinions in all candor. For centuries it was the subject of philosophical and comparative investigations.1392 Among these, the most thorough and profound is the Cuzari by the Jewish philosopher and poet, Jehuda ha Levi. But the parable of the three rings also has been traced through Jewish and Christian collections of tales dating back to the thirteenth century, and seems to be originally the work of a Jewish author. Standing between the two powerful faiths with their appeal to the temporal arm, the Jew had to resort to his wit as almost his only resource for escape. Two Jewish works have preserved earlier forms of the parable. In Ibn Verga's collection of histories of the fifteenth century, it is related that "Don Pedro the Elder, King of Aragon (1196-1213), asked Ephraim Sancho, a Jewish sage, which of the two religions, the Jewish or Christian, was the better one. After three days' deliberation, the sage told the king a story of two sons who had each received a precious stone from their father, a jeweler, when he went on a journey. The sons then went to a stranger, threatening him with violence, unless he would decide which of the jewels was the more valuable. The king, believing the story to be a fact, protested against the action of the two sons, whereupon the Jew explained: Esau and Jacob are the two sons who have each received a jewel from their heavenly Father. Instead of asking me which jewel is the more precious, ask God, the heavenly Jeweler. He knows the difference, and can tell the two apart."1393

An older and probably more original form of the parable was discovered by Steinschneider in a work by Abraham Abulafia of the thirteenth century, running as follows: "A father intended to bequeath a precious jewel to his only son, but was exasperated by his ingratitude, and therefore buried it. His servants, however, knowing of the treasure, took it and claimed to have received it from the father. In the course of time they became so arrogant that the son repented of his conduct, whereupon the father gave him the jewel as his rightful possession." The story ends by stating that Israel is the son and the Moslem and Christian the servants.

Beside this witty solution of a delicate problem, some Mohammedans made attempts very early, doubtless on account of discussions with learned Jews, to prove the justification of the three religions from the Jewish Scriptures themselves. Thus they referred the verse speaking of the revelation of God on Sinai, Mount Seir, and Mount Paran1394 to the religious teachings of Moses, Jesus, and Mohammed. Naturally, the Jewish exegetes and philosophers objected vigorously to such an interpretation.

6. The question which religion is the best, has been most satisfactorily answered for Judaism by R. Joshua ben Hanania, who said that "the righteous of the heathen have also a share in the world to come."1395 The question which religion is true, has been, alas, too long arbitrated by the sword, and will be decided peacefully only when the whole earth will be full of the knowledge of God. Our own age, however, has begun to examine the title to existence of every religion from the broad standpoint of history and ethnology, assigning to each its proper rank. In this large purview even the crude beliefs of savages are shown to be of value, and the various heathen religions are seen to have a historical task of their own. Each of them has to some extent awakened the dormant divine spark in man; one has aided in the growth of the ideal of the beautiful in art, another in the rise of the ideal of the true in philosophy and science; a third in the cultivation of the ideal of the good and in stimulating sympathy and love so as to ennoble men and nations. Thus after a careful examination of the historical documents of the Christian and Mohammedan religions, it is possible to state clearly their great historic mission and their achievements in the whole domain of civilization. The Jewish religion, as the mother who gave birth to both, must deliver the verdict, how far they still contribute to the upbuilding of God's kingdom on earth. In fulfilling their appointed mission, each has given rise to valuable and peculiar institutions, and each has fallen short of the Messianic ideal as visualized by our great prophets of old. Only an impartial judgment can say which one has reached the higher stage of civilization.

7. Christianity's origin from Judaism is proved by its religious documents as well as by its very name, which is derived from the Greek for the title Messiah (Christos), bestowed on the Nazarene by his followers. Still the name Christianity arose in Antioch among non-Jews who scarcely knew its meaning. All the sources of the New Testament, however much they conflict in details, agree that the movement of Christianity began with the appearance of John the Baptist, a popular Essene saint. He rallied the multitude at the shore of the Jordan, preparing them for the approaching end of the Roman world-kingdom with the proclamation, "Wash yourselves clean from your sins!" that is, "Take the baptismal bath of repentance, for the kingdom of heaven is nigh."1396 He conferred the baptismal bath of repentance upon Jesus of Nazareth and the first apostles.1397 Jesus took up this message when John was imprisoned and finally killed by Herod Antipas on account of his preachment against him.1398 The life of Jesus is wrapt in legends which may be reduced to the following historical elements:1399 The young Nazarene was of an altogether different temperament from that of John the Baptist, the stern, Elijah-like preacher in the wilderness;1400 he manifested as preacher and as a healer of the sick a profound love for, and tender sympathy with suffering humanity, a trait especially fostered among the Essenes. This drew him toward that class of people who were shunned as unclean by the uncompromising leaders of the Pharisees, and also by the rigid brotherhoods of the Essenes, whose chief object was to attain the highest degree of holiness by a life of asceticism. His simple countrymen, the fishers and shepherds of Galilee, on hearing his wise and humane teachings and seeing his miraculous cures, considered him a prophet and a conqueror of the hosts of demons, the workers of disease. In contrast to the learned Pharisees, he felt it to be his calling to bring the good tidings of salvation to the poor and outcast, to "seek the lost sheep of the house of Israel" and win them for God. He soon found himself surrounded by a multitude of followers, who, on a Passover pilgrimage to Jerusalem, induced him to announce himself as the expected Messiah. He attracted the people in Jerusalem by his vehement attacks upon the Sadducean hierarchy, which he threatened with the wrath of heaven for its abuses, and also by his denunciations of the self-sufficient Pharisean doctors of the law. Soon the crisis came when he openly declared war against the avarice of the priests, who owned the markets where the sacrificial fowl for the Temple were sold, overthrowing the tables of the money-changers, and declaring the Temple to have become "a den of robbers."1401 The hierarchical council

delivered him to Pontius Pilatus, the Roman prefect, as an aspirant to the royal title of Messiah, which in the eyes of the Romans meant a revolutionary leader. The Roman soldiers crucified him and mocked him, calling him, "Jesus, the king of the Jews."1402

The fate of crucifixion, however, did not end the career of Jesus, as it had that of many other claimants to the Messiahship in those turbulent times. His personality had impressed itself so deeply upon his followers that they could not admit that he had gone from them forever. They awaited his resurrection and return in all the heavenly glory of the "Son of Man," and saw him in their ecstatic visions, attending their love-feasts,1403 or walking about on the lake of Nazareth while they were fishing from their boats, or hovering at the summit of the mountains.1404 This was but the starting point of that remarkable religious movement which grew first among the lower classes in northern Palestine and Syria,1405 then gradually throughout the entire Roman Empire, shaking the whole of heathendom until all its deities gave way to the God of Israel, the divine Father of the crucified Messiah. The Jewish tidings of salvation for the poor and lowly offered by the Nazarene became the death-knell to the proud might of paganism.

8. But the ways of Providence are as inscrutable as they are wonderful. The poor and lowly members of the early Christian Churches, with their leaders, called "apostles" or "messengers" of the community,—elected originally to carry out works of charity and love,1406—would never have been able to conquer the great world, if they had persisted in the Essene traditions. They owed their success to the large Hellenistic groups who joined them at an early period and introduced the Greek language as their medium of expression. Henceforth the propaganda activity of the Alexandrian Jews was adopted by the young Church, which likewise took up all the works of wisdom and ethics written in Greek for the instruction of the proselytes and the young, scarcely known to the Palestinian schools. The Essene baptism for repentance was replaced by baptism for conversion or initiation into the new faith, while the neophyte to be prepared for this rite was for a long time instructed mainly in the doctrines of the Jewish faith.1407 Subsequently collections of wise sayings and moral teachings ascribed to the Nazarene and handed down in the Aramaic vernacular, orally or in writing, were translated into Greek. These together with the manuals for proselytes were the original Church teachings. The Greek language paved the way for the Church to enter the great pagan world, exactly as the Greek translation of the Bible in Alexandria brought the teachings of Judaism to the knowledge of the outside world.

At first the same obstacle confronted the early Church which had prevented the Synagogue from becoming a world conqueror, namely, the rite of circumcision, which was required for full membership. Without this, baptized converts were only half-proselytes and could not be fully assimilated. This classification was still upheld by the Apostolic Convention, which met under the presidency of James the Elder.1408 The time was ripe for a bold and radical innovation, and at this psychological moment arose a man of great zeal and unbridled energy as well as of a creative genius and a mystical imagination,—Saul of Tarsus, known by his Roman name Paulus.1409 He had been sent by the authorities at Jerusalem to pursue the adherents of the new sect, but when he had come as far as Damascus in Syria, he suddenly turned from a persecutor into the most ardent promoter of the nascent Church, impelled by a strange hallucination. Paul was a carpet weaver by trade, born and reared in Tarsus, a seaport of Asia Minor, where he seems to have had a Greek training and to have imbibed Gnostic or semi-pagan ideas beside his Biblical knowledge. In this ecstatic vision on his journey he beheld the figure of Jesus, "the crucified Christ," whose adherents he was pursuing, yet whom he had never seen in the flesh, appearing as a heavenly being whom Paul identified as the heavenly Adam, the archetypal "godlike" man.

Upon this strange vision he constructed a theological system far more pagan than Jewish in type, according to which man was corrupt through the sin of the first couple, and the death of Jesus on the cross was to be the atoning sacrifice offered by God himself, who gave His own son as a ransom for the sins of humanity. This doctrine he used as a lever with which, at one bold stroke, he was to unhinge the Mosaic law and make the infant Church a world-religion. Through baptism in the name of the Christ, the old sin-laden Adam was to be cast off and the new heavenly Adam, in the image of Christ, put on instead. The new covenant of God's atoning love was to replace the old covenant of Sinai, to abolish forever the old covenant based upon the Jewish law, and to set mankind free from all law, "which begets sin and works wrath." In Christ, "who is the end of the law," the sinfulness of the flesh should be overcome and the gates of salvation be opened to a world redeemed from both death and sin.1410 The one essential for salvation was to accept the mystery concerning the birth and death of Christ, after the manner of the heathen mystery-religions, and to employ as sacramental symbols of the mystery the rites of baptism and communion with Christ.

9. This system of Paul, however, demanded a high price of its votaries. Acceptance of the belief meant the surrender of reason and free thinking. This breach in pure monotheism opened the door for the whole heathen mythology and the worship of the heathen deities in a new form. But the saddest result was the dualism of the system; the kingdom of God predicted by the prophets and sages of Israel for all humanity was transferred to the hereafter, and this life with all its healthy aspirations was considered sinful and in the hands of Satan. The cross, originally a sign of life,1411 became from this time and through the Middle Ages a sign of death, casting a shadow of sin upon the Christian world and a shadow of terror upon the Jew.

The greatest harm of all, however, was done to Judaism itself. Paul made a caricature of the Law, which he declared to be a rigid, external system, not elevating life, but only inciting to transgression and engendering curse. He even aroused a feeling of hatred toward the Law, which grew in intensity, until it became a source of untold cruelty for many centuries. This spirit permeated the Gospels more and more in their successive appearance, even finding its way into the Sermon on the Mount. In the simple form given in the Gospel of Luke this was a teaching of love and tenderness; in Matthew, Jesus is represented as offering a new dispensation to replace the revelation of Sinai.1412 Here the Mosaic law is presented as a system of commandments demanding austere adherence to the letter with no regard to the inner life, whereas, on the other hand, the actual teachings of the Nazarene were animated by love and sympathy, emanating from the ethical spirit of the Law. Yet the very words of Jesus in this same sermon disavow every hint of antinomianism: "Verily I say unto you, till heaven and earth pass, one jot or one tittle shall in no wise pass from the Law till all be fulfilled."1413 As a matter of fact, the very teachings of love and inwardness which are embodied in both the Sermon on the Mount and the epistles of Paul were largely adopted from the Pharisean schools and Hasidean works as well as from the Alexandrian Propaganda literature and the Proselyte Manuals preserved by the Church.

In fact, part of this criticism was voiced by the Pharisees, as they attacked the Saducean insistence upon the letter of the Law. The Pharisean spirit of progress applied new methods of interpretation to the Mosaic Code and especially to the Decalogue, deriving from them a higher conception of God and godliness, breaking the fetters of the letter, and working mainly for the holiness of the inner life and the endeavor to spread happiness about.1414 Taking no heed of the actual achievements of the Synagogue, the Paulinian Church rose triumphantly to power after the downfall of the Jewish State and impregnated the Christian world with hostility to Judaism and the Jew, which lasts to this very day, thus turning the gospel of love into a source of religious hatred.

10. Nevertheless it cannot be denied that Paulinian Christianity, while growing into a world-conquering Church, achieved the dissemination of the Sinaitic doctrines as neither Judaism nor the Judæo-Christian sect could ever have done. The missionary zeal of the apostle to the heathen caused a fermentation and dissolution in the entire neo-Jewish world, which will not end until all pagan elements are eliminated. Eventually the whole of civilization will accept, through a purified Christianity, the Fatherhood of God, the only Ruler of the world, and the brotherhood of all men as His children. Then, in place of an unsound overemphasis on the principle of love, justice will be the foundation of society; in place of a pessimistic other-worldliness, the optimistic hope for a kingdom of God on earth will constitute the spiritual and ethical ideal of humanity. We must not be blind to the fact that only her alliance with Rome, her holding in one hand the sword of Esau and in the other the Scriptures of the house of Jacob, made the Church able to train the crude heathen nations for a life of duty and love, for the willing subordination to a higher power, and caused them to banish vice and cruelty from their deep hold on social and domestic life. Only the powerful Church was able to develop the ancient Jewish institutions of charity and redeeming love into magnificent systems of beneficence, which have led civilization forward toward ideals which it will take centuries to realize.

Nor must we overlook the mission of the Church in the realm of art, a mission which Judaism could never have undertaken. The stern conception of a spiritual God who tolerated no visible representation of His being made impossible the development of plastic art among the Jews. The semi-pagan image worship of the Christian Church, the representation of God and the saints in pictorial form, favored ecclesiastical art, until it broadened in the Renaissance into the various arts of modern times. Similarly, the predominance of mysticism over reason, of the emotions over the intellect in the Church, gave rise to its wonderful creation of music, endowing the soul with new powers to soar aloft to undreamed-of heights of emotion, to be carried along as upon Seraph's wings to realms where human language falters and grows faint. Beyond dispute Christianity deserves great credit for having among all religions opened wide the flood gates of the soul by cultivating the emotions through works of art and the development of music, thereby enriching human life in all directions.

11. Islam, the other daughter of Judaism, for its part, fostered the intellectual side of humanity, so contemptuously neglected by the Church. The cultivation of philosophy and science was the historical task assigned to the Mohammedan religion. From the sources of information we have about the life and revelation of Mohammed, we learn that the origin of the belief in Allah, the God of Abraham, goes back to an earlier period when Jewish tribes settled in south Arabia. Among these Jews were traders, goldsmiths, famous warriors, and knights endowed with the gift of song, who disseminated Jewish legends concerning Biblical heroes.1415 Amid hallucinations and mighty emotional outbursts this belief in Allah took root in the fiery soul of Mohammed, who thus received sublime conceptions of the one God and His creation, and of the world's Judge and His future Day of Judgment. The sight of idolatry, cruelty, and vice among his countrymen filled him with boundless indignation, so that he began his career as a God-sent preacher of repentance, modeling his life after the great prophets of yore. With drastic threats of the last Judgment he tried to force the idolaters to return to Allah in true repentance. But few of his hearers believed in his prophetic mission, and the leading men of the city of Mecca, who derived a large income from the heathen sanctuary there, opposed him with fierce and violent measures.

Thus he was forced to flee to the Jewish colony of Yathrib, afterwards called Medina, "the city" of the prophet. He hoped for recognition there, especially after he had made certain concessions, such as turning the face toward Jerusalem in prayer, and keeping the Day of Atonement on the tenth of Tishri. In addition, he emphasized the unity of God in the strongest possible manner, and opposed every encroachment upon it by the belief in additional powers or persons, attacking the Christians on the one hand and his Arabian countrymen on the other, with the sarcastic phrase: "Verily, God has neither a son, nor has He any daughter." In spite of all these facts, the Jews could not be brought to recognize the uneducated son of the desert as a prophet. Therefore his proffered friendship was turned to deadly hatred and passionate revenge. His whole nature underwent a great change; his former enthusiasm and prophetic zeal were replaced by calculation and worldly desire, so that the preacher of repentance of Mecca became at the last a lover of bloodshed, robbery and lust. Instead of Jerusalem he chose Mecca with its heathen traditions as the center of his religious system and aimed chiefly to win the Arabian tribes for his divine revelation.

Thus the entire Arabian nation, full of youthful energy, burning with the impulse of great deeds, bore the faith of the One God to the world by the sword. Like Israel of old, it stepped forth from the desert with a divine revelation contained in a holy book. It conquered first the Christian lands of the East, which under the Trinitarian dogma had lapsed from pure monotheism, then the northern coast of Africa, and it finally unfurled the green flag of Islam over the lands of the West to free them from the fanatical Church. Henceforth war was waged for centuries between the One God of Abraham and the triune God of the Church in both Spain and Palestine. Then might the genius of history ask: "Watchman, what of the night? Watchman, what of the night?" And again the words are heard, as from on high: "The morning cometh, and also the night." The final victory is yet to come.

12. It cannot be denied that the Mohammedan monotheism has a certain harshness and bluntness. It cannot win the heart by the mildness of heaven or the recognition of man's individuality. Islam, as the name denotes, demands blind submission to the will of God, and it has led to a fatalism which paralyzes the sense of freedom, and to a fanaticism which treats every other faith with contempt. Islam has remained a national religion, which has never attained the outlook upon the whole of humanity, so characteristic of the prophets of Israel. Its view of the hereafter is crude and sensuous, while its picture of the Day of Judgment bears no trace of the divine mercy. On the other hand, we must recognize that the reverence of the Koran lent the "Men of the Book," the representatives of culture, greater dignity, and provided a mighty incentive to study and inquiry. Damascus and Bagdad became under the Caliphs centers of learning, of philosophical study and scientific investigation, uniting Nestorian, Jew, and Mohammedan in the great efforts towards general enlightenment. The consequence was that Greek science and philosophy, banished by the Church, were revived by the Mohammedan rulers and again cultivated, so that Judaism also felt their fructifying power. Our modern Christian civilization, so-called by Christian historians, is largely the fruit of the rich intellectual seeds sown by Mohammedans and Jews, after the works of ancient Greeks had been translated into Syrian, Arabic, and Hebrew by a group of Syrian Unitarians (the Nestorians) assisted by Jewish scholars.1416

As for instance the Hohenstaufen Emperor Frederick II, the friend of Jewish and other liberal thinkers, was much more of an investigator than a believer, so did the spirit of investigation derived from Islam and Judaism pervade Christendom, and create the great intellectual movements which finally undermined its creeds and shattered its solidarity into contending sects. Return to the Bible and the God of the Bible, to a Sabbath devoted to instruction in the word of God, and to the recognition of human freedom and the sanctity of the family—this was the watchword of the Reformation. Return to the right of free thought and free conscience, which implies the pure worship of God as He lives in the heart, is now the watchword of those who endeavor to reform the Protestant Church. That is, both are moved by a desire to return to the principles and ideals set forth by Israel's prophets of old.

13. Both the Church, Protestant and Catholic, and the Mosque have a Providential mission which they must fulfill through the ages of history, until all the heathen have learned to worship God as the spirit of holiness in man, instead of seeking Him in the blind forces of nature or of destiny. True, the Mohammedan religion is predisposed to sensuality and still awaits the process of purification to become completely spiritualized; yet indications are not lacking that a process of reform is approaching to bring out the gold of pure monotheism and cast off the dross of Oriental voluptuousness and superstition. We must remember that during the dark night of medieval ignorance and barbarism Islam carried throughout all lands the torch of philosophy and scientific investigation and of the pure faith in God. Even to-day it accomplishes far more for the advancement of life in the east of Asia and the south of Africa than did the Russian Church with her gross superstition and idolatry, or even some branches of Protestantism, with their deification of a human being.

Between Church and Mosque, hated and despised by both, stood and still stands the Synagogue, proudly conscious of its divine mission. It feels itself the banner-bearer of a truth which brooks no compromise, of a justice which insists on the rights of all men. It offers the world a religion of peace and love, admitting no division or discord among mankind, waiting for the day when the God of Sinai shall rear high His throne in the hearts of all men and nations. To-day the Synagogue, rejuvenated by the influences of modern culture, looks with ever greater confidence to a speedy realization of its Messianic hope for all humanity.

Hitherto Judaism was restrained by its two daughter-religions from pursuing its former missionary activity. It was forced to employ all its energy in the single effort for self-preservation. But in the striking contrasts of our age, when the enlightened spirit of humanity struggles so bitterly with the forces of barbarism and brutality, we may well see the approaching dawn of a new era. That glorious day, we feel, will witness the ultimate triumph of justice and truth, and out of the day which is "neither day nor night" will bring forth the time when "the Lord shall be King over all the earth, the Lord shall be One and His name One."1417 This will be an auspicious time for Israel to arise with renewed prophetic vigor as the bearer of a world-uniting faith, as the triumphant Messiah of the nations. Through Israel the monotheistic faiths of the world may find a union so that, in fulfillment of the ancient prophecy,1418 its Sabbath may be a world-Sabbath and its Atonement Day a feast of at-one-ment and reconciliation for all mankind. "He that believeth shall not make haste."1419

Yet just because of this universalistic Messianic hope of Judaism it is still imperative, as it has been throughout the past, that the Jewish people must continue its separateness as "a Kingdom of priests and a holy nation," and for the sake of its world-mission avoid intermarrying with members of other sects, unless they espouse the Jewish faith.1420 Israel's particularism, says Professor Lazarus,1421 has its universalism as motive and aim.

Chapter LVIII. The Synagogue and its Institutions

1. Every religion, as soon as it attains any degree of self-consciousness, aims to present a convincing form of truth to the individual and to win adherents in increasing numbers. Nevertheless the maintenance of a religion does not rest upon its doctrines, which must differ according to the intellectual capacity of the people and the prevailing views of each age. Its stability is based upon those forms and institutions which lend it a peculiar character, and which express, symbolically or otherwise, definite ideas, religious, ethical, and historical. For this reason many exponents of Judaism would entirely discard the idea of a systematic theology, and insist on the observance of the ceremonial laws as the one essential. In following tradition in this manner, they forget that the forms of religious practice have undergone many changes in the course of time. In fact, the vitality of Judaism lies in its unique capacity for development. Its ever youthful mind has constantly created new forms to express the ideas of the time, or has invested old ones with new meanings.1422

2. The greatest and, indeed, the unique creation of Judaism is the Synagogue, which started it on its world-mission and made the Torah the common property of the entire people. Devised in the Exile as a substitute for the Temple, it soon eclipsed it as a religious force and a rallying point for the whole people, appealing through the prayers and Scriptural lessons to the congregation as a whole. The Synagogue was limited to no one locality, like the Temple,

but raised its banner wherever Jews settled throughout the globe. It was thus able to spread the truths of Judaism to the remotest parts of the earth, and to invest the Sabbath and festivals with deeper meaning by utilizing them for the instruction and elevation of the people. What did it matter, if the Temple fell a prey to the flame for a second time, or if the whole sacrificial cult of the priesthood with all its pomp were to cease forever? The soul of Judaism lived indestructibly in the house of prayer and learning. In the Synagogue was fanned the holy flame which kindled the heart with love of God and fellow-men; here were offered sacrifices more pleasing to God than the blood and fat of beasts, sacrifices of love and charity.1423

3. The Synagogue has its peculiar institutions and ceremonies, but no sacraments like those of the Church. Its institutions, such as the festivals, aim to preserve the historic memory of the people; its ceremonies, called "signs" or "testimonies" in the Scripture, are to sanctify the life of the nation, the family, or the individual. Neither possesses a sacramental power, as does baptism or communion in the Church, in giving salvation, or imparting something of the nature of the Deity, or making one a member of the religious community. The Jew is a member of the Jewish community by his birth, which imposes upon him the obligations of the covenant which God made with Israel at Mount Sinai. Judaism is a religious heritage intrusted to a nation of priests, and is not acquired by any rite of consecration or confession of faith. Such a form of consecration and confession is required only in the case of proselytes.1424 It is superfluous to state that Confirmation does not bestow the character of Jew upon the young, any more than the former rite of Bar Mizwah did upon the young Israelite who was called up to the reading from the Law in his thirteenth year as a form of initiation into Jewish life.1425

4. The rite of circumcision is enjoined upon the father in the Mosaic Code as a "sign" of the covenant with Abraham, to be performed on every son on the eighth day after birth.1426 Therefore it is held in high esteem, and the father terms the act in his benediction "admission into the covenant of Abraham";1427 but in spite of this it is not a sacrament and does not determine membership in the Jewish community. The operation was not to be performed by a person of sacred calling such as priest or rabbi, but in ancient Biblical times was performed by women,1428 and in the Talmudic period by the surgeon.1429 In fact, if no Jewish surgeon was at hand, some Talmudic authorities held that a non-Jewish surgeon could perform it. Moreover, where hygienic reasons forced the omission of the rite, the man was still a Jew.1430 The rite itself underwent a change; it was performed with stone knives in Biblical times, just as in Egypt and even to-day in Arabia and Syria.1431 It became a mark of distinction for the people during the Exile.1432 But the act was invested with special religious sanctity during the Syrian persecution, when many Jewish youths "violated the covenant" in order to appear uncircumcised when they appeared in the arena with the heathen.1433 At this time new methods were introduced to guard the "seal" of the covenant,1434 while pious mothers faced martyrdom willingly to preserve the rite of Abraham among their children. Later on the rabbis even declared circumcision to be a safeguard against the pit of Gehenna1435 and made Elijah the guardian of the covenant.1436 The rite may be traced back to primitive life, when the operation was usually performed at the time of puberty and as a preliminary to marriage,1437 but in Jewish life it assumed a religious meaning and became endeared to the people as the consecration of the child as the future head of a family. The idea underlying the institution (as Zunz correctly calls it)1438 is the sanctification of the Jewish household as represented by its male members. The member of a people that is to be holy unto God must bear the seal of the covenant on his flesh; as a potential father of another generation, the sign he bore had a deeper meaning for the future of the people.1439 The rationalistic view that the Mosaic law is merely hygienic, although found as early as Philo, is quite erroneous.1440

5. The same rationalist view1441 is often applied to the dietary laws of the Mosaic Code, but without any justification from the Biblical point of view. These laws prohibit as unclean various species of animals, or such as have fallen dead or as the prey of wild beasts, or certain portions like blood and suet.1442 The Holiness Code states its reason for these prohibitions very emphatically: "I am the Lord your God, who have set you apart from the peoples. Ye shall therefore separate between the clean beast and the unclean, and between the unclean fowl and the clean; and ye shall not make your souls detestable by beast, or by fowl, or by any thing wherewith the ground teemeth, which I have set apart for you to hold unclean. And ye shall be holy unto Me; for I the Lord your God am holy, and have set you apart from the peoples, that ye should be Mine."1443 The Deuteronomic Code gives the same reason for the prohibition of the unclean beasts: "For thou art a holy people unto the Lord thy God." It seems that these prohibitions of "unclean" foods were intended originally for the priesthood and other holy men, as appears in Ezekiel and elsewhere.1444 As a matter of fact, the same class of animals from which the Israelites were commanded to abstain were also forbidden to the priests or saints of India, Persia, Mesopotamia, and partly

of Egypt.1445 The natural conclusion is that the Mosaic law intended these rules as a practical expression of its general principle that Israel was to be "a kingdom of priests and a holy nation."1446 In other words, Israel was to fill the usual place of the priest among the nations of the ancient world, a priest-people observing the priestly laws of sanctification. Whatever the origin of these customs may have been, whether they were tabu laws in connection with totemism or some other primitive view, the Priestly Code itself admits their lack of an Israelitish origin by recognizing that they were known to Noah.1447 They were simply adopted by the law-giver of Israel to make the whole people feel their priestly calling.

In later times the dietary laws, especially abstinence from the flesh of swine, became a mark of distinction which separated the Jew from his heathen surroundings; and they became a symbol of Jewish loyalty in the Syrian persecutions when pious Jews faced martyrdom for them as willingly as for the refusal to adore the Syrian idols.1448 In fact, Pharisaism adopted the principle of separation from the heathen in every matter pertaining to diet, and this spirit of separatism was strengthened by the scorn of the Greeks and Romans and afterward by the antinomian spirit of Christianity. While Hellenistic writers, eager to find a universal meaning in these laws, assigned certain physical or psychic reasons for them,1449 the rabbis of the Talmud insisted that they were given solely for the moral purification of Israel. Thus they were to be observed as tests of Israel's submission to the divine will and not because of personal distaste. In their own words, "We must overcome all desire for the sake of our Father in heaven"; and "Only to those who wrestle with temptation does the kingdom of God come."1450 In the course of time these prohibitions were steadily extended, until they encircled the whole life of the Jew, forming an insurmountable wall which secluded him from his non-Jewish environment. Finally, separation from the world came to be regarded as an end in itself.1451

Now, it cannot be denied that these laws actually disciplined the medieval Jew, so that during centuries of wild dissipation he practiced sobriety and moderation; as Maimonides says,1452 they served as lessons in self-mastery, in curbing carnal desire, and keeping him clean in soul as well as body. The question remains whether they still fulfill their real object of consecrating Israel to its priestly mission among the nations. Certainly the priestly character of these laws is no longer understood, and the great majority of the Jewish people who live among the various nations have long discarded them. Orthodox Judaism, which follows tradition without inquiring into the purpose of the laws, is entirely consistent in maintaining the importance of every item of the traditional Jewish life. Reform Judaism has a different view, as it sees in the humanitarianism of the present a mode of realizing the Messianic hope of Israel. Therefore it cannot afford to encourage the separation of the Jew from his environment in any way except through the maintenance of his religion, and cannot encourage the dietary laws as a means of separatism. Its great problem is to find other methods to inculcate the spirit of holiness in the modern Jew, to render him conscious of his priestly mission, while he lives in unison and fellowship with all his fellow-citizens.1453

6. The tendency to distinguish the Jew from his non-Jewish neighbor in the course of time found expression in the laws for wearing phylacteries (tefillin) on his forehead and arm, a special sign on the doorpost of his house (mezuzzah) and fringes (zizith) on the four corners of his shawl (tallith).1454 As a matter of fact, the original Biblical passages had no such meaning, but acquired it through rabbinical interpretation. The Mosaic law said: "And thou shalt bind them for a sign upon thy hand, and they shall be for frontlets between thine eyes. And thou shalt write them upon the doorposts of thy house and upon thy gates." This refers clearly to the words of God, admonishing the people to keep them in mind, as the preceding verse indicates. Likewise, the precept regarding the fringes upon the four-cornered garment emphasizes rather the blue thread in the fringes, which is to help the people remember the commandments of the Lord, that they may not go astray, "following after the promptings of their own hearts and eyes." As the name phylacteries shows, these were originally talismans or amulets. True, the law as stated in Deuteronomy may be taken symbolically;1455 but the corresponding passage in Exodus, which is traditionally referred to the phylacteries, indicates its origin by its close relation to the Passover sacrifice. The blood of this was, no doubt, put originally on the arm and forehead,1456 which is still done by the Samaritans1457 and has striking parallels in the practice of the Fellahin in Palestine and Syria.1458 Originally the sacrificial blood was supposed to ward off evil spirits from men, beasts and houses or tents, and gradually this pagan custom was transformed into a religious precept to consecrate the body, life, and home of the Jew. In more ancient times the phylacteries were worn by pious men and women all day and not merely during the time of prayer, and seem to have served both as a religious symbol and an amulet. This was certainly the case with the mezuzzah on the doorpost and probably with the blue thread at the corners of the tallith.1459 As both phylacteries and tallith came

into use at the divine service in connection with the recital of the Shema and the chapter on the zizith, the symbols assumed a higher meaning. Arrayed in his vestments, the pious Jew offered daily allegiance to his Maker, feeling that he was thereby protected from evil within and without; similarly, the sacred sign upon the door both consecrated and protected his home. Even with this conception the talismanic character was never quite forgotten. Throughout the Middle Ages these ceremonies were observed as divine commandments; and tradition having seemingly fixed them for all time, the Jew took great pride in the fact that he was "distinguished" in many ways, and especially in his forms of worship.1460 Of course, they distinguished him far more when these ceremonies were practiced for the entire day. Since the modern era has brought the Jew nearer to his neighbors and he has opened the Synagogue to invite the non-Jewish world to hear its teachings, these practices have lost their hold upon the people, becoming meaningless forms. The wearing of these sacred symbols while at prayer seems superfluous as a means of "turning men's hearts away from frivolous and sinful thoughts."1461

7. The most important institution of the Synagogue, and the one most fraught with blessing for all mankind, is the Sabbath. Although its name and existence point to a Babylonian origin,1462 it is still the peculiar creation of the Jewish genius and a chief pillar of the Jewish religion. As a day of rest crowning the daily labor of the week, it testifies to the Creator of the universe who made all that is in accordance with His divine plan of perfection. The underlying idea expressed in Scripture is that the Sabbath is a divine institution. As God himself worked out His design for the world in absolute freedom and rested with delight at its completion, so man is to follow His example, working during six days of the week and then enjoying the rest of the Sabbath with a mind elated by higher thoughts. Moreover, the day of rest observed by Israel should recall his redemption from the slavery and continual labor of Egypt. Thereby every creature made in God's image, the slave and stranger as well as the born Israelite, is given the heavenly boon of freedom and recreation to hallow the labor of the week. There are thus two explanations given for the Sabbath, one in the Decalogue of Exodus, the Holiness Code and Priestly Code,1463 the other in the Decalogue of Deuteronomy and the Book of the Covenant.1464

These two views, in turn, gave rise to different conceptions of the Sabbath laws. Many ancient teachers laid chief stress on the letter of the law which bids men cease from labor. Others, who penetrated farther into the spirit of Deuteronomy and the Covenant Code, emphasized the human need for relaxation and refreshment of soul. The older school, especially the Sadducees, demanded absolute cessation of labor on pain of death for any work, however insignificant, and even for the moving from one place to another. They thought of the Sabbath as a sign of the covenant between God and Israel, and hence held that it should be observed as punctiliously as possible.1465 In the same measure as the Pharisees, with their program of religious democracy and common sense, obtained the upper hand, the Biblical strictness of the Sabbath law was modified. The term labor was defined by analogy with the work done for the tabernacle, and so restricted as to make the death penalty much more limited.1466 Moreover, the Pharisees held that the Sabbath was made for man, not man for the Sabbath;1467 so, although they adhered strictly to the prohibition of labor, the Sabbath received at their hands more of the other element, and became a day for the elevation of the soul, "a day of delight" for the spirit.1468 The whole man, body and soul alike, should enjoy God's gifts more fully on this day; he should cast off care and sanctify the day by praise offered to God at the family table. At a very early period in Israel the Sabbath was distinguished by the words of instruction and comfort offered by the prophets to the people who consulted them on the day of rest.1469 During the Exile and afterward the people assembled on the Sabbath to hear the word of God read from the Torah and the prophets and to join in prayer and song, which soon became a permanent institution.1470 Thus the Sabbath elevated and educated the Jewish people, and afterward transferred its blessings also to the Christian and Mohammedan world. Especially during the Middle Ages the Sabbath became an oasis, a refreshing spring of water for the Jew. All through the week he was a Pariah in the outside world, but the Sabbath brought him bliss in his home and spiritual power in his Synagogue and school. Cheerfully he bore the yoke of statutes and ordinances that grew ever heavier under the rabbinical amplification; for he hailed the Sabbath as the "queen" that raised him from a hated wanderer to a prince in his own domain.1471

Modern life has worked great changes in the Jewish observance of the Sabbath. Caught up in the whirl of commercial and industrial competition, the Jew, like Ixion in the fable, is bound to his wheel of business, and enjoys neither rest for his body nor elevation for his soul on God's holy day. True, the Synagogue still preserves the sanctity of the ancient Sabbath, however small may be the attendance at the divine service, and in many pious homes the family still rallies around the festive table, lighted by the Sabbath lamp and decorated by the symbolic cup of wine. But for the majority of Western Jews the Sabbath has lost its pristine sanctity and splendor, to the great detriment of Jewish religious life. Therefore many now ask: "Is it sufficient to have a vicarious observance of the historical Sabbath, the 'sign between God and Israel,' by an hour or two in the Synagogue, but without rest for the entire day? Or shall the civic day of rest, though Christian in origin and character, take the place of the Jewish Sabbath with its sacred traditions, so that possibly at last it may become the Sabbath day predicted by the seer upon which 'all flesh shall come to worship before the Lord'?"1472 In the halcyon days of the reform movement in Germany this view was often expressed when the radical reformers celebrated the civic day of rest as the Jewish Sabbath, not in the spirit of dissension, but for the sake of giving Judaism a larger scope and a wider outlook. In America, too, the idea of transferring the Sabbath to Sunday was broached by some leading Reform rabbis and met with hearty support on the part of their congregations. Since then a more conservative view has taken hold of most of the liberal elements of Jewry also in America. While divine service on Sundays has been introduced with decided success in many cities and eminent preachers bring the message of Judaism home to thousands that would otherwise remain strangers to the house of God and to the influence of religion, the conviction has become well established that the continuity with our great past must be upheld, and the general feeling is that the historical Sabbath should under no condition be entirely given up. It is inseparably connected with the election of Israel as a priest-people, while the Christian "Lord's Day" represents views and tendencies opposed to those of Judaism, whether considered in its original meaning or in that given it by the Church.1473 The Jew may properly use the civic day of rest in common with his Christian fellow-citizen for religious devotion and instruction for young and old; it will supplement his neglected Sabbath service, until conditions have changed. Perhaps the Jew in Mohammedan countries may even at some time observe Friday as is done by the Mosque, and accordingly consecrate this day in common with his fellow-citizens. Still, between the Sabbath observed by the Church and the one of the Mosque stands the Jewish Sabbath in solemn grandeur and patriarchal dignity, waiting with Israel, its keeper and ally, for the day when all humanity will worship the one holy God of Abraham, and when our ancient Sabbath may truly become the Sabbath of the world.

8. In all lands time was originally regulated by the movements of the moon, which are within the observation of all. The alternation of its increase and decrease divided the month into two parts, which were then subdivided into four. Therefore the original month among both the Babylonians and the Hebrews consisted of four weeks of seven days each, the last day of each week being the Sabbath, the "day of standstill," and two days of the new moon.1474 Both the new moon and full moon were special days of celebration,1475 and later two other Sabbath days were added between them to correspond to the four phases of the moon. Still later the week was detached altogether from the moon and made a fixed period of seven days, solemnly ended by the Sabbath. Thus Judaism raised the Sabbath above all dependence on nature and into the realm of holiness. The Jewish Sabbath became the witness to God, the Creator ruling above nature in absolute freedom.1476

Still the ancient festival of the new moon was preserved as an observance in the Temple, and it afterward survived only in the liturgy of the Synagogue. While ancient Israel had observed the New Moon as a day of rest even more sacred than the Sabbath,1477 the Priestly Code placed it among the festivals only as a day of sacrifice, but as neither a day of rest nor of popular celebration.1478 Beside the recital of the Hallel Psalms and the Mussaf ("additional") prayer in the Synagogue no religious significance was attached to it in the daily life of the people. Still the fact that the Jewish calendar was regulated by the moon, while that of other nations depended on the solar year, led the rabbis to compare the unique history of Israel to the course of the moon. As the moon changes continually, waxing and waning but ever renewing itself after each decline, so Israel renews itself after every fall; while the proud nations of the world, which count their year by the course of the sun, rise and set, as it does, with no hope of renewal.1479 At the same time, assurance was found in the prophetic words that "the light of the moon shall be as the light of the sun and the light of the sun shall be sevenfold as the light of the seven days" and "thy (Israel's) sun shall no more go down, neither shall thy moon withdraw itself, for the Lord shall be thine everlasting light."1480

9. The various Jewish festivals, like the Sabbath, were detached from their original relation to nature and turned into historical memorials, eloquent testimonies to the great works of God and of Israel's power of rejuvenation. The Passover was originally the spring festival of the shepherds when they hallowed the thresholds,1481 but was later identified with the agricultural Feast of Unleavened Bread in Palestine, and at an early period was further transformed into a festival of redemption. The former rites of consecration of tent and herd were taken as symbols of the wondrous deliverance of the Hebrews from the Egyptian yoke. The sacrifice of the "passing over the threshold," with the sprinkling of the blood on the doorposts and lintels of each house, observed each spring

exactly as is still done among the semi-pagan inhabitants of Syria and Arabia, was reinterpreted. According to the Mosaic code it indicated the wondrous passing of the angel of death over the thresholds of the Israelites in Egypt, while he entered the homes of the Egyptians to slay the first-born and avenge the wrongs of Israel.1482 Likewise the cakes of bread without leaven (the Mazzoth) baked for the festival were taken as reminders of the hasty exodus of the fathers from the land of oppression. Thus the spring festival became a memorial of the springtime of liberty for the nation and at the same time a consecration of the Jewish home to the covenant God of Israel. God was to enter the Jewish home as He did in Egypt, as the Redeemer and Protector of Israel. Young and old listened with perennial interest to the story of the deliverance, offering praise for the wonders of the past and voicing their confidence in the future redemption from oppression and woe.

However burdensome the Passover minutiæ, especially in regard to the prohibition of leaven, became to the Jewish household, the predominant feature was always an exuberance of joy. In the darkest days of medievalism the synagogue and home resounded with song and thanksgiving, and the young imbibed the joy and comfort of their elders through the beautiful symbols of the feast and the richly adorned tale of the deliverance (the Haggadah). The Passover feast with its "night of divine watching" endowed the Jew ever anew with endurance during the dark night of medieval tyranny, and with faith in "the Keeper of Israel who slumbereth not nor sleepeth."1483 Moreover, as the springtide of nature fills each creature with joy and hope, so Israel's feast of redemption promises the great day of liberty to those who still chafe under the yoke of oppression. The modern Jew is beginning to see in the reawakening of his religious and social life in western lands the token of the future liberation of all mankind.1484 The Passover feast brings him the clear and hopeful message of freedom for humanity from all bondage of body and of spirit.

10. The Feast of Weeks or Festival of the First Fruits in Biblical times was merely a farmer's holiday at the end of the seven weeks of harvest. At the beginning of the harvest parched grains of barley were offered, while at its end two loaves of the new wheat flour were brought as a thank-offering for the new crop.1485 Rabbinical Judaism, however, transformed it into a historical feast by making it the memorial day of the giving of the Ten Words on Mount Sinai. It was thus given a universal significance, as the Midrash has it, "turning the Feast of the First Fruits into a festival commemorating the ripening of the first fruits of the spiritual harvest for the people of the covenant."1486 Henceforth the Ten Words were to be solemnly read to the congregation on that day, and the pledge of loyalty made by the fathers thereby renewed each year by Israel's faithful sons. The leaders of Reform Judaism surrounded the day with new charm by the introduction of the confirmation ceremony,1487 thus rendering it a feast of consecration of the Jewish youth to the ancient covenant, of yearly renewal of loyalty by the rising generation to the ancestral faith.

11. The main festival in Biblical times was the Feast of Sukkoth, or Tabernacles, the great harvest festival of autumn, when the people flocked to the central sanctuary in solemn procession, carrying palms and other plants. Hence this was called the Hag or Pilgrimage Feast.1488 In the post-exilic Priestly Code this festival also was made historical, and the name Feast of Sukkoth (which denoted originally Feast of Pilgrimage Tents) was connected with the exodus from Egypt, when the town of Sukkoth (possibly named from the tents of their encampment) was made the rallying point of the fugitive Hebrews at their departure from Egypt. The commentators no longer understood this connection, and traced the name to the tents erected by the people in their wanderings through the wilderness.1489 It seems that from very ancient times popular rites were performed at this feast, which took a specially solemn form in the holding of a procession from the pool of Shiloah at the foot of the Temple mount to the altar in the Temple, to offer there a libation of water, which was a sort of symbolic prayer for rain for the opening year. Obviously, it is this feast which is referred to in the last chapter of Zechariah, while this outburst of popular joy found a deep response among the pious leaders of the people and is echoed in the liturgy of the medieval Synagogue.1490 The Halakic rules concerning the tabernacle and the four plans for it tended to obscure the real significance of the festival;1491 yet in the synagogue and the home it retained its original character as a "season of gladness." The joyous gratitude to God for His protection of Israel during the forty years of wanderings through the wilderness expanded into thanksgiving for His guidance throughout the forty centuries of Israel's pilgrimage through all lands and ages. This joy culminated on the last day in the Feast of Rejoicing in the Law, when the annual cycle of readings from the Pentateuch was completed in the Synagogue amid overflowing pride in the possession of God's law by Israel.1492 The rabbis gave Sukkoth a universal significance by taking the seventy bullocks prescribed for the seven days as offerings for the salvation of the seventy nations of the world, while the one bullock offered on the last day suggested the uniqueness of Israel as God's peculiar people.1493

12. The highest point of religious devotion in the synagogue is reached on the New Year's day and the Day of Atonement preceding the Feast of Sukkoth. These are first mentioned in the Priestly Code and were undoubtedly instituted after the time of Ezra;1494 they were then brought into closer connection by the Pharisees and permeated with lofty ideas which struck the deepest chords of the human heart and voiced the sublimest truths of religion for all time to come.

The New Year's Day on the first of Tishri appears in the Mosaic Code simply as the memorial "Day of the Blowing of the Trumpet," because of the increased number of trumpet blasts to usher in the seventh or Sabbatical month with its great pilgrim feast. Under Babylonian influence, however, it received a new name and meaning. The Babylonian New Year was looked upon as a heavenly day of destiny when the fates of all beings on earth and in heaven were foretold for the whole year from the tables of destiny. The leaders of Jewish thought also adopted the first day of the holy month of Tishri as a day of divine judgment, when God allots to each man his destiny for the year according to his record of good and evil deeds in the book of life.1495 Accordingly, the stirring notes of the Shofar were to strike the hearts of the people with fear, that they might repent of their sins and improve their ways during the new year. As fixed by tradition, the liturgy contained three blasts of the Shofar to proclaim three great ideas of Judaism:1496 the recognition of God as King of the world; as Judge, remembering the actions and thoughts of men and nations for their reward and punishment; and as the Ruler of history, who revealed Himself to Israel in the trumpet-blasts of Sinai and will gather all men and nations by the trumpet-blasts of the Judgment Day at the end of time.

The main purpose of the New Year was to render it a day of renewal of the heart, so that man might put himself in harmony with the great Judge on high and receive life anew from His hand, while he fills his spirit with new and better resolves for the future. Judaism does not place the day of judgment after death, when repentance is beyond reach and the sinner can only await damnation, as is done by Christianity after the apocalyptic views adopted from the Parsees. The Jewish judgment day occurs at the beginning of every year, a day of self-examination and improvement of men before God. On this day—in the orthodox Synagogue on the second day of the New Year—the chapter is read from the Torah describing Abraham's great act of faith on Mount Moriah, the heroic pattern of Jewish martyrdom, and stirring prayers, litanies, and songs prepare the worshiper for the "great day" of the year, the Day of Atonement, which is to come on the tenth day of Tishri, the last of the ten Days of Repentance.

13. The Day of Atonement figures in the Mosaic Code as the day when the high priest in the Temple performed the important function of expiation for the sanctuary, the priesthood, and the people. The mass of the people were to observe the day from evening to evening as a Sabbath and a fast day to obtain pardon for their sins before God.1497 A very primitive rite which survived for this day was the selection of two goats, one of which was to be sent to Azazel, the demon of the wilderness, to bear away the sins of the people, while the other was to be offered to the Lord as a sacrifice. We learn from the Mishnaic sources that the sending forth of the scapegoat was accompanied by strange practices betraying intense popular interest, and its arrival at the bottom of the wild ravine, where Azazel was supposed to dwell, was announced by signals from station to station, until they reached the Temple mount, and the news of it was then received with wild bursts of joy by the people. The young men and maidens assembled on the heights of Jerusalem, like the men at the pilgrimage feast at Shiloh, and held, as it were, nuptial dances.1498 The day was one of communion with God for the high-priest alone; he confessed his sins and those of the people and implored forgiveness, and it was actually believed that he beheld the Majesty of God on that day when he entered the Holy of Holies with the incense shrouding his face.1499

In contrast to this priestly monopoly of service with its external and archaic forms of expiation, the founders of the Synagogue invested the Day of Atonement with a higher meaning in accord with the spirit of the prophets of old, the doctrine of God's mercy and paternal love. Atonement could no longer be obtained by the priest with the sacrificial blood, the incense, or the scapegoat; it must come through the repentance of the sinner, leading him back from the path of error to the way of God. As the high-priest in the Temple, so now every son of Israel was to spend the day in the house of prayer, confessing his sins before God with a contrite heart, awaiting with awe the realization of God's promise to Moses: "I have pardoned according to thy word."1500 Indeed, a forward step in the history of religion is represented in the interpretation of the verse: "For on this day he—that is, the high-priest—shall make atonement for you to cleanse you," which was now understood to refer to God: "He shall make atonement for you through this day."1501 Therefore R. Akiba could exclaim proudly, as he thought of the Paulinian doctrine of vicarious atonement: "Happy are ye Israelites! Before whom do you cleanse yourselves from sin, and who cleanses you? Your Father in heaven!"1502 No mediator was needed between man and his heavenly Father from the moment that each individual learned to approach God in true humility on the Day of Atonement, imploring His pardon for sin and promising to amend his ways. With profound intuition the rabbis attributed God's pardon to the petition of Moses, saying that He revealed Himself in His attribute of mercy on the very tenth of Tishri, foreshadowing for all time the divine forgiveness of sin on the Day of Atonement.1503

As the Mishnah expressly states, even the Day of Atonement cannot bring forgiveness so long as injustice cleaves to one's hand or evil speech to the lips and no attempt is made to repair the injury and appease one's fellow-man.1504 Where justice is lacking, divine love cannot exert its saving power. God's mercy and long-suffering cannot remove sin, unless the root of evil is removed from the heart and every wrong redressed in sincere repentance. The spirit of God is invoked on these great days at the year's commencement only that the penitent soul may thus receive strength to improve its ways, that good conduct in the future may atone for the errors of the past. Surely no religion in the world can equal the sublime teachings of the New Year's day and the Day of Atonement, first filling the heart of mortal man with awe before the Judge of the world and then cheering it with the assurance of God's paternal love being ever ready to extend mercy to His repentant children. While the other festivals of the year are specifically Jewish in historic associations and meaning, these two days on the threshold of each new year are universally human, and the chief prayers for this day are of a universal character, appealing to every human heart. Indeed, it is characteristic that both the concluding service for the day, the Neilah, and the Scriptural reading of the Minhah Service, selected from the book of Jonah, tell that God's all-forgiving mercy extends to the non-Jewish world as well as to the Jew.1505

14. Altogether, the Synagogue gave to the annual cycle of the Jewish life a beautiful rhythm in its alternation of joy and sorrow, lending a higher solemnity to general experience. All the festivals mentioned above were preceded by a series of Sabbaths to prepare the congregation for the coming of the sad or the joyful season with its historical reminiscences. So the memorial day of the destruction of Jerusalem, the ninth of Ab, had three weeks previously to herald in a day commemorating the siege of Jerusalem, the seventeenth of Tammuz; but it had also seven Sabbath days to follow, which afforded words of consolation and hope of a more glorious future for the mourning nation.1506 Of course, the brighter days of the present era have greatly modified the lugubrious character of these eventful days of the past, even in those circles where the hope for the restoration of the Jewish nation and Temple is still expressed in prayer. At the same time, the commemoration of the destruction of State and Temple, the great turning-point in the history of the Jew, ought to be given a prominent place in the Reform Synagogue as well, though celebrated in the spirit of progressive Judaism.

The feast of Hanukkah with its lights and song, jubilant with the Maccabean victory in the battle for Israel's faith, still resounds in the Jewish home and the house of God with the prophetic watchword: "Not by might, nor by power, but by My spirit, saith the Lord of Hosts."1507

The mirthful feast of Purim, with its half-serious, half-jovial use of the scroll of Esther and its popular rejoicing, assumed in the course of time a more earnest character, because the plot of Haman and the rescue of the Jews became typical in Jewish history. Therefore the story of Amalek, the arch-foe of Israel, is read in the Synagogue on the preceding Sabbath as a reminder of the constant battle which Israel must wage for its supreme religious task.1508

15. Through the entire history of Judaism since the Exile, the Synagogue brought its religious truth home to the people each Sabbath and holy day through the reading and expounding of the Torah and the prophets. These words of consolation and admonition struck a deep chord in the hearts of the people, so that learning was the coveted prize of all and ignorance of the law became a mark of inferiority. Beside these stated occasions, all times of joy or sadness such as weddings and funerals were given some attention in the Synagogue, as linking the individual to the communal life, and linking his personal joy and sorrow with the past sadness and future glory of Jerusalem, as if they but mirrored the greater events of the people. Thus the whole life was to be placed in the service of the social body, and could not be torn asunder or divided into things holy and things profane. Religion must send forth its rays like the sun, illumining and warming all of man's deeds and thoughts.

16. The weakness of the Synagogue was its Orientalism. Amid all the changes of time and environment, it remained separated from the surrounding world to such an extent that it could no longer exert an influence to win outsiders for its great truths. Until recently the Hebrew language was retained for the entire liturgy, although it had become unintelligible to the majority of the Jews in western lands, and even though the rabbis had declared in Talmudic times that the verse: "Hear O Israel, the Lord is our God, the Lord is One" indicates that the words should be spoken

in a language which can be heard and understood by the people.1509 The Torah likewise was, and in the ancient Synagogue is still read exclusively in the Hebrew original, in spite of the fact that the original reading under Ezra was accompanied by a translation and interpretation in the Aramaic vernacular. Thus only could the Torah become "the heritage of the whole congregation of Jacob," which fact gave rise to both the Aramaic and Greek translations of the Bible which carried the truths of Judaism to the wider circle of the world. These plain facts were ignored through the centuries to the detriment of the Jewish faith, and this neglect, in turn, engendered a false conception of Judaism, making it seem ever more exclusive and narrow. Instead of becoming "our wisdom and understanding before all the nations,"1510 knowledge of the Torah dwindled to a possession of the few, while the ceremonial laws, observed by the many, were performed without any understanding of their origin or purpose. But in the last century under the banner of Reform Judaism many of these points were altered. The vernacular was introduced into the Synagogue, so that the modern Jew might pray in the same tongue in which he feels and thinks, thus turning the prayers from mechanical recitations into true offerings of the soul, and bringing the Scriptural readings nearer to the consciousness of the congregation. Likewise the reintroduction of the sermon in the vernacular as part of the divine service for Sabbath and holy days became the vehicle to awaken religious sentiments in the hearts of the people, and thereby to revive the spirit of the ancient prophets and Haggadists.1511

17. This Orientalism is especially marked in the attitude of the older Synagogue to women. True enough, woman was honored as the mistress of the home. She kindled the Sabbath light, provided for the joy and comfort of domestic life, especially on the holy days, observed strictly the laws of diet and purity, and awakened the spirit of piety in her children. Still she was excluded from the regular divine service in the Synagogue. She did not count as a member of the religious community, which consisted exclusively of men. She had to sit in the gallery behind a trellis during the service and could not even join the men in saying grace at table. A few rare women were privileged to study Hebrew, such as the daughter of Rashi, but as a rule woman's education was neglected as if "she had no claim on any other wisdom than the distaff."1512 More and more Judaism lost sight of its noble types of women in antiquity; it forgot the Biblical heroines such as Miriam and Deborah, Hannah and Hulda, and Talmudic ones such as Beruria the wife of Rabbi Meir. Such women as these might have repeated the words: "Hath the Lord indeed spoken only through Moses? Hath He not also spoken through us?"1513 Aside from the sphere of religion, in which woman always manifests a splendid wealth of sentiment, she was held in subjection by Oriental laws in both marital and social relations,1514 and her natural vocation as religious teacher of the children in the home failed to receive full recognition also.

The first attempt to liberate the Jewish woman from the yoke of Orientalism was made in the eleventh century by Rabbi Gershon ben Jehudah of Mayence, at that time the leading rabbi of Germany. Under the influence of Occidental ideas he secured equal rights for men and women in marriage.1515 But only in our own time were full rights accorded her in the Synagogue, owing to the reform movement in Germany and Austria. As a matter of fact, the confirmation of children of both sexes, which was gradually introduced in many conservative congregations also, was the virtual recognition of woman as the equal of man in Synagogue and school.1516 Finally, upon the initiative of Isaac M. Wise, then Rabbi in Albany, N. Y., family pews were introduced in the American Synagogue and woman was seated beside her husband, son, father, and brother as their equal. With her greater emotional powers she is able to lend a new solemnity and dignity to the religious and educational efforts of the Synagogue, wherever she is admitted as a full participant in the service.

18. Another shortcoming of the Synagogue and of Rabbinical Judaism in general was its formalism. Too much stress was laid upon the perfunctory "discharge of duty," the outward performance of the letter of the law, and not enough upon the spiritual basis of the Jewish religion. The form obscured the spirit, even though it never quite succeeded in throttling it. This formalism of the ignorant, but observant multitude was censured as early as the eleventh century by Bahya ben Joseph ibn Pakudah in his "Duties of the Heart," a philosophical work in which he emphatically urges the need of inwardness for the Jewish faith.1517 Later the mystics of Germany and Palestine, while strong supporters of the law, opposed the one-sidedness of legalism and intellectualism, and endeavored to instill elements of deeper devotion into the Jewish soul through the introduction of their secret lore, Cabbalah, or "esoteric tradition."1518 Their offering, however, was anything but beneficial to the soul of Judaism. A mysticism which attempts to fathom the unfathomable depth of the divine accords but ill with the teaching of Judaism, which says: "The secret things belong unto the Lord our God, but the things that are revealed belong unto us and to our children forever, that we may do all the words of this law."1519 The Cabbalah was but the reaction to the excessive rationalism of the Spanish-Arabic period. As the ultimate source of religion is not reason but the heart, so the

cultivation of the intellect at the expense of the emotions can be only harmful to the faith. The legalism and casuistry of the Talmud and the Codes appealed too much to the intellect, disregarding the deeper emotional sources of religion and morality; on the other hand, the mysticism of the Cabbalists overemphasized the emotional element, and eliminated much of the rational basis of Judaism. True religion grasps the whole of man and shows God's world as a harmonious whole, reflecting in both mind and heart the greatness and majesty of God on high. In order to open the flood-gates of the soul and render religion again the deepest and strongest force of life, the Synagogue must revitalize its time-honored institutions and ceremonies. Thus only will they become real powers of the Jewish spirit, testimonies to the living God, witnessing to the truth of the Biblical words: "For this commandment which I command thee this day, it is not too hard for thee, neither is it too far off. It is not in heaven, that thou shouldest say, 'Who shall go up for us to heaven and bring it unto us, and make us to hear it, that we may do it?' Neither is it beyond the sea, that thou shouldest say, 'Who shall go over the sea for us and bring it unto us, and make us to hear it, that we may do it?' But the word is very nigh unto thee, in thy mouth and in thy heart, that thou mayest do it."1520

19. The Synagogue need no longer restrict itself to the ancient forms of worship in its appeal to the Jewish soul. It must point to the loftiest ideals for the future of all humanity, if it is to be true to its prophetic spirit of yore. "My house shall be called a house of prayer for all peoples," exclaimed the seer of the exile.1521 "Hear O Israel, the Lord our God, the Lord is one" must be echoed in all lands and languages, by all God-seeking minds and hearts, to realize the prophetic vision: "And the Lord shall be King over all the earth; in that day the Lord shall be One, and His name One."1522 Just as there is but one truth, one justice, and one love, however differently the various races and classes of men may conceive them, so Israel shall uphold God, the only One, as the bond of unity for all men, despite their diversity of ideas and cultures, and His truth will be the beacon-light for all humanity. As the Psalms, prophets, and the opening chapters of the Pentateuch speak a language appealing to the common sense of mankind, so the divine worship of the Synagogue must again strike the deeper chords of humanity, in its weal and woe, its hope and fear, its aspirations and ideals. Therefore it is not enough that the institutions and ceremonies of the Synagogue are testimonies to the great past of Israel. They must also become eloquent heralds and monitors of the glorious future, when all mankind will have learned the lessons of the Jewish festivals, the ideals of liberty, law, and peace, the thoughts of the divine judgment and the divine mercy. They must help also to bring about the time when the ideal of social justice, which the Mosaic Code holds forth for the Israelitish nation, will have become the motive-power and incentive to the reëstablishment of human society upon new foundations.

Jehudah ha Levi, the lofty poet of medieval Jewry,1523 speaks of Israel as the "heart of humanity," because it has supplied the spiritual and moral life-blood of the civilized world. Israel provides continually the rejuvenating influence of society. Israel's history is the history of the world in miniature. As the Midrash says,1524 the confession of God's unity imposes upon us the obligation to lead all God's children to love Him with heart and soul and might, thus working toward the time when "the earth shall be filled with the knowledge of the glory of the Lord as the waters cover the sea."1525 All the social, political, and intellectual movements of our restless, heaven-storming age, notwithstanding temporary lapses into barbarism and hatred, point unerringly to the final goal, the unity of all human and cosmic life under the supreme leadership of God on high. In the midst of all these movements of the day stands the Jew, God's witness from of old, yet vigorous and youthful still, surveying the experiences of the past and voicing the hope of the future, exclaiming in the words of his traditional prayers: "Happy are we; how goodly is our portion! how pleasant our lot! how beautiful our inheritance!"1526 Our faith is the faith of the coming humanity; our hope of Zion is the kingdom of God, which will include all the ideals of mankind.

Chapter LIX. The Ethics of Judaism and the Kingdom of God

1. The soul of the Jewish religion is its ethics. Its God is the Fountainhead and Ideal of morality. At the beginning of the summary of the ethical laws in the Mosaic Code stands the verse: "Ye shall be holy, for I the Lord your God am holy."1527 This provides the Jew with the loftiest possible motive for perfection and at the same time the greatest incentive to an ever higher conception of life and life's purpose. Accordingly, the kingdom of God for whose coming the Jew longs from the beginning until the end of the year,1528 does not rest in a world beyond the grave, but (in consonance with the ideal of Israel's sages and prophets) in a complete moral order on earth, the reign of truth, righteousness and holiness among all men and nations. Jewish ethics, then, derives its sanction from God, the

Author and Master of life, and sees its purpose in the hallowing of all life, individual and social. Its motive is the splendid conception that man, with his finite ends, is linked to the infinite God with His infinite ends; or, as the rabbis express it, "Man is a co-worker with God in the work of creation."1529

2. Both the term ethics (from the Greek ethos) and morality (from the Latin mores) are derived from custom or habit. In distinction to this, the Hebrew Scripture points to God's will as perceived in the human conscience as the source of all morality. Those ethical systems which dispense with religion fail to take due cognizance of the voice of duty which says to each man: "Thou shalt" or "Thou shalt not!" Duty distinguishes man from all other creatures. However low man may be in the scale of freedom, he is moved to action by an impulse from within, not by a compulsion from without. Of course, morality must travel a long road from the primitive code, which does not extend beyond the near kinsmen, to the ideal of civilized man which encompasses the world. Still man's steps are always directed by some rule of duty. The voice of conscience, heard clearly or dimly, is not, as is so often asserted, the product, but the original guiding factor of human society. The divine inner power of morality has made man, not man morality. Morality and religion, inseparably united in the Decalogue of Sinai, will attain their perfection together in the kingdom of God upon the Zion heights of humanity.

3. Ethical elements, greater or smaller, enter into all religions and codes of law of the various nations. Ancient Egypt, Persia and India even connected ethical principle and the future of the soul so closely, that certain ethical laws were to determine one's fate in heaven or hell. This led to the idea that this life is but the preparatory stage to the great hereafter. But antiquity also witnessed more or less successful attempts to emancipate ethics from religion. When the old beliefs no longer satisfied the thinking mind and no longer kept men from corruption, various philosophers attempted to provide general principles of morality as substitutes for the departed deities. Confucius built up in China a system of common-sense ethics based upon the communal life, but without any religious ideals; this satisfied the commonplace attitude of that country, but could not pass beyond the confines of the far East. A semi-religious ascetic system was offered at about the same time by Gautama Buddha of India, a prince garbed as a mendicant friar, who preached the gospel of love and charity for all fellow creatures. His leading maxims were blind resignation and self-effacement in the presence of the ills, suffering and death which rule the entire domain of life. All existence was evil to him, with its pleasure, passion and desire, its thought and feeling; his aim was a state of apathy and listlessness, Nirvana; while sympathy and compassion for fellow creatures were to offer some relief to a life of delusion and despair. The Hindu conception of the unbearable woe of the world corresponded more or less with the hot climate, which renders the people indolent and apathetic. In striking contrast to this was the vigorous manhood of the ethical systems developed on the healthy soil of Greece, under the azure canopy of a sky that fills the soul with beauty and joy. Life should be valued for the happiness it offers to the individual or to society. The good should be loved for its beauty, the just admired for its nobility. Greek ethics was thus both aristocratic and utilitarian; it took no heed of the toiling slave, the suffering poor, or the unprotected stranger. Both the Buddhist and the Hellenic systems lacked the energizing force and motive of the highest purpose of life, because both have left out of their purview the great Ruler who summons man to his duty, saying: "I am the Lord thy God; thou shalt and thou shalt not!"

4. Between the two extremes, the Hellenic self-expansion and the Buddhist self-extinction, Jewish ethics labors for self-elevation under the uplifting power of a holy God. The term which Scripture uses for moral conduct is, very significantly, "to walk in the ways of God." The rabbis explain this as follows: "As God is merciful and gracious, so be thou merciful and gracious. As God is called righteous, so be thou righteous. As God is holy, so do thou strive to be holy."1530 Another of their maxims is: "How can mortal man walk after God, who is an all-consuming fire? What Scripture means is that man should emulate God. As He clothes the naked, nurses the sick, comforts the sorrowing, and buries the dead, so should man."1531 In other words, human life must take its pattern from the divine goodness and holiness.

5. Obviously, Jewish ethics had to go through the same long process of development as the Jewish religion itself. A very high stage is represented by that disinterested goodness taught by Antigonus of Soko in the second pre-Christian century and by ben Azzai in the second century of the present era, which no longer anticipates reward or punishment, but does good for its own sake and shuns evil because it is evil.1532 As long as the law tolerated slavery, polygamy, and blood vengeance, and man's personality was not recognized on principle as being made in the image of God, the practical morality of the Hebrews could not rise above that of other nations, except in so far as the shepherd's compassion for the beast occasioned sympathy also for the fellow-man. After all, Jewish ethics became the ethics of humanity because of the God-conception of the prophets,—the righteous, merciful, and holy

God, the God "who executeth the judgment of the fatherless and the widow, and loveth the stranger in giving him food and raiment."1533 The conception of Jewish ethics as human ethics is voiced in the familiar verse: "It hath been told thee, O man, what is good and what the Lord doth require of thee: only to do justly and to love mercy and to walk humbly with thy God."1534 The all-ruling and all-seeing God of the Psalmist made men feel that only such a one can stand in His holy place "who hath clean hands and a pure heart, who hath not lifted up his soul unto falsehood, nor sworn deceitfully."1535 After law-giver, prophet, and psalmist came the wise, who gave ethics a more practical and popular character in the wisdom literature, and then came the Hasidim or Essenes, who, while seeking the highest piety or saintliness as life's aim, deepened and spiritualized their ethical ideals. Some of these considered the essential principles of morality to be love of God and of the fellow-man;1536 while rabbinical ethics in general laid great stress on motive as determining the value of the deed. The words, "Thou shalt fear the Lord thy God," so often repeated in the law, are taken to mean: Fear Him who looks into the heart, judging motives and intentions.1537

6. As the Mosaic Code presented the ceremonial and moral laws together as divine, so the rabbinical schools treated them all as divine commandments without any distinction. Hence the Mishnah and the Talmud fail to give ethics the prominent place it occupies in the prophetic and wisdom literature of the Bible and did not even make an attempt to formulate a system of ethics. The ethical rules in the "Sayings of the Fathers" and similar later collections make no pretensions to being general or systematic. The ethical teachings became conspicuous only through contact with the Hellenic world in the propaganda literature, with its aim to win the Gentile world to Judaism. Thus at an early period handbooks on ethics were written and circulated in the Greek language, some of which were afterward appropriated by the Christian Church. This entire movement is summed up in the well-known answer of Hillel to the heathen who desired to join the Jewish faith: "What is hateful to thee, do thou not unto thy fellow man; this is the law, and all the rest is merely commentary."1538

On the whole, rabbinical Judaism elaborated no ethical system before the Middle Ages. Then, under Mohammedan influence, the Aristotelian and Neo-Platonic philosophies in vogue gave rise to certain ethical works more or less in accord with their philosophic or mystic prototypes. In addition, ethical treatises were often written in the form of wills and of popular admonitions, which were sometimes broad and human, at other times stern and ascetic. One thought, however, prevailed through the ages: as life emanates from the God of holiness, so it must ever serve His holy purposes and benefit all His earthly children. "All the laws given by God to Israel have only the purification and ennobling of the life of men for their object," say the rabbis.1539

7. Perhaps the best summary of Jewish ethics was presented by Hillel in the famous three words: "If I am not for myself, who will be for me? But if I am for myself alone, what am I? And if not now, when then?"1540 We find here three spheres of duty: toward one's self, toward others, and toward the life before us. In contrast to purely altruistic or socialistic ethics, Jewish morality accentuated the value of the individual even apart from the social organism. Man is a child of God, a. self-conscious personality, who is to unfold and improve the powers implanted by his divine Maker, in both body and soul, laboring in this way toward the purpose for which he was created. Man was created single, says one of the sages in the Mishnah,1541 that he might know that he forms a world for himself, and the whole creation must aid him in unfolding the divine image within himself. Accordingly, self-preservation, self-improvement and self-perfection are duties of every man. This implies first the care for the human body as the temple which enshrines the divine spirit. In the eyes of Judaism, to neglect or enfeeble the body, the instrument of the soul, is altogether sinful. As the Sabbath law demands physical rest and recreation after the week's work, so the Jewish religion in general trains men to enjoy the gifts of God; and the rabbis declare that their rejection (except for disciplinary reasons) is ingratitude for which man must give an account at the last Judgment Day.1542 The Pharisean teacher who opposed the Essenic custom of fasting and declared it sinful, unless it be for special purposes, would have deprecated even more strongly the ascetic Christian or Hindoo saint who castigated his body as the seat of sin.1543 As Hillel remarked: "See what care is bestowed upon the statue of the emperor to keep it clean and bright; ought we not, likewise, keep God's image, our body, clean and free from every blemish?"1544

In regard to our moral and spiritual selves the rabbinical maxim is: "Beautify thyself first, and then beautify others."1545 Only as we first ennoble ourselves can we then contribute to the elevation of the world about us. Our industry promotes the welfare of the community as well as of ourselves; our idleness harms others as well as ourselves.1546 Upon self-respect rest our honor and our character. Virtue also is the result of self-control and self-conquest.1547 "There shall be no strange God in thee." This Psalm verse is taken by the rabbis to mean that no anger and passion nor any evil desire or overbearing pride shall obtain their mastery over thee.1548 Man asserts himself in braving temptation and trial, in overcoming sin and grief. Greater still is the hero who, in complete self-mastery, can sacrifice himself in a great cause. Martyrdom for the sake of God, which the rabbis call sanctification of the name of God,1549 is really the assertion of the divine life in the midst of death. But desertion of life from selfish motives through suicide is all the more despicable. He who sells his human birthright to escape pain or disgrace, though greatly to be pitied, has forfeited his claim and his share in the world to come.1550

Not only our life is to be maintained amid all trials as a sacred trust, but also our rights, our freedom, and our individuality, for we must not allow our personality to become the slave or tool of others. Job, who battled for his own convictions against the false assumption of his friends, was at last praised and rewarded by God.1551 The Biblical verse: "For they are My servants whom I brought forth out of the land of Egypt, they shall not be sold as slaves," is explained by the rabbis: "My servants, but not servants to servants," and is thus applicable to spiritual slavery as well.1552

8. Therefore the Jewish conception of duty to our fellow-men is by no means comprised in love or benevolence. Long before Hillel, other Jewish sages gave the so-called Golden Rule: "Love thy neighbor as thyself," a negative form: "What is hateful to thee do not do unto thy fellow men."1553 Taken in the positive form, the command cannot be literally carried out. We cannot love the stranger as we love ourselves or our kin; still less can we love our enemy, as is demanded by the Sermon on the Mount. According to the Hebrew Scriptures1554 we can and should treat our enemy magnanimously and forgive him, but we cannot truly love him, unless he turns from an enemy to a friend. The real meaning given by the rabbis to the command, "Love thy neighbor as thyself" is: "Put thyself in his place and act accordingly. As thou dost not desire to be robbed of thy property or good name or to be injured or insulted, so do not these things unto thy fellow man."1555 They then take the closing words, "I am the Lord thy God," as an oath by God: "I am the Lord, the Creator of thy fellow man as well as of thee; therefore, if thou showest love to him, I shall surely reward thee, and if not, I am the Judge ready to punish thee."1556 Love of all fellow-men is, in fact, taught by both Hillel1557 and Philo.1558 Love and helpful sympathy are implied also by the verse from Deuteronomy: "He (the Lord) loveth the stranger in giving him bread and raiment. Love ye therefore the stranger."1559 All members of the human household are dependent on each other for kindness and good will, whether we are rich or poor, high or lowly, in life or in death; so do we owe love and kindness to all men alike.

9. However, love as a principle of action is not sufficiently firm to fashion human conduct or rule society. It is too much swayed by impulse and emotion and is often too partial. Love without justice leads to abuse and wrong, as we see in the history of the Church, which began with the principle of love, but often failed to heed the admonitions of justice. Therefore justice is the all-inclusive principle of human conduct in the eyes of Judaism. Justice is impartial by its very nature. It must right every wrong and vindicate the cause of the oppressed. "When Thy judgments are in the earth, the inhabitants of the world will learn righteousness," said the prophet,1560 describing the just man as he "that walketh righteously and speaketh uprightly, that despiseth the gain of oppressions, that shaketh his hands from holding of bribes, that stoppeth his ear from hearing of blood, and shutteth his eyes from looking on evil."1561 Justice is the requisite not only in action, but also in disposition,1562 implying honesty in intention as in deed, uprightness in speech and mien, perfect rectitude, neither taking advantage of ignorance nor abusing confidence.1563 It is sinful to acquire wealth by betting or gambling,1564 or by cornering food-supplies to raise the market price.1565 The rabbis derive from Scripture the thought that, just as "your balances and weights, your ephah and hin" must be just, so should your yea and nay.1566 The verse, "Justice, justice shalt them follow,"1567 is explained thus in a Midrash which is quoted by Bahya ben Asher of the thirteenth century: "Justice, whether to your profit or loss, whether in word or in action, whether to Jew or non-Jew."1568 This category of justice covers also regard for the honor of our fellow-men, lest we harm it by the tongue of the back-biter,1569 by the ear that listens to calumny,1570 or by suspicion cast upon the innocent.1571 "God in His law takes especial care of the honor of our fellow-men," say the rabbis, and "he who publicly puts his fellow man to shame forfeits his share in the world to come."1572

10. But the Jewish conception of justice is broader than mere abstention from hurting our fellow-men. Justice is a positive conception. Righteousness (Zedakah) includes also charity and philanthropy. It asserts the claim of the poor upon the rich, of the helpless upon him who possesses the means to help. "He who prevents the poor from reaping the corners of the field or the gleanings of the harvest, or in any way withholds that which has been assigned them by the law of Moses, is a robber," says the Mishnah, "for it is written: 'Remove not the old landmark, and enter not into the field of the fatherless.' "1573 Jewish ethics holds that charity is not a gift of condescending love, but a duty. It is incumbent upon the fortunate to rescue the unfortunate, since all that we possess is only lent

to us by God, the Owner of the world, with the charge that we provide for the needy who are under His special protection. Those who refuse to give the poor their share abuse the divine trust. "If thou lendest money to My people, to the poor with thee,"1574 says Scripture, and the rabbis comment on this to the effect that "the poor are called God's people; do not forget that the turn of fortune which made you rich and them poor may turn, and that you may then be in need."1575 Nor is it sufficient merely to give to him who is poor; we are bidden to uphold him when his powers fail.1576

This is the very principle of ethics of the Mosaic law, the principle for which the great prophets fought with all the vigor and vehemence of the divine spirit—social justice. The cry: "Woe unto them that join house to house, that lay field to field, till there be no room,"1577 the condemnation of those "that swallow the needy and destroy the poor of the land,"1578 the curse hurled at him who withholdeth corn,1579 laid the foundations of a higher justice, which is not satisfied with mitigating the misery of the unfortunate by acts of charity, but insists on a readjustment of the social conditions which create poverty. This spirit created the poor laws of the Mosaic Code, which were partially adopted by both Christians and Mohammedans. It dictated the Mosaic institutions of the seventh year of release and the Jubilee year for the restoration of fields and houses, to prevent the tyranny of wealth from becoming a permanent source of oppression. While these were scarcely ever put into practice, they remained as a protest and an appeal. Their aim and permanent influence tended toward relations between the upper and lower classes, which would insure the latter some degree of independence and dignity. In fact, the foundations laid by the Hebrew Scripture underlie all our great modern efforts to turn the forces of charity so as to check the sources of evil in our social organism. Modern philanthropy, taking its clue from the old Hebrew ideal, aims not to alleviate but to cure, and to stimulate the natural good in society, material, moral and intellectual, that it may overcome the evil. We are recognizing more and more the principle of mutual responsibility and interdependence of men and classes. Yet this very principle, modern as it seems, was recognized by the Jewish sages, as we see in the remarkable passage where the rabbis comment on the law concerning the case of a slain body found in the field, with the murderer unknown. The Bible commands that in such a case the elders of the city should kill a heifer, wash their hands over it, and say: "Our hands have not shed this blood, neither have our eyes seen it."1580 The rabbis then ask: "How could the elders of a city ever be suspected of the crime of murder?" and their reply is: "Even if they only failed to provide the poor in their charge with the necessary food, and he became a highway robber and murderer; or if they left him without the necessary protection, and he fell a victim to murderers, they are held responsible for the crime before the higher court of God."1581 That is, according to our station we are all responsible for the social conditions which create poverty and crime, and it is our duty to establish such relations between the individual and the community as will remove the causes of all the evils of society.

11. This, in a way, anticipates the third maxim of Hillel: "If not now, when then?" Judaism cannot accept the New Testament spirit of other-worldliness, which prompted the teaching: "Take no thought for your life, what ye shall eat or what ye shall drink, nor yet for your body what ye shall put on," or "Resist not evil."1582 Such a view disregards the values and duties of domestic, civic, and industrial life, and creates an inseparable gulf between sacred and profane, between religion and culture. In contrast to this, Jewish ethics sets the highest value upon all things that make man more of a human being and increase his power of doing good. To Judaism marriage and home life are regarded as the normal conditions of human welfare and sane morality, while celibacy is considered abnormal.1583 Labor establishes the dignity of man,1584 while wealth is a source of blessing, a stewardship in the service of society.1585 In opposition to the practice fostered by the Essenes and afterwards adopted by the early Church, of devoting one's whole fortune to charity, the rabbis decreed that one should not give over one fifth of one's possessions.1586 As has well been said, Judaism teaches a "robust morality."1587 It regards life as a continual battle for God and right against every sort of injustice,1588 for truth against every kind of falsehood. At the same time it fosters also the gentler virtues of meekness,1589 kindness to animals,1590 peaceableness and modesty.1591

12. Jewish ethics excels all other ethical systems, especially in its insistence on purity and holiness. Not only is any unchaste look, thought, or act condemned, exactly as in the Sermon on the Mount,1592 as approaching adultery,1593 but all profanity of act or speech is declared to be an unpardonable offense against the majesty of God.1594 Modesty in demeanor and dress was both preached and practiced by the Jews throughout the Middle Ages, while in non-Jewish circles coarseness and lewdness prevailed among high and low, in minstrel song and monastic life. "The Lord thy God walketh in the midst of thy camp ... therefore shall thy camp be holy, that He see no unseemly thing in thee, and turn away from thee."1595 These Biblical words created among the Essenes (the

Zenuim) and later among the entire Jewish people a spirit of chastity and modesty which made the Jewish home of old a model of purity and sanctity. The great problem for modern Israel, amid our present allurements of luxury and pleasure, is to restore the home to its pristine glory as a sanctuary of God, a training school for virtue, so that its influence may extend over the whole of life.

13. Thus Jewish ethics derives its sanction from the idea of a God of holiness. But it never made life austere, depriving it of joy, or begrudging man his cheerfulness and laughter. On the contrary, the Sabbath and many of the holy days are seasons of joy, for gladness should bring the spirit of God near to man.1596 Moreover, the Talmud holds that we should encourage every means of promoting cheer among men. This is illustrated by one of the popular legends of the prophet Elijah, who told the saintly Rabbi Beroka, who prided himself upon his austerity, that his companions in Paradise were to be two jesters, because they cheered the depressed and increased the joy in the world.1597

As a matter of fact, the Jewish ideal of holiness is all-inclusive. It aims to hallow every pursuit and endeavor, all social relations and activities, insisting only on a pure motive and disinterested service. As the Ruler of life is the source of all morality, so all of life should be made holy with duty. Man becomes a child of God through his responsibility, instead of remaining a mere product of the social forces about him or of claiming self-sufficient sovereignty and refusing to acknowledge a higher Will. Jewish ethics is autonomous, because it insists on the divine spirit in man.1598 As we follow the divine Pattern of holiness, all that we have and are, body and soul, weal and woe, wealth and want, pain and pleasure, life and death, become stepping-stones on the road to holiness and godliness. Life is like a ladder on which man can rise from round to round, to come ever nearer to God on high who beckons him toward ever higher ideals and achievements. Man and humanity are thus given the potentiality of infinite progress in every direction. Science and art, industry and commerce, literature and law, every pursuit of man comes within the scope of religion and ethics. For God's kingdom of truth, righteousness and peace, as beheld by Israel's seers of old, will be fully established on earth only when all the forces of material, intellectual, and social life have been unfolded, when all the prophetic ideals, the visions and aspirations of all the seers of humanity have been realized, and the Zion heights of human perfection have at last been attained. "The wise have no rest, neither in this world nor in the world to come, for it is said: 'they go from strength to strength, [until] they appear before God on Zion.'"159

List Of Abbreviations

A. d. R. N. Aboth di Rabbi Nathan

A. T. Altes Testament

Ab. Z. Aboda Zarah

Ag. Agada

Ann. Annotations

Ant. Antiquities (of Josephus)

Ap. Apionem, contra

Apoc. Apocalyptic

Arak. Arakin

Art. Article

B. Babli (Babylonian)

b. ben

B. B. Baba Bathra

B. H. Beth ha Midrash

B. K. Baba Kamma

B. M. Baba Metzia

Beitr. Beitraege

Ber. Berakoth

Bibl. Bible or Biblical

C. C. A. R. Central Conference of American Rabbis

Cant. Canticles

Chron. Chronicles

Ch. Chapter

Comm. Commentary, -ies

Comp. Compare

Cor. Corinthians, Epistle to

Dan. Daniel

Deut. Deuteronomy

Dict. Dictionary

Eccl. Ecclesiastes

Enc. Encyclopedia

(a) Brit. Britannia

(b) R. a. Eth.... of Religion and Ethics

Ep. Epistle

Eph. Ephesians, Epistle to

Ethnol. Ethnologische

Ex. Exodus

Ez. Ezekiel

G. J. Geschichte der Juden (Graetz)

G. Jud. Geschichte des Judenthums (Jost)

G. V. I. Geschichte des Volkes Israel (Schuerer)

Gal. Galatians, Epistle to

Gen. Genesis

Ges. Abh. Gesammelte Abhandlungen

Ges. Schrf. Gesammelte Schriften

Gesch. u. Lit. Geschichte und Literature

Gottesd. Gottesdienstliche

H. Hilkoth

H. B. Handbuch

H. J. History of Jews (Graetz)

H. U. C. Hebrew Union College

Hab. Habakkuk

Hag. Hagigah

Hist. History

Hor. Horayoth

Hul. Hullin

Introd. Introduction

Isai. Isaiah

Israel. Israelitisch

J. Journal

J. E. Jewish Encyclopedia

J. Q. R. Jewish Quarterly Review

J. W. Jewish War (Josephus)

Jahrb. Jahrbuch

Jer. Jeremiah

Jew. Jewish

Josh. Joshua

Jud. Judenthums

Judg. Judges

Jued. Juedisch

K. A. T. "Die Keilinschriften und das Alte Testament"

Ker. Kerithoth

Keth. Kethuboth

Kil. Kilayim

L. Literature

l. c. loco citato, the same place;

libro citato, the same book (for the usual o. c. = opere citato).

Lam. Lamentations

Lev. Leviticus

M. K. Moed Katan

Macc. Maccabees, Book of

Maim. Maimonides

Mak. Makkoth

Mal. Malachi

Mas. Masseketh

Meg. Megillah

Mek. Mekiltha

Men. Menahoth

Mid. Midrash

Mtschr. Monatsschrift fuer Geschichte und Wissenschaft des Judenthums

Mitth. Mittheilungen

Nachgel-Schr. Nachgelassene Schriften

Neh. Nehemiah

Nid. Niddah

Numb. Numbers

P. d. R. El. Pirke di Rabbi Eliezer

Pars. Parsisch

Pes. Pesahim, -ee

Pes. R. Pesikta Rabbathi

Pesik. Pesikta di Rab Kahana

Phil. Philosophy or Philosophical

Prov. Proverbs

Prot. Protestantisch

Ps. Psalms

Psych. Psychologisch

Quel. Quellen

R. Rabbah, also Rabbi, Rabban

R. h. Sh. Rosh ha Shanah

R. W. B. Real-Woerterbuch

ref. referring or reference

Rel. Religion

S. O. Seder Olam

s. v. sub verbo

Sam. Samuel

Sanh. Sanhedrin

Sh. A. Shulhan Aruk

Shab. Shabuoth

Sibyl. Sibylline Books

Slav. Slavonic

Soc. Society

Stud. Studien or Studies

Suk. Sukkah

Syst. System or Systematic

T. d. b. E. Tanna di be Eliahu

Tanh. Tanhuma

Teh. Tehillim

Theol. Theologisch

Tos. Tosefta

Tosaf. Tosafoth

u. und or ueber

W. B. Woerterbuch

Wiss. Wissenschaft or Wissenschaftlich

Yalk. Yalkut

Y. B. Yearbook

Yeb. Yebamoth

Yer. Yerushalmi

Zech. Zechariah

Zeitschr. Zeitschr

Footnotes

1.

Compare Heinrici Theologische Encyclopaedie, p. 4; Enc. Brit. art. Theology.

2.

Heinrici, l. c., p. 14 f., 212; Hagenbach-Kautsch: Encyc. d. theolog. Wiss., p. 28-30; Rauwenhoff: Religionsphilosophie, Einl., xiii; Margolis: "The Theological Aspect of Reformed Judaism," in Yearbook of C. C. A. R., 1903, p. 188-192. Lauterbach, J. E., art. Theology.

3.

See, however, Geiger: Nachgel. Schriften, II, 3-8; also Margolis, l. c., p. 192-196.

4.

A fine beginning in this direction has been made by Professor Schechter in Some Aspects of Rabbinic Theology, New York, 1909.

5.

See Joel: "D. Mosaismus u. d. Heidenthum," in Jahrb. f. Jued. Gesch. und Lit., 1904, p. 70-73.

6.

See Schaff-Herzog's Encycl., art. Apostles' Creed and Symbol.

7.

See Schechter: Studies in Judaism, Intr., XXI-XXII; p. 147, 198 f.; Foster: The Finality of the Christian Religion, Chicago, 1906; Friedr. Delitzsch: Zur Weiterentwicklung der Religion, 1908; and comp. Orelli: Religionsgeschichte, 276 f., and Dorner: Beitr. z. Weitrentwicklung d. christl. Religion, 173.

8.

For the origin of the name Judaism, see Esther VIII, 17. Compare Yahduth, Esther Rabbah III, 7; II Macc. II, 21; VIII, 1, 14, 38; Graetz: G. d. J., II, 174 f.; Jost: G.d. Jud., I, 1-12; J. E., art. Judaism. Regarding the unfairness of Christian authors in their estimate of Judaism, see Schechter, l. c., 232-251; M. Schreiner: D. juengst. Urtheile u. d. Judenthum, p. 48-58. Dubnow, Asher Ginsberg and the rest of the nationalists underrate the religious power of the Jew's soul, which forms the essence of his character and the motive power of all his aspirations and hopes, as well as of all his achievements in history.

9.

Erub. 13 b.

10.

Neh. VIII, 1-18; Ez. VII, 12-28.

11.

See M. Bloch: Tekanot, and art. Tekanot J. E. Regarding inspiration see J. E.; Sanh, 99 a; Meg. 7 a; Maim.: Moreh, II, 45; comp. Yerush. Ab. Zar., I, 40; Horay. III, 48 c; Levit. R. VI, 1; IX, 9; and Yoma 9 b. The laying on of hands for ordination (Semikah) implied originally the imparting of the holy spirit, see J. E., art. Authority.

12.

See Geiger, J. Z., I, p. 7.

13.

Aboth d. R. Nathan, I; Shab. 30 b with reference to Ezek. XLIII-XLIV.

14.

See Geiger: Z. D. M. G., XII, 536; Schechter, Wisdom of Ben Sira, p. 35.

15.

See J. E., art. Jubilees, Book of. Very instructive in this connection is a comparative study of the Falashas, the Samaritans, especially the Dosithean sect, and the still problematical sect discovered through the document found by Schechter, edited by him under the title Fragments of a Zadokite Sect.

16.

See Yer. Hag., I, 76, and elsewhere.

17.

Ethics of Judaism, I, 8-10; Geiger: J. Z., IX, 263.

18.

See Pesik. R., V, p. 146; Midr. Tanhuma, ed. Buber, Wayera 6 and Ki Thissa, 17. Comp. the legend of Moses and Akiba, Men. 29 b.

19.

Comp. Geiger: Nachgel. Schr., II, 37-41; also his Jud. u. s. Gesch., I, 20-35; Beck: D. Wesen d. Judenthums; Eschelbacher: D. Judenthum u. d. Wesen d. Christenthums; Schreiner, l. c., 26-34.

20.

Deut. VI, 7; XI, 19.

21.

See Geiger: Nachgel. Schr., II, 37 f.

22.

John XIV, 6. Comp. Dorner, l. c., 173; and his Grundprobleme d. Religionsphilosophie; Orelli: Religionsgeschichte, 276 f.

23.

Gen. R. VIII, 5.

24.

See Schechter: Studies, 147-181 and notes 351 f.; Mendelssohn: Ges. Schr., III, 321. Comp. Schlesinger: Buch Ikkarim, 630-632; Bousset: Religion d. Judenthums, 170 f., 175, and thereto Perles: Bousset, 112 f.; Martin Schreiner: l. c., 35 f.; J. E., art. Faith and Articles of Faith (E. G. Hirsch); Felsenthal, Margolis, and Kohler, in Y. B. C. C. A. R., 1897, p. 54; 1903, p. 188-193; 1905, p. 83; Neumark: art. Ikkarim in Ozar ha Yahduth; D. Fr. Strauss: D. christl. Glaubenslehre, I, 25.

25.

See Gen. XV, 6; Mek. to Ex. XIV; J. E., art. Faith.

26.

Deut. VI, 1-6; XI, 13-21; Num. XV, 37-41.

27.

See Bousset, II, 224 f. The term Pistis = faith, assumes a new meaning in Hellenistic Literature.

28.

See J. E., art. Emeth we Yatzib.

29.

See J. E., art. Alenu.

30.

See J. E., art. Abraham in Apocryphical and Rabbinical Lit.

31.

Sifra Behukothai, III, 6; Sanh. 38 b; Targ. Y. to Gen. IV, 8.

32.

Ber. II, 2; see Kohler: Monatsschrift, 1883, p. 445.

33.

Kohler, l. c.

34.

The Mishnaic Apicoros corresponded to the Greek, Epicoureios, and was no longer understood by the Talmudists; see Schechter: Studies in Judaism, I, 157. It is defined by Josephus: Antiquities, X, 11, 7: "The Epicureans ... are in a state of error, who cast Providence out of life, and do not believe that God takes care of the affairs of the world, nor that the universe is governed by a Being which outlives all things in everlasting self-sufficiency and bliss, but declare it to be self-sustaining and void of a ruler and protector ... like a ship without a helmsman and like a chariot without a driver." Comp. also Oppenheim in Monatsschr., 1864, p. 149.

35.

See Rappaport; "Biography of R. Hananel," in Bikkure ha Ittim, 1842.

36.

Contra Apionem, II, 22. See J. G. Mueller: Josephus' Schrift gegen Apion, 311-313.

37.

See Alfred v. Kremer: Gesch. d. herrsch. Ideen d. Islam, 39-41; Goldziher, D. M. L. Z., XLIV, p. 168 f.; XLI, p. 72 f., which passages cast much light upon the Jewish Ani Maamin.

38.

See Jost: Gesch. d. Jud., II, 330 f.; Frankl: art. Karaites in Ersch und Gruber's Encyclopaedie; Loew: Juedische Dogmen, Ges. s. I, 154; Schechter, l. c.

39.

J. Guttman: D. Religionsphil, v. Abraham Ibn Daud; David Kaufmann, Gesch. d. Attributenlehre; Neumark: Gesch. d. juedisch. Phil. vols. I and II.

40.

Maimonides: Commentary on Mishnah, Sanh., X, 1; Schechter, l. c., 163; Holzer: Gesch. d. Dogmenlehre, Berlin, 1901.

41.

See Loew, l. c., 156; Schechter, l. c, 165.

42.

See P. Bloch: "Luzzatto als Religionsphilosoph" in Samuel David Luzzatto, p. 49-71. Comp. Hochmuth: Gotteskenntniss und Gottesverehrung, Einleitung.

43.

See Schechter, l. c., 167 and the notes.

44.

See Horowitz: D. Psychologie u. d. jued. Religionsphilosophie, 1883.

45.

See J. E., art. Albo by E. G. Hirsch, and the bibliography there.

46.

See Schechter, l. c., p. 162.

47.

Isa. XLIX, 9, and elsewhere.

48.

See Schechter, l. c., p. 169.

49.

Aboth, III, 1; Gen. R. XXI, 5.

50.

See Schechter, l. c.

51.

See Loew, l. c., 157, and his "Mafteah," p. 331; Schechter, l. c.

52.

Makk. 23 b.

53.

See J. E., art. Catechism by E. Schreiber.

54.

Gen. XX, 11.

55.

Ps. CXI, 10; Prov. IX, 10; Job XXVIII, 28.

56.

Ex. XX, 20.

57.

Hos. IV, 1, 6; II. 3; XIII, 4-5.

58.

Jer. IX, 23; XXII, 16; XXXI, 32-33.

59.

Deut. IV, 39; VII, 9.

60.

Knowledge as intellect is brought out as early as the Book of Wisdom, XIII, 1; see especially Maimonides: Yesode ha Torah, I, 1-3; Moreh, I, 39; III, 28. In opposition, see Rosin: Ethik des Maimonides, 101; Luzzatto and Hochmuth, l. c.; also Dillmann: H. B. d. alttestamentl. Theol., 204 f.

61.

Ch. IV.

62.

Gen. XV, 6; see J. E., art. Abraham.

63.

Shab. 97 a.

64.

Mek. Beshallak 6, p. 41 ab.

65.

Deut. VI, 5; X, 12; XI, 1; XIII, 22; XXX, 6, 16, 20.

66.

Sifre to Deut. VI, 5.

67.

Judges V, 31.

68.

Shab. 88 b.

69.

See Testament of Job, and notes by Kohler, in Semitic Studies in Memory of Alexander Kohut, 271, and Sota, V, 5.

70.

Sifre, l. c.

71.

See Yoma, 86 a; T. d. El. R., XXIV; Maimonides, H. Teshubah, X; Crescas: Or Adonai, I, 3. Comp. Testaments Twelve Patriarchs, Simeon 3, 4; Issachar, 5; Philo: Quod omnis probus liber, 12 and elsewhere.

72.

Song of Songs VII, 6, 7.

73.

See Sifre Deut. XXVI, 8; Sanh. X, 1; J. E., art. Revelation; Dillmann, 61 f.; Geiger, D. Jud. u. s. Gesch. I, 34 f.

74.

See Deut. XIII, 2-6, where prophet forms a parallel to dreamer of dreams. God appears in a dream to Abraham (Gen. XV, 1, 12), to Abimelek (Gen. XX, 3, 6), to Jacob (XXVIII, 12; XXXI, 11; XLVI, 2), to Laban

(XXXI, 24), to Balaam (Num. XXIV, 3), and to Eliphaz (Job IV, 3-6). Dream-like visions open the prophetic career of Moses (Exod. III, 3-6), Samuel (I Sam. III, 1, 15, 21), Isaiah (Is. VI, 1 f.), Jeremiah (Jer. I, 11 f.), Ezekiel (Ezek. I, 4), and others. Revelation in the Bible is Mahazeh, hazon, and hizayon, "vision"—whence hozeh, "seer"; or mareh, "sight," whence roeh, "seer." See also Geiger: Urschrift, 340; 390. Prophecy without dream or vision is claimed for Moses (Num. XII, 6-8; Exod. XXX, 11; Deut. XXXIV, 10; see Maimonides: Moreh, II, 43-47; Albo, Ikkarim, III, 8). The revelation on Sinai is described as "the great vision," or mareh: Exod. III, 3; XXIV, 17; compare Deut. IV, 11-V, 23, according to which only a "voice" is heard. Instead of God the later prophets see an angel, as Zach. I, 8, 11; II, 2 f. Compare Yebam. 49 b, as to the difference between Isaiah, who saw God in a vision, and Moses, who saw Him "in a shining mirror." He will appear in the latter way to the righteous in the future world, Suc. 45 b; Lev. R. I, 14; I Cor. XIII, 12.

75.

See Gen. XX, 6; XXXI, 29; Num. XXIV; Job IV, 16 f.; XXXVIII, 1.

76.

The Hebrew word for prophecy is passive,—nibba' or hithnabbe', "to be made to speak," or "to bubble forth,"—the Deity being the active power, while the prophet is His mouthpiece.

77.

Ex. XXXIII, 11; Deut. XXXIV, 10.

78.

Ex. XIX, 19; XX, 19.

79.

Ex. XIX, 1-8.

80.

Shab. 88 a after Ex. XXIV, 7.

81.

Seder Olam R., I and XXI; Lev. Rab. I, 12-14; B. B. 15 b.

82.

Hag. 13 b; Sanh. 89 a; Lev. R. l. c.

83.

See Schmiedl: Stud. u. jued.-arabische Religionsphilosophie, 191-192; S. Horowitz: D. Prophetologie i. d. jued. Religionsphilosophie; Sandler: D. Problem d. Prophetie i. d. jued. Religionsphilosophie; J. E., art. Prophets and Prophecy; Emunoth III, 4; Cuzari, I, 95; II, 10-12; Emunah Ramah, II, 5, 1; Moreh, II, 32-48; Yesode ha Torah, VII; Or Adonai, II, 4, 1; Ikkarim, III, 8-12, 17; Nachmanides to Gen. XVIII, 2; Abravanel to Gen. XXI, 27; Comp. Husik, Hist. Med. Jew. Phil., Index s. v. Prophecy; Enc. Rel. Ethics, art. Philosophy and Prophecy.

84.

Horowitz, l. c. p. 11-16; Gen. R. XVII, 6; Lev. R, l. c; Sanh. 17 b; Philo: De Decalog., 21; de Migratione Abrahami, 7; comp. I Corinth. XIII, 12.

85.

Moreh, l. c.

86.

Cuzari, l. c.

87.

Kol Nibra: Moreh, I, 65; Emunoth, II, 8; Cuzari, I, 89.

88.

According to the rabbis, the working of the holy spirit ceased with Haggai, Zechariah, and Malachi, who, with Ezra, were included also among the "Men of the Great Synagogue." See Tos. Sota XIII, 2; Seder Olam R. XXX; Sanh. 11 a. See J. E., art. Synagogue, Men of the Great; Holy Spirit; Inspiration. Comp. B. B. 14 b, 15 a; Yoma 9 b; Meg. 3 a, 7 a; I Macc. IV, 46; Ps. LXXIV, 9; Josephus, Con. Apion., I, 8; Philo: Vita Mosis, II, 7; Aristeas, 305-307. As to the difference between the spirit of prophecy and the holy spirit, see Cuzari, III, 32-35; Moreh, II, 35-37. The Essenes claimed the holy spirit for their apocryphal writings; see IV Esdras XIV, 38; Book of Wisdom VII, 27.

89.

On the disputes concerning canonical books, see Yadayim III, 5; Ab. d. R. N., I, ed. Schechter, 2-3; Shab. 30 b; Meg. 7 a. Comp. B. K. 92 b, where Ben Sira is quoted as one of the Hagiographa.

90.

See Tos. Pes. I, 27; IV, 2; Sota XIII, 3; Yer. Horay. III, 48 c; Lev. R. XXI, 7.

91.

R. h. Sh. 27 a; Mak. 22 b.

92.

Sifre Deut. VI, 4.

93.

On the term Torah see Smend: Lehrb. d. alttest. Religionsgesch.; Stade: Bibl. Theol. d. Alt. Test., Index s. v. Torah; W. J. Beecher: Jour. Bibl. Lit., 1905, 1-16; "Thora a Word Study in the Old Testament." For Torah as Law, see Neh. VIII, 1; Joshua I, 7, and throughout the Pentateuch; as moral instruction, see Hos. IV, 6; VIII, 1; Is. I, 10; V, 24; XXX, 9; LI, 4; Mic. IV, 2; Jer. XXXVI, 4 f.; XXXI, 32; Ps. XVI, 8; Prov. VI, 22; VII, 2; Guedeman: Quell. z. G. d. Unterrichts, at the beginning; Claude Montefiore: Hibbert Lectures, 1892, p. 465 f.

94.

Nehematha, which means the Messianic hope; see Kohut: Aruch V, 328 and Appendix 59.

95.

See B. B. 13 b; Meg. III, 1; IV, 4; comp. Ned. 22 b; Taan. 9 a; Shab. 104 a; Sifra Behukothai at end; Eccl. R. I, 10; Ex. R. XXXVIII, 6. Zunz: Gottesd. Vortr., 46 f., and art. Canon and Bible in the various encyclopedias. As to Torah for the whole Bible, see Mek. Shira I; Sanh. 37 a, 91 b; Ab. Zar. 17 a; M. K. 5 a; comp. I Cor. XIV, 21; John X, 34; XII, 34; XV, 25. For Torah as Nomos, or Law, see II Macc. XV, 9.

96.

Bousset, l. c., 128-129.

97.

On the divine origin of the Torah, see Sanh. 99 a; Sifra Kedoshim 8; Behar I; Behukothay 8. Regarding the meaning of metammin eth ha yadayim in the sense of taboo for the holy writings, see Geiger: Urschrift, p. 146.

98.

Sanh. 99 a; Maim. H. Teshubah III, 8.

99.

Comp. Kohler: Hebrew Union College Annual, 1904, "The Four Ells of the Halakah."

100.

Deut. XXXIII, 4.

101.

Mak. 23 b.

102.

Jerem. XXXI, 32.

103.

Comp. Schechter, Aspects, p. 120-136, and see Ben Sira, XXIV, 8-23; XVII, 11; Baruch III, 38 f.; Apoc. Baruch XXXVIII, 4; XLIV, 16; IV Esdras VIII, 12; IX, 37; Philo: Vita Mosis, II, 3, 9; Gen. R. I; P. d. R. El. III.

104.

This apotheosis of the Torah is put in a wrong light by Weber, Juedische Theologie, 157 f., 197, but is stated better in Bousset, l. c., 136-142.

105.

Dibre Kabbalah, R. h. Sh. 7 a, 19 a; Yer. Halla I, 57 b; see Levy, W. B., s. v. Kabbalah.

106.

The personality of Moses was at first exalted to almost superhuman height; see Ben Sira, XLV, 2; Assumptio Mosis, I, 14; XI, 16; Philo: Vita Mosis, III, 39; Josephus: Antiquities, IV, 32 b; Bousset, l. c., 140 f. In contrast to the Church view of Jesus the rabbis later emphasized the human frailties of Moses: "Never did divine majesty descend to the habitations of mortal man, nor did ever a mortal man such as Moses and Elijah ascend to heaven, the dwelling-place of God," taught Rabbi Jose (Suk. 5 a).

107.

See Deut. IV, 6-8; Jer. XXXI, 34-35; Philo: Vita Mosis, II, 14; Josephus: Apion, II, 277.

108.

See Herodotus, III, 8; IV, 70; Jer. XXIV, 18; H. Clay Trumbull: The Blood Covenant, New York, 1885; Kraetschmar: D. Bundervorstellung i. A. Test., 1896; J. E. and Encyl. of Rel. and Ethics, art. Covenant.

109.

See Gen. IX, 1-17; Tos. Ab. Zar. VIII, 4; San. 56 a; Gen. R. XVI, XXIV; Jubilees VI, 10 f.; Bernays: Ges. Abh. I, 252 f., 272 f.; II, 71-80.

110.

Gen. XV, 18; XVII, 2 f.; XVIII, 19; Lev. XXVI, 42; Jubilees I, 51.

111.

Ex. XIX, 5; XXIV, 6-8; XXXIV, 28; Deut. IV-V, XXVIII, XXIX; Comp. I Kings XIX, 10, 14; Jer. XI; XXXI; XXXIV, 13; Ezek. XVI-XVII.

112.

Hos. II, 18-20.

113.

113. Jer. XXXI, 30-32, 34-35; XXXIII, 25; Deut. XXIX, 14.

114. See Ep. Hebrews VIII, 8 f.; Gal. III, 15; I Cor. XI, 25; Matt. XXIV, 21, and parallels.

115. Gen. XVII, 11.

116. Ex. XXXI, 13-17; comp. Deut. X, 16; Josh. V, 9; Isa. LVI, 4-6. See Mek. to Ex. XIX, 5, the controversy between R. Eliezer and R. Akiba, whether the Sabbath or circumcision was the essential sign of the covenant.

117. Ker. 9 a; Yeb. 45-48 and see Chapter LVI below.

118. Ps. XXII, 28 f.; CXV, 11; CXVIII, 4; Is. LVI, 6.

119. Isaiah XLIX, 6-8.

120. Acts XV, 20, 29.

121. See J. E., art. Saul of Tarsus; Enc. Rel. Eth. art. Paul.

122. Isaac ben Shesheth: Responsa, 119. Comp, J. E., art. Christianity.

123. See further, Chapter XLIX.

124. Jer. X, 11; 16 and 10.

125. Shab. 89 b.

126. Lev. XVIII, 2, 27 f.; Num. XXV, 3-8; Hos. IV, 10; V, 4.

127. Num. XV, 39; Ex. XXIII, 24; Deut. XX, 18; Sanh. XII, 5; X, 4-6; Ab. Zar. II-IV; Sanh. 106 a: "Israel's God hates lewdness."

128. Ex. XX, 5; Deut. IV, 24; VI, 15.

129. See Philo: De Humanitate; Doellinger: Heidenthum u. Judenthum, 682, 700 f.; I. H. Weiss: Dor Dor we Doreshav, II, 19 f.

130. See J. E., art. Christianity.

131. Isa. XLII, 8. Scripture always emphasizes the contrast between Israel's God and the heathen gods. See Ex. XII, 12; XV, 11; XVIII, 11; Deut. X, 17; also in the prophets, Isa. XL; XLIV, 9; Jer. X; and the Psalms, XCVI, CXV, CXXXV. Absolute monotheism was a slow growth from this basis.

132. See Ex. R. V, 18.

133. Deut. VII; XVII, 2 f.; XX, 16; Maimonides: H. Akkum, II-VII; Melakim, VI, 4; Yoreh Deah, CXII-XLVIII.

134. Ps. XCVI-XCIX.

135. See Singer's Prayerbook, p, 76-77, and J. E., art. Alenu.

136. See Cheyne's Dict. Bibl. art. Name and Names with Bibliography; Jacob: Im Namen Gottes; Heitmueller, Im Namen Jesu, 1903, p. 24-25. The Name for the Lord occurs Lev, XXIV, 11, 16; Deut. XXVIII, 58; Geiger, Urschrift, 261 f.

137. See Baudissin, Stud. z. Sem. Religionsgesch., I, 47; 177; Robinson Smith: Religion of the Semites; Max Mueller, Chips from a German Workshop, I, 336-374.

138. See J. E., art. God. Comp. also Encycl. of Religion and Ethics, art. God. Primitive and Biblical; Name of God, Jewish.

139. Gen. XVII, 11; Ex. VI, 3, and commentators; Gen. R. XLVI. The Book of Job, where the name Shaddai is constantly used, refers to the patriarchal age.

140. Ex. III, 14, and commentators, espec. Dillmann. Comp. art. Jahweh in Prot. Realencyc. and Cheyne's Dict.

Bible, art. Names, § 109 ff., where different etymologies are given.

141.

Ex. III, 14.

142.

Ex. XIX, 5, 6.

143.

See Prot. Enc., art. Jahveh, p, 530 f.

144.

See J. E., art. Adonai; Bousset, l. c., 352 f.

145.

Ber. 40 b. On the alleged "Judaisirung des Gottesbegriffs," see Weber, l. c., 148-158.

146.

Sifre to Deut. VI, 4.

147.

Gen. XXIV, 3.

148.

Gen. R. XXIV, 3.

149.

Shab. 87 a, 89 b; Mek. Yithro IV.

150.

See J. E., art. Alenu.

151.

See J. E., art. Abba and Names of God; Weber, l. c, 148 f.; Bousset, II, 356-361; Schechter: Aspects, II, 21-28.

152.

See J. E., art. Heaven; Levy, W. B.: "Shamayim."

153.

See Pes. X, 5; Ber. 16 b; Ab. Zar. 40 b; Gen. R. LXVIII, 9, referring to Gen. XXVIII, 11 and Ex. XXXIII, 21; P. d. R. El. XXXV; Pes. Rab. 104 a; comp. LXX, Ex. XXIV, 10; see also Siegfried: Philo, p. 202, 204, 217; Schechter, l. c., 26, 34. The passage in Mekilta on Ex. XVII, 7, which refers Makom to the Sanhedrin (after Deut. XVII, 8), seems originally to have been a marginal note belonging to Ex. XXI, 13, where Makom is the equivalent of Makam, a place of refuge, and put here at the wrong place by an error;—Against Schechter, l. c., 27 note 1, Bousset (p. 591) thinks that ha Makom for God is Persian, where both space and time were deified. See Spiegel: Eranisches Alterthum, II, 15 f.

154.

See Gen. R. XII, 15; XXX, 3; Targum to Psalm LVI, 11; comp. Philo, I, 496; Siegfried, l. c., 203, 213.

155.

Metaphysical proofs for God's existence have been outlawed since Kant. God is the postulate of man's moral consciousness. See Rauwenhoff, l. c., 236-357.

156.

See art. Atheism, in J. E. and in Enc. Reli. and Ethics, II, 18 f.

157.

Jer. V, 12; Psalm X, 4; XIV, 1; LIII, 1.

158.

B. B. 16 b; Targ. to Gen. IV, 8.

159.

See above, Chapter IV, 3.

160.

Isa. XL, 12-26; XLVI, 10.

161.

See Bousset, l. c., 295-298.

162.

See J. E., art. Abraham.

163.

Ch. XIII.

164.

Philo: De Somniis, I, 43, 44; Zeller: D. Philosophie d. Griechen, III, 2, 307 f.; Drummond: Philo Judæus, II, 4-5.

165.

See D. F. Strauss: Christl. Glaubenslehre, I, 364-399; Windelband: Hist. of Phil., transl. by J. H. Tufts, 2d ed., 1914, p. 54, 98, 128, 327.

166.

See Windelband-Tufts, l. c., 145, 292.

167.

See Strauss, l. c.; Kaufmann, l. c., 2-3, 58; D. Theologie d. Bachya, p. 222 f.; Husik: Hist. Jew. Phil., p. 32 ff., 89 ff.

168.

Kaufmann, l. c., p. 341 f., 431 f.; Husik, l. c., 218 f., 254 f.

169.

See D. F. Strauss, l. c.; Windelband-Tufts, p. 292, 393.

170.

D. F. Strauss, l. c., 375, 394; Windelband-Tufts, l. c., 450.

171.

See Windelband-Tufts, l. c., 549-550.

172.

See Kaufmann, l. c., p. 223 f., and, opposed to him, Neumark: Jehuda Halevi's Philosophy, Cincinnati, 1909. See also Husik, l. c., 157 ff.

173.

Compare C. Seligman: Judenth. u. moderne Anschauung. The philosophy of Bergson, which eliminates design and purpose from the cosmos and places Deity itself into the process as the vital urgent of it all, and thus sees God forever in the making, is pantheistic and un-Jewish, and therefore cannot be considered in a theology of Judaism. This does not exclude our accepting minor elements of his system, which contains suggestive hints. H. G. Wells' God the Invisible King (Macmillan, 1917) is likewise a God in the making, man-made, not the Maker and Ruler of man.

174.

Job XI, 7.

175.

Ex. XXXIII, 23; Maim.; Yesode ha Torah, I, 8, 10; Moreh, I, 21 a; Kaufmann, l. c., 431; Philo: Mutatio Nom., 2; Vita Mosis, I, 28; Leg. All., I, 29, and elsewhere. See J. Drummond: Philo Judæus, II, 18-24.

176.

Ex. R. XXIX, at the close.

177.

Jer. X, 10.

178.

Isaiah XLIV, 6.

179.

Comp. Dillmann, l. c., 226-235; D. F. Strauss, l. c., I, 525-553.

180.

See J. E., art. Anthropomorphism and Anthropopathism. Comp. Schmiedl, l. c., 1-30.

181.

Ps. XXXIII, 13-14.

182.

Deut. IV, 36; Ex. XIX, 20. Comp. Gen. XI, 5.

183.

Isa. XLVI, 1.

184.

Ps. CXXXIX, 7-10.

185.

Ps. XCIV, 9.

186.

See Ab. d. R. Nathan II; Bacher: D. Exegetische Terminologie, I, 8; Schechter, l. c., 35.

187.

Gen. R. XXVII; Mek. Ex. XV; Pes. d. R. K. 109 b; Tanh. to Ex. XXII, 16; Schechter, l. c., 43 f.

188.

Gen. R. IV, 3; comp, Pes. d. R. K. 2 b; Schechter, l. c., 29 f.

189.

Hul. 59, 60; Sanh. 39 a; Philo: De Abrahamo, 16.

190.

Mid. Teh. Ps. CIII, 1; Sanh. 39 a.

191.

See Weber, l. c., 149 f., 157; Bousset, l. c., 302, 313; von Hartman: Das religioese Bewusstsein. Against this Schreiner, l. c., 49-58, and Schechter, Aspects 33 f.

192.

Mek. and Tanh. to Ex. XV, 11.

193.

Deut. IV, 7; Yer. Ber. IX, 13 a.

194.

Isa. LVII, 15. See also Deut. X, 17-18; Ps. LXXXVI, 5-6. Comp. R. Johanan, Meg, 31 a.

195.

Ex. R. II, 9; Mid. Teh. Ps. LXVIII, 7.

196.

Ps. XLVI, 2.

197.

Ab. Zar. 3 b.

198.

Ps. CXIII, 5, 6.

199.

Ber. 60 b. Singer's Prayerbook, 291.

200.

On pantheism in Judaism see Seligman, l. c.

201.

See Sachs: D. religioese Poesie d. Juden. in Spanien, 225-228; Kaufmann: Stud u. Solomon Ibn Gabirol.

202.

See Siegfried: Philo, 199-203, 292; Gen. R. LXVIII, 10; comp. Geiger: Zeitschr., XI, 218; Hamburger: R. W. B., II, 986.

203.

See Graetz: G. d. J., X, 319.

204.

See Maimonides: H. Teshubah, III, 7 and R. A. B. D., notes.

205.

Jer. XXIII, 23.

206.

Isa. XL, 25.

207.

Lev. XIX, 4; XXVI, 1; Isaiah II, 8, 11; Psalm XCVI, 5.

208.

Comp. Ex. XX, 3; XXII, 19; XXIII, 13; with Deut. VI, 4; IV, 35, 39; XXXII, 39; Isaiah XL to XLVIII.

209.

See Dillmann, l. c., 235-241; D. F. Strauss, l. c., 402-408; A. B. Davidson: Theology of O. T., p. 105; 149 f.

210.

Zach. XIV, 9.

211.

Deut. IV, 19; Jer. X, 2.

212.

Bousset, l. c., 221 f., 348.

213.

See Chapter LVI, below.

214.

Isa. XLV, 5-7.

215.

Lam. III, 38.

216.

Shethe Reshuyoth, see Hag. 15 a; Deut. R. I. 10; Eccl. R. II, 12; Weber, l. c., 152; Joel, Blicke in d. Religionsgesch., II, 157.

217.

D. F. Strauss, l. c., 409-501; J. E., art. Christianity.

218.

Meg. 13 a.

219.

Comp. Lange: Gesch. d. Materialismus, I, 149-158.

220.

Alfred v. Kremer, l. c., 9-33; J. E., art. Arabic and Arabic-Jewish Philosophy.

221.

See Draper's Conflict between Religion and Science.

222.

Maim.: Yesode ha Torah, I, 7.

223.

Sachs, l. c., 3.

224.

See Schmiedl, l. c., 239-258.

225.

See Hebrew Dictionary, El; comp. Dillmann, l. c., 210, 244.

226.

See Levy, W. B.: Geburah.

227.

See Septuagint to Job V, 17; VIII, 3, and II Sam. V, 10; VII, 8, and Ber. 31 b.

228.

See Schmiedl, l. c., 67 ff. David Neumark thinks that both the prophet Jeremiah and the Mishnah knew and rejected the belief in angels. See his article Ikkarim in Ozar Ha Yahduth.

229.

Gen. XVIII, 14; Num. XI, 13; Is. XL, 12; Jer. V, 22; X, 12; XXVII, 5; XXXII, 17; Zach. VIII, 6; Job XXXVIII, 7; XLII, 1.

230.

Deut. III. 24; XI, 3; XXVI, 8; XXIX, 2; Jer. X, 6; Ps. LXV, 7; LXVI, 7; LXIV-LXXVIII; I Chron. XXIX, 11, 12.

231.

Ex. XII, 12; Judges V, 10.

232.

Daniel IV, 35.

233.

Ps. XI, 4; XXXIII, 13 f.; CXXXIX; Jer. XI, 20; XVII, 10; Job XII, 13; Dan. II, 20 f.

234.

Aboth II, 1.

235.

Mal. III, 16; Ps. LVI, 9.

236.

See New Year liturgy, Singer's Prayerbook, 249.

237.

Amos III, 7.; Gen. XVIII, 17.

238.

Gen. VI, 5; XI, 5; XVIII, 21.

239.

Isa. LV, 8, 9.

240.

Gen. IV, 16; XI, 5; XVIII, 21; XXVIII, 16; Deut. XXVI, 15; Micah I, 3; see Strauss, l. c., I, 548 f.

241.

I Kings VIII, 27; Isa. LXVI, 1.

242.

See above, Chapter XII, 5.

243.

Comp. Amos IX, 2; Jer. XXIII, 24.

244.

Sanh. 39 a.

245.

Comp. Kaufmann, l. c., 70 and 71, notes 130, 131; Strauss, l. c., I, 551.

246.

Makom, see above, Chapter X, 8-9; Schechter, Aspects, 26 f.

247.

Luk. 45 b; comp. I Corinth. XIII, 12, based on Ex. XXXIII, 28; Ps. XVII, 15.

248.

See Kaufmann, l. c., 100 f.

249.

Isa. XLVIII, 12; Ps. XC, 2 f.; CII, 26, 27. On the process of development of the idea of eternity, see Neumark, l. c., II, 77.

250.

Adon Olam, Singer's Prayerbook, p. 3.

251.

See Strauss, l. c., 562, 651; Kaufmann, l. c., 306 f.; Drummond: Philo, II, 46.

252.

See Chapter XXV below.

253.

Tanh. Naso ed. Buber, 8; Gen. R. IX, 9 with reference to Jer. XXIII, 24.

254.

Lev. XIX, 1.

255.

Comp. Dillmann, l. c., 252 f.; Strauss, l. c., 593 f.; Rauwenhoff, l. c., 498-505; Lazarus: Ethics of Judaism, Chapters IV-V.

256.

I Sam. II, 21.

257.

Ps. LXXVII, 14.

258.

Deut. X, 12; XI, 22, and elsewhere.

259.

Gen. XVIII, 19.

260.

Ex. XXXIII, 13-23.

261.

See J. E., art. Holiness. The Assyrian Kuddisu denotes "bright," "pure," according to Zimmern in Religion und Sprache, K. A. T., 3d ed., 603.

262.

Deut. XXXIII, 3; Job V, 1; VI, 10; XV, 15; Ps. LXXXIX, 6, 8.

263.

Ex. XIX, 21 f.; XXIV, 17; I Sam. VI, 20; Josh. XXIV, 19; Isa. IV, 3; VI, 3, 13; X, 17; XXXI, 9; XXXIII, 14; Hab. I, 13.

264.

Deut. IV, 24; Ex. XXIV, 17.

265.

Comp. the name Kadesh and Kedesha for the hierodules consecrated to Astarte. See Deut. XXIII, 18; I Kings XIV, 24; XV, 12; Hosea IV, 14. Comp. Zimmern, l. c., p. 423.

266.

Isa. I, 4; V, 12; X, 20; XII, 6; XLI, 14; XLIII, 3 f.; XLV, 11; and elsewhere.

267.

Ezek. XX, 12; XXXVII, 28; Ex. XXXI, 13, and elsewhere.

268.

See Sifra and Rabba to Lev. XIX, 2.

269.

Cusari IV, 3; Kaufmann, l. c., 162 f.

270.

Aboth, I, 3.

271.

Rauwenhoff, l. c., 504.

272.

Hab. I, 13.

273.

Psalm XXIV, 4-5.

274.

L. Lazarus: Z. Characteristik d. juedisch. Ethik, 40-45; M. Lazarus: Ethics of Judaism, p. 184.

275.

Isa. V, 16.

276.

Comp. Dillmann, l. c., 258 f.; J. E., art. "Anger."

277.

Ex. XX, 5; Isa. XXX, 27 f.; Nahum I, 5 f.

278.

Ex. XXII, 23; Num. XVII, 10 f.; XXV, 3; Deut. XXIX, 19; XXXII, 21; Isa. IX, 16.

279.

Hosea XI, 9.

280.

Psalm XXX.

281.

Targum to Ex. XX, 3; Sanh. 27 b.

282.

Isa. XXXIII, 14-17.

283.

Mal. III, 2, 19 f.

284.

Deut. XXXII, 35; comp. Sifre, 325; Geiger: Urschrift, 247, regarding Samaritan text. Zeph. I, 15; Isa. LXVI, 15-16.

285.

Isa. XVLI, 24.

286.

See J. E., art. "Gehenna"; Mid. Teh. to Ps. LXXVI, 11, and LXXIX; Ned. 32 a; Taan. 9 b; Yer. Taan. II, 65 b; Ab. Zar. 4 a and b; 18 b; Ber. 7 a; Shab. 118 a; Sanh. 110 b; Gen. R. VI, 9; XXVI, 11, et al.; comp. Romans II, 5; Eph. V, 6; I Thess. I, 10.

287.

Sibyll. II, 170, 285; III, 541, 556 f., 672-697, 760, 810; Enoch XCI, 7-9.

288.

Ber. 10 a; Midr. Teh. to Ps. CIV, 35.

289.

Tan. 23 b.

290.

Cusari IV, 5; Moreh I, 36, and Commentary to Sanh. X, I.

291.

Testament of Abraham, A, X.

292.

Hab. III, 2.

293.

Ezek. XVIII, 23, 32; XXXIII, 11.

294.

Ex. XXXII-XXXIV, 7. Comp. Num. XIV, 18.

295.

Gen. XIX, 1-28; Ex. XX, 5-6.

296.

Hosea I-III; XI, 1-9; XIV, 5. Comp. Micah XIII, 18; Jer. III, 8-12; Isa. LIV, 6-8; LVII, 16 f.; Joel II, 13; Jonah IV, 2, 10 f.; Lam. III, 31; Ps. LXXVIII, 38 et al. See Dillmann, l. c., 263 f.; Davidson Theology of O. T., 132 f.

297.

Gen. VI, 6; I Sam. XV, 11; Jer. XVIII, 7-10; Joel II, 14; Jonah III, 10; IV, 2.

298.

Num. XXIII, 19; I Sam. XV, 29; see Targum and commentaries.

299.

See J. E., art. Anthropomorphism and Allegorical Interpretation.

300.

Tanh. Waethhanan, ed. Buber, 3.

301.

Gen. R. VIII, 4-5. See Morris Joseph: Judaism as Creed and Life, p. 59, 90-95.

302.

R. h. Sh. 17 b; compare, J. Davidson, 134; Koeberle: Suende und Gnade, 1905, p. 625, 634 f.; but p. 658, 614, are misleading; Weber, l. c., 154, 260, 303 f., altogether misrepresents the Jewish doctrine of grace.

303.

Gen. XVIII, 19.

304.

Gen. XVIII, 25.

305.

Jer. XII, 1.

306.

Ps. LXXIII, 12.

307.

Job X, 22 f.

308.

Yer. Hag. II, 1; Elisha ben Abuyah.

309.

Ps. LXXXIX, 15.

310.

Ps. XXXVI, 7; see Davidson, l. c., 143 f.; J. E., art. Justice; Hamburger: Realencyclopaedie, art. Gerechtigkeit; Dillmann, l. c., 270 f.; Strauss, l. c., 596-604. Bousset, 437 f., is misleading.

311.

Deut. XXXII, 4.

312.

Tanh., Jithro 5.

313.

Deut. X, 17-18.

314.

Deut. I, 17.

315.

Yeb. 92 a; Yer. Sanh. I, 18 b.

316.

Amos V, 24; Isa. I, 17, 28; XXVIII, 17; LIV, 14.

317.

Ps. V, 5-6.

318.

Isa. LXVI, 16.

319.

Ps. XCIX, 4; Tanh. Mishpatim 1.

320.

Ps. XCVI, 13; XCVIII, 9.

321.

See Bousset, l. c., 357-366; Weber, l. c., 259-279, and comp. Suk. 30 a, where it is stated, referring to Isa. LXI, 8, that "good deeds can never justify evil acts."

322.

Hosea VI, 6; Ps. XXXVII, 6; I Sam. II, 9.

323.

Sota I, 7-8; Tos. Sota III; Mek. Shirah 4; B. Wisdom XV, 3; XIX, 17 Jubilees IV, 3, elsewhere, comp. Math. VII, 2, and parallels.

324.

Aboth IV, 2.

325.

See Levy, W. B.: Zidduk; comp. Ex. IX, 27; Lam. I, 18; Neh. IX, 33.

326.

Gen. R. XLIX, 19; Yoma 37 a.

327.

Prov. X, 25.

328.

See Tos. Sanh. XIII, 2; Sanh. 105 a; Yalkut Isaiah 296; Crescas: Or Adonai, III, 44.

329.

Gen. R. VIII, 4-5; XII, 15; Midr. Teh. to Ps. LXXXIX, 2; comp. Ben Sira, XVIII, 11; Testaments of XII Patr.: Zebulon 9; Ap. Baruch XLVIII, 14; IV Esdras VIII, 31; Psalms of Solomon IX, 7; Prayer of Manasseh, 8, 13.

330.

See J. E., art. "Love." Both Weber, l. c., 57 f. and Bousset, l. c., 443 f. show Christian bias.

331.

Ps. CXXX, 4.

332.

Aboth III, 19; comp. B. Wisdom XI, 23, 26; XII, 16, 18; Ben Sira, II, 18.

333.

Ps. CXLIV, 8-9; comp. Ben Sira, XVIII, 13.

334.

Tos. Sanh. XIII, 3.

335.

Yer. R. h. Sh. I, 57 a.

336.

Ber. 7 a.

337.

Tos. Sota IV, 1, with reference to Ex. XX, 5-6. The plural, laalafim, is taken to mean two thousand.

338.

Ex. XXII, 26; comp. 21, 23.

339.

See Harper: Code of Hammurabi, 1900; Oettli: D. Gesetz Hammurabis und d. Thora Israels, 1903; Cohn: D. Gesetz Hammurabis, Zürich, 1903; Grimm: D. Gesetz Chammurabis und Moses, Cologne, 1903. Also M. Jastrow, Hebrew and Babylonian Traditions, p. 255-319.

340.

Deut. X, 18; Ps. LXXIII.

341.

Isa. XXV, 4.

342.

Ex. XXII, 24.

343.

Ex. R. XXVII, 5; Eccles. R. to III, 15.

344.

Gen. XXIV, 19.

345.

Ex. XXIII, 5.

346.

Deut. XXV, 4.

347.

Lev. XX, 28; Deut. XXII, 6.

348.

Git. 62 a, with reference to Deut. XI, 15.

349.

Ps. CXLV, 9.

350.

B. M. 85 a; Yer. Kil. IX, 4.

351.

Tos. B. K. IX, 30; Sifre, Deut. 96.

352.

Sifre, Deut. § 49; Shab. 133 b; comp. Philo: De Humanitate.

353.

See Concordance to ahabah and hesed. Note especially Hos. VI, 6.

354.

Hos. III, 1; XI, 1, 4; XIV, 5.

355.

Jer. XXXI, 2, 19.

356.

Deut. VII, 8; X, 15.

357.

Deut. VIII, 5; see Sifre, Deut. 32.

358.

Prov. III, 13.

359.

Ber. 5 a; Sifre, l. c.; Mek. Yithro 10.

360.

See Mek. and Sifre, l. c.

361.

Ex. IV, 22.

362.

Deut. XXXII, 6, 10 f.

363.

Jer. II, 2.

364.

Song of Songs, R. to III, 7. Comp. Davidson, l. c., 235-287.

365.

See Schreiner, l. c., 103-112; Perles: Bousset, 58 f.

366.

Pesik, 16-17; Mek. Yithro 6, at end.

367.

Aboth III, 14.

368.

XI, 23-26.

369.

IV Esdra VIII, 47.

370.

III, 10.

371.

Zohar I, 44 b; II, 97 a.

372.

See Or Adonai, I, 3, 5, and Joel: Crescas 36-37.

373.

Dialoghi di Amore; see Zimmels: Leo Hebraeus, 1886.

374.

Ethics V, proposition XXXV.

375.

"The Theosophy of Julius": "God."

376.

Middath tobah.

377.

Gen. I, 4, 10, 12, 18, 21, 23, 31.

378.

Gen. R. IX, 5, 9; Ber. 60 a; Yer. Ber. IX, 13 c-14 b; Taan. 21 a.

379.

Isa. LXV, 16.

380.

Deut. XXXII, 40.

381.

Deut. XXXII, 4.

382.

Num. XXIII, 19; Isa. XL, 8; Jer. X, 10; Ps. XXXI, 6; comp. Dillmann, l. c. 269 f.

383.

Ps. XXXVI, 6; LXXXIX, 3, 38; CXLVI, 6; Benediction at seeing the rainbow, Singer's Prayerbook, p. 291.

384.

Gen. IX, 11.

385.

Ps. CIV, 9; Job XXXVIII, 11; Jer. XXXI, 34.

386.

Deut. XXXIII, 27.

387.

Jer. X, 10, 15.

388.

Emuna Rama 54. See Kaufmann, l. c., 333 f., 352 f.; comp. Guttmann: Religionsphilosophie des Ibn Daud, 136 f.; Albo II, 27, at the end; Maimonides: Yesode ha Torah, I, 3-4; Hillel of Verona refers even to Aristotle's "Metaphysics." See Kaufmann, l. c., 334, note; Neumark, l. c., and Husik., l. c. passim.

389.

See Yer. Sanh. I, 18 a.

390.

Contra Apionem, II, 22; compare J. E., art. "Alpha and Omega."

391.

See Yer. Sanh. I, 18 a.

392.

Ber. 33 b.

393.

Jedayah ha Penini.

394.

Ps. LXV, 2.

395.

Jer. X, 12; Amos IV, 13; Job XXXVIII-XXXIX.

396.

Prov. VI, 6.

397.

Job XXXVIII-XXXIX.

398.

Ps. CIV, 24.

399.

Gen. L, 20; see Dillmann, l. c., 280; Strauss, l. c., 575 f.; Hamburger, l. c., art. "Weisheit Gottes"; A. B. Davidson, l. c., 180-182.

400.

Gen. XLI, 38; I Kings III, 12; Ex. XXXV, 31; Prov. II, 6.

401.

Isa. XXV, 1; XXVII, 29.

402.

Isa. XL-LV.

403.

Prov. IX, 1. Comp. A. Jeremias: D. A. Test. i. L. d. i. alt. Orients, 5, 80, 336, 367.

404.

Ben Sira XXIV, 3-6, 14, 21; Enoch XLII, 1-2; Slavonic Enoch XXX, 8; Baruch III, 9-IV, 4; comp. Bousset, l. c., 337 f.; J. E., art. Wisdom; Bentwich: Philo, pp. 141-147.

405.

Targ. Ver. to Gen. I, 1. Gen. R. I. 2, 5. See Schechter: Aspects, 127-137.

406.

Kaufmann, l. c., 16, 107, 113, 163, 325, 418.

407.

Job IX, 4; Cuzari, II, 2.

408.

Sachs, cl, 6, 227.

409.

Ps. XVIII, 36.

410.

Meg. 35 a.

411.

Isa. LVII, 15.

412.

Deut. X, 17-18.

413.

Ps. LXVIII, 5-6.

414.

Ps. CXIII, 5-6.

415.

Weber, l. c., 154.

416.

Deut. IV, 7; Yer. Ber. IX, 19 a, where the plural, Kerobim, suggests the idea, "all kinds of nearness."

417.

Ps. XXIX, 4; Tanh. Yithro, ed. Buber, 17.

418.

Ps. XCI, 15; Isa. LXIII, 9; Sifre Num. 84.

419.

Ber. 6 a; 7 a; R. ha Sh. 17 b; Hag. 5 b; Sanh. 39 a. Comp. Schechter, Aspects, p. 21-50.

420.

Weber, l. c., 157-160.

421.

Plutarch: "De placitis philosophiae," II, 1; comp. for the entire chapter Dillmann, l. c., 284-295; Smend: 1. c., 454 f.; H. Steinthal: "Die Idee der Schöpfung" in J. B. z. Jued. Gesch. u. Lit., II, 39-44.

422.

Ps. XXXIII, 9.

423.

Job XXXVIII; Ps. CIV.

424.

Comp. Albo I, 12, and Schlesinger's Notes, 625.

425.

Ps. CII, 25-27.

426.

Job XXV, 2.

427.

Ber. 60 b.

428.

Gam su le tobah, an allusion to his own name. Taan. 21 b.

429.

Gen. R. IX, 5.

430.

Gen. R. IX, 9-10.

431.

Sifre Deut. 307.

432.

Jer. X, 11-12 and 10.

433.

See his commentary to Gen. I, 1; comp. Neumark, l. c., I, 70, 71, 80 f., 87, 412, 439, 515; Husik, l. c., p. 190; D. Strauss, l. c., 619-660.

434.

II Macc. VII, 28.

435.

Gen. R. I, 12; X. 3; Hag. II b-13 a; Slavonic Enoch, XXV; see J. E., art. Cosmogony and Creation; Enc. Rel. and Eth., 151 ff., 167 f.

436.

Gen. R. IX, 1.

437.

See Strauss, l. c., 645 f.

438.

See Schmiedl, l. c., 91-128; Kaufmann, l. c., 280 f., 306, 387 f.

439.

See C. Seligman, Judenthum und Moderne Weltanchauung.

440.

The first benediction before the Shema.

441.

Gen. VII, 11; VIII, 2.

442.

Isa. XL, 26.

443.

Job XXXVI, 6.

444.

Job XXXVIII, 25.

445.

Gen. XX, 17-18; XXX, 22.

446.

Ps. CXLVII, 8-9.

447.

Ps. CIV, 27-30.

448.

Gen. I, 11.

449.

Ps. CIV, 8.

450.

Gen. VIII, 22; Job XXXVIII, 33.

451.

Jer. XXXI, 39; XXXIII, 25.

452.

Gen. IX, 12 f.

453.

Job XXV, 2.

454.

See Dillmann, l. c., 295 f.; D. Strauss, l. c., 629-643.

455.

Enoch LXIX, 15-25; Prayer of Manasseh, 3; Suk. 53 a b; Hag. 12 a.

456.

See Singer's Prayerbook, 37, 96, 290, 292.

457.

Ps. CIII, 20.

458.

Shab. 119 b.

459.

Ps. CII, 27; Isa. XXXIV, 4.

460.

Isa. LXV, 17.

461.

See J. E. and Enc. of Rel. and Eth., art. "Eschatology"; Schuerer, G. V. I. II, 545.

462.

Ex. XV, 11.

463.

Oth, sign for miracle, Ex. IV, 8, 17, and elsewhere.

464.

Mopheth, Ex. VII, 3, and elsewhere.

465.

Gen. XVIII, 14.

466.

Num. XI, 23.

467.

Ex. XXXIV, 10; Num. XVI, 30.

468.

Ex. IV, 11.

469.

Josh. X, 12-14. See Joel: "D. Mosaismus u. d. Wunder," in Jb. d. Jued. Gesch. u. Lit., 1904, p. 66-94.

470.

Mek. Beshallah 3; Gen. R. V, 4.

471.

Aboth V, 6; comp. Ab. d. R. N., ed. Schechter, 95; Mek. Beshallah, 5; Sifre Debarim, 355; Pes. 54 a; P. d. R. Eli., XIX; Targ. Y. to Num. XXII, 28, where a different list of ten wondrous things is given.

472.

Emunoth we Deoth II, 44, 68. Comp. Ibn Ezra to Gen. III, 1, and Num. XXII, 28.

473.

Moreh, II, 25, 35, 37; III, 24; Yesode ha Torah, VII, 7; VIII, 1-3. Comp. Joel: Moses Maimonides, p. 77.

474.

Ikkarim, I, 18.

475.

Or Adonai, III, 5; comp. Joel: Don Chasdai Crescas, p. 70.

476.

Milhamoth Adonai, last chapters; comp. J. E., art. Levi ben Gershom.

477.

Cuzari, II, 54.

478.

The Anshe maaseh, mentioned together with the Hasidim in Suk. V, 4, and Sot. IX, 15, are wonderworkers, of whom Haninah ben Dosa, the last, is singled out. The same epithet was given to Simeon ben Yochai in Aramaic, Iskan, see Lev. Rabba XXII, 2, and to R. Assi, eod. XIX, 1,—where it means, worker in nature's realm. Thus Nahum of Gimzo is called "trained in the skill to perform miracles"—Taan. 21 a; Phinehas ben Jair was also a wonderworker—Hul. 7 a. The whole portion regarding rain-miracles seems to be taken from a work on the miracles of saints.

479.

Taan, 18 b.

480.

Pes. 118 a; Ned. 41 a.

481.

Shab. 53 b.

482.

Ab. Za. IV, 7; comp. Ber. 4 a, 20 a; Sanh. 97 b.

483.

B. M. 59 b.

484.

Deut. XIII, 2-6.

485.

Yesode ha Torah, VIII, 1-5.

486.

Ikkarim, I, 18.

487.

Mendelssohn: G. Sch., III, 65, 120 f., 320 f.

488.

II Kings VI, 6.

489.

Joshua X, 13.

490.

Moreh, II, 33.

491.

The Hebrew term Hashgaha—Providence—is derived from Ps. XXXIII, 14, hishgiah, "He observes." See J. E., art. Providence; Davidson, l. c., 178-182; Hamburger, R. W. B. II, art. Bestimmung; Rauwenhoff, l. c., 538 f.; Ludwig Philippson: "Israel. Religionsl.," II, 98 f.; Formstecher: "Religion des Geistes," 114-119.

492.

Jer. X, 2. See art. Divination, in J. E.; Dict. Bible; Enc. R. and Eth.

493.

See Lev. XVI, 8 f.; Num. XXVI, 56; Josh. XVIII-XIX; Prov. XVIII, 18.

494.

Ex. XVIII, 30; I Sam. see LXX; XIV, 41.

495.

Ex. XXXIII, 32; Ps. LVI, 9; CXXXIX, 16; comp., however, the Babylonian "tables of destinies."

496.

Isa. XL, 21; XLI, 4, 22 f.; Amos III, 7.

497.

Isa. LIV, 16.

498.

Isa. X, 5, 15.

499.

Isa. VIII. 11; Ps. II, 2 f.; Deut. XXIII, 6.

500.

Jer. X, 33.

501.

Aboth III, 15.

502.

Hul. 7 a.

503.

Gen. XXIV, 50; M. K. 18 b.

504.

Ch. XXXIV.

505.

Ber. 33 b.

506.

R. h. Sh. 17 b; New Year's liturgy.

507.

H. Teshubah, V, 1-2.

508.

See, on the Zagmuk festival, Zimmern, K. A. T., p. 514 f.

509.

Tos. R. h. Sh, I, 13; R. h. Sh. 16 a.

510.

Saadia: Emunoth, IV, 7; Bahya: Hoboth ha Lebaboth, III, 8; IV, 3.

511.

H. Teshubah V; Moreh, I, 23; III, 16-19; comp. Cuzari, V, 20-21; Albo: Ikkarim, IV, 1-11; Gersonides: Milhamoth, III, 2; VI, 1-18; Isaac ben Shesheth: Responsa, 119; Lipman Heller to Aboth III, 15. See Joel: Levi ben Gerson, p. 56.

512.

See Or Adonai, II, 3; comp. Joel: Hasdai Crescas, 41-49, 54-55; Neumark: "Crescas and Spinoza," in Y. B. C. C. A. R., 1908, vol. XVIII, p. 277-319.

513.

Or Adonai, III, 24.

514.

Gen. R. LXXIX, 16; comp. Matt. X, 29.

515.

B. B. 16 a; comp. Matt. X, 30; Luke XII, 7.

516.

Deut. XXXII, 11.

517.

Mek. Yithro 2; Sifre ad loc.

518.

Shab. 119 b.

519.

Ps. XLVI, 2; CXXI, 4.

520.

See David Kaufmann: "Theol. d. B. b. Pakudah," p. 240.

521.

Mid. Teh. to Ps. XXXIV; L. Ginzberg, Legends of the Jews, IV, 89-90; Alphabet of Ben Sira.

522.

Comp. Maasehhbuch; Tendlau: Sagen d. jued. Vorzeit.

523.

See Gen. R. IX, 5, 10, 11; Dillmann, l. c., 309-318; D. F. Strauss, l. c., II, 343-384.

524.

Shab. 55 a.

525.

Ber. 5 a, after Deut. VIII, 5; Prov. III, 12.

526.

Isa. XLV, 7.

527.

Deut. XI, 27; see the Midrash ad loc.

528.

Emunah Ramah, ed. Weil, 93 f.; Moreh, III, 10.

529.

See M. Lefkovitz, "The Attitude of Judaism to Christian Science," in Y. B. C. C. A. R. XXII, 300-318.

530.

See Morris Joseph, l. c., p. 108, 127 ff.; C. Seligman, l. c., 50-68.

531.

Gen. VI, 2; Job I, 6; II, 1; XXXIII, 7; Gen. XXXII, 29; XXXIII, 10; Jud. XIII, 22; Ps. VIII, 6.

532.

Comp. Mek. Yithro 7 through 10; Hul. 40; Tos. Hul. II, 18; Ab. Z. 42 b; Maimonides to Sanh. X; Targ. Y. to Ex. XX, 3.

533.

Deut. IV, 39.

534.

Deut. XXXII, 39.

535.

Isa. XLIV, 24; XL, 5.

536.

Gen. XVIII and XVII, 11, 13.

537.

Gen. VI, 1 f.

538.

Comp. Ezek. XXVIII, 13 f.

539.

Ps. LXXVIII, 25.

540.

See Dillmann, l. c., 318-333; Davidson, l. c., 289-300; J. E., art. Angelology; Enc. Rel. and Eth. IV, 594-601, art. Demons.

541.

Lev. XVII, 7; Deut. XXXII, 17; Isa. XXXIV, 14.

542.

Gen. XVIII.

543.

Ex. XXIII, 20; II Sam. XXIV, 16; II Kings XIX, 35 et al. See J. E., art. Angelology.

544.

Ex. III, 2-4; XXIII, 20-21; Isa. LXIII, 9.

545.

Zech. I, 9 f.; II, 1 f.

546.

See J. E., art. Angelology.

547.

Ezek. I, 4-24; X, 1-22; Isa. VI, 2; Dan. IV, 10 f.; VII, 9 f.; VIII, 16 f.; X, 13 f; Enoch XV, 1 f., and elsewhere.

548.

See J. E., art. Merkabah, though still doubted by Bousset, l. c., p. 406. For Akathriel see Ber. 7 and J. E., art. Sandalfon.

549.

Jubilees II, 2; Slav. Enoch. XXIX, 3; I, 3; Gen. R, III, 11.

550.

Yer. Ber. IX; Sanh. 93 a; Hul. 91 b; Ned. 32 a; Gen. R. VIII, XXI; Midr. Teh. to Ps. CIII, 18; CIV, 1.

551.

Neumark, l. c.

552.

Schmiedl, l. c., 69-87.

553.

Yesode ha Torah, II, 4-9; Moreh, I, 43; II, 3-7, 41; III, 13; Husik, l. c., 303 f.

554.

Emunoth, IV, 1; VI, 2; Hoboth ha Lebaboth, I, 6; Cuzari, IV, 3; Emunah Ramah, IV, 2; VI, 1; Ikkarim, II, 28, 31.

555.

Zohar, III, 68; Joel: Religionsphilosophie des Zohar, 278 f.

556.

Ned. 20 b; Midr. Teh. Ps. CIII, 17-18; Ibn Ezra: Introduction to his commentary on the Pentateuch.

557.

Compare Gen. R. to Gen. I, 31.

558.

Ps. CIII, 19-20.

559.

Job I, 6.

560.

See J. E., art. Demonology; Satan; Belial; Enc. Rel. and Eth., art. Demons and Spirits, Jewish; Davidson, l. c., 300-306; Dillmann, l. c., 334-340; D. F. Strauss, l. c., II, 1-18.

561.

Lev. XVII, 7; Deut. XXXII, 17; Isa. XIII, 21; XXXIV, 14.

562.

Lev. XVI, 8; see Ibn Ezra; J. E. and Enc. Rel. and Eth., art. Azazel.

563.

J. E., art. Beelzebub.

564.

J. E., art. Belial.

565.

Enoch VI, 7; J. E., art. Ashmodai; Levy: W. B., Shemachzai.

566.

Levy: W. B., Lilith; Iggereth.

567.

J. E., art. Demonology.

568.

Aboth V, 6; P. d. R. El., XIX; Gen. R. VII, 7.

569.

Enoch VII; Yalkut Gen. 44, 47.

570.

Erubin, 18 b.

571.

P. d. R. El., XIII; Yalkut Gen. 25.

572.

See Abrahams' Ann. to Singers' Prayerb. XLIV f. and for the Church, Enc. Rel, and Eth., Demons and Spirits, Christian.

573.

Abrahams, l. c., p. 7, 196; XX, CCXV.

574.

Ps. CIX, 6.

575.

Zech. III, 1; Job I, 6.

576.

I Chron. XXI, 1.

577.

See B. Wisdom II, 24; P. d. R. El., XIII.

578.

Shab. 146 a; Yeb. 103 b; Ab. Zar. 22 b.

579.

Suk. 52 a.

580.

Targ. to Isa. XI, 4.

581.

B. B. 16 a.

582.

De Gigantibus, 2-4.

583.

Sifra Lev. XVI, 8; Yoma, 67 b.

584.

See the Ethiopic "Adam and Eve"; C. Bezold, Die Schalzhochle, p. 18; comp. Gen. R. XXVI.

585.

See D. Cassel: Cuzari, p. 402 note.

586.

Moreh III, 29-37, 46; Ibn Ezra to Job I, 6; comp. Finkelscherer: Maimunis' Stellung zum Aberglauben, 1894, p. 40-51.

587.

Christliche Glaubenslehre, II, 18.

588.

Euken, D. Wahrheitsgehalt d. Religion, p. 384, 402; Bousset, Wesen d. Rel., p. 239.

589.

See H. Cohen: Ethik des reinen Willens, 282 f., 341 f., 428 f., 593: "Eine Macht des Boesen gibt es nur im Mythos." "Dieser Mythos fuehrt folgerichtig sum mythologischen Gottmenschen." M. Joel, in his article, "Der Mosaismus und das Heidenthum," in J. B. j. Gesch. u. Lit, 1904, p. 49-66, ascribes the belief in demons to Greek influence. He holds that the prophetic teaching of God's unity was the best bulwark against demonology and mysticism.

590.

See Dillmann, l. c., 341-351; Weber, l. c., 177-190; Bousset, l. c., 336, 346; Davidson, l. c, 36-38, 115-129; Schechter, Aspects, p. 21-45; Schmiedl, l. c., 35-48; J. E., art. Holy Spirit; Logos; Memra; Metatron; Name of God; Shekinah; Enc. Rel. and Eth., I, 308-312.

591.

Ps. LXXXII, 1.

592.

Ex. XXV, 8.

593.

Ber. 17 a.

594.

See Ber., l. c., Rab's reference to Ex. XXIV, 11.

595.

John I, 1-6.

596.

Singer's Prayerbook, p. 96, 292.

597.

Ch. XXII. See Prov. VIII, 22.

598.

XXIV, 9 f.

599.

Weber, l. c., 197 f.

600.

L. c., 178 f.

601.

See Kohut: Jued, Angelologie, 36-38; Schorr: He Halutz, VIII, 3; J. E., art. Merkabah.

602.

See Targ. Yer. to Gen. V, 24; J. E., art. Metatron. Comp. Eth. Enoch LXX, 1, and Slav. Enoch III-XXIV.

603.

Gen. I, 2.

604.

Gen. II, 7; VI, 3; Job XXXII, 8.

605.

Num. XI, 17 f.; XXIV, 2; XXVII, 18; Ex. XXVIII, 3; XXXI, 3 f.; Isa. XI, 2; LXI, 1; Ezek. I, 12, 20.

606.

Isa. LXIII, 10; Ps. LI, 13.

607.

See J. E., art. Holy Spirit.

608.

See J. E. art., Bath Kol.

609.

See Tos. Sota XIII, 2; XXLV, 11; compare Levy: W. B., Shem; Geiger: Urschrift, 273 f.

610.

Deut. XII, 5, 11; II Sam. XII, 28; Neh. I, 9; Jer. VII, 12, 14.

611.

Ex. XXIII, 21.

612.

Jer. XLIV, 26; Isa. XLV, 23.

613.

Midr. Teh. to Ps. XXXVIII, 8; XCI, 8.

614.

Taan. III, 8.

615.

Prayer of Manasses, 3.

616.

P. d. R. El. III.

617.

See Levy: W. B., Geburah.

618.

Ex. XXI, 6.

619.

Ex. XXXIV, 5 f.

620.

Gen. R. XXI, 8; Targ. Ps. LVI, 11, and see Siegfried: Philo, 213 f.

621.

Gen. R. VIII, 5, after Ps. LXXXV, 11-12.

622.

P. d. R. El. III; Midr. Teh. Ps. L, 1, ref. to Prov. III, 19-20.

623.

A. d. N. XXXVII, ref. to Prov. III, 19 f.; Ps. LXV, 7; LXXXV, 21-22; Job XXVII, 11.

624.

Ref. to Hosea II, 21-22.

625.

Hag. 12 a.

626.

See J. E., art. Sefiroth, the Ten; Yezirah, Sefer.

627.

See J. E., art. Shekinah; Cuzari, II, 4; IV, 3.

628.

Gen. I, 26, and the commentaries.

629.

Gen. R. VIII, 9.

630.

Gen. R. XIV, 1.

631.

Gen. I, 28.

632.

Gen. R. VIII, 12; P. d. R. El., XI.

633.

Sanh. IV, 5, correctly preserved in the Yerushalmi, and the addition in the Babli, Me Yisrael, ought not to have been inserted by Schechter, Ab. d. R.N., p. 90.

634.

Lev. R. XXXIV, 3.

635.

Ab. d. R. N. XXXI.

636.

See Jubilees XV, 27; comp. Gen. R. VIII, 7-9; Ab. d. R. N., ed. Schechter, p. 153.

637.

See Jellinek: Bezelem Elohim; Philippson, l. c., II, 58-72; Dillmann, l. c., 325. The words of Plato (State, X, 613, and Theætetos, 176), "Man should strive for God-likeness through virtue, and be holy, righteous and wise like the Deity," may have influenced the ethical interpretation of the Biblical term.

638.

Gen. R. VIII, 1.

639.

See Gen. I, 26; Comm. of Rashi, Saadia, Ibn Ezra, Nahmanides, and Ob. Sforno.

640.

Job XXXII, 8.

641.

Zach. III, 7; see comm.

642.

Gen. VI, 12, 19.

643.

Gen. IX, 21; Lev. XVII, 11, 14.

644.

See Dillmann, l. c., 355-361; Davidson, l. c., 182-203; comp. Gen. R. XIV, 11, where these three terms are given, and also yehidah, Ps. XXII, 21; XXXV, 17, and hayah, Ps. XCLIII, 3; Job XXXIII, 1.

645.

De Leg. Alleg. III, 38.

646.

See Horovitz: D. Psychologie Saadias; Scheyer: D. psycholog. System d. Maimonides; Cassel's Cuzari, p. 382-400; Husik, l. c., IX, 41; and see also Index: Soul.

647.

Sanh. 91 a, b; Nid. 30 b-31 b; Sifre Deut. 306, ref. to Deut. XXXII, 1; Lev. IV, 5-8.

648.

Ab. Z. 5 a; Gen. R. VIII, 1.

649.

B. Wisdom, VIII, 20; Slav. Enoch XXIII, 5; Philo I, 15, 32; II, 356; comp. Bousset, l. c., p. 508 f.

650.

Gen. VI, 5; VIII, 21; B. Sira XV, 14; XVII, 31; XXI, 11; Ber. 5 a; Kid. 30 b; Suk. 52 a, b; Shab. 152 b; Eccl. R. XII, 7; comp. F. Ch. Porter: "The Yezer ha Ra" in Biblical and Semitic Studies, 93-156; Bousset, l. c., 462 f.

651.

Suk. 52 a, b.

652.

Gen. R. VIII, 11.

653.

Ab. d. R. N. XXXI.

654.

Aboth III, 18.

655.

Ber. 10 a; Midr. Teh. Ps. CIII, 4-5.

656.

Gen. XVIII, 19; Deut. VIII, 6; X, 12; XXXII, 4.

657.

Micah VI, 8.

658.

Gen. V. 22; VI, 9; XVII, 1-2.

659.

Gen. R. XII, 8; XIV, 6, ref. to Josh. XIV, 15.

660.

Ezek. XXVIII, 14.

661.

Prov. III, 18.

662.

Gen. R. XVI, 10; Shab. 55 b.

663.

B. B. 15 a.

664.

Shab. 146 a; Yeb. 103 b; Ab. Zar. 22 b; Shab. 55 b.

665.

B. Wisdom, II, 24.

666.

Romans V, 12 f.

667.

Shab. 146 a.

668.

Deut. XXIV, 16; Ezek. XVIII, 4.

669.

Shab. 55 a, b.

670.

Shab. 32 b.

671.

B. Sira XXV, 24.

672.

Yer. Shab. II, 5 b.

673.

Gen. R. XIX, 10, ref. to Gen. III, 6-7.

674.

Apoc. Baruch XXIII, 4; XLVIII, 42 f.; LVI, 6; and especially LIV, 14-19; IV Esdras III, 7; VII, 11, 118.

675.

Pesik. 160 b; Num. R. XIII, 5.

676.

P. d. R. El., XX; comp. Adam and Eve, I; Erub. 18 b.

677.

Gen. R. XII, 5; XIX, 11; XXI, 4 f.; comp. Shab. 55 b.

678.

See Windishman: Zoroastrische Studien, p. 27 f.

679.

Eccl. VII, 29.

680.

Tanh. Yelamdenu to Gen. III, 22.

681.

Eccl. XII, 7.

682.

Shab. 152 b.

683.

Ber. 80 a. The rabbis did not have the belief that the body is morally impure and therefore the seat of the yezer ha ra, as is stated by Weber, l. c., 228 f. See Potter, l. c., 98-107; Schechter: Aspects, 242-292. It is wrong also to explain Ps. LI, 7, "Behold I was brought forth in iniquity, and in sin did my mother conceive me," as inherited sinfulness, as Delitzsch and other Christian commentators have done, following Ibn Ezra, who refers this to Eve, the mother of all men. The correct interpretation is given by R. Ahha in Lev. R. XIV, 5; "Every sexual act is the work of sensuality, the Yezer ha ra." Comp. Yoma 69 b. Needless to say that Hosea VI, 7; Isa. XLIII, 37; Job XXXI, 33 do not refer to the sin of Adam.

684.

See Ibn Ezra to Gen. III, 1.

685.

See Taan. 10 a; Ber. 34 b; D. comp. Enoch XXIX-XXXII; Seder Gan Eden, in Jellinek, Beth ha Midrash, II, III.

686.

Moreh, II, 30; Nahmanides to Gen. III, 1.

687.

Gen. R. XVI, 8, ref. to Gen. II, 15.

688.

Pes. 111 a; Gen. R. XX, 24.

689.

Seder Olam at the close; Gen. R. XXIV, 2.

690.

Prov. XX, 27.

691.

Job XXXII, 8.

692.

Isa. XI, 2.

693.

Dan. II, 20-21.

694.

Tanh. Miketz 9; comp. Tanh. Yelamdenu Wayakhel, where the story is told differently.

695.

Singer's Prayerbook, p. 46.

696.

Cuzari III, 19.

697.

Ber. 58 a; Singer's Prayerb., p. 291.

698.

Yesode ha Torah, II, 2.

699.

Nethibot Olam, XIV.

700.

Pes. 94 b.

701.

Shaare Shamayim, IV, 3.

702.

R. h. Sh. 21 b.

703.

II Sam. XXIII, 2.

704.

Job IV, 12-16.

705.

Gen. R. XXIV, 7; comp. Jubilees III, 12.

706.

See Dillmann, l. c., 301 f., 375; J. E., art. Freedom of Will.

707.

Gen. IV, 7.

708.

Deut. XXX, 15-19.

709.

Jer. XXI, 8.

710.

See Sifre Deut. 53-54; J. E., art. Didache.

711.

Gen. III, 22; Mek. Beshallah 6; Gen. R. XXI. 5; Mid. Teh. Ps. XXXVI, 3; LVIII, 2.

712.

Aboth III, 15, but see Schechter: Aspects, 285, note 4.

713.

Ben Sira XV, 11-20.

714.

Enoch XCVIII, 4.

715.

IX, 7.

716.

IV Ezra VII, 127-129; IX, 10-11.

717.

Quod deus immutabilis, 10, I, 279; Di confusione linguarum, 35, I, 432; Quod deterius potiori insid.

718.

Josephus, J. W., II, 8, 14; Ant. XVIII, I, 3.

719.

Ber. 33 b.

720.

Gen. R. LXVII, 7. Comp. P. R. El. XV.

721.

Tanh. Toledoth, ed. Buber, 21.

722.

Shab. 104 a; Yoma 38 b-39 a; Yer. Kid. I, 67 d.

723.

Mak. 10 b; ref. to Ex. XXI, 12; Num. XXII, 12; Isa. XLVIII, 17; Prov. III, 34.

724.

Ex. IV, 21; VII, 3, and elsewhere; see the Jewish commentaries to these passages. Comp. Pes. 165 a; Num. R. XV, 16. See Schechter, Aspects, 289-292.

725.

Saadia: Emunoth, III, 154; IV, 7 f.; Bahya: Hoboth haleboboth, III, 8; Cuzari, V, 20; Moreh I, 23; III, 16; H. Teshuba, V; Gersonides: Milhamoth, III, 106; Albo: Ikkarim, IV, 5-10; see Cassel notes, Cuzari, p. 414.

726.

Or Adonai II, 4; comp. Bloch: Willensfreiheit des Hisdai Crescas; Neumark: Crescas and Spinoza, Y. B. C. C. A. R. 1908.

727.

Ex. XX, 5.

728.

Sanh. 27 b.

729.

Job XIV, 4.

730.

Pesik. 29 b.

731.

H. Teshubah, V.

732.

See Morgenstern, "The Doctrine of Sin in the Babylonian Religion," in Mitth. Vorderas. Gesellsch. 1905.

733.

Gen. VI, 3; Ps. LXXVIII, 39.

734.

Sota 3 a.

735.

Suk. 52 a, b. Comp. Schechter, "The Evil Yezer, Source of Rebellion and Victory over the Evil Yezer," l. c., 242-292.

736.

Prov. XX, 9.

737.

Eccl. VII, 20.

738.

Job IV, 17; XV, 14 f; XXV, 5.

739.

Num. XX, 12; XXVII, 14.

740.

Yeb. 121 b.

741.

Mid. Teh. Ps. XVI, 2.

742.

Job XV, 15.

743.

Midr. Teh. eodem.

744.

Morgenstern, l. c.

745.

Ex. XXX, 33, 38; Lev. X, 2; XVI, 1-2; Num. XVII, 28; XVIII, 7.

746.

Ezek. XVIII, 6 f.; XX, 13 f.; Isa. LVI, 2 f.

747.

Hos. VI, 6; Mic. VI, 8; Isa. I, 11 f.

748.

I Sam. XV, 22-23.

749.

Job XXXV, 6-8.

750.

Ps. LI, 6.

751.

Sanh. 107 a.

752.

Isa. LIX, 2.

753.

Gen. IV, 13; XV, 16; XIX, 15; Ps. XL, 13.

754.

Gen. XXVI, 10; XLII, 21; Ps. XXXIV, 22.

755.

Lev. IV, 13 f.; Num. V, 6.

756.

Ps. XIX, 13.

757.

Num. R. XXI, 19.

758.

Num. XVI, 22.

759.

Tanh. Korah, ed. Buber, 19.

760.

Habak. I, 13.

761.

Isa. XXXIII, 14.

762.

Isa. VI, 5-7.

763.

Pes. 45 b; Gen. R. XXIII, 9.

764.

See J. E., art. Cabala; Abelson, Jewish Mysticism, p. 127 f., 171 f.

765.

See J. E., art. Repentance; Claude Montefiore: "Rabbinical Conceptions of Repentance," in J. Q. R., Jan. 1904; Schechter, Aspects, 313-343. The works of Weber (p. 261 f.), Bousset (p. 446 f.), and Davidson (l. c., 327-338) do not do justice to the Jewish teachings.

766.

Ezek. XVIII, 4; Ps. XXXIV, 21; Prov. XIV, 12.

767.

Ezek. XVIII, 32; XXXIII, 11.

768.

Prov. XIII, 21.

769.

Ezek. XVIII, 4.

770.

Lev. I, 4; IV, 26-31.

771.

Ps. XXV, 8.

772.

Yer. Mak. II, 37 d; Pesik. 158 b. See Schechter, l. c., p. 294, note 1.

773.

Amos V, 4.

774.

Isa. LV, 7.

775.

Deut. IV, 30; XXX, 2-3.

776.

Amos IV, 6 f.

777.

Hos. VI, 1; XIV, 2 f.

778.

Jer. III, 12-13; IV, 3; 14; XVIII, 11.

779.

Ezek. XVIII, 1-32.

780.

Zech. I, 3.

781.

Mal. III, 7.

782.

Joel II, 12-13.

783.

See Ps. XXXII, 1 f.

784.

Jonah III-IV.

785.

The Hebrew teshubah is translated in Greek metanoia, meaning a change of mind.

786.

Pes. 119 a; P. d. R. El. XLIII.

787.

Pes. 54 a; Gen, R. I, 5; P. d. R. El. III; Singer's Prayerb. 267 f.

788.

Shab. 56 a; Ab. Z. 4 b-5 a; Midr. Teh. Ps. XL, 3; LI, 13.

789.

Ter. Sanh. X, 78 c; Sanh. 103 a; Pes. 162; Prayer of Manasseh.

790.

Pesik. 160 a-162; Shab. 56 a, b; Gen. R. XI, 6; XXII, 12-13; XXXVIII, 9; XLIX, 6; P. R. El. XX; XLIII; Num. R. XVIII, 6; Ab. d. R. N. I, 32; Sanh. 102 b.

791.

Yoma 86 a, b; Pes. R. XLIX.

792.

Mek. Shira 5; Gen. R. XXI, 6; XXX, 4; XXXII, 10; XXXVIII, 14; LXXXIV, 18; Ex. R. XII, 1; Num. R. XII, 13; B. Wisdom XI, 23; XII, 10, 19.

793.

Sanh. 108; Sibyllines, I, 125-198.

794.

Cant. R. VII, 5, ref. to the name Hadrach, Zech. IX, 1.

795.

Weber, l. c., 261 f.; Bousset, l. c., 446 f.; comp. Perles: Bousset.

796.

Gen. R. XXII, 27; comp. Sanh 107 b.

797.

Mek. Yithro I.

798.

Erub. 19 a.

799.

Mid. Teh. Ps. I, 21 f.; IX, 13, 15; XI, 5.

800.

See Maimonides, Bahya, and others on Teshubah; comp. J. E., art. Repentance; Tobit XIII, 6; XIV, 6; Philo II, 435.

801.

See Schechter, l. c., 323 f.

802.

Sanh. 99 a, Luke XV, 7. The third Gospel more than the others preserved the original Jewish doctrines of the Church.

803.

Job XIX, 25. The Hebrew Goel signifies kinsman as well as redeemer and avenger, implying blood-relationship. In Job it means vindicator.

804. Deut. XIV, 1.

805. Mal. II, 10.

806. Ps. CIII, 13.

807. Jer. II, 27.

808. Hosea II, 1.

809. See Jer. III, 4.

810. Jer. XXXI, 9; Deut. XXXII, 7; Isa. LXIII, 16; LXIV, 7; Mal. I, 4; I Chron. XXIX, 10.

811. Yoma VIII, 9.

812. Sota IX, 15.

813. See next paragraph, and the art. Abba in J. E.

814. II Sam. VII, 14.

815. Ps. LXXXIX, 27-28.

816. Jubilees I, 24.

817. Wisdom II, 16; V, 5.

818. Psalms of Solomon XVII, 27.

819. Taan. III, 8.

820. Ber. V, 1.

821. Midr. Teh. Ps. CXXI, 1.

822. Mek. Yithro 11.

823. Sifre Deut. 96; Hosea I, 10.

824. Ex. IV, 22.

825. Sifre Deut. 49.

826. Sifre Deut. 96.

827. Beza 32 b.

828. Yeb. 61 a.

829. Aboth III, 13, quoted above, Chap. XXXIV, par. 6.

830. Sifra Ahare 13, p. 86.

831. Ps. XLII, 3.

832. Mal. I, 11.

833. With its azkarah, the flame of incense rising in "pyramidal" form, generally translated "memorial," or "memorial-part." Lev. II, 9, 16. For sacrifice as means of atonement see Schechter: Aspects, 295-301.

834. Amos V, 21-24.

835. Hosea VI, 6.

836. Isa. I, 11-18.

837. Jer. VII, 21-23.

838. Ps. L, 7-13.

839.

Ps. XL, 7.

840.

I Sam. I, 13-14.

841.

Often mentioned in the Psalms, under such terms as "the congregation of the righteous," "the holy ones," "the devout ones," etc.

842.

See I Kings VIII, 48; Dan. VI, 11.

843.

Isa. LVI, 7.

844.

Tamid V, 1; comp. Kohler: Monatsschr., 1893, p. 441.

845.

Sifre Deut. 41: "What is meant by, 'To serve Him with all your heart?' this is prayer."

846.

Ber. 26 a.

847.

Ber. 32 b; Midr. to Sam. I, 7.

848.

P. d. R. El. XVI.

849.

R. ha Sh. 17 b.

850.

Meg. 31 b; Yer. Taan. IV, 68 c. But compare Isaac Aboab: Menorath ha Maor, III, 3 a; Bahya ben Asher: Kad ha Kemah, art. Tefillah.

851.

Jer. VI, 22.

852.

Lev. R. XXII, 5.

853.

Cuzari, II, 25, see note by Cassel; Moreh, III, 32; comp. Midrash Tadshe 12; I, 177 f.; comp. Hebrews IX-X; Barnabas, I, 25. S. R. Hirsch in Horeb p. 639 f.

854.

See Philipson: The Reform Movement in Judaism for the various views and debates on sacrifice and prayer. I. Elbogen: D. jued. Gottesdienst i. s. geschichtl. Entwicklung, p. 374 f., 435 f., is written in a more conservative spirit and unfavorable to American Reform Judaism. Comp. for the traditional liturgy: Dembitz: Jewish Services in the Synagogue and Home, especially on the Prayerbook, p. 233-246, and for America, 497-499.

855.

Ex. XV, 2.

856.

Ps. LXV, 3. See Wm. James: Varieties of Rel. Experience, 463-477; Foster: Function of Religion, 183-185; Abelson: Jewish Mysticism, p. 15 and elsewhere.

857.

Yoma 53 b.

858.

Yeb. 64 a; Ex. R. XXI, 6.

859.

Ber. 55 a.

860.

Ber. 10 a.

861.

Ber. 7 a.

862.

Taan. III, 8; Ber. V, 6; Babl. 34 b; Yer. 9 d.

863.

Pes. R. XXII, p. 114 b; Midr. Teh. Ps. XCI, 8; see Schechter: Aspects, 156; 42.

864.

I Sam. II, 31.

865.

Prov. XVI, 32.

866.

Gen. R. LIX, 1; Yeb. 105 a, where R. Johanan ben Zakkai is mentioned instead of R. Meir; Albo: Ikkarim, IV, 18.

867.

See Steinschneider: Abraham Ibn Ezra, 126 ff.

868.

Ps. CXLV, 18.

869.

Ps. CXXXIX, 4.

870.

Ps. LV, 23.

871.

Ber. 29 b; Tos. Ber. III, 7; comp. Albo: Ikkarim, IV, 24.

872.

Job XVI, 17; Ex. R. XXII, 4; comp. Schechter: Aspects, 228.

873.

Ab. Z. 76.

874.

Ber. 8 a.

875.

Ber. 30 a.

876.

Hab. II, 20.

877.

Sifre Deut. 41.

878.

Isa. LV, 6.

879.

Ps. LXXIII, 25, 28.

880.

Gen. III, 22.

881.

Gen. V, 24; II Kings II, 1.

882.

Isa., XXV, 8.

883.

Isa. XXXVIII, 11; Ps. CXVI, 9.

884.

Ps. XVIII, 5, and J. E., art. Belial.

885.

Ps. CXV, 17; LXXXVIII, 13.

886.

Isa. XXVI, 14, 19; Ps. LXXXVIII, 11; Prov. IX, 18; Job XXVI, 5.

887.

Ps. XLIX, 15.

888.

See Isa. VIII, 19; XXVIII, 15, 18; I Sam. XXIX, 7-14.

889.

Job XVIII, 14; Ps. XLIX, 15.

890.

Ps. XLIX, 16; Job XIV, 13.

891.

Ps. CXXXIX, 8.

892.

Ps. XVI, 10-11; Hosea XIII is a late emendation of the text.

893.

Deut. XXX, 19; Jer. XXI, 8; Ezek. XX, 11; Lev. XVIII, 5; Ps. XXXIV, 3; Prov. III, 22; V, 5 f.

894.

Isa. XXXVIII, 10-20.

895.

Ps. LXXIII, 25-28.

896.

Job XIX, 25 f., challenges God to be his vindicator on earth or on his tomb, testifying to his righteousness. Resurrection is denied directly: VII, 8-21; XIV, 12-22. The whole argument of the book excludes the thought.

897.

Ber. 64 a, with ref. to Ps. LXXXIV, 4.

898.

Isa. XXVI, 19. Read, "thy dead instead of My dead." The translation given here differs from the new translation.

899.

I Sam. II, 6.

900.

II Kings IV, 20-37.

901.

Ezek. XXXVII, 1-14.

902.

Dan. XII, 2, and comp. II Macc. VII, 9-36; XII, 43, and the Apocalyptic books such as Enoch, Test. Twelve Patriarchs, Jubilees, Psalms of Solomon, IV Ezra and Baruch Apocalypse, whereas I Macc., Judith and Tobit, belonging to the Sadducean circles, never allude to the future life.

903.

Passages like Ps. IX, 18; XI, 6; XLIX, 15, comp. with Isa. XXXIII, 14; LXV, 24; Mal. III, 19, lent themselves especially to this conception of Sheol as a fiery place of punishment identified afterwards with Gehinnom. Jer. VII, 31 f.; XIX, 6. See J. E., art. Gehenna, and R. H. Charles, Hebrew, Jewish and Christian Eschatology, 2d, 1913, p. 75 f., 132, 160 f., 292 f.

904.

Midr. Teh. Ps. XI, 5-6; Erub. 19 a.

905.

Sanh. 90 b; comp. Matt. XXII, 32.

906.

Sanh. X, 1; see J. E., art. Resurrection, and Neumark, art. Ikkarim in l. c.

907.

See Singer's Prayerb., 44 f., and Abrahams' Notes, LIX.

908.

Prov. XII, 28, comp. LXX, and see Kittel: Bibl. Hebr., note.

909.

Ps. XLVIII, 15; see Kittel, note; Midr. Teh. to Psalms and note by Buber; Yer. Meg. II, 73 b; M. K. 83 b; Lev. R. XI, 9.

910.

See Tylor: Primitive Culture, Index, s. v. Soul.

911.

Gen. II, 7.

912.

Eccl. XII, 7.

913.

See J. E., art. Birds as Souls.

914.

Prov. XX, 27.

915.

Ber. 60 b; Singer's Prayerb., 5.

916.

Isa. XXVI, 19; Dan. XII, 2.

917.

Ezek. XXXVII, 1 f.

918.

Eccl. R. XII, 5: J. E., art. Luz.

919.

Judg. I, 26.

920.

Sota 46 b.

921.

Brugsch: Religion u. Mythologie d. alt. Aegypten, p. 618, 634.

922.

P. d. R. El. XXXIV.

923.

Ber. 18 b.

924.

Shab. 152 b.

925.

Midr. Teh. Ps. CIII, 1.

926.

Sanh. 39 b.

927.

Nid. 30 b.

928.

B. Wisd. VIII, 19; Slav. Enoch XXII, 4, comp, Bousset, l. c., 313 f.

929.

Philo: Leg. All. III, 38; Migrat. Abrah. 12; De Concupiscentia, 2; De Fortitudine, 3; Drummond: Philo, I, 318 f.; Bentwich: Philo, 178, 181; Windleband-Tufts on Plato, 123 f., on Philo, 231, comp. Bousset, l. c., 508; Rhode: Psyche, 557 f.

930.

Emunoth, Ch. VI; Schmiedl, l. c., 135 f.; Neumark, l. c., I, 536 f.; Husik, l. c., 376.

931.

931. Neumark, l. c., 495; Husik, l. c., 108 f.; J. E., art. Bahya.

932. Cuzari, V, 12. See Cassel, notes; Schmiedl, l. c., 141; Neumark, l. c., 561; Husik, l. c., 179 f.

933. Schmiedl, l. c., 149; Neumark, l. c., 536 f., 551, 558, 573, 586; Husik, l. c., 281 f. Comp. Scheyer: d. Psychol. Syst. d. Maim.; Simon, Aspects of the Hebrew Genius, 75-78, 86.

934. Or Adonai, II, 6; Joel: "Crescas"; Husik, l. c., 400.

935. Emunah Ramah, 39; Husik, l. c., 259 b.

936. Emunoth, VII.

937. H. Teshubah, VIII, 2.

938. Maamar Tehiyyath ha Metim, see Schmiedl, l. c., 172.

939. In Schaar ha Gemul.

940. Ikkarim, IV, 35.

941. Zohar, I, 96 b; Yalk. Reubeni to Deut. XIX, 2; J. E., art. Cabala.

942. See Kayserling: Moses Mendelssohn, 148 ff.

943. Ps. XVII, 15.

944. See J. Jastrow: Fact and Fable in Psychology.

945. Singer's Prayerb., 45. The Rabb. Conf. of Philadelphia in 1869 passed the resolution: "The belief in the Resurrection of the Body has no religious foundation (in Judaism), and the doctrine of Immortality refers to the after-existence of the Soul only," Comp. D. Philipson: l. c., p. 489 and 492.

946. Jer. XXXII, 18.

947. Targ. to Ex. XX, 5; Sanh. 27 b.

948. Deut. XXIV, 16.

949. Ezek. XVIII, 2.

950. Ezek. XVIII, 20.

951. XVIII, 23, 32.

952. Ex. XVIII, 11; XXI, 23-25; Sota I, 7-9; Tos. Sota III-IV; Sanh. 90 a; B. Wisdom XVI-XIX; Jubilees IV, 31; II Macc. V, 10; XV, 32.

953. Prov. XI, 31; XIII, 21.

954. See especially Sanh. 90 b-92 b, ref. to Ex. VI, 4; Deut. XI, 9; IV, 5; XXXI, 16; Isa. XXVI, 19; Dan. XII, 13; Ps. LXXII, 16; also Ex. XV, 1; Josh. VIII, 30; and Song of Songs, VII, 10. On the Second Death see Targ. to Deut. XXXIII, 6; Isa. XIV, 19; LXV, 6; Jer. LI, 39; and Revelation XX, 6, 14; XXI, 8.

955. IV Ezra VII, 31 f.; comp. Baruch Apoc. 42 ff.; Adam et Eva, 42; II Sibyll., 220-236; IV Sibyll., 180 f.

956. Aboth IV, 22.

957. See Stave, Ueb. d. Einfluss d. Parsismus a. d. Judenth., 145 ff.; Boecklen: D. Verwandtschaft d. jued, christl. u. d. pars. Eschatologie; Schorr: He Haluz, VII-VIII.

958. Sanh. 91 a, b; Matt. XXII, 31 f.

959. The parable is found in an Apocryphon ascribed to the prophet Ezekiel, see Epiphanius Haeres, LXIV, ed. Dindorf, II, 683 f. and ascribed to R. Ishmael, Lev. R. IV, 5; in Sanh. 91 a, b it is given in a dialogue with Antonius; in Tanh. Wayithro, ed. Buber, § 12, it is anonymous.

960.

Ps. L, 4.

961.

Isa. LXVI, 24; see Yalkut; Bousset, 308-321; J. E., art. Eschatology.

962.

Aboth III, 1, 19, 20; Ber. 28 b.

963.

Aboth IV, 21.

964.

Tos. Sanh. XIII, 3; R. H. 16 b; see J. E., art. Purgatory.

965.

See Testament of Abraham XIV; comp. Kohler in J. Q. R. VII, 587.

966.

T. d. b. El. Zuta XVII, ed. Friedman, p. 23. See note, Kalla R. II., J. E., art. Kaddish, but comp. IV Ezra VII, 102-115.

967.

Tos. Sanh. XIII, 2; Sanh. 105 a; Midr. Teh. Ps. IX, 18: "The wicked shall return to Sheol, all the nations that forget God," R. Joshua taking the last sense as restrictive and R. Eliezer as a generalization.

968.

For the banquet of the pious see Aboth. III, 16; Shab. 153 a; Pes. R. XLI; comp. Luke XIII, 28; XXII, 30, and parallels. The idea rests on Isa. LXV, 13, which is taken literally, and Ps. XXIII, 5; see Midr. Teh., ad loc. For the Leviathan and Behemoth see Job XL, 15-30; B. B. 74 b-75 a; Enoch LX, 7 f.; IV Ezra VI, 52; Baruch Apoc. XXIX, 4; Targ. Ps. CIV, 26; Lev. R. XIII, 3. For the giant bird Ziz see Ps. L, 40-41; Targ. and Midr. Teh., ad loc.; Tanh. Beshallah, ed. Buber, 24; Jellinek, B. H. III, 76, 80. For the heavenly manna Ps. LXXVIII, 24; Joma 75 b; Hag. 12 b; Tanh. Beshallah, ed. Buber, 21; Sibyll. Prœmium 87; II, 318; III, 746; IV Ezra IX, 19. For the wine see Ex. R. XXV, 10; Ber. 34 b; Sanh. 99 a; Matt. XXVI, 29; comp. also Num. R. XIII, 3 for other fruits of Paradise. For the Persian origin of these ideas see Bundahish, XIX, 13; XXX, 25. The Behemoth corresponds with the primeval ox Hadhayos, whose flesh produces the sap of immortality; the giant fish and bird with Bundahish, XVIII, 5-8; XIX, 16-19; the wine corresponds with the Parsee Hom: Bundahish, XXX, 25. See Windishman: Zoroastr. Stud., 92 f., 252 f., and Boeklen, l. c., p. 68.

969.

Shab. 153 a, with ref. to Isa. LXV, 13-14; LXVI, 24; IV Ezra VII, 83, 93.

970.

Ber. 17 a.

971.

Ber. 34 b; with ref. to Isa., LXIV, 3.

972.

Ab. Zar. 36 with ref. to Mal. III, 19-22.

973.

See Jellinek, B. H. I, II and III, the Treatise on Gehinnom and Gan Eden.

974.

Emunoth VII, IX, and comp. J. Guttman; Religionsphil. des Saadia, 208 f., 249 f.

975.

See Joel, Religionsphil. d. Mose b. Maimon., p. 40.

976.

Cuzari, I, 15; V, 14; Or Adonai III, 4, 2. See Joel: Crescas, p. 74 f.; Albo: Ikkarim, IV, 29-41.

977.

Nahmanides, l. c., last chapter; Manasse b. Israel in Nishmat Chayim.

978.

Aboth. IV, 2.

979.

Com. to Sanh. XI and H. Teshubah, VIII.

980.

Ps. LXXIII, 28.

981.

Or Adonai, II, 55; VI, 1; comp. Joel, l. c., 56-62; comp. Bahya: Hoboth, Halebaboth, Shaar Bitahon.

982.

See Joel: Z. Gen. d. Lehre Spinoza, p. 64.

983.

Ikkarim, IV, 35-38.

984.

Ber. 64 a, with ref. to Ps. LXXXIV, 8; see also Midr. Teh. ad loc.

985.

See J. E., art. Adam, and Jellinek: Bezelem Elohim, Sermon IV. The term humanity arose among the Stoics. See Reizenstein: Wesen u. Werden d. Humanität; comp. Schmidt, Ethik d. Griechen, II, 324, 477; and Zeller, Griech. Philo. III, 1, 287, 299. For the rabbinical Berioth for humanity see B. Sira, XVI, 16.

986.

Ps. CXXXIX, 16.

987.

Midr. Teh., ad loc.; Pesik. R. XXIII; Gen. R. XXIV, 2; Sanh. 38 b after Seder Olam at the close.

988.

Gen. R. VIII, 1.

989.

Eodem; Midr. Teh. to Ps. CXXXIX, 5; Ber. 61 a.

990.

Gen. R. XXIV, 8.

991.

Tos. Ber. VII, 2; Ber. 58 a.

992.

Ber. 6 b; Shab. 30 b; see Rashi (against Bacher: Ag. Tann., I, 432).

993.

I Sam. II, 2.

994.

Gen. R. LVI, 9.

995.

Isa. LXV, 18; see Yeb. 62 a.

996.

Gen. R. XVII, 2.

997.

For the term Aguddah Ahath in the New Year and Atonement Day Prayer, Singer's Prayerbook, p. 239, comp. Gen. R. LXXXVIII, 6, and XXXIX, 3.

998.

Isa. XLV, 18.

999.

Yeb. 62 a, b

1000.

Yoma I, 1.

1001.

Prov. XXII, 29.

1002.

Ps. CXXVIII, 2.

1003.

Ber. 8 a.

1004.

Ned. 49 b.

1005.

Keth. V, 5, 59 b.

1006.

Kid. 29 a; comp. R. Simeon b. Yohai, Mek. Beshallah, 56.

1007.

Kid. 82 a.

1008.

Abot. I, 10; II, 2; B. B. 11 a.

1009.

Taan. 11 a.

1010.

Yer. Kid. IV at the close.

1011.

Taan. 23 a.

1012.

Abot. V, 19.

1013.

Prov. XXVII, 17.

1014.

Taan. 7 a.

1015.

See J. E., art. Abraham.

1016.

Abot. IV, 1; B. K. 79 b; Ber. 19 b.

1017.

Sota 14 a.

1018.

Jer. XXIX, 7; comp. Abot. III, 2.

1019.

B. K. 113 a and elsewhere.

1020.

Ber. 58 a.

1021.

Ex. XIX, 4-5.

1022.

Deut. VII, 6-8; X, 15; XIV, 2. Comp. Schechter: Aspects, 57 ff.

1023.

See Singer's Prayerbook, 226 f.

1024.

Hos. XI, 1; XII, 10; XIII, 4.

1025.

Jer. II, 3.

1026.

Amos III, 2.

1027.

Isa. XLI, 8 f.; XLII, 6; XLIII, 10; XLIX, 8.

1028.

CV, 7 f., comp. Neh. IX, 7.

1029.

Singer's Prayerb., p. 40.

1030.

Isa. LII, 3-LIII, 12.

1031.

Meg. 16 a.

1032.

Beza 25 b.

1033.

Yeb. 79 a.

1034.

Shab. 88 a.

1035.

Cant. R. IV, 2; Tanh. Tezaveh 1.

1036.

Menah. 53 b with ref. to Jer. XI, 16.

1037.

Sifre to Deut. XIV, 2.

1038.

Deut. VII, 6; XIV, 2.

1039.

Isa. II, 3; Micah IV, 2—passages considered by modern critics to be of exilic origin.

1040.

See Bousset, l. c., 60-99.

1041.

Gen. R. to Gen. XII, 4, and see J. E., art. Abraham.

1042.

Pes. 87 b. with ref. to Hosea II, 25.

1043.

Cuzari IV, 23; Maim. H. Melakim XI, 4.

1044.

See Geiger: Zeitschr. 1868, p. 18 ff.; 1869, 55 ff.

1045.

J. E., art. Alenu; Singer's Prayerb., 76 f.

1046.

J. E., art. Kaddish.

1047.

Zech. XIV, 9.

1048.

See Schechter: Aspects, 89 f., 93 f.

1049.

Isa. XLIX, 6.

1050.

Isa. LII, 10

1051.

Micah V, 6.

1052.

Judg. VIII, 23.

1053.

I Sam. VIII, 7; XII, 12, 17 f.

1054.

1055.

Hos. XIII, 11.

1056.

Isa. IX, 5; XI, 1-10.

1057.

Isa. IV, 2; Jer. XXIII, 5; XXXII, 15; and Zech. III, 8; VI, 12. Here Zerubbabel is referred to.

1058.

Isa. XLI, 21; XLIII, 15; XLIV, 6. Comp. XLIII, 22.

1059.

Isa. XLV, 1.

1060.

Isa. XI, 9; Hab. II, 14.

1061.

Isa. VI, 5; XXIV, 23. Comp. Jer. XLVI, 18; XLVIII, 15.

1062.

Zech. XIV, 9; Mal. I, 14.

1063.

Ps. XXII, 29; XCIII, 1; XCV, 99.

1064.

Jer. X, 7. This chapter is post-exilic; comp. Jer. XLVI, 18; XLVIII, 15 and I Chron. XXIX, 11.

1065.

Singer's Prayerb., 239.

1066.

Ps. XLVIII, 3.

1067.

Cont. Apion, II, 16, 7.

1068.

Dan. VII, 27.

1069.

See J. E., art. Zealots.

1070.

Shab. 31 a.

1071.

Ps. XXII, 28; LXVII, 3; LXXXVI, 10; CXVII, 1.

1072.

Ps. CV, 15.

1073.

Ps. LXXXVII, 5. See Commentaries and LXX.

1074.

Ruth II, 12. Comp. Lev. R. II, 8.

1075.

See both Enoch books and B. Sira XLIV, 16.

1076.

Sibyll. I, 128-170; Sanh. 108 a.

1077.

Gen. R. XXXIX, 21.

1078.

Sifre Deut. 313, with ref. to Gen. XXIV, 3.

1079.

See Dillmann's Comm. to Gen. XII, 2; XXII, 18; and Kuenen: The Prophets and Prophecy, 373, 457.

1080.

Gen. XVII, 5.

1081.

Ezek. XX, 33.

1082.

Sifre, l. c.

1083.

P. D. R. El. XI; Mek. Yithro 6; Lev. R. II, 4.

1084.

Sifra Behukkothai VIII with ref. to Ezek. XX, 33; Sanh. 105 a.

1085.

Mek. Beshallah X, p. 52.

1086.

Tanh. Lek leka 6.

1087.

Tobit XIII, 1-11; Sibyll. III, 47, 76 b.

1088.

Ps. CXVII; CXVIII, 4. See chapter LVI.

1089.

Singer's Prayerb., 48.

1089.
Mek. Amalek at close; Cant. R. II, 28; IV Ezra VI, 9-10.
1090.
B. Wisdom V, 16; Sibyll. III, 76 b.
1091.
Sifra Kedoshim at close; Sifre Deut. 323.
1092.
Cuzari IV, 23; Maim. H. Melakim XI, 4.
1093.
Maim.: Commentary to Eduyoth at close.
1094.
Pes. R. XXXIV, p. 158 ref. to Zeph. III, 8. See Friedman's note.
1095.
Zech. IV, 6.
1096.
Tos. Sanh. XIII, 2.
1097.
P. 374-378.
1098.
Isa. LXVI, 22.
1099.
Part II, p. 332.
1100.
Isa. LXI, 6.
1101.
Ex. XIX, 22 f.
1102.
Lev. XXI, 6; XXII, 2.
1103.
Lev. VIII, 2, 8.
1104.
Num. XVIII, 7.
1105.
M. K. 28 b.
1106.
Ezek. XL-XLVIII.
1107.
Deut. X, 16. Comp. Jer. IX, 24.
1108.
Gen. XVII, 9.
1109.
Lev. XXV, 1-24.
1110.
Deut. XIV, 2-11; Lev. XI. Comp. Ezek. XLIV, 31, and Judg. XIII, 4.
1111.
Num. XV, 40.
1112.
See J. E., art. Pharisees.
1113.
II Macc. II, 17.
1114.
Aboth. I, 1.
1115.
See Perles: Bousset, 68, 89.
1116.
Aristeas 139-152.
1117.
Ned. 20 a.
1118.
See Schechter, Studies, I, 233 ff. I. Abrahams in J. Q. R. XI, 62; b ff., and Claude Montefiore, J. Q. R. XIII, 161-217.
1119.
Lev. XXII, 32.
1120.
Sifra Emor. IX.
1121.
Yesode ha Torah V. Comp. Lazarus: Ethics, 29, 184.
1122.
Isa. XLIII, 12.
1123.
Pesik. 102 b.
1124.
Perles, l. c., 68 f.

1125.

Yer. B. M. II, 8 c.

1126.

Sifra Kedoshim 1.

1127.

Mak. 23 b.

1128.

Ps. XXIV, 3-4; XV, 1-5.

1129.

Deut. XXXIII, 4.

1130.

Num. XI, 29.

1131.

Jer. XXXI, 34.

1132.

Isa. LIV, 13.

1133.

Deut. IV, 6.

1134.

Isa. XLII, 4.

1135.

Isa. II, 3; Micah IV, 2.

1136.

See Guedemann: Das Judenthum, 67 f.; Jued. Apologetik, 12b; Schechter: Studies, I, 233 f., and Aspects, I, 116 f.

1137.

II Kings XXII, 8 f.

1138.

Neh. VIII-X.

1139.

See Gunkel: Israel u. Babylonien; Jeremias: Moses u. Hammurabi; H. Grimme: D. Gesetz Chammurabi's u. Moses'; George Cohen: D. Gesetze Hammurabi's; D. M. Mueller: D. Gesetz Hammurabi's u. d. mosaische Gesetzgebung.

1140.

See Chapter LIX.

1141.

Sota 14 a.

1142.

Yer. Kid. IV, 1; 65 c.

1143.

Sifra Ahare Moth 13.

1144.

Deut. VI, 7; XI, 19; XXX, 14; Ex. XIII, 9.

1145.

Deut. XXXI, 12.

1146.

See Elbogen: D. Jued. Gottesdienst, 174 f.

1147.

Isa. LI, 4, 7-8.

1148.

Ps. XIX, 7-10.

1149.

Aboth I, 2.

1150.

Mek. Beshallah 45 b, note by Friedman; Yalkut Yithro 286.

1151.

B. Sira XXIV, 8-10; comp. Bousset, l. c., 136 f.

1152.

See Josephus: Cont. Apion. II, 36 f., 39; Aristobulus in Eusebius: Prep. Ev. XIII, 121, 413; Cuzari, I, 63 f.; II, 66; comp. Cassel, l. c. ad loc.

1153.

Josephus, l. c., I, 22; Gutschmidt: Kleine Schriften, IV, 578; Th. Reinach: Textes Relatifs au Judaism, 11-13.

1154.

J. E., art. Adonai.

1155.

Ps. CXV, 11; CXVIII, 4; comp. Bernays: Ges. Abh., II, 71; Schuerer, l. c., III, 124 f.

1156.

Shab. 88 b.; Ex. R. V, 9; Tanh. Shemoth, ed. Buber, 22; Midr. Teh. Ps. LXVIII, 6; Acts II, 6; Spitta: Apostelgeschichte, 27, referring to Philo II, 295.

1157.

Sifre Deut. XXXIII, 2; XXVII, 8; Sota 35 b.

1158.

Shab., 88 a, b.

1159.

Aboth I, 12.

1160.

J. E., art. Zealots.

1161.

Ber. 61 b.

1162.

Weber, l. c., 46-56; he fails completely to grasp this spirit.

1163.

Song of Songs, V, 2.

1164.

Aboth. III, 21.

1165.

Deut. XXXIII, 18. See Gen. R. XCIX, 11.

1166.

Gen. L, 20.

1167.

See J. E., art. "Commerce"; American Encyclopedia, art. Jewish Commerce; Publ. Am. Hist. Soc. X, 47; Schulman in Judaean Addresses, II, 77 ff., and Lecky: Rationalism in Europe, II, 272.

1168.

See Saadia: Emunoth, III, 17, quoted by Schechter: Aspects, 105.

1169.

Isa. II, 2; Micah IV, 1; see Pesik 144 b; Midr. Teh. Ps. XXXVI, 6; LXXXVII, 3.

1170.

Ps. XLIV, 12-25.

1171.

Ezek. XXXIX, 23-26.

1172.

Lev. XXVI, 40-42.

1173.

I Kings VIII, 47-50.

1174.

Ps. CXIX, 92.

1175.

Pesik. 139 b.

1176.

Ezek. XVIII, 2.

1177.

Isa. XL, 2.

1178.

Job I, 8; II, 3; XLII, 7, 8.

1179.

Isa. XLII, 1 f.; XLIX, 1; L, 4; LII, 13-LIII, 12.

1180.

See Ibn Ezra, quoting Saadia; Ewald and Giesebrecht, commentaries; Sellin: Serubabel, 96 f., 144 f.; also Davidson, l. c., p. 356-398.

1181.

Isa. LII, 13-LIII, 12. In LIII, 9, we should read "the evil-doers" instead of "the rich" by a slight amendment of the text.

1182.

Isa. L, 6.

1183.

Isa. XLII, 4.

1184.

Isa. XLIX, 1-6.

1185.

Job XLII, 10-17.

1186.

The disappointment is especially voiced in Ps. LXXX, 16 f.; LXXIX, 40-46.

1187.

See Targum and Abravanel to Isa. LII, 13; comp. Pes. R. XXXVI-XXXVII; Sanh. 98 b.

1188.

He is called Taeb "Moses redivivus," after Deut. XVIII, 18. Merk, E. Samarit. Fragment ueb. d. Taeb. See Bousset, l. c., 258; J. E., art. Samaritans.

1189.

1189.
Suk. 52 a; Jellinek: B. H. III, 141 f; Schuerer, l. c., II, 535.

1190.
J. E., art. Messiah.

1191.
Contra Celsum I, 155.

1192.
See commentaries of Cheyne, Duhm, Giesebrecht, and others.

1193.
Isa. L, 8-9.

1194.
Comp. Pesik. 131 b; Ex. R. II, 7.

1195.
Zech. II, 12. See Geiger: Urschrift, 324, as to the Soferic Emendation.

1196.
Pesik. 76 a; Eccl. R. III, 19; Lev. R. XXVII, 5.

1197.
Yoma 23 a, referring to Jud. V, 31.

1198.
See Gressmann: Urspr. d. israel. u. jued. Eschatologie,—an instructive work, but full of unsubstantiated assertions, thus failing to do justice to the creative genius of the Jewish prophets.

1199.
Isa. XI, 1-8.

1200.
Isa. IX, 5; the note in the new Jewish translation takes the words in a different sense.

1201.
Jer. XXIII, 5; XXXIII, 15; Zech. III, 8; VI, 12; see Sellin. l. c. Compare Ps. LXXX, 16 f.; LXXXIV, 10; LXXXIX, 39, 52; CXXX, 10; see Ewald's commentary.

1202.
Ezek. XXXVIII-XXXIX; Sibyll. III, 663; J. E., art. Gog u. Magog; Bousset, l. c., 231 f.

1203.
For the prince of peace, see, for example, Zech. IX, 9.

1204.
See Bousset, l. c., 255-261.

1205.
See Targum to Isa. XI, 4, where the older Mss. read Arimalyus, later on corrupted into Armillus. See Bousset, l. c., 589.

1206.
Dan. II; VII; IX; see J. E., art. Eschatology.

1207.
Sota IX, 15; Enoch XCIX, 4; C, 1; Matt. XXIV, 8; Bousset, l. c., 286.

1208.
Mal. III, 23; B. Sira XLVIII, 10 f.; Sibyll. II, 187.

1209.
Isa. XXVII, 13; B. Sira XXXVI, 13; Tobit XIII, 13; Enoch XC, 32; II Macc. II, 18; Bousset, l. c., 271.

1210.
See Chap. LII.

1211.
IV Ezra VIII, 28.

1212.
Sanh. 96 f.; J. E., art. Eschatology; Bousset, l. c.

1213.
Sanh. 97 a, b, 99.

1214.
Midr. Teh. Ps. CXLVI, 4; see Buber's note.

1215.
Ket. 111-112; comp. Irenæus: Adver. Haeres. V, 32.

1216.
See Ekah. R. II, 2; J. E., art. Bar Kokba.

1217.
Pesik. 144 a, b.

1218.
Ber. 34 b.

1219.
Sanh. 97 b.

1220.
Sanh. 97 a.

1221.

Sanh. 98 b.

1222.

Commentary to San. X; Yad, H. Melakim, XI-XII; H. Teshubah VIII-IX.

1223.

Notes of R. A. B. D. to Maimuni.

1224.

Ikkarim, IV, 42.

1225.

See Philipson: The Reform Movement in Judaism, 246 f.

1226.

See Einhorn: Sinai I, 133; Leopold Stein: Schrift des Lebens, 320, 336. For the term Messiah comp. Ps. LV, 15; Hab. III, 13; also Ps. XXVIII, 8; LXXXIV, 10; LXXXIX, 39, 52.

1227.

See J. E., art. Resurrection.

1228.

Deut. XXXII, 39; see Sifre ad loc.

1229.

I Sam. II, 6; see Midr. Sh'muel, ad loc.

1230.

Isa. XXVI, 19; Dan. XII, 2.

1231.

Hosea VI, 1-2; comp. XIII, 14.

1232.

Ezek. XXXVII, 1-14.

1233.

Isa. XXV, 8.

1234.

Isa. XXVI, 19. Instead of "my dead bodies" in the new Bible translation, read "thy dead," and instead of "light" translate oroth, after II Kings IV, 39, "herb," which means "dew of revival"; the last is also a rabbinic term.

1235.

Dan. XII, 2.

1236.

See II Macc. VII, 9-36; XII, 43; XIV, 46; Sibyll. II, 47; Midr. Teh. Ps. XVII, 13.

1237.

See Joel IV, 2; Erub. 19 a, ref. to Isa. XXXI., 9; Enoch XXVIII, 1.

1238.

Isa. LX, 21.

1239.

Sanh. X, 1.

1240.

Kid. I, 10; Matt. V, 5, ref. to Ps. XXXVII, 11; Enoch V, 7.

1241.

Ezek. XXVI, 20.

1242.

Isa. XLII, 5.

1243.

Keth. 111 a.

1244.

Ps. CXVI, 9; Yer. Keth. XII, 35 b; Pesik. R, I, 2 b.

1245.

Ber. 15 b; Alphabet d. R. Akiba in Jellinek, B. H. III, 31; Targum Yer. to Ex. XX, 15; I Cor. XV, 52.

1246.

Keth. l. c.

1247.

Ex. IV, 22.

1248.

Isa. XIX, 25.

1249.

Isa. XLII, 4; XLV, 23; LI, 5; Zeph. III, 9; Zech. VIII, 22; XIV, 9.

1250.

Lev. XX, 26; Deut. XX, 16-18; comp. Gen. R. II, 4; III, 10.

1251.

Weber. l. c., 57-79.

1252.

Gen. XIV, 13; XXI, 32.

1253.

1253. I Kings XX, 31.

1254. Amos I-II; Isa. XXIX-XXXIII; Jer. XXV f.; Hab. I.

1255. Gen. XVIII, 25.

1256. Gen. XX, 3.

1257. Job XXXI.

1258. Kid. 31 a.

1259. Tos. Sanh. XIII, 2; B. B. 10 b.

1260. See Lazarus: Ethics, 49 and appendix.

1261. Ex. XXIII, 32.

1262. Deut. VII, 2; XX, 16 f.

1263. Shab. 27 b; Jubil. XXII, 16.

1264. Isa. LX, 12; LXIII, 6; LXVI, 14 f.; Zech. XIV, 2 f.; Joel IV, 9-19; Jer. X, 25; Ps. IX, 16, 18, 20; X, 17.

1265. Tos. Sanh. XIII, 2.

1266. Jonah III-IV.

1267. Isa. LXVI, 19-21.

1268. Zech. IX, 1; Cant. R. VII, 10.

1269. Sanh. 108 a; Sibyll. I, 129 f.

1270. B. B. 15 b; Seder Olam R. XXI.

1271. Mek. Yithro V; Ab. Z. 2 b-3 a.

1272. Deut. IV, 19; XXIX, 25; Jer. X, 16; B. Sira XVIII, 17; comp. Bousset, l. c., 350.

1273. Jubil. XI, 3-5; XIX, 20; Enoch XV; XIX; XCIX, 7; see Bousset, l. c., 350-351.

1274. Yeb. 98 a, ref. to Ezek. XXIII, 20; Ab. Z., l. c. In this sense we must take the Talmudic passage: "Israel are really men, not the heathen," Yeb. 61 a; B. M. 114 b; B. B. 16 b; whereas the passage, Lev. XVIII, 5, "which man doth to live thereby," is declared to include all who observe the laws of humanity, Sifra eodem; Midr. Teh. Ps. I, 1-2.

1275. Lazarus, l. c., 49.

1276. Tos. Sanh. XIII, 2.

1277. Yer. R. Sh. I, 57 a.

1278. Ezek. XXVIII, 10; XXXI, 18; XXXII, 19-32. Possibly the prophet in speaking of arelim had in mind the Babylonian Arallu, "the nether-world"; see Ex. R. XIX, 5; Gen. R. XL; VIII, 7; Tanh. Lek Leka, ed. Buber, 27.

1279. Tos. Sanh. XIII, 4-5; Rosh ha Shana, 17 a.

1280. B. B. 10 b; A. d. R. N. IV.

1281. Suk. 55 b; Pesik. 193 b; Philo; Vita Mosis, 2 f; De Special; I, 3; II, 104, 227. 238.

1282. Sifra, Ahare Moth 13.

1283. Gen. R. L; LXV, 16; Ruth R. I, 8; J. E., art. Œnomaos.

1284. J. E. art. Antoninus in the Talmud; Kraus: Antoninus.

1285. Ab. Z. 30 a.

1286.

Deut. VII, 3; Sanh. 57 a-59 b.

1287.

H. Melakim VIII, 9-10.

1288.

H. Shemitta we Yobel XIII, 13.

1289.

Mal. I. 11.

1290.

Ex. XXII, 26; Philo II, 166; Josephus: Ant., IV, 8, 10; Con. Apio., II, 34; comp. Kohler: "The Halakic Portions in Josephus' Antiquities," in H. U. C. Monthly III, 117.

1291.

See Meg. 16 a; J. E., art. Aristotle; Neumark, l. c., Index: Aristoteles, Plato, Plotin; comp. Bahya: Hoboth ha Lebaboth, and other medieval philosophic works.

1292.

Deut. IV, 37.

1293.

Ex. XXXIII, 12; Lev. XXVI, 42; Ex. R. XLIV, 7-8; Lev. R. XXXVI, 2-5.

1294.

Cant. R. I, 5.

1295.

Isa. LIV, 10; Shab. 55 a; comp. S. Hirsch: "The Doctrine of Original Virtue" in Jew. Lit. Annual, 1905; Schechter, l. c., 170 f.

1296.

Ex. XXII, 20; XXIII, 9.

1297.

Deut. X, 18-19.

1298.

Lev. XIV, 22.

1299.

Gen. XXIII, 4; Lev. XX, 35. On the term Ger see W. R. Smith: The Religion of the Semites, 75 ff.; Bertholet: Die Stellung d. Israeliten und Juden zu den Fremden, 28, 178; Schuerer, l. c., III, 150-188; Encyc. Biblica, art. Stranger and Sojourner; Cheyne, Bampton Lectures, 1889, p. 429. Commerce between the Phoenicians and Greeks was protected by the Greek god of the stranger (Zeus Xenios); see Ihering: D. Gastfreundschaft im Alterthum, Deutsche Rundschau, 1887, showing how the Phoenicians developed the Ger idea in the direction of international commerce, just as the Jews developed it toward international religion; M. J. Kohler: "Right of Asylum" in Am. Law Review, LI, p. 381.

1300.

Ex. XX, 10.

1301.

Lev. XVI, 29; XVII, 8-15; XVIII, 26; XXIV, 16-29.

1302.

Ex. XII, 48; see Yeb., 46 a-47 b; Mas. Gerim I-III. The opinion of Bertholet and Schuerer concerning the semi-proselyte or Ger Toshab is contradicted by both the Book of Jubilees and the Talmudic sources, as will be shown below.

1303.

Jer. XVI, 19.

1304.

Zech. VIII, 21-23.

1305.

Isa. XIV, 1.

1306.

Ps. XXII, 30; LXVII, 3; LXVIII, 30 f; LXXXVII, 4 f.

1307.

II. Chron. II, 16; XXX, 25.

1308.

Ps. CXV, 11; CXVIII, 4; CXXXV, 20; comp. LXVII, 8; CII, 16; Job I, 1; Tobit LXIV, 6; Sibyll. III, 572, 756; Acts X, 2; XXI, 13; V, 26 f.; XVI, 44; XVII, 4; XVIII, 7; Midr. Teh. Ps. XXII, 29; Lev. III, 2; Mek. to Ex. XXII, 20; see Bernays: Ges. Abh., II, 74.

1309.

Tos. Ab. Z. IX, 4; Sanh. 56 b-57; Gen. R. XXXIV, 7; Jubil. VII, 20 f.; Sibyll. III, 38, 762. For the thirty commandments, see Yer. Ab. Z. II, 40 c; Midr. Teh. Ps. II. 5; Gen. R. XCVIII, 9; J. Q. R., 1894, p. 259. Comp. also Pseudo-Phocylides in Bernays' Ges. Abh., I, 291 ff.; Seeberg: D. beiden Wege u. d. Aposteldecret, p. 25. Klein: Der aelteste christl. Katechismus; J. E., art. Commandments.

1310.

See Schuerer, l. c., 165, 175; Harnack, D. Mission u. Ausbreitung d. Christentums, chapter I.

1311.

Ant. XVI, 7.

1312.

Gen. R. XXVIII, 5; Cant. R. I, 4; see Matt. XXIII, 15; Jellinek, B. H. VI, Introd., p. XLVI.

1313.

II Kings C, 1-15; see LXX to verse 14; Sanh 96 b.

1314.

See Sota, 12 b; Sibyll. IV, 164; comp. Gen. R. II, 5; J. E., art. Baptism and Birth, New; Enc. Religion and Ethics, art. Baptism, Jewish.

1315.

See J. E., art. Asenath, and the passages quoted there.

1316.

Sifre and Targum to Deut. XXIII, 16-19.

1317.

Tos. Negaim VI, 2; Mas. Gerim III.

1318.

Philo, De Monarchia, I, 7.

1319.

Ps, XV, 1-2; see Cheyne's Commentary.

1320.

The article ha Zedek seems to point to Jerusalem, called "the city" or "dwelling place of righteousness" (Zedek). See Isa. I, 21; Jer. XXXI, 23; L, 7. Comp. "Gates of righteousness" (Zedek) for the Temple gates, in Ps. CXVIII, 19, and the ancient legendary hero of Jerusalem, Malki-Zedek, Gen. XIV, 18; Josephus, J. W. VI, 10; Epis. Heb. VII, 10; and Adoni Zedek, first king of Jerusalem, Josh. X, 3.

1321.

Sifre and Targum to Deut. XXXIII, 19.

1322.

Singer's Prayerb. p. 48.

1323.

See Mek. Mishpatim XVIII; comp. A. d. R. N. XXXVI ref. to Isa. XLIV, 5.

1324.

Arak. 29 a.

1325.

Vita 25.

1326.

J. W. II, 20, 2.

1327.

Josephus: Ant. XIII, 9, 1; 11, 3; XVIII, 3, 5; XX, 8, 11; Mek. Bo XV: Beluria (Fulvia or Valeria); Schuerer, III, 176; Gemeindeverf. v. Juden in Rome; Graetz: D. juedisch, Proselyten im Roemerreich; Radin: Jews among Greeks and Romans, p. 389. See also Crooks: The Jewish Rate in Ancient and Roman History.

1328.

Josephus: Ant. XX, 2-4; Yoma III, 10; Yoma 37 a.; Suk. 2 b; B. B. 11 a; Gen. R. XLVI, 8.

1329.

Midrash Tadshe in Jellinek: B. H. III, 111; Epstein: Jued. Alierthumskunde, XLIII.

1330.

See J. E., art. Asenath.

1331.

Comp. Sifre Num. 178.

1332.

I Chron. IV, 18; Meg. 13 a.

1333.

Meg. 15 b.

1334.

Philo: De Nobilitate, 6; II, 443.

1335.

Ruth II, 12.

1336.

Ab. d. R. N., ed. Schechter, 53 f.; Shab. 31 a; Lev. R. II, 8.

1337.

See Bertholet, l. c., 285-287.

1338.

Ab. d. R. N., l. c.

1339.

Mek. to Ex. XVIII, 27.

1340.

Gen. R. XXXIX, 14; Yeb. 22 a; comp. Pes. VIII, 8.

1341.

Yeb. 46 a; comp. Josephus: Ant. XX, 2-4.

1342.

Shab. 31 a.

1343.

Lev, R. II, 8.

1344.

Gen. R. LXX, 5; B. M. 59 b.

1345.

Mekilta, l. c.; comp. Ab. d. R. N. XXXVI, ed. Schechter, 107.

1346.

Midr. Teh. Ps. CXLVI, 9; Num. R. VIII, 2.

1347.

Prov. VIII, 17; Num. R., l. c.

1348.

Schuerer, l. c., III, 4; Radin, l. c.

1349.

Yeb. 24 b; Yer. Kid., IV, 65 b.

1350.

Apion, II, 10, 3.

1351.

Yeb. 47 a; comp. Mas. Gerim I.

1352.

See J. E., art. Didache and Klein, l. c.

1353.

Git. 56 b; Ab. Z. 10 b; on Clemens see Graetz: H. J. II, 387-389; but see literature in Schuerer, l. c., III, 169.

1354.

Git. 56 b-57.

1355.

Ex. R. XIX, 4; comp. Midr. Teh. Ps. LXXXVII, 4, ref. to I Sam. II, 36 and Isa. LXVI, 2; comp. Bacher: Agada d. Palest. Amorder., III, 45, 363.

1356.

Yeb. 47 b; 109 b; Kid. 70 b, ref. Isa. XIV to Lev. XIV, 56.

1357.

Ex. R. XIX, 5.

1358.

See Bacher, l. c., II, 115-118.

1359.

Num. R. VIII, 1.

1360.

Gen. R. LXX, 5.

1361.

Ab. Z. 3 b.

1362.

B. M. 59 b.

1363.

Midr. Teh. Ps. XXII, 34; here also a later Haggadist removes the reference to the half-proselytes. See Buber, l. c.; Yer. Meg. I, 72 b.

1364.

Num. R. VIII, 10.

1365.

Shab. 31 a.

1366.

See com. to Ps. LXXXVII, and LXX version.

1367.

Yearb. C. C. A. R., 1891, 1892, 1895.

1368.

Isa. XXVI, 2.

1369.

Philo, De Penitentia, 2.

1370.

See J. E., art. Apostasy and Apostates.

1371.

See J. E., art. Apologetic and Polemical Literature.

1372.

Ber. 28 a; Singer's Prayerb. 48.

1373.

Cant. R. I. 6.

1374.

Deut. XXV, 3 and Sifre ad loc.; Sanh. 44 a.

1375.

Sifra Wayikra 2.

1376.

Sifre Num. 112; R. H., 17 a; Tos. Sanh. XIII, 5.

1377.

Zech. XIV, 8-9.

1378.

Cusari, IV, 23; Maim.: H. Melakim XI, 41; Responsa, 58; Nahmanides: Derashah, ed. Jellinek, 5; see Rashi and Tosafot to Ab. Z. 2 a, 57 b; Sanh. 63 b.

1379.

Solomon ben Adret; Responsa, 302; Yore Deah CXLVIII, 12; Jacob Emden, Comm. to Abot. V, 17; comp. Chwolson: D. Blutanklage, 64-79.

1380.

Isaac ben Sheshet's Responsa, 119.

1381.

Yer. Shab. XIV, 14 d; Ab. Z. II, 40 d; Sota, 47 a; Sanh. 103 a; Eccl. R. I, 24-25.

1382.

See J. E., art. Christianity; Ebionites; Minim; and comp. the various Church Histories.

1383.

See J. E., art. Saul of Tarsus.

1384.

Sanh. 97 a.

1385.

Lev. XIII, 13: Kullo happak laben, instead of laban.

1386.

Ab. d. R. N. XXXIV; Lev. R. XIII, 4 ref. to Ps. LXXX, 14; Midr. Teh. Ps., l. c.

1387.

H. Akkum IX, 4.

1388.

Tosaf. Sanh. 63 b; Isserles Sh. Ar. Orah Hayim, 156; comp. J. E. art. Sanhedrin, Napoleonic.

1389.

Edom, the name for Rome since the time of the Idumean Herod, became the name for the Church of Rome, while Yavan = Greek was the name given to the Greek Church.

1390.

On Ishmael and Edom see Steinschneider: Polemisch. u. Apologet. Literatur, 256-273; on Mohammed, eodem, 302-388.

1391.

See Wuensche: "Urspr. d. Parabel v. d. drei Ringen" in Lessing-Mendelssohn Gedenkbuch, Leipzig, 1879; comp. Steinschneider, l. c., 37, 317, 319; Hebr. Bibliogr. IV, 79; XII, 21; Dunlop-Liebrecht: Gesch. d. Prosadichtung, p. 221, note to 294 f.

1392.

See Schreiner: D. juengst. Urteile u. d. Judenth., 3-5.

1393.

Shebet Yehudah, ed. Wiener, p. 107. See Steinschneider: Heb. Bibl., l. c.

1394.

Deut. XXXIII, 2; see Steinschneider: "Pol. u. Apol. Lit.," 317 f.

1395.

Tos. Sanh. XIII, 2; Sanh. 105 a; Maimonides: H. Teshubah III, 5.

1396.

Matt. III, 2; Luke III, 3; Josephus: Ant. XVIII, 5, 2; see J. E., art. John the Baptist. Perhaps John was identical with Hanan, "the hidden one," a popular saint called "father" by the people, and believed to be a descendant of Moses, a grandson of Onias the rainmaker, and a rain-invoking saint himself. See Taan. 23 b; Tanh. Waera, ed. Buber, II, 37.

1397.

Matt. III, 33; Mark I, 7; Luke III, 21; John I, 29-40.

1398.

Matt. IV, 12; XIV, 10.

1399.

J. E., art. Christianity; Jesus; New Testament; Simon Kaifa. Among the Gospels, that of Luke has the oldest records, rather than Mark. See also Spitta: D. Synoptische Grundschrift.

1400.

See J. E., art. John the Baptist.

1401.

Matt. XXI, 12, and parallels; comp. Yer. Taan. IV, 8; Tos. Menah. XIII, 21.

1402.

Matt. XXVII, 37-42, and parallels.

1403.

John XX; the latter part of the Gospel of John belonged originally to Matthew.

1404.

Matt. XIV, 24 f.; XVII, 1; see Wellhausen: Comm.

1405.

See J. E., art. Ebionites.

1406.

See J. E., art. Apostles.

1407.

J. E., art. Didache and Didascalia; Klein, l. c.

1408.

Acts XV, 5-29; comp. R. Seeberg: Das Aposteldecret; Didache u. d. Urchristenheit.

1409.

J. E., art. Saul of Tarsus.

1410.

Paul's opposition to the law includes the moral law, and even the Decalogue. See Romans VII-VIII; X, 4; XIV; I Cor. VI, 1-3, 15; VII, 31; VIII; II Cor. III, 3.

1411.

See J. E., art. Cross.

1412.

Luke VI, 20-49; comp. with Matt. V-VII; XXIII, 15-36. See Claude Montefiore, The Synoptic Gospels, I and II; G. Friedlander, Jewish Sources of the Sermon on the Mount; Kohler: "D. Naechstenliebe im Judenth.," Judaica, Berlin, 1912.

1413.

Matt. V, 17-18.

1414.

See J. E., and Enc. Rel. and Ethics, art. Pharisees; Lauterbach, "The Sad. and Phar.," in Stud. in Jew. Lit., Berlin, 1913; Herford: Pharisaism; Wuensche: Neue Beitr. z. Erläuterung d. Evangelien.

1415.

See J. E., art. Mohammed; Islam; and the works of Muir, W. Robertson Smith, Hirschfeld; of Geiger, Weil, Sprenger, von Kremer, Noeldeke, Grimme, Dozy, and above all Goldziher, on the Koran, Mohammed and Islam; also Enc. Religion and Ethics, VIII, 871-907.

1416.

See Draper, Conflict of Religion with Science; Intellectual Development of Europe; Lecky, History of Rationalism; Andrew D. White: Warfare between Religion and Science; Krauskopf: Jews and Moors in Spain.

1417.

Zech. XIV, 6-9.

1418.

Isa. LXVI, 20.

1419.

Isa. XXVIII, 16.

1420.

Ex. XIX, 6; Num. XXIII, 9; Deut. VII, 2-6; Isa. LXI, 6; 9; Maim. H. Issure Biah XII, 1; Sh. A. Eben ha Ezer XVI, 1; Einhorn in Jewish Times 1876, against Sam. Hirsch; Samuel Schulman in Y. B. C. C. A. R. 1909, comp. D. Philipson, l. c. Index s. v. Intermarriage; J. E., art. Intermarriage; also Mielziner: The Jewish Law of Marriage and Divorce, p. 45-54, where the opinions of L. Philippson, Geiger, Aub, Einhorn and I. M. Wise are quoted.

1421.

Lazarus, l. c., § 159.

1422.

See Kohler: "Origin a. Function of Ceremonies in Judaism," in Y. B. C. C. of Am. R., 1907. Rosenau: Jewish Ceremonies, Institutions a. Customs, 1912.

1423.

See art. Synagogue, in various encyclopedias; Enelow: The Synagogue in Modern Life; Schuerer, l. c., II, 429; Bousset, l. c., 197 ff.

1424.

See Chapter LVI above; J. E., art. Proselyte.

1425.

See J. E., art. Bar Mizwah and Confirmation.

1426.

Gen. XVII, 10-14.

1427.

Singer's Prayerb., p. 305.

1428.

Ex. IV, 25; see commentaries; Ebers: Ægypten, B. M. I, 183.

1429.

Josephus: Ant. XX, 2,4; Shab. 130 b, 133 b, 156 a; Men. 42 a; Ab. Z. 26 b; comp. Gen. R. XLVI, 9.

1430.

Ab. Z. 27 a.

1431.

Ex. IV, 25; Josh. V, 2; comp. Tylor: Early History of Mankind, 217-222; J. E. and Encyc. of Rel. and Ethics, art. Circumcision; Ploss: Knabenbeschneidung, p. 11.

1432.

Gen. XVII, 10-14; comp. Deut. X, 16; Jer. IX, 25; Claude Montefiore: Hibbert Lectures, 229, 337.

1433.

I Macc. I, 15, 48, 60; Josephus: Ant. XII, 5, 1; Aboth III, 11; Tos. Shab. XV, 9; Yer. Peah I, 16 b; Gen. R. XLVI, 9; Jubil. XV, 26 f.

1434.

Yer. Shab. XIX, 6; Yeb. 71 b.

1435.

Gen. R. XLVIII, 7; Tanh. Lek Leka, ed. Buber, 27; Singer's Prayerb., 304, after Tos. Ber. VI, 12, 13; Shab. 137 b.

1436.

P. d. R. El. XIX.

1437.

Ploss: Geschicht. u. Ethnol. ue. Knabenbeschneidung, 1844; Encyc. Rel. and Ethics, art. Circumcision.

1438.

Zunz: Ges. Schr. II, 197; comp. Rabbin Gutachlen ue. d. Beschneidung, 1844; Frankel: Zeitsch., 1844, p. 66-67.

1439.

See J. E., art. Circumcision; Sam. Cohn: Gesch. d. Beschneidung b. d. Juden (Hebrew), Cracaw, 1903, for the extensive literature.

1440.

Philo II, 210; Josephus: Con. Apion. II, 13; Saadia: Emunoth, III, 10; Maimonides: Moreh, III, 49; Michaelis: Mosaisches Recht, IV, 184-186.

1441.

Maimonides, l. c., III, 48; Samuel ben Meir to Lev. XI, 3; Michaelis, l. c., IV, 202.

1442.

Lev. XI; Deut. XIV, 3-21; Ex. XXII, 30; Lev. VII, 23; XVII, 9 f.; see Kalisch's: commentary to Lev. vol. II, 2-189; J. E., art. Dietary Laws.

1443.

Lev. XX, 24-26, which belongs to Lev. XI, 1-47; comp. Deut. XIV, 3-21.

1444.

See Ezek. XLIV, 31; IV, 14; Jud. XIII, 7, 14. The law in Ex. XXII, 30, "Ye shall be holy men unto Me, therefore ye shall not eat any flesh that is torn of beasts in the field," seems to have been originally only for priests and other holy men.

1445.

See Laws of Manu, V, 7; 11-20 in Sacred Books of the East, XXV, 171 f.; comp. II, 64; XIV, 38-48; 74; 184; Bundahish, XIV; S. B. E. V, 47; Chwolson: Die Szabier, II, 7; 102; Porphyrius: De Abstinentia, IV, 7; Sommer, Bibl. Abh. 271-322; J. E., l. c., 599.

1446.

Ex. XIX, 6.

1447.

Gen. VII, 2, 8.

1448.

II Macc. VI, 18; VII, 41.

1449.

Aristeas, 144-170.

1450.

Sifra to Lev. XX, 26; Tanh. to Lev. XI, 2.

1451.

Shab. 17 b; Ab. Z. 36 b, 38 a, 8 a; Sanh. 104 a; P. d. R. El. XXIX.

1452.

Moreh, III, 25; see also Morris Joseph, l. c., 180-189.

1453.

For the orthodox view, see S. R. Hirsch: Horeb, Chap. LXVIII; M. Friedlander: The Jewish Religion, 237; for the reform, Einhorn: Sinai, 1859; Kohler: Jewish Times, 1872; Geiger: Ges. Schr. I, 253 f.

1454.

Deut. VI, 8-9; XI, 18-20; Num. XV, 38-39.

1455.

Comp. Prov. III, 3; Samuel ben Meir to Ex. XIII, 9.

1456.

Ex. XIII, 9 and commentaries.

1457.

Stanley: Hist. of the Jewish Church, I, 561; Peterman: Reisen im Orient, I, 237.

1458.

Curtiss: Ursemitische Religion, Chap. XX-XXI; Kohler: Monatsschrift, 1893, p. 445, note.

1459.

Ber. 6 a, 14 b, 23 a, b; Tos. Ber. VII, 25; Midr. Teh. to Ps. VI, 1; Yer. Peah I, 15 d; Targum Song of Songs, VIII, 3; Pes. III b; Schorr: HeHalutz, VII, 56-57; Baentsch: Comm. to Num. XV, 37; also Schuerer, G. V. II, 483-486.

1460.

Cant. R. III, 11; Sifre Deut. 43; M. K. 16 b.

1461.

Kohler, l. c.: comp. Schechter: Studies, I, 249; Morris Joseph, l. c., p. 178, where he quotes Maimonides H. Tefillin IV, 25.

1462.

See art. Sabbath in various encyclopedias and the Babel-Bibel controversies; Zimmern and Schrader: K. A. T., II, 592 f.; Jastrow: American Journal of Theology, 1898, p. 315-352.

1463.

Ex. XX, 8-11; XVI, 23-29; XXXV, 2-3; XXXI, 13; comp. Jer. XVIII, 21-27; Neh. XIII, 15-18.

1464.

Deut. V, 12-15; Ex. XXIII, 12; XXXIV, 21; comp. Isa. LVIII, 13.

1465.

See Jubilees II, 23-30; L, 6; Geiger, Zeitsch., 1868, 116; Nachgel. Schr., III, 286 f.; V, 142 f.; Schechter: Document of a Jewish Sect, I; XXV; XLVIII-L; Halevi: The Commandments of the Sabbath for the Falashas, 1902; Harkavy L. K., II, 69 f., for the Karaites.

1466.

Shab. VII, 2, 70 a; Mek. Wayakhel.

1467.

Mek. Ki Thisla I, comp. Mark II. 2 f.

1468.

Isa. LVIII; Shab. 118 a, b; Mek. Yithro VII; Pes, R. XXIII, p. 121.

1469.

II Kings IV, 23.

1470.

Philo II, 137, 166, 281, 631.

1471.

See Schechter: Studies, I, 249 f.; Morris Joseph, l. c., 202-214.

1472.

See David Philipson: Reform Movement in Judaism, 275-302, 503-508; E. G. Hirsch in J. E., art. Sabbath; Sabbath and Sunday.

1473.

See Schaff-Herzog Encyc., art. Sunday.

1474.

See I Sam. XX, 5-27, where the two new-moon days are spoken of as approaching, proving the use of the Babylonian month of four weeks of seven days each, and two new-moon days.

1475.

II Kings IV, 23; Prov. VII, 20; comp. Ps. LXXXI, 4, Kese.

1476.

Ex. XX, 11; Gen. II, 2-3.

1477.

II Kings IV, 23; Isa. I, 13; LXVI, 23.

1478.

Num. XXVIII, 11 f.

1479.

Mek. Bo I; Pes. R. XV; P. d. R. El. LI; Sanh. 42 a; Singer's Prayerb., 292.

1480.

Isa. XXX, 26; LX, 20.

1481.

Ex. XII, 11-27; Deut, XVI, 1; see the commentaries, also Clay Trumbull: The Threshold Covenant; Curtiss, l. c.

1482.

In Deut. the Passover sacrifice was the first-born of the flock, see Deut. XVI, 2, comp. with Ex. XIII, 2-16, and the celebration took place on the night of the new moon. The Priestly Code observed it on the full moon, with a lamb instead of the first-born sheep or cattle. Ex. XII, 3 f.; Lev, XXIII, 5 (the Holiness Code); Josh. V, 10.

1483.

About the watch-night, see Jubilees XLVIII, 5; Pesah. 109 b.

1484.

See Einhorn's Prayerbook, 485; Holdheim: Prediglen, 1853, II, 189, referring to Jer. XXIII, 7-8; Tos. Ber. I, 12; Ber. 12 b.

1485.

Ex. XXIII, 16; XXXIV, 22; Deut. XVI, 9; Lev. XXIII, 10-17.

1486.

Ex. R. XXXI, 17, with reference to Ex. XIX, 1; Jubilees VI, 17-21.

1487.

See J. E., art. Confirmation.

1488.

Deut. XVI, 13; Lev. XXIII, 34-43; comp. I Kings VIII, 65; Ezek. XLV, 23; R. h. Sh. I, 2.

1489.

See Ex. XII, 37; XIII, 20; Num. XXXIII, 5, and comp. Mek. Bo 14; Sifra Emor XVII.

1490.

Zech. XIV, 16-19; comp. Is. XII, 3; Suk. V, 1-4; Tos. Suk. IV, 1-9; Piyut to the Sukkoth festival.

1491.

Suk. I-IV; Talmud and Codes.

1492.

Ibn Yarchi: Manhig, H. Suk. 53-60; T. O. Ch. DCLXIX; J. E., art. Simhath Torah.

1493.

Pesik. 193 b; Suk. 55 b; Philo: De Victimis, I, 2, II, 238-239.

1494.

Lev. XXIII, 24-32; comp. Neh. VIII, 1-18.

1495.

J. E., art. New Year's Day; Life, Book of.

1496.

R. h. Sh. IV, 6-7; Tos. R. h. Sh. IV, 4-9; R. h. Sh. 27 a; Singer's Prayerb., 247-254, and Abrahams Ann. CXCV, 111 f.; and Union Prayer Book, II, 70-75.

1497.

Lev. XVI, 2-34; comp. Ezek. XLV, 18-20.

1498.

Yoma VI; Kalish's commentary to Lev. XVI; Taan. IV, 8; comp. Jud. XXI, 21; see Morgenstern in Journal Oriental Soc., 1917, and J.Q.R. 1917, p. 94.

1499.

Yoma IV-VI; comp. Lev. R. XXI, 11; V, 1.

1500.

Num. XIV, 20; XV, 26.

1501.

Lev. XVI, 30; Sifra Ahare VI; Yoma 30 b; Yer. Yoma V, 42 c.

1502.

Yoma VIII, 9.

1503.

P. d. R. El. XLVI; Taan. 30 b; B. B. 121 a; S. Olam R. VI; T. d. El. Zutta IV; Ex. R. LI, 4. Jubilees XXXIV, 18-19 connects the Day of Atonement with the repentance of Joseph's brethren.

1504.

Yoma, l. c.

1505.

Comp. above, Chapter XXXIX.

1506.

Josephus J. W. VI, 4, 5; Meg. Taan. V; Taan. IV, 4; Taan. 12 a, 29 ab. J. E., art. Ab, Ninth of; see also Pes. R. XXVI-XXXIII; Pesik. 110 b-148 a.

1507.

Zech. IV, 6; J. E., art. Hanukka; Maccabees.

1508.

Meg. IV, 5; 18 a, 21 b; J. E., art. Purim; Esther; Sifre to Deut. 296.

1509.

Ber. 13 a.

1510.

Deut. IV, 6.

1511.

See Zunz: Gottesdienstliche Vortraege.

1512.

Yoma 66 b; comp. R. Eliezer's other dictum, Sota III, 4.

1513.

Num. XII, 2.

1514.

See Geiger's Zeitschr., 1836, 1 f., 354; 1839, 333 f.

1515.

Graetz, H. J. III, 244 f.; L. Loew: Ges. Sch. III, 57.

1516.

See Landsberg in J. E., art. Confirmation; L. Loew: Lebensalter, 17.

1517.

See his Introduction.

1518.

Comp. Schechter: Studies, II, 148 f., 202 f.

1519.

Deut. XXIX, 28.

1520.

Deut. XXX, 11-14.

1521.

Isa. LVI, 7.

1522.

Zech. XIV, 9.

1523.

Cuzari, I, 103; II, 12.

1524.

Sifre to Deut. VI, 5.

1525.

Hab. II, 14.

1526.

Singer's Prayerb., 8.

1527.

Lev. XIX, 2; comp. on the whole E. G. Hirsch in J. E., art. Ethics.

1528.

See Alenu in Singer's Prayerb., 67 f.; Union Prayerbook, I, 48, 104 f.

1529.

Shab. 119 b.

1530.

Deut. XI, 22; Sifre Deut. 49.

1531.

Deut. XIII, 5; Sota 14 a; see Schechter: Aspects, 200-203.

1532.

Aboth. I, 3; IV, 2; E. G. Hirsch in J. E., art Ethics. See Toy: Judaism and Christianity, p. 260.

1533.

Deut. X, 19.

1534.

Micah VI, 8.

1535.

Ps. XXIV, 3-4.

1536.

See J. E., art. Essenes, Hasidim and Test. Twelve Patriarchs: Iss. V, 2; VII, 6; Dan. V, 3.

1537.

Lev. XIX, 14, 32; Sifra ad loc. B. M. 58 b.

1538.

Shab. 31 a; comp. J. E., art. Didache and Klein, l. c.

1539.

Tanh. Shemini, ed. Buber, § 12; comp. Lauterbach, Ethics of Halakah, p. 12.

1540.

Aboth. I, 14.

1541.

Sanh. IV, 5.

1542.

Yer. Kid. IV, 66 d.

1543.

Taan. 22 b; Ned. 10 a.

1544.

Lev. R. XXXIV, 3, ref. to Prov. XI, 17.

1545.

Sanh. 18 a, 19 a.

1546.

Keth. V, 5.

1547.

Prov. XVI, 32; Shab. 105 b; Ned. 22 b; Sota 4 b; Ber. 43 b.

1548.

Ps. LXXXI, 10.

1549.

See above, chapter L, par. 6.

1550.

Semakot II; R. Eleazar in B. K. 91 b with reference to Gen. IX, 5. Prof. Lauterbach referred me to Shebet Mussar, XX, obviously a quotation from some lost Midrash.

1551.

Job XLII, 7.

1552.

Lev. XXV, 42, 55; Tos. B. K. VII, 5; Kid. 22 d.

1553.

Targ. to Lev. XIX, 18; Tobit IV, 15; Philo II, 236.

1554.

Ex. XXIII, 4-5; Prov. XXIV, 17; XXV, 21.

1555.

Ab. d R. N., ed. Schechter, 53, 60.

1556.

Eodem, 64.

1557.

Aboth. I, 12.

1558.

Philo II, 284 f.

1559.

Deut. X, 18-19.

1560.

Isa. XXVI, 9.

1561.

Isa. XXXIII, 15.

1562.

Sifra Behar IV; B. M. 58 b.

1563.

Tos. B. K. VII, 8; B. M. III, 27; B. B. 88 a-90 b; Makk. 24 a.

1564.

Sanh. 24 b.

1565.

B. B. 90 b.

1566.

Lev. XIX, 36; B. M. 49 a.

1567.

Deut. XVI, 20.

1568.

Kad ha Kemah, s. v. Gezelah.

1569.

Ps. XV, 3.

1570.

Pes. 118 a.

1571.

Shab. 97 a; Yoma 19 b.

1572.

Mek. Mishpatim 82; B. K. 79 b; B. M. 58 b-59 a; Lauterbach l. c. 20-21.

1573.

Peah V, 6; Prov. XXIII, 10.

1574.

Ex. XXIII, 24.

1575.

Tanh. Mishpatim. ed. Buber, 8.

1576.

Lev. XXV, 35; Sifra ad loc.

1577.

Isa. V, 8.

1578.

Amos VIII, 4.

1579.

Prov. XI, 26.

1580.

Deut. XXI, 1-8.

1581.

Sifre ad loc.; Sota IX, 7.

1582.

Matt. VI, 25-28, V, 39; comp. Cor. VI, 6-7.

1583.

Yeb. 62 a, 63 a.

1584.

Prov. XXII, 29; Ned. 49 b.

1585.

Ber. 8 a, ref. to Ps. CXXVIII, 2.

1586.

Keth. 50 a.

1587.

Morris Joseph in Religious Systems of the World, 1892, p. 701.

1588.

Deut. I, 17; see Schmiedl: D. Lehre v. Kampf um's Recht, 1875.

1589.

Ps. XXXVII, 11; Shab. 88 b.

1590.

Ex. XXIII, 5; Deut. XXV, 4; Prov. XII, 10; Git. 62 a.

1591.

Aboth. I, 12; IV, 4, 12; Taan. 20 b.

1592.

Matt. V. 17-30.

1593.

Job XXXI, 1; Pes. R. XXIV; Lev. R. XXIII, 12; Ber. 12 b; Nid. 13 a.

1594.

Shab. 33 a, referring to Isa. IX, 17; Ben Sira XXIII, 13; Test. Twelve Patriarchs, passim.

1595.

Deut. XXIII, 14.

1596.

Deut. XVI, 11; 14 f.; Shab. 118 a; Pes. R. XXIII; Meg. 16 b; Shab. 30 b; Ber. 31 a; comp. M. Lazarus, l. c., 254-261.

1597.

Taan. 22 a.

1598.

See Lazarus, l. c., 99.

1599.

Ber. 64 a, refer. to Ps. LXXXIV, 8; comp. Lazarus, l. c., p. 280.

Made in the USA
Lexington, KY
03 April 2017